LOUIS MOREAU GOTTSCHALK

Louis Moreau Gottschalk. Photograph courtesy of the Music Division, The New York Public Library for the Performing Arts, Astor, Lenox and Tilden Foundations.

LOUIS MOREAU GOTTSCHALK

A Bio-Bibliography

James E. Perone

Bio-Bibliographies in Music, Number 91
Donald L. Hixon, Series Adviser

GREENWOOD PRESS
Westport, Connecticut • London

Library of Congress Cataloging-in-Publication Data

Perone, James E.
    Louis Moreau Gottschalk : a bio-bibliography / James E. Perone.
        p.   cm.—(Bio-bibliographies in music, ISSN 0742–6968 ; no. 91)
    Includes bibliography (p.   ), filmography/videography (p.   ), and index.
    ISBN 0–313–31824–7 (alk. paper)
    1. Gottschalk, Louis Moreau, 1829–1869—Bibliography.   I. Title.   II. Series.
ML134.G68P47   2002
780′.92—dc21   2002067923
    [B]

British Library Cataloguing in Publication Data is available.

Library of Congress Catalog Card Number: 2002067923
ISBN: 0–313–31824–7
ISSN: 0742–6968

First published in 2002

Greenwood Press, 88 Post Road West, Westport, CT 06881
An imprint of Greenwood Publishing Group, Inc.
www.greenwood.com

Printed in the United States of America

The paper used in this book complies with the
Permanent Paper Standard issued by the National
Information Standards Organization (Z39.48–1984).

10 9 8 7 6 5 4 3 2 1

Copyright Acknowledgment

The author and publisher gratefully acknowledge the Music Division, The New York Public
Library for the Performing Arts, Astor, Lenox and Tilden Foundations, for use of the photograph of Louis Moreau Gottschalk.

Contents

Preface

While following the general format of other volumes in Greenwood's *Bio-Bibliographies in Music* series, I have used some slight stylistic variations due to the nature of the compositions of the subject of the present volume, the nineteenth-century American composer/pianist Louis Moreau Gottschalk. The book is divided into (1) Biography; (2) Vocal Works; (3) Orchestral and Band Works; (4) Chamber Works; (5) Solo Piano Works; (6) Works for Multiple Pianists; (7) General Bibliography; and (8) Index. There are also smaller chapters devoted to Miscellaneous Works, Filmography and Videography, and an alphabetical listing of Gottschalk's compositions.

Within the Vocal Works chapter, I have arranged the compositions first by genre (Opera, Choral, and Music for Solo Voice) and then chronologically within each category by date (or, in some cases, approximate date). Each composition is designated by the mnemonic "W" for "Work" followed by a sequential number. I have listed details such as date of composition, publisher information, contents, dedicatory information, author of text, manuscript location, other catalog numbers (RO numbers for Robert Offergeld's designations and D numbers for John Doyle's listings) and other information for each work. The Orchestral and Band Works, Chamber Works, Solo Piano Works, Works for Multiple Pianists, and Miscellaneous Works chapters use a similar format, except that they are not broken down into subgenres.

Representative performances are listed after the descriptive details of each work. I have listed the performances chronologically. They are designated by the Work number followed by sequential lower-case letters. Following the listings of representative performances for each work is a listing of recordings, which are designated by mnemonic "R" for Recording. The recordings then receive the Works number, followed by sequential lower-case letters to show their chronology; hence R37b would be the second ("b") recording issued of W37. I have opted to include the recording information within the Works chapters so as to minimize redundancy and keep the number of pages down. I have used the mnemonic "R," rather than the more familiar "D" (commonly found in Discographies) to avoid confusion with the John Doyle catalog numbers.

Following the listings of representative performances and recordings for each work are bibliographical references to the work and its performances. These references are numbered sequentially with the designation "WB" for "Works Bibliography" and the entries are arranged chronologically under each composition. Pertinent references are made to the performances reviewed or to other citations for further information with "See" or "See also" notes. In an effort to avoid redundancy, especially with several of the recordings of Gottschalk's short works including up to forty pieces on one release, I have placed all recording reviews in the General Bibliography. "See" and "See also" references will direct the reader from the recording listing to reviews and from the reviews to the recordings.

The General Bibliography is arranged chronologically and contains primarily biographical references, reviews of some of Gottschalk's thousands of concerts and recitals, references to the general aesthetics of his music, as well as detailed studies that focus on the totality of Gottschalk's career. Gottschalk's own writings are cited as well. All of these citations are numbered sequentially with the mnemonic "B" for "Bibliography."

The reader should be aware that Gottschalk's thousands of performances were announced, previewed, and reviewed by North American, European, South American, and Caribbean newspapers, in cities and towns large and small. A complete listing of all of these probably would be impossible to assemble, and inclusion of those citations is certainly outside the scope of this book. John Doyle's 1982 *Louis Moreau Gottschalk, 1929-1869: A Bibliographical Study and Catalog of Works* (See: B484) and S. Frederick Starr's *Bamboula! The Life and Times of Louis Moreau Gottschalk* (See: B524) both include partial listings of newspaper sources; the lists, sketchy though they are, are daunting.

Acknowledgments

I am indebted to a number of individuals for their assistance in preparing the present book. In particular, I wish to thank my wife, Karen L. Perone, whose 1991 bio-bibliography on American composer Lukas Foss for Greenwood Press first inspired me to enter the book-writing side of academe. I also wish to thank Donald Hixon, Series Advisor of Greenwood's *Bio-Bibliographies in Music* series, as well as the entire editorial staff at Greenwood Press, especially Acquisitions Editor Eric Levy.

Biography

Born in New Orleans, Louisiana, May 8, 1829, Louis Moreau Gottschalk was certainly the most multi-cultural American musician of the nineteenth century, generations before the term "multi-culturalism" would find its way into the dictionary. His father, Edward Gottschalk, of German-Jewish heritage, was born in London, but moved to the United States in the 1820s. His mother, Marie-Aimée Gottschalk (née Bruslé), of French-Roman Catholic background, had lived in Haiti until the slave revolt of the 1790s forced her family to flee to New Orleans. Gottschalk's youth in New Orleans continued the multi-cultural trend, with the boy absorbing not only the French and Caribbean music sung by his mother, grandmother, and his grandmother's slave, Sally, but also the influences of African-American music on the streets of what was probably America's culturally richest city; Haitian, African-American, Hispanic, and French folk music abounded, as did music in the European classical tradition. As a first generation New Orleans resident, Louis Moreau Gottschalk can rightly be labeled a Creole. Although the accepted meaning of the term during Gottschalk's childhood and today is "one who is of first generation New Orleans birth," the term has been widely misinterpreted in the past, leading to unfounded speculation that Gottschalk was of mixed race (See: B205, B374, and B416). Confusion over the use of the term, and the fact that Edward Gottschalk apparently did not actively practice his faith (although he did provide the synagogue with financial contributions), has also caused some writers to question the younger Gottschalk's Jewish heritage (See: B194). It may be interesting for the reader to note that, this controversy aside, Gottschalk would eventually find his way onto the Nazi's official list of Jewish musicians (See: B211).

A child prodigy, Moreau, as family and friends knew him, began study with François Letellier, organist and choirmaster at St. Louis Cathedral in New Orleans. Gottschalk would later dedicate his early 1850s solo piano work, *La jota aragonesa, caprice espagnol*, Op. 14 (See: W105), to his first teacher. Keyboard lessons with Letellier progressed to the point that Gottschalk was able to substitute for his teacher at Mass by the age of seven. Nineteenth-century America suffered from a musical inferiority complex; the feeling that a child prodigy could fully develop only with European training caused Edward Gottschalk to send his son to Paris. Moreau, against his mother's wishes, left for France one week shy of his twelfth birthday.

Gottschalk's Parisian piano teachers included Carl Hallé and Camille Stamaty (later the teacher of Camille Saint-Saëns). From the latter, Gottschalk learned the famous arm-restricting piano techniques developed by Stamaty's teacher, Frédéric Kalkbrenner. Throughout his pianistic career Gottschalk would be recognized for both his virtuosic technique and his emotional expression. It was during his stay in France that Gottschalk began the study of composition, taking private lessons with Pierre Maleden. His first compositions appeared in 1842, with his first published work being the *Polka de salon*, Op. 1 (See: W64), issued by A. Lafont in 1846.

On April 2, 1845, Gottschalk gave his informal Paris debut, receiving praise in the press (See: B1 and B2), and public acknowledgment by Frédéric Chopin, the reigning master of the piano, who had attended the Gottschalk recital and was most impressed with how the teenager performed Chopin's own *Piano Concerto in E minor*. With Gottschalk's professional debut on April 17, 1849 and Chopin's death in the same year, it appeared that Gottschalk was heir to the Pole's throne. Most noteworthy of Gottschalk's professional debut was his performance of several of his Creole compositions, such as *Bamboula*, Op. 2 (See: W68) and *La savane*, Op. 3 (See: W76). These works, inspired in large part by the African-American folk music the composer had heard in the New Orleans of his childhood, created an instant sensation in Paris. The two previously named works, along with *La bananier*, Op. 5 (See: W78) and *Le mancenillier* (See: W88), fit the European Romantic era's fascination with all things exotic. In bringing the melodies of the American Negro to Europe, Gottschalk anticipated the spiritual, ragtime, and early jazz-influenced works of Dvořák, Debussy, and Stravinsky by over a half-century.

The inspiration of Chopin, exhibited in several 1840s polkas and waltzes (as well as ballades that would appear throughout Gottschalk's career), and the inspiration of New Orleans were not the only two influences to come together in the early works of Gottschalk. He received mentorship from the famed composer/conductor Hector Berlioz and expanded his interest in European traditions with his *Ossian*, Op. 4 (See: W69), a composition that began a series of works in which the composer explored the stories and musical styles of Scandinavia. As a budding world traveler, however, Gottschalk's interests tended toward points farther south; he undertook a tour of Switzerland in 1850 and spent an extended period of time in Spain in 1851-52. Isabella II strongly supported the young composer/pianist and, as he would continue to do throughout his career, Gottschalk reciprocated by thoroughly absorbing the music surrounding him, making it his own in a series of compositions. *La jota aragonesa*, Op. 14 (See: W105) and *Minuit à Séville*, Op. 30 (See: W112) are two of the better-known Spanish-influenced solo piano works of the period. During his year-and-a-half stay in Spain, Gottschalk began seriously dealing with larger instrumental resources; the composer scored *El sitio de Zaragoza* (See: W279) for ten pianos. Throughout his career, Gottschalk's primary compositional focus would remain single-movement works for piano solo, with piano, four-hands compositions and works for multiple pianos being of secondary importance. Although he would compose in every European-based genre, orchestral music, chamber music, choral music, opera, and song would never receive the amount of attention his performance medium would.

Early in his career as a composer and traveling pianist, Gottschalk recognized that audiences loved hearing familiar operatic airs given virtuosic treatment at the piano. Gottschalk composed fantasies on airs from several operas from the 1840s on, favoring the works of Verdi (See: W54, W55, W93, W159, W162, W276, W294, and W303) and Donizetti (See: W123, W125, W129, W147, W148, W194, W238, W240, W263, W299, and W314). In a similar vein, Gottschalk arranged opera overtures and the music from famous operatic scenes for solo piano and for multiple pianists, with his piano, four hands version of Rossini's *Overture de "Guillaume Tell"* (See: W277) remaining one of the most frequently performed today.

After a brief return to France in 1852, Gottschalk set sail for the United States, arriving in New York on January 1853. His February 11, 1853 New York debut proved to be a success (See: B33), with its mixture of Creole works and the ever-popular Italian opera fantasies. Among the works performed by Gottschalk and pianist Richard Hoffman on the concert was *Jerusalem, grande fantaisie triomphale*, Op. 84 (See: W276), a work based on themes from Verdi's opera *I lombardi*. It might be surprising for the reader to note the rather advanced opus number assigned to *Jerusalem*. The work was not published until approximately five years after Gottschalk's death. Gottschalk composed many works that were either near improvisations or were written out in a shorthand notation that only the composer and a few close associates could decipher. Even a cursory glance at the works list later in this book will reveal numerous works not published until years after their composition and even more lost works. In many cases, Gottschalk probably never bothered to write down the lost works for solo piano; these pieces were part of his repertoire, he had them memorized, and he had little chance of many of them ever being published, since few other pianists of the time could perform them with Gottschalk's brilliance.

October 1853 marked a turning point in Gottschalk's career; his father, Edward, died. The pianist/composer became the breadwinner for his younger siblings and his mother. Ironically, the rest of Gottschalk's family was now living in Paris. The musician was now forced to concertize extensively and write compositions in the popular vein of the time; he had to become concerned with sheet music sales. Like his contemporary Stephen Foster, Gottschalk found that sentimental songs and piano pieces enjoyed great popularity in the home. *The Last Hope* (See: W139), an 1854 work, remained a popular favorite in this style. *The Last Hope* was, in fact, one of the first Gottschalk compositions to be commercially recorded; the Victor label issued Ferdinand Himmelreich's 78-rpm recording in 1913 (See: R139a). The principle theme from the sentimental work, which reportedly was based on an 1853 improvisation in Satiago de Cuba to ease the last moments of life for a Cuban woman (See: B523), perhaps is better known today as the hymn tune *Mercy*, in its arrangement by Edwin P. Parker. Charles Ives quoted the melodic theme used by Parker in his 1923-24 setting of *Psalm 90*. *The Last Hope* was certainly not the last sentimental work Gottschalk based on the theme of death; *The Dying Poet* (See: W227), an 1863 composition enjoyed great success in its day and became a staple of silent film pianists in the early twentieth century, and *Morte!!* (See: W249), an 1868 composition based on the death of a young girl, continued the trend.

As a result of works in the sentimental style, Gottschalk's reputation suffered among music critics and serious musicologists. Influential Boston critic John Sullivan Dwight took the composer/pianist to task in numerous reviews (See: B326) both for catering to low public tastes in the sentimental pieces and for seeking inspiration from African-American and Caribbean folk sources. Dwight also complained about Gottschalk's tendency to program primarily his own works, neglecting the Germanic classics that Dwight held in such high esteem. Gottschalk's letters, many of which are now housed at the New York Public Library, find the musician complaining bitterly about his treatment in Dwight's influential music journal. Ironically, while it is true that Gottschalk avoided the classics in his public concerts—he knew what American audiences wanted to hear and what they did not care to hear—he studied and performed the Beethoven repertoire quite extensively in private concerts given for more knowledgeable audiences (See: B82 and B162). S. Frederick Starr, writing in his 1995 Gottschalk biography *Bamboula!* (See: B524), devotes an entire chapter to the Gottschalk/Dwight controversy, delving into the various social issues that caused the Jewish/Roman Catholic, New Orleans-born composer to have considerable difficulty being accepted by the conservative, largely Protestant musical establishment of mid-century Boston.

Gottschalk continued to tour the United States, Cuba, and Canada quite extensively, composing all the time. His tour of Cuba in 1854, however, proved to be most inspiring, with Gottschalk composing several obscure sacred choral works, *Pange linguae* (See: W5) and *Rex altissime* (See: W6), the solo song *Alone* (See: W10), and several piano pieces based on Cuban dance styles, most notably *El cocoyé, grand caprice cubain de bravura*, Op. 80 (See: W135). The Gottschalk scholar Robert Offergeld labeled the pianist/composer's January 31, 1856 performance in New York City "musicologically extraordinary" (See: B378, p23). Gottschalk took the highly unusual step of featuring music that was either from, or directly influenced by Peninsular Spain and Cuba, music probably previously unheard in New York concert circles. The lure of the exotic melodic turns and rhythms of the Caribbean, as well as a very publicly played out affair (See: B41-B44, B49, and B80) with the New York bohemian Ada Clare (pseudonym of Jane McElhenny), which was rumored to have produced a child, led to Gottschalk's decision to spend an extended period of time on the islands; he set sail from New York for Havana in early February 1857 and did not return to the United States until February 1862. The fourteen-year-old soprano and sometimes pianist Adelina Patti, who had previously performed with the famed Norwegian violinist Ole Bull, accompanied Gottschalk on his 1857 trip to Cuba. Gottschalk and Patti concertized extensively, performing such now lost Gottschalk works as *Le Carnaval de Venise* (See: W12a) and *Chant des oiseaux* (See: W47a). In 1858 Patti, appearing as a pianist, performed Gottschalk's difficult *Souvenir de Porto Rico*, Op. 31 (See: W165b). Gottschalk would later perform with Patti's older sister Carlotta (See: W15a and W15b, for example).

During his five years in the islands, Gottschalk lived in Cuba, Puerto Rico, Guadeloupe, and Martinique. In addition to the aforementioned *Souvenir de Porto Rico*, Gottschalk wrote numerous works for solo piano based on the contradanza and other island dance styles. The melodic twists and syncopated rhythms of works such as *La Gallina*, Op. 53 (See: W204), *Suis-moi!*, Op. 45 (See: W216), *Danza*, Op. 33 (See: W167), as well as *Souvenir de Porto Rico*, anticipate ragtime; Scott Joplin's 1909 composition *Solace: A Mexican Serenade*, in particular, bears a striking stylistic resemblance in its habañera rhythms to the latter three of these mid-nineteenth-century Gottschalk works. Festivals in the islands also provided the opportunity for Gottschalk to write music for orchestra, military band, and opera. Although many of these works have not survived, the fourteen-minute opera *Escenas campestres* (See: W4), based in part on *Danza*, Op. 33, and the *Marcha Triunfal y Final de Opera* (See: W36), a transcription for combined orchestra and military band of the finale of the lost opera *Charles IX* (See: W2), are extant, with scores and parts presently available on rental.

Certainly the most famous Gottschalk orchestral composition, *Symphonie romantique ("La nuit des tropiques")* (See: W34), was premiered in Havana on February 17, 1860. Gottschalk conducted the two-movement symphony, lasting less than twenty minutes, several times before his return to the United States, employing huge instrumental forces of festival orchestras and bands. The first movement, Andante ("Noche en los Tropicos"), resembles a sentimental song of the era in structure and style. In the second movement ("Festa Criolla"), Gottschalk incorporates syncopated Caribbean melodies and a percussion section, which uses Cuban instruments and plays traditional Latino clave and drum rhythmic ostinati. Gottschalk's scoring in both movements is bright and clear. Since the work's revival in the mid-1950s, several editions have been recorded. In most of these, arrangers have "corrected" Gottschalk's sometimes-unorthodox voice leadings and scoring; however, like earlier American composers such as William Billings, and later American composers such as Charles Ives, Gottschalk's breaking of the established "rules" of composition and orchestration give his writing a unique sound. The present-day trend is to follow Gottschalk's original intent as closely as possible.

By 1861, Cuban audiences had perhaps grown too accustomed to Louis Moreau Gottschalk; festivals early in that year in Havana proved to be less successful than those of the past. A stint as an opera conductor also proved to be a failure (See: B66 and B403). With the United States now being torn apart by the Civil War, and with the cooling of audience reaction in the Caribbean to his music, Gottschalk returned to the United States. Although he had been born in Louisiana and had written and performed *Variations on "Dixie's Land"* (See: W214) early in the 1860s, Gottschalk firmly believed in the Union cause. He believed that the Union must be preserved and had developed an anti-slavery sentiment. This is probably easily understandable given the strong influence upon his music from people of color; Gottschalk valued the culture of blacks in the United States and in the Caribbean like no other well-known white public figure of his day.

Gottschalk's February 11, 1862 concert in New York City set the stage for the next three years. The musician performed transcriptions of music from Italian opera favorites such as Rossini's *Guillaume Tell* (See: R277b) and Verdi's *Rigoletto* (See: R218a), as well as his Creole and Caribbean works. Gottschalk erased the lines between popular and art music, much like John Philip Sousa would do a generation later, when the band master would program transcriptions, marches, virtuoso showpieces, and even ragtime. Like Sousa, Gottschalk was easily the most famous musician of his day. Gottschalk achieved his fame, as he had done earlier in his U.S. career, through extensive travel, covering, by his own estimate, 95,000 miles by rail between 1862 and 1865. His over 1000 recitals during the period took place in major cities and in small cities and towns all across the North. During this period of war, Gottschalk frequently programmed his *L'Union (The Union), paraphrase de concert*, Op. 48 (See: W220). An 1862 work dedicated to Union Major General George B. McClellan, *L'Union* features melodic material from "The Star-Spangled Banner," "Yankee Doodle," and "Hail Columbia," interspersed with battle music episodes drawn from the composer's own decade-old *El sitio de Zaragoza* (See: W101). The work is a virtuoso *tour de force* for the pianist and finds Gottschalk combining the various themes contrapuntally so as to paint a vivid picture of the battle. Although he did not do so often, Gottschalk's use of quotations of familiar popular and patriotic themes anticipated the more famous work of Charles Ives by approximately a half-century. Another patriotic favorite of Gottschalk's Unionist audiences of the 1863-65 period was his *Battle Cry of Freedom, grand caprice de concert*, Op. 55 (See: W229), a brilliant fantasy on the well-known George F. Root song "The Battle Cry of Freedom." As a counterpoint to the patriotic works, Gottschalk also composed and performed his solo piano work *Pasquinade*, Op. 59 (See: W228), yet another syncopated precursor of ragtime, during the same period.

During the Civil War era, Gottschalk left ample evidence of what life was like for a traveling virtuoso, as well as what the general musical climate was in mid-nineteenth-century America. He wrote articles for American and French publications and his concert books, containing biographical details as well as quotations from newspaper reviews, were widely distributed (See: B53, B60, B63, B64, B67-B69, and B75-B77, for example). The composer's sister, Clara Gottschalk Peterson, collected many of these observations into the 1881 book *Notes of a Pianist* (See: B113). The extant Gottschalk letters also describe his compositional work and the day-to-day activities of America's most popular concert performer. Long before the word "spin" was used to describe the slant a spokesperson or a news reporter would put on a story, Gottschalk demonstrated acute attention to spin in his writings. He was a consummate self-promoter, which probably helped fuel his immense popularity. As a serious chronicle of his work as composer, Gottschalk's writings must be taken with the proverbial grain of salt; he sometimes confused dates and would refer to pieces by working titles or by their subtitles, thereby making it difficult to determine exactly to which composition he was referring. Jeanne Behrend's commentary in her 1964 edition of *Notes of a Pianist* (See: B296) clears up some of the confusion.

Gottschalk's travel to the San Francisco Bay area in spring 1865 marked the end of his stay in the United States. While staying in San Francisco, he was persuaded to spend an evening socializing with a friend who brought along two young women from the Oakland Female Seminary. When the women did not return to the boarding school before curfew, a scandal developed. Although all the evidence suggests that there was no amorous liaison between the musician and the student, anti-Gottschalk forces in the press fabricated a story linking the two and seriously damaging Gottschalk's reputation. As he had done when Ada Clare compromised his reputation in her published articles of December 1856 (See: B41-B44), Gottschalk left the United States. When he left the country in September 1865, however, he fled a near mob hysteria over the scandal, which had not yet been cleared up.

Gottschalk's four years in Central and South America found him touring and staying in Argentina, Uruguay, Panama, Chile, Brazil, and Peru. Expanding on what he had done in his U.S. concerts of the previous three years, Gottschalk brought together music based on Creole melodies, Italian and German opera—he is credited with introducing the music of Richard Wagner to South America (See: B489) with his transcriptions of music from *Tannhauser* (See: W39 and W304)—Caribbean melodies, and works based on themes from the various South American cultures. As Lowens and Starr so aptly write, "He also championed public education and the republican form of government, and used his music festivals as showcases for a pan-American model of civic life and culture; in the process, he became the first pan-American cultural figure" (See: B543, p. 200). Gottschalk's South American festivals were some of the most mammoth musical events ever witnessed, involving hundreds of performers, including one such event in Brazil featuring 650 musicians. Pianist Eugene List, who organized major Gottschalk commemorative concerts in the 1970s and 1980s, has revived the "monster concert" concept. Present-day festival get-togethers of musicians performing solo or chamber arrangements *en masse* also certainly carry on the Gottschalk tradition.

The best-remembered orchestral compositions dating from Gottschalk's South American years include his *Symphony No. 2 ("À Montevideo")* (See: W41), a work premiered in Montevideo in November 1868. The twelve-minute composition, written in one movement consisting of seven sections, has been revived and received several performances during 1969, the centennial of Gottschalk's death; the American Symphony Orchestra, under the baton of Leopold Stokowski, gave the New York premiere October 6, 1969 (See: W41d). The *Grande tarantelle (Célèbre Tarantelle)*, Op. 67 (See: W37), an even more successful work that evolved between 1858 and 1868 and eventually existed in chamber, solo piano, piano duet, and piano and orchestra versions (See also: W48, W247, W311, and W312), has received numerous performances in the past several decades, particularly as a work for piano and orchestra (See: W37f-W37k). Just as they had during Gottschalk's years in the United States, patriotic fantasies on national airs generated considerable audience applause in every South American country the musician visited. The *Grande fantaisie triomphale sur l'hymne national brésilien*, Op. 69 (See: W258) and the *Variations de concert sur l'hymne portugais*, Op. 91 (See: W42 and W260) are two extant works that were particularly popular in Gottschalk's concerts.

The end of Gottschalk's life was marked by a case of malaria. Known to provide relief from the tropical disease with its abilities to regulate heart rhythm, quinine was used by the musician. The speculation today is that an overdose of the drug, whose side effects were not adequately understood during Gottschalk's era, caused Gottschalk's collapse at his November 25, 1869 concert at the Theatro Lyrico Fluminense in Rio de Janeiro, and his death two weeks later at age forty. The legend quickly developed that Gottschalk finished playing his solo piano work *Morte!! (She Is Dead)*, Op. 60 (See: W249), arose from the keyboard and collapsed. Reports from the concert indicate that he finished the aforementioned, eerily titled work and actually was just beginning the virtuosic *Tremelo, grande étude de concert*, Op. 58 (See: W250) when he collapsed and had to be carried from the stage.

In the years following Gottschalk's death, his close associate, pianist/composer Nicolás Ruiz Espadero edited several previously unpublished works and issued them. Works from the 1850s that Espadero edited for publication include: *Le carnaval de Venice, grand caprice et variations*, Op. 89 (See: W90); *Danse des sylphes, caprice de concert*, Op. 86 (See: W96); *Scherzo Romantique*, Op. 73 (See: W99); and *Banjo*, Op. 82 (See: W110). We have documentary evidence that Gottschalk performed these works during his 1850s and 1860s tours. It is most likely that some of the more virtuosic compositions were not thought to be suitable for publication; since very few pianists would be able to play them, the works would generate few sales. Although Gaspar Agüero y Barreras claimed in his 1939 book *El Compositor Nicolás Ruiz Espadero* (See: B209, pp. 11-15) that Gottschalk composed only the melodies of these posthumously published works, with Espadero supplying the harmony and accompaniment texture, it seems more likely that Espadero based his editions both on Gottschalk's sketches—Espadero was one of the few musicians who understood Gottschalk's shorthand notational system—and on his experience of having heard the composer perform the works over the period of many years, going all the way back to Gottschalk's first travels to Cuba in the early 1850s.

In 1871, the composer's former friend, hosiery importer Charles Vezin, "absconded with the major portion of the Gottschalk estate, including jewels and decorations, traveling to Rio de Janeiro in an attempt to obtain the balance of Gottschalk's estate still involved in litigation there since his death" (See: B514, p. 64). Over the years, the composer's letters and other memorabilia would surface and go on exhibit. Today, most of the extant Gottschalk material, including photographs, portraits, manuscripts, and letters, is owned by the New York Public Library.

For several decades after Gottschalk's death, his works remained in publication; in 1900 the Oliver Ditson Company, one of the composer's primary American publishers, listed over 100 Gottschalk works in print (See: B136). Critical assessment of Gottschalk generally allowed that he had been a highly musical, technically brilliant pianist who wrote music of highly uneven quality. By 1908, Frederic S. Law included Gottschalk among the undeservedly forgotten great musicians of the past (See: B157). Indeed, by 1915 the Oliver Ditson Company included only 55 Gottschalk works in its catalog (See: B180).

The revival of interest in Gottschalk goes back to 1940s performances by pianist John Kirkpatrick, followed by the concert work of Jeanne Behrend and Eugene List in the 1950s and 1960s. Recordings by List, Behrend, Leonard Pennario, Philip Martin, and Alan Mandel, among others, have continued to perpetuate Gottschalk's music into the era of the compact disc.

Scholarly interest in Gottschalk began to take hold in the 1940s with such works as Paul Henry Lang's 1941 book *Music in Western Civilization* (See: B214), a work in which the composer is treated as a virtual equal of his European contemporaries; Gilbert Chase's 1941 book *The Music of Spain* (See: B213), in which Gottschalk is discussed in the chapter "Hispanic Music in the Americas," and Chase's 1945 book *A Guide to Latin American Music* (See: B222), in which the author credits Gottschalk with bridging inter-American musical cultures. Gottschalk-specific studies appeared more frequently beginning in the 1940s, with theses such as Sister Mary Rachel Rooks' *The Life and Piano Music of Louis Moreau Gottschalk* (See: B218) and Carl E. Lindstrom's 1945 *Musical Quarterly* article, "The American Quality in the Music of Louis Moreau Gottschalk" (See: B223). Lindstrom deals with Gottschalk's compositions as precursors of ragtime, jazz, and Tin Pan Alley music.

The principle Gottschalk scholarship of the 1950s includes Franciso Curt Lange's 1951 study *Vida y muerte de Louis Moreau Gottschalk en Rio de Janeiro, 1869*, a book that is still considered the standard in documenting the musician's activities at the end of his life. As Jeanne Behrend and Eugene List issued recordings of Gottschalk piano music in the late 1950s and more public attention was focused on the Creole master, Vernon Loggins' much-anticipated, 1958 biography *Where the Word Ends: The Life of Louis Moreau Gottschalk* (See: B267) appeared. Unfortunately, the book included fictionalized conversations between Gottschalk and his contemporaries and was received by many reviewers as a work closer to historical fiction than a true biography (See: B270, B271, and B276, for example).

The 1960s, 1970s, and 1980s were notable for even more serious documentary study being given to Gottschalk. John Doyle's 1960 dissertation, *The Piano Music of Louis Moreau Gottschalk, 1829-1869* (See: B279), included important systematic study of the various folk melodies used by the composer. Robert Offergeld's 1970 booklet *The Centennial Catalogue of the Published and Unpublished Compositions of Louis Moreau Gottschalk* (See: B378), published under the auspices of *Stereo Review*, remains the principal catalog of Gottschalk's works, published and unpublished, lost and extant, even though subsequent scholarship has answered some of the questions Offergeld raised about some of the lost works. John Doyle's 1982 *Louis Moreau Gottschalk, 1929-1869: A Bibliographical Study and Catalog of Works* (See: B484) is an inclusive bibliographical source for information on Gottschalk, including much iconography study.   Doyle's works catalog is considerably smaller than Offergeld's, as Doyle includes only published compositions.   A comprehensive, scholarly biography of Gottschalk was not published until 1995 when S. Frederick Starr's *Bamboula!   The Life and Times of Louis Moreau Gottschalk* (See: B524) appeared.   Combining excellent scholarship with a writing style that brings Gottschalk to life, Starr's book remains the premiere Gottschalk biography to date.

At the time of this writing, Louis Moreau Gottschalk is still acknowledged as America's leading concert artist of the nineteenth century.   His compositions receive more sympathetic consideration than ever, with even the sentimental pot-boilers like *The Last Hope* and *The Dying Poet* acknowledged as accurate reflections of the aesthetic of a large segment of mid-century American popular culture.   Although formally and harmonically he was far from being a progressive composer, in terms of his creative use of quotation and his catholic treatment of every folk music style he heard around him, no matter how obscure and no matter how denigrated by the musical establishment of his day, Louis Moreau Gottschalk is now considered to have been one of the most ground-breaking composers in all of American musical history.

Vocal Works

OPERA

W1. **Isaura di Salerno** (1859; lost.)

Contents: Three acts, all lost.
Other indices: RO125.

Bibliography

WB1. Offergeld, Robert. *The Centennial Catalogue of the Published and Unpublished Compositions of Louis Moreau Gottschalk*. New York: *Stereo Review*, 1970.
Offergeld provides extensive commentary on the possible history and historical subject matter of the piece.

W2. **Charles IX [Carlos IX]** (1859-1860; lost.)

Other indices: RO52.
(See also: W36)

Bibliography

WB2. Tolon, Edwin T. and Jorge A. Gonzales. *Operas cubanas y sus autores*. Havana: Imprenta Ucar, Garcia, 1943.
Includes information on the performance of part of the opera later cited by Doyle (See: B484) and used by Starr (See: B524).

W3.   **Amalia Warden** (1860; unpublished; lost.)

Other indices: RO4, D3.
Contents: Three acts, all lost except Act I libretto.
Act I libretto manuscript is located at the New York Public Library.
Libretto by Alessandro Lorenzana.

W4.   **Escenas campestres** (1860; New York: MCA Music, 1969 [full score and parts available for rental only].)

For soprano, tenor, baritone, and orchestra.
Contents: one act.
Dedication: Countess de San Antonia.
Libretto by Manuel Ramirez.
Manuscript is located at the New York Public Library.
Other indices: RO77, D47.

Performances

W4a.   February 17, 1860. Teatro di tacón, Havana, Cuba.
            The world premiere of the work.

W4b.   February 25, 1969. New Orleans Louisiana; various soloists; New Orleans Philharmonic Orchestra; Werner Torkanowsky, conductor.
            The United States premiere of the work.

Recordings

R4a.   *A Gottschalk Festival.* Trinidad Paniagua, soprano; Jose Alberto Esteves, tenor; Pablo Garcia, baritone; Wiener Staatsopernorchester; Igor Buketoff, conductor. Two compact discs. Vox Box 5009, n.d.
            (See also: R34e, R36b, R37g, R41a, R42a, R44a, R191h, R220m, R228t, R258k, R298b, R302d, R305c, R310c)

Bibliography

WB3.   "Symphony Plans Concert in Honor of Composer." *New Orleans Times-Picayune* February 16, 1969.
            A preview of the United States premiere (See: W4b).

WB4.   "Rare Gottschalk Works to Be Played Tuesday." *New Orleans Times-Picayune* February 23, 1969.
    A preview of the United States premiere (See: W4b).

WB5.   Dufour, Charles L. "Works and Performers Glow in Première Here." *New Orleans States-Item* February 26, 1969.
    A favorable review of the United States premiere (See: W4b).

WB6.   Gagnard, Frank. "Music of 100 Years Ago Heard Again in Concert." *New Orleans Times-Picayune* February 26, 1969.
    A favorable review of the United States premiere (See: W4b).

WB7.   Schonberg, Harold C. "Music: Southern Original." *New York Times* February 27, 1969:33.
    A favorable review of the United States premiere (See: W4b).

WB8.   Korf, William E. *The Orchestral Music of Louis Moreau Gottschalk*. Dissertation: The University of Iowa, 1974. Also published as *Wissenschaftliche Abhandlungen*, Vol. 28. Henryville, Pennsylvania: Institute of Mediaeval Music, 1983.
    Also indexed in *Dissertation Abstracts International* 35-A/7 (January 1975), p. 4589.

WB9.   Korf, William E. "Gottschalk's One-Act Opera Scene, *Escenas Campestres*." *Current Musicology* 26:62-73 (1978).
    A description of the work with examples of the thematic relationships between the piece and *Danza, Op. 33* (See: W167).

CHORAL WORKS

W5.   **Pange linguae** (1854-5; unpublished; lost.)

For male voices.

Bibliography

WB10.   Starr, S. Frederick. *Bamboula! The Life and Times of Louis Moreau Gottschalk.* New York: Oxford University Press, 1995. Paperback edition: Urbana: University of Illinois Press, 2000.
         Starr cites newspaper evidence of the composition of this work in Cuba (p. 193). According to the author, the piece is not mentioned in any previous study of Gottschalk.

W6.   **Rex altissime** (1854-5; unpublished; lost.)

Possibly for SATB choir.

Bibliography

WB11.   Starr, S. Frederick. *Bamboula! The Life and Times of Louis Moreau Gottschalk.* New York: Oxford University Press, 1995. Paperback edition: Urbana: University of Illinois Press, 2000.
         Starr cites newspaper evidence of the composition of this work in Cuba (p. 193). According to the author, the piece is not mentioned in any previous study of Gottschalk.

MUSIC FOR SOLO VOICE

W7.   **The Clermont Mass** (1848; lost.)

For voice and organ.
Other indices: RO56.
(See also: W8)

W8.   **Agnus Dei** (1853; lost.)

Precise medium unknown.
Other indices: RO3.

Bibliography

WB12.   *The Life of Louis Moreau Gottschalk.* New York, 1863.
The works list (p. 11) seems to be the only source
suggesting the existence of *Agnus Dei.* Several writers
suggest that the piece may have been a movement of *The
Clermont Mass* (See: W7).

W9.   **Mélodie pour voix d'homme** (1855; unpublished; lost.)

For male voice and piano.
Other indices: RO168.

W10.   **Alone** (1855-6; Philadelphia: Hatch Music Co., 1902. Pub. pl. no.
2062-3; Newton Centre, Massachusetts: Margun Music, 1992 (*The
Complete Published Songs of Louis Moreau Gottschalk, with a
Selection of Other Songs of Mid-Nineteenth-Century America*, ed.
Richard Jackson).)

For voice and piano.
Text by William H. Morris.
Other indices: RO278, D2.
Note: While Offergeld lists this piece as an untitled song, Doyle and
later writers identify it by name.

W11.   **Grande Valse poétique concertante** (1856; unpublished; lost.)

For voice and piano.
Written for Madame Anna de la Grange.

Performances

W11a.   October 14, 1856. Philadelphia. Madame Anna de la
Grange, voice; Louis Moreau Gottschalk, piano.

Bibliography

WB13.   Concert Notice. *Dwight's Journal of Music.* p23
(October 18, 1856).

W12.   **Le Carnaval de Venise** (1857; unpublished; lost.)

For soprano and piano.
Other indices: RO46.

Performances

W12a.   February 1857. West Indies. Adelina Patti, soprano;
        Louis Moreau Gottschalk, piano.

W13.   Paulina, sérénade pour voix d'homme (1859; lost.)

For male voice and piano.
Other indices: RO192.
Note: Lowens and Starr (See: WB16) suggest that the lost *Paulina,
      sérénade* and *Idol of Beauty* (See: W14) are the same piece.
      The earlier Offergeld (See: WB14) cites evidence to the
      contrary. Jackson (See: WB15, pp50-51), discusses the
      differences between the songs, considering them substantive
      enough to constitute two separate compositions.

Bibliography

WB14.   Offergeld, Robert. *The Centennial Catalogue of the
        Published and Unpublished Compositions of Louis
        Moreau Gottschalk.* New York: Stereo Review, 1970.

WB15.   Jackson, Richard. Notes to *The Complete Published
        Songs of Louis Moreau Gottschalk, with a Selection of
        Other Songs of Mid-Nineteenth-Century America.*
        Newton Centre, Massachusetts: Margun Music, 1992.

WB16.   Lowens, Irving and S. Frederick Starr. *The New Grove
        Dictionary of Music and Musicians*, 2nd ed. s.v.
        "Gottschalk, Louis Moreau." London: Macmillan, 2000.

W14.   Idol of Beauty (Viens o ma belle), serenade (1861; New York:
        Wm. Hall & Son, 1863. Pub. pl. no. 4816; Newton Centre,
        Massachusetts: Margun Music, 1992 (*The Complete Published
        Songs of Louis Moreau Gottschalk, with a Selection of Other Songs
        of Mid-Nineteenth-Century America*, ed. Richard Jackson).)
For voice and piano.
French text by Louis Moreau Gottschalk. English translation by
        William Jarvis Wetmore.
Manuscript is located at the New York Public Library.
Dedicated to Pasquale Grignoli.
Other indices: RO120, D71.
Note: Lowens and Starr (See: WB22) suggest that the lost *Paulina,
      sérénade* (See: W13) and *Idol of Beauty* are the same piece.

The earlier Offergeld (See: WB19) cites evidence to the contrary.

Performances

W14a.   October 1861. Guanabacoa, Cuba. Constant Hayet, voice; Louis Moreau Gottschalk, piano.

Recordings

R14a.   *A Gottschalk Gala.* Various artists. Compact disc. Premiere Recordings PRCD 1063, 1998.

Bibliography

WB17.   Concert review. *Gaceta de la Habana* October 2, 1861.

WB18.   Concert review. *Gaceta de la Habana* October 17, 1861.

WB19.   Offergeld, Robert. *The Centennial Catalogue of the Published and Unpublished Compositions of Louis Moreau Gottschalk.* New York: Stereo Review, 1970.

WB20.   Doyle, John G. *Louis Moreau Gottschalk 1829-1869: A Bibliographical Study and Catalog of Works.* Detroit: Information Coordinators, Inc. for the College Music Society, 1983.
            Doyle (p. 292) is the source for the above citations from *Gaceta de la Habana* (See: WB17 and WB18).

WB21.   Jackson, Richard. Notes to *The Complete Published Songs of Louis Moreau Gottschalk, with a Selection of Other Songs of Mid-Nineteenth-Century America.* Newton Centre, Massachusetts: Margun Music, 1992.

WB22.   Lowens, Irving and S. Frederick Starr. *The New Grove Dictionary of Music and Musicians,* 2nd ed. s.v. "Gottschalk, Louis Moreau." London: Macmillan, 2000.

W15.   Le Papillon (Fair Butterfly) (1862; Boston: Oliver Ditson & Co., 1874, ed. Clara Gottschalk Peterson. Pub. pl. no. 28130; Newton Centre, Massachusetts: Margun Music, 1992 (*The Complete Published Songs of Louis Moreau Gottschalk, with a Selection of*

Other Songs of Mid-Nineteenth-Century America, ed. Richard Jackson).)

For voice and piano.
French text by Louis Moreau Gottschalk. English adaptation by
    Louis C. Elson.
Dedicated to Carlotta Patti, who possibly premiered the work (See:
    W15a).
Manuscript sketches are located at the New York Public Library.
Other indices: RO188, D112.

Performances

W15a.   November 5, 1862. Washington, D.C. Carlotta Patti,
    soprano; Louis Moreau Gottschalk, piano.
        Possibly the premiere (See: WB24, p. 87)

W15b.   January 1863. Rochester, New York. Louis Moreau
    Gottschalk, piano; Carlotta Patti, soprano.

W15c.   May 2, 1979. Carnegie Hall, New York City. Geanie
    Faulkner, soprano.

W15d.   November 1984. New York City. Lucy Shelton,
    soprano; Lambert Orkis, piano.
        (See also: WB23)

Recordings

R15a.   *A Gottschalk Gala*. Various artists. Compact disc.
    Premiere Recordings PRCD 1063, 1998.

Bibliography

WB23.   Crutchfield, Will. *New York Times* November 7, 1984:
    III/21.
        Reviewing Shelton and Orkis' performance (See:
    W15d), Crutchfield describes the piece as "irresistible"
    and "splendidly flamboyant."

WB24.   Jackson, Richard. Notes to *The Complete Published
    Songs of Louis Moreau Gottschalk, with a Selection of
    Other Songs of Mid-Nineteenth-Century America*.
    Newton Centre, Massachusetts: Margun Music, 1992.

W16. **Slumber on, Baby Dear (La ninnarella), a Mother's Cradle Song**
(c1862; New York: William Hall and Son, 1863. Pub. pl. no. 4820;
Newton Centre, Massachusetts: Margun Music, 1992 (*The Complete
Published Songs of Louis Moreau Gottschalk, with a Selection of
Other Songs of Mid-Nineteenth-Century America*, ed. Richard
Jackson).)

For voice and piano.
English text by Henry C. Watson. Italian text by J. Debrin.
Dedicated to Mrs. Marie Abbott, a singer who had appeared with
Gottschalk after his 1862 return to the United States from the
Caribbean.
Other indices: RO28, D21.
Note: This song is based on the piano piece *Berceuse* (See: W212).

Recordings

R16a.   *Louis Moreau Gottschalk: A Night in the Tropics*. Paul
Rowe, baritone; Barbara Richards, piano. Compact disc.
Naxos 8.559036, 2000
Note: This recording was of Lucièn Lambert's 1898
edition of the song. (See also: R34f, R37i, R78t, R95n,
R103g, R165x, R203i, R227l, R311a)

Bibliography

WB25.   Jackson, Richard. Notes to *The Complete Published
Songs of Louis Moreau Gottschalk, with a Selection of
Other Songs of Mid-Nineteenth-Century America*.
Newton Centre, Massachusetts: Margun Music, 1992.

W17. **The Mountaineer's Song (Il canto del montanaro)** (c1862-3; New
York: Wm. Hall, 1863. Pub no. 4781; Newton Centre,
Massachusetts: Margun Music, 1992 (*The Complete Published
Songs of Louis Moreau Gottschalk, with a Selection of Other Songs
of Mid-Nineteenth-Century America*, ed. Richard Jackson).)

For high voice and piano.
English text by William Jarvis Wetmore.
Dedicated to William Castle.
Other indices: RO175, D101.

Performances

W17a.   April 20, 1863. Irving Hall, New York City. William
        Castle, tenor; Louis Moreau Gottschalk, piano.
        The New York premiere.

Recordings

R17a.   *A Gottschalk Gala*. Various artists. Compact disc.
        Premiere Recordings PRCD 1063, 1998.

Bibliography

WB26.   Minor, Andrew C. *Piano Concerts in New York, 1849-
        1865*. Thesis: University of Michigan, 1947.
            Minor (p. 387) documents the New York premiere
        (See: W17a).

WB27.   Jackson, Richard. Notes to *The Complete Published
        Songs of Louis Moreau Gottschalk, with a Selection of
        Other Songs of Mid-Nineteenth-Century America*.
        Newton Centre, Massachusetts: Margun Music, 1992.

W18.   **My Only Love, Good Bye! (Addio, mio solo amor)** (1863; New
        York: Wm. Hall, 1863. Pub. pl. no. 4760; Newton Centre,
        Massachusetts: Margun Music, 1992 (*The Complete Published
        Songs of Louis Moreau Gottschalk, with a Selection of Other Songs
        of Mid-Nineteenth-Century America*, ed. Richard Jackson).)

    For high voice and piano.
    English text may be by Louis Moreau Gottschalk (See: WB28).
        Italian translation by E.C. Sebastiany.
    Dedicated to Mrs. Charles Vezin, a friend of the composer.
    Other indices: RO177, D103.

Recordings

R18a.   *A Gottschalk Gala*. Various artists. Compact disc.
        Premiere Recordings PRCD 1063, 1998.

Bibliography

WB28.   Jackson, Richard. Notes to *The Complete Published
        Songs of Louis Moreau Gottschalk, with a Selection of*

Other Songs of Mid-Nineteenth-Century America.
Newton Centre, Massachusetts: Margun Music, 1992.
    Jackson speculates (p. 64) that Gottschalk may have been the author of the text and that the text was written in response to the composer's brother Edward's dying of tuberculosis.

W19.   **O Loving Heart, Trust On! (Amor y fé) (O Waiting Heart)** (1863; New York: Wm. Hall & Sons, 1864. Pub. pl. no. 6618; Chicago: Clayton F. Summy Co., 1907 ("O Waiting Heart" version); Boston: Oliver Ditson & Co., 1908 (includes added violin obligato by N. Clifford Page). Pub. pl. no. 5-47-67092-8; New York: University Society, c1910; New York: M. Witmark & Sons, 1913 (*The Artistic Soprano, Volume One: A Collection of Standard Ballads and Arias by Celebrated Composers*); Boston: Oliver Ditson & Co., 1916 (*Songs with Violin*, edited and violin and violoncello parts arranged by N. Clifford Page; Newton Centre, Massachusetts: Margun Music, 1992 (*The Complete Published Songs of Louis Moreau Gottschalk, with a Selection of Other Songs of Mid-Nineteenth-Century America,* ed. Richard Jackson).)

For high voice and piano.
"O Loving Heart, Trust On!" text by Henry C. Watson.
"O Waiting Heart" text by Frederick W. Root.
Dedication: "To my Friend Sherwood C. Campbell." (Campbell
        was a baritone who first appeared with Gottschalk in 1863.)
Other indices: RO181, D106 ("O Waiting Heart" version listed as
        D111).
Note: Despite the above dedication, found on the 1864 Wm. Hall &
        Sons publication, Starr claims that Gottchalk dedicated the
        piece to "the fair Turkish maiden Oseilu Lylcek," "an anagram
        for Louise Kelly," a woman whom Gottschalk was reportedly
        about to marry (See: B524, p. 352). Doyle (p. 307) indicates
        that the c1910 University Society edition bears a dedication to
        Adelaide Neilson.

Recordings

R19a.   *A Gottschalk Gala.* Various artists. Compact disc.
        Premiere Recordings PRCD 1063, 1998.

Bibliography

WB29.   Jackson, Richard. Notes to *The Complete Published*

> *Songs of Louis Moreau Gottschalk, with a Selection of Other Songs of Mid-Nineteenth-Century America.* Newton Centre, Massachusetts: Margun Music, 1992.
>
> Jackson quotes the sales figures for the song, indicating that, with over 14,000 copies sold between 1880 and June 1897, it was easily Gottschalk's best-selling song; "Slumber On, Baby Dear," the composer's second best-selling song of the period, sold just over 3,000 copies (p. 71). Jackson also quotes lyricist Henry C. Watson's assessment of the song as "one of the best, if not the best song that Gottschalk has written" (p. 71).

W20.   **I Don't See It, Mamma!** (c1863-4; New York: Wm. Hall & Son, 1864; Newton Centre, Massachusetts: Margun Music, 1992 (*The Complete Published Songs of Louis Moreau Gottschalk, with a Selection of Other Songs of Mid-Nineteenth-Century America*, ed. Richard Jackson).)

For voice and piano.
Text by Henry C. Watson.
Dedication: "To Osielu Lyleek."
Sketches are located at the New York Public Library.
Other indices: RO119, D72.

Recordings

R20a.   *A Gottschalk Gala.* Various artists. Compact disc. Premiere Recordings PRCD 1063, 1998.

W21.   **Stay, My Charmer** (c1864; New York: Wm. Hall & Son, 1864; Newton Centre, Massachusetts: Margun Music, 1992 (*The Complete Published Songs of Louis Moreau Gottschalk, with a Selection of Other Songs of Mid-Nineteenth-Century America*, ed. Richard Jackson).)

For voice and piano.
Text by Robert Burns.
Dedication: "To Osielu Lyleek."
Other indices: RO252, D149.
Note: This is Gottschalk's shortest song, being only 48 measures in length.

Recordings

R21a.   *A Gottschalk Gala.* Various artists. Compact disc.
Premiere Recordings PRCD 1063, 1998.

Bibliography

WB30.   Jackson, Richard. Notes to *The Complete Published
Songs of Louis Moreau Gottschalk, with a Selection of
Other Songs of Mid-Nineteenth-Century America.*
Newton Centre, Massachusetts: Margun Music, 1992.
    Jackson discusses some of the unique formal and
harmonic features of the song, as well as some of the
history around its publication.

W22.   **Canadian Boat Song** (c1864; Philadelphia: Reed Meyer, 1870. Pub.
pl. no. RM171; Newton Centre, Massachusetts: Margun Music,
1992 (*The Complete Published Songs of Louis Moreau Gottschalk,
with a Selection of Other Songs of Mid-Nineteenth-Century America*,
ed. Richard Jackson).)

For voice and piano.
Also arranged for four male voices.
Dedication: "Composed for the Wissahickon Glee Club."
Text by Thomas Moore.
Other indices: RO34, D24 (male quartet arrangement, D24a).
Sketches are located at the New York Public Library.

W23.   **Pastorella e cavalliere (The Young Shepherdess and the Knight)**
(c1865; New York: Wm. Hall & Son, 1865. Pub. pl. no. 6007;
Boston: Oliver Ditson & Co., 1865. Pub. pl. no. 6007; Newton
Centre, Massachusetts: Margun Music, 1992 (*The Complete
Published Songs of Louis Moreau Gottschalk, with a Selection of
Other Songs of Mid-Nineteenth-Century America*, ed. Richard
Jackson).)

For voice and piano.
Text by Henry C. Watson.
Dedicated to Mrs. Varian Hoffman.
An arrangment of W185.
Other indices: RO191, D114a.

Bibliography

WB31.   Jackson, Richard. Notes to *The Complete Published
          Songs of Louis Moreau Gottschalk, with a Selection of
          Other Songs of Mid-Nineteenth-Century America.*
          Newton Centre, Massachusetts: Margun Music, 1992.
             Jackson's assessment is that "the song's length is
          deadly; its prosody atrocious" (p. 109). He submits that
          the piano piece upon which the song is based is in every
          way superior to the song.

W24. **Ave Maria** (1864-6; Boston: Oliver Ditson & Co., 1873, ed. Clara
          Gottschalk Peterson. Pub. pl. no. 28062; Paris: L. Escudier, 1875.
          Pub. pl. no. L.E.3431; Paris: O. Bornemann, 1886; Newton Centre,
          Massachusetts: Margun Music, 1992 (*The Complete Published
          Songs of Louis Moreau Gottschalk, with a Selection of Other Songs
          of Mid-Nineteenth-Century America,* ed. Richard Jackson).)

          For voice and piano.
          Dedication: "à mon amie Madame M. Buckler."
          An arrangement of *Marguerite* (See: W244).
          Anonymous Biblical text.
          Other indices: RO10, D6.

Recordings

R24a.   *A Gottschalk Gala.* Various artists. Compact disc.
          Premiere Recordings PRCD 1063, 1998.

W25. **Rapelle-toi (Pensez à moi)** (c1863-8; Paris: Escudier, 1879
          ("Pensez à moi," ed. Clara Gottschalk Peterson); Newton Centre,
          Massachusetts: Margun Music, 1992 (*The Complete Published
          Songs of Louis Moreau Gottschalk, with a Selection of Other Songs
          of Mid-Nineteenth-Century America,* ed. Richard Jackson).)

          For voice and piano.
          "Rapelle-toi" text by Alfred de Musset. "Pensez à moi" text by Jules
              Ruelle.
          Manuscript is located at the New York Public Library.
          Other indices: RO219 (RO195), D118.
          Note: As documented by Jackson (See: WB32, pp. 94-95), only
              four minor, yet musically interesting, exceptions distinguish
              "Rapelle-toi" (RO219) and "Pensez à moi" (RO195).
          (See also: W27)

Recordings

R25a.   *A Gottschalk Gala.* Various artists. Compact disc.
Premiere Recordings PRCD 1063, 1998.

Bibliography

WB32.   Jackson, Richard. Notes to *The Complete Published
Songs of Louis Moreau Gottschalk, with a Selection of
Other Songs of Mid-Nineteenth-Century America.*
Newton Centre, Massachusetts: Margun Music, 1992.

W26.   **La flor que ella me envia** (c1866-8; Buenos Aires: Edigiones A.
Demarchi y C., 1868; Newton Centre, Massachusetts: Margun
Music, 1992 (*The Complete Published Songs of Louis Moreau
Gottschalk, with a Selection of Other Songs of Mid-Nineteenth-
Century America,* ed. Richard Jackson).)

For high voice and piano.
Text by Guillermo Blest Gana.
Dedicated to Amalia Gordillo de Tarnassi, an Argentinian pupil of
Gottschalk.
Note: Doyle lists the piece as a piano solo (D57) and Offergeld does
not list it.
Note: Jackson (See: WB35, p. 31) gives the Argentinian publisher's
name as A. Dimarchi, although the reproduction of the title
page gives A. Demarchi.
(See also: W248)

Recordings

R26a.   *A Gottschalk Gala.* Various artists. Compact disc.
Premiere Recordings PRCD 1063, 1998.

Bibliography

WB33.   Stevenson, Robert M. "Gottschalk in Buenos Aires."
Inter-American Bulletin 74:1-7 (November 1969).

WB34.   Stevenson, Robert M. "Gottschalk in Western South
America." *Inter-American Bulletin* 74:7-16 (November
1969).

WB35.   Jackson, Richard. Notes to *The Complete Published*

> *Songs of Louis Moreau Gottschalk, with a Selection of Other Songs of Mid-Nineteenth-Century America.* Newton Centre, Massachusetts: Margun Music, 1992.

W27.   **L'exile** (unknown date; possibly published after 1869; lost.)

For voice and piano.
Other indices: RO90.
Note: Offergeld suggests that the piece may be spurious and its listing in early Gottschalk sources may have been the result of confusion about the publication of *Pensez à moi* (See: W25).

W28.   **Berceuse (O mon trésor, dors d'un calme sommeil)** (unknown date; lost.)

For voice and piano.
Other indices: D22.
Note: The piece is possibly spurious.

Orchestral and Band Works

W29.   **Concerto in F minor for Piano and Orchestra** (fragment) (1853; unpublished; lost.)

For piano and orchestra.
Other indices: RO197.
Note: Gottschalk's *Concerto in F minor* seems to be a work of considerable controversy, with Doyle (See: WB36) claiming that the piece was actually composed by Henselt and with Offergeld (See: WB37) citing evidence to the contrary. Offergeld (p. 26) also discusses the conflicting dates and venues for possible Gottschalk performances of the piece. There seems to be no evidence that Gottschalk ever completed more than a fragmentary version of the composition.

Bibliography

WB36.   Doyle, John Godfrey. *The Piano Music of Louis Moreau Gottschalk, 1829-1869*. Dissertation: New York University, 1960.

WB37.   Offergeld, Robert. *The Centennial Catalogue of the Published and Unpublished Compositions of Louis Moreau Gottschalk*. New York: *Stereo Review*, 1970.

W30.   **La Puertorrequeña, gran marcha triunfal** (1857; unpublished; lost.)

For military band (See note below).

Other indices: RO215.

Note: Although the exact instrumentation of this work has not been
determined, Offergeld (p. 27) reports that it was scored for "at
least forty performers, including five military snare drums,
eight maracas, eight gourds, two contrabasses, three violins,
and two grand pianos played by four pianists."

Performances

W30a.   Late 1857. Ponce, Puerto Rico.

Bibliography

WB38.   Pasarell, Emilio J. "El Centenario de los conciertos de
Andelina Patti y Luis Moreau Gottschalk en Puerto Rico."
Revista del Instituto de Cultura Puertorriqueña 2:52-5
(no. 2; January-March 1959).
      Pasarell (pp. 52-53) provides information on the 1857
performance of the work in Puerto Rico (See: W30a).

WB39.   Muñoz, María Luisa. *La Musica en Puerto Rico*. Sharon,
Connecticut: Troutman Press, 1966.
      The author mentions several Gottschalk works
performed in Puerto Rico, including the lost
Puertorrequeña.

W31.   **Valse poétique** (1857; unpublished; lost.)

Other indices: RO286.

Note: Although Offergeld suggests that the piece may be related to
Sospiro, Valse poétique (See: W152), based on similar titles
and the composition dates, there is no independent evidence to
document such a relationship.

W32.   **Las Ponceñas, Contradanzas: Quadrilles** (1857; unpublished;
lost.)

For military band.
Other indices: RO211.
Dedication: "respetuosamente a las hochiceras hijas de esta villa."

Performances

W32a.   Late 1857. Ponce, Puerto Rico.

Bibliography

WB40.   Pasarell, Emilio J. "El Centenario de los conciertos de
          Andelina Patti y Luis Moreau Gottschalk en Puerto Rico."
          Revista del Instituto de Cultura Puertorriqueña 2:52-5
          (no. 2; January-March 1959).
               Pasarell (pp. 52-53) provides information on the 1857
          performance of the work in Puerto Rico (See: W32a).

WB41.   Gottschalk, Louis Moreau. *Notes of a Pianist*, ed. Jeanne
          Behrend. New York: Alfred A. Knopf, 1964.
               Editor Jeanne Behrend (p. 19) discusses this work.

WB42.   Muñoz, María Luisa. *La Musica en Puerto Rico*. Sharon,
          Connecticut: Troutman Press, 1966.
               The author mentions several Gottschalk works,
          including the lost *Las Ponceñas*, providing information on
          the work's dedication (pp. 112-14).

W33.   **Valse di bravura** (1858; unpublished; lost.)

          For military orchestra.
          Other indices: RO283.

W34.   **Symphonie romantique [Symphony No. 1] ("La nuit des
          tropiques")** (1858-9; New York: Edition Musica, 1937, ed. Quinto
          Maganini (Andante only); New York, 1965, ed. Gaylen Hatton. Pub.
          pl. no. F.S. 299; Newton Centre, Massachusetts, 1998, ed. Gunther
          Schuller.)

          For orchestra.
          Contents: Two movements: Andante ("Noche en los Tropicos"),
               Allegro moderato ("Festa Criolla").
          Manuscript is located at the New York Public Library.
          Duration: 16-19 minutes.
          Other indices: RO255, D104.
          (See also: W50 and W297)

Performances

W34a.   February 17, 1860. Teatro Tacón, Havana, Cuba. Louis
        Moreau Gottschalk, conductor.
            Note: Offergeld suggests that possibly only the first
        movement was performed at this concert.

W34b.   April 17, 1861. Havana, Cuba. Louis Moreau
        Gottschalk, conductor.

W34c.   May 5, 1955. McMillin Theater, Columbia University,
        New York City. Columbia University Symphony;
        Howard Shanet, conductor; Columbia University Band,
        Hunter Wiley, conductor.
            The United States premiere. Note that the
        performance utilized Howard Shanet's unpublished
        arrangement/recreation of the piece. (See also: WB43,
        WB44, WB45, WB46)

W34d.   November 21, 1959. Carnegie Hall, New York City.
        New York Philharmonic; Howard Shanet, guest
        conductor.
            Shanet guest conducted this "Young People's
        Concert" in his own reconstruction of the Gottschalk
        score. (See also: WB47)

W34e.   January 13, 1960. Carnegie Hall, New York City.
        Orchestra of America; Richard Korn, conductor.
            This performance was of the Howard Shanet
        reconstruction. (See also: WB48, WB49)

W34f.   June 3, 10, 11, 1966. Avery Fisher Hall, New York City.
        New York Philharmonic; André Kostelanetz, conductor.
            Note: The performance was of the second
        movement, "Allegro moderato," only. (See also: WB52)

W34g.   May 8, 11, 1969. Avery Fisher Hall, New York City.
        New York Philharmonic; André Kostelanetz, conductor.
            Kostelanetz and the New York Philharmonic
        performed only the second movement of the work. (See
        also: WB53)

W34h.   June 11, 12, 13, 1970. Avery Fisher Hall, New York
         City. New York Philharmonic. André Kostelanetz,
         conductor.
             As had been the case over the course of the previous
         several years, Kostelanetz and the Philharmonic
         performed only the second movement of the work.

W34i.   December 2, 1975. McMillin Theater, Columbia
         University, New York City. Columbia University
         Orchestra; Howard Shanet, conductor.
             (See also: WB56)

W34j.   May 21, 1976. Carnegie Hall, New York City. New
         York Philharmonic; André Kostelanetz, conductor.
             Note: Only the second movement, "Allegro
         moderato," was performed. (See also: WB57)

W34k.   July 4, 1976. Battery Park, New York City. American
         Symphony Orchestra; Morton Gould, conductor.
             (See also: WB58)

Recordings

R34a.   *A Panorama of American Orchestral Music.*
         Philharmonia Orchestra; Richard Korn, conductor. 33-1/3
         rpm phonodisc. Allegro 3148, c1959.
             With various works by Samuel Barber, Morton
         Gould, William Henry Fry, Hans Gram, and Paul Creston.
         Note: Only the "Andante" is performed, and in Quinto
         Maganini's orchestration.

R34b.   *The World of Louis Moreau Gottschalk.* Various
         performers. *Symphony No. 1* performed by Utah
         Symphony Orchestra; Maurice Abravanel, conductor.
         Two 33-1/3 rpm phonodiscs. Vanguard VSD-723; VSD-
         724, 1973. Reissued on compact disc. Vanguard VCD
         72026, 1988. Some material originally issued on
         Vanguard VSC 2141, 1964.
             For a review of this recording, see: B417. (See also:
         R37a, R68e, R76b, R78f, R95d, R139g, R142i, R165g,
         R191c, R216d, R227c, R228g, R230c)

R34c.   *Louis Moreau Gottschalk.* Utah Symphony Orchestra; Maurice Abravanel, conductor. Compact disc. Vanguard Classics OVC 4051, 1992. Reissued as part of the two compact disc set *Piano Music.* Vanguard Classics 08 9143 72/08 9144-72, 1993.

        (See also: R37f, R100e, R220h, R250a, R275a, R282b, R291b, R292a, R300b, R302b, R305b, R307b, R310b)

R34d.   *Music & The Arts.* Virginia Symphony; JoAnn Falletta, conductor. Compact disc. Connell Communications CRD0497, 1997. Recorded December 1, 1996 at the L. Douglas Wilder Performing Arts Center, Norfolk State University, Norfolk, Virginia.

        With: compositions by Adolphus Hailstork and Mary Howe.

R34e.   *A Gottschalk Festival.* Wiener Staatsopernorchester; Igor Buketoff, conductor. Two compact discs. Vox Box 5009, n.d.

        (See also: R4a, R36b, R37g, R41a, R42a, R44a, R191h, R220m, R228t, R258k, R298b, R302d, R305c, R310c)

R34f.   *Louis Moreau Gottschalk: A Night in the Tropics.* Hot Springs Music Festival Symphony Orchestra; Richard Rosenberg, conductor. Compact disc. Naxos 8.559036, 2000.

        Note: This recording is of Richard Rosenberg's reconstruction of the work, based on Gottschalk's manuscripts and descriptions. (See also: R16a, R37i, R78t, R95n, R103g, R165x, R203i, R227l, R311a)

Bibliography

WB43.   Schonberg, Harold C. "Concert at Columbia." *New York Times* May 6, 1955.

        A review of W34c.

WB44.   Trimble, Lester. "Columbia Orchestra." *New York Herald-Tribune* May 6, 1955.

        A review of W34c.

WB45.   Kamien, Roger. "Lion about Music—Musical
         Novelties." *Columbia Daily Spectator* May 9, 1955.
         A report on W34c.

WB46.   Seder, Theodore. "Letter to the Editor: Our Early
         Composers." *New York Times* May 22, 1955.
         An editorial concerning W34c.

WB47.   Salzman, Eric. "Music for Young at Carnegie Hall." *New
         York Times* November 22, 1959.
         Review of W34d.

WB48.   Schonberg, Harold C. "Music of America at Carnegie
         Hall." *New York Times* January 14, 1960.
         A review of W34e.

WB49.   Kammerer, Rafael. "Orchestra of America Offers
         Kirchner Work." *Musical America* 80:253 (February
         1960).
         A review of W34e.

WB50.   Shanet, Howard. "En garde, Vanguard!" *Saturday
         Review* p118 (March 14, 1964). Reprinted in *Music
         Journal* p68 (February 1965).
         Concerning the editing of the symphony on Vanguard
         VSC 2141 (See: R34b).

WB51.   Solomon, Seymour. "Vanguard Replies." *Saturday
         Review* (April 11, 1964).
         Concerning the editing of the symphony on Vanguard
         VSC 2141 (See: R34b).

WB52.   Klein, Howard. "Exotic Night at Philharmonic." *New
         York Times* June 4, 1966:18.
         A review of W34f.

WB53.   Hughes, Allen. "Eugene List Is Soloist with the
         Philharmonic." *New York Times* May 10, 1969:53.
         Review of W34g.

WB54.   Offergeld, Robert. *The Centennial Catalogue of the
         Published and Unpublished Compositions of Louis*

Moreau Gottschalk. New York: *Stereo Review*, 1970.

WB55.   Korf, William E. *The Orchestral Music of Louis Moreau Gottschalk*. Dissertation: The University of Iowa, 1974. Also published as *Wissenschatliche Abhandlungen*, Vol. 28. Henryville, Pennsylvania: Institute of Mediaeval Music, 1983.
Also indexed in *Dissertation Abstracts International* 35-A/7 (January 1975), p. 4589.

WB56.   Ericson, Raymond. "An Evening of Musical Rediscovery." *New York Times* December 4, 1975:50.
A favorable review of the Columbia University Orchestra's performance of the work (See: W34i).

WB57.   Sherman, Robert. "Philharmonic Plays Classic Americana." *New York Times* May 23, 1976:61.
A review of W34j.

WB58.   Davis, Peter G. "American Symphony in Rousing Holiday Fare." *New York Times* July 5, 1976:8.
A review of W34k.

W35.   La Bataille de Carabova (1859; lost.)

Probably for military band.
Commissioned by Venezuelan General-President José Antonio Paëz.
Other indices: RO26.

W36.   Marcha Triunfal y Final de Opera (1860; New York: MCA Music, Inc., 1969.)

For orchestra.
Manuscript is located at the New York Public Library.
Other indices: RO157, D87.
Note: This work is an orchestral transcription of the finale from Gottschalk's opera *Charles IX* (See: W2).

Performances

W36a.   February 17, 1860. Havana, Cuba.

W36b.   February 25, 1969. New Orleans, Louisiana. New
        Orleans Philharmonic Orchestra; Werner Torkanowsky,
        conductor.
        The United States premiere.

Recordings

R36a.   *The Best of Louis Moreau Gottschalk.* Berlin Symphony
        Orchestra; Samuel Adler, conductor. 33-1/3 rpm
        phonodisc. Turnabout TV-S 34449, c1979.
        Note: This performance is of a realization and
        orchestration of the work by Donald Hunsberger. (See
        also: R37b, R220e, R258e)

R36b.   *A Gottschalk Festival.* Wiener Staatsopernorchester; Igor
        Buketoff, conductor. Two compact discs. Vox Box
        5009.
        (See also: R4a, R34e, R37g, R41a, R42a, R44a,
        R191h, R220m, R228t, R258k, R298b, R302d, R305c,
        R310c)

Bibliography

WB59.   "Symphony Plans Concert in Honor of Composer." *New
        Orleans Times-Picayune* February 16, 1969.
        A preview of W36b.

WB60.   "Rare Gottschalk Works to Be Played Tuesday." *New
        Orleans Times-Picayune* February 23, 1969.
        A preview of W36b.

WB61.   Dufour, Charles L. "Works and Performers Glow in
        Première Here." *New Orleans States-Item* February 26,
        1969.
        A favorable review of W36b.

WB62.   Gagnard, Frank. "Music of 100 Years Ago Heard Again
        in Concert." *New Orleans Times-Picayune* February 26,
        1969.
        A favorable review of W36b.

WB63.   Schonberg, Harold C. "Music: Southern Original." *New*

York Times February 27, 1969:33.
A favorable review of W36b.

WB64.   Korf, William E. *The Orchestral Music of Louis Moreau Gottschalk*. Dissertation: The University of Iowa, 1974. Also published as *Wissenschaftliche Abhandlungen*, Vol. 28. Henryville, Pennsylvania: Institute of Mediaeval Music, 1983.
Also indexed in *Dissertation Abstracts International* 35-A/7 (January 1975), p. 4589.

W37.   **Grande tarantelle (Célèbre Tarantelle), Op.** 67 (1858-68; Paris: Escudier, c1874, ed. Nicolás Ruiz Espadero; New York: Boosey and Hawkes, 1964 (arr. Hershy Kay). Pub. pl. no. F.S. 298.)

For piano and orchestra.
Manuscript sketches are located at the New York Public Library.
Duration: 7-1/2 minutes.
Other indices: RO259, D66.
Note: The unusually large range of possible composition dates results from conflicting evidence in various sources. Gottschalk's own writings suggest 1868 as the date of the present work (See: WB71); however, there is evidence that he performed a tarantelle of his own composition in 1864. Doyle (See: WB80, p. 288) cites evidence that Gottschalk and violinist José White improvised a chamber version of the piece (See: W48) in Havana as early as 1858; Starr (See: WB81, p. 289) suggests that Nicolás Ruiz Espadero was also involved in the initial 1858 performances, suggesting a work for violin and two pianists.
(See also: W48, W247, W311, W312)

Performances

W37a.   October 29, 1864. Academy of Music, Philadelphia. Louis Moreau Gottschalk, piano; Adolph Birgfeld, conductor.

W37b.   November 24, 1869. Rio de Janeiro. Louis Moreau Gottschalk, piano; "Monster Concert" festival orchestra.
Although Gottschalk performed the work numerous times in South America during the final years of his life,

this performance was notable as his last. (See: WB80)

W37c.   November 17, 1957. Carnegie Recital Hall, New York
City. Eugene List, piano; Knickerbocker Players; George
Koutzen, conductor.
Hershy Kay's reconstruction for piano, trumpet, and
strings. (See also: WB67)

W37d.   November 7, 1962. Carnegie Hall, New York City.
Eugene List, piano; Orchestra of America; Richard Korn,
conductor.
A performance of Hershy Kay's reconstruction for
piano and orchestra. (See also: WB68, WB69, WB70)

W37e.   May 29, 30, 1963. New York City. Theodore Lettvin,
piano; New York Philharmonic; André Kostelanetz,
conductor.

W37f.   March 16, 1965. New Orleans, Louisiana. Theodore
Lettvin, piano; New Orleans Philharmonic Symphony
Orchestra; Werner Torkanowsky, conductor.

W37g.   February 25, 1969. New Orleans, Louisiana. Theodore
Lettvin, piano; New Orleans Philharmonic Symphony
Orchestra; Werner Torkanowsky, conductor.

W37h.   May 8, 11, 1969. Avery Fisher Hall, New York City.
Eugene List, piano; New York Philharmonic; André
Kostelanetz, conductor.
(See also: WB72)

W37i.   June 2, 3, 5, 1971. New York City. Theodore Lettvin,
piano; New York Philharmonic; André Kostelanetz,
conductor.

W37j.   May 2, 1979. *Monster Concert*. Carnegie Hall, New
York City. Eugene List, piano; various wind and string
performers.
(See also: WB74-79)

W37k.   January 27, 1984. Coolidge Auditorium, Library of
Congress, Washington, D.C. Eugene List, piano;

chamber ensemble.

Recordings

R37a.   *The World of Louis Moreau Gottschalk.* Various
performers. *Grand tarantelle* performed by Reid Nibley,
piano; Utah Symphony Orchestra; Maurice Abravanel,
conductor. Two 33-1/3 rpm phonodiscs. Vanguard VSD-
723; VSD-724, 1973. Reissued on compact disc.
Vanguard VCD 72026, 1988.

    For a review of this recording, see: B417. (See also:
R34b, R68e, R76b, R78f, R95d, R139g, R142i, R165g,
R191c, R216d, R227c, R228g, R230c)

R37b.   *The Best of Louis Moreau Gottschalk.* Eugene List,
piano; Vienna State Opera Orchestra; Igor Buketoff,
conductor. 33-1/3 rpm phonodisc. Turnabout TV-S
34449, c1979.

    Note: This performance is of a reconstruction and
orchestration of the work by Hershey Kay. (See also:
R36a, R220e, R258e)

R37c.   *The Piano Concerto in America.* Various performers.
Grande tarantelle performed by Eugene List, piano;
Vienna State Opera Orchestra; Igor Buketoff, conductor.
Three 1-7/8 ips audio cassettes. Murray Hill Records &
Tapes, 1982.

    With works by Aaron Copland, William Schuman,
Amy Cheney Beach, Samuel Barber, Edward MacDowell,
and Miklós Rózsa.

R37d.   *The Monster Concert in Celebration of Louis Moreau
Gottschalk.* Various performers. *Grande tarantelle*
performed by Eugene List, piano; chamber ensemble of
string quintet, flute, and clarinet. 33-1/3 rpm phonodisc.
Musicmasters MM 20061, 1983. Reissued as Musical
Heritage Society MHS 4924, 1984.

    Contains a number of Gottschalk compositions and
other works from the era. (See also: R273b, R279a,
R297b, R307a)

R37e.   *Library of Congress Music Division Concert, 1984-01-27.*
Eugene List, piano; chamber ensemble (Ronald Neal,
violin; Patmore Lewis, violin; Alex Sobolevsky, violin;
Virginia Barron, viola; Gayane Manasjan, violoncello;
Linda Draper, bass). Three 7-1/2 ips reel-to-reel tapes.
Library of Congress. Recorded live at the Coolidge
Auditorium of the Library of Congress, Washington,
D.C., January 27, 1984.

R37f.   *Louis Moreau Gottschalk.* Reid Nibley, piano; Utah
Symphony Orchestra; Maurice Abravanel, conductor.
Compact disc. Vanguard Classics OVC 4051, 1992.
Reissued as part of the two compact disc set *Piano Music.*
Vanguard Classics 08 9143 72/08 9144-72, 1993.
        (See also: R34c, R100e, R220h, R250a, R275a,
R282b, R291b, R292a, R300b, R302b, R305b, R307b,
R310b)

R37g.   *A Gottschalk Festival.* Eugene List, piano; Wiener
Staatsopernorchester; Igor Buketoff, conductor. Two
compact discs. Vox Box 5009, n.d.
        (See also: R4a, R34e, R36b, R41a, R42a, R44a,
R191h, R220m, R228t, R258k, R298b, R302d, R305c,
R310c)

R37h.   *American Piano Classics.* William Tritt, piano;
Cincinnati Pops Orchestra; Erich Kunzel, conductor.
Simultaneously issued on 1-7/8 ips audio cassette and
compact disc. Telarc 80112, n.d.
        With: various works by George Gershwin, Euday L.
Bowman, Scott Joplin, Leroy Anderson, and Morton
Gould.

R37i.   *Louis Moreau Gottschalk: A Night in the Tropics.* Gary
Hammond, piano; Hot Springs Music Festival Symphony
Orchestra; Richard Rosenberg, conductor. Compact disc.
Naxos 8.559036, 2000.
        Note: This recording is of the 1874 Espadero
arrangement of the piece. (See also: R16a, R34f, R78t,
R95n, R103g, R165x, R203i, R2271, R311a)

Bibliography

WB65.   Apthorp, William Foster. "Recent Music." *Atlantic Monthly* 35:380-81 (March 1875).
   A review of several of Gottschalk's posthumously published works, including the *Grand tarantelle*. (See also: WB66)

WB66.   "Gottschalk's Posthumous Works." *Music* (March 1875).
   Like WB65, this article reviews *Grand tarantelle*, suggesting that only those who had actually heard Gottschalk play the piece would fully appreciate the composition.

WB67.   "Knickerbocker Players Heard." *New York Times* November 18, 1957:36.
   Review of W37c.

WB68.   Biancolli, Louis. Concert Review. *New York World Telegram* Novmeber 8, 1962.
   Review of W37d.

WB69.   Schonberg, Harold C. "Orchestra of America Heard." *New York Times* November 8, 1962:51.
   Review of W37d.

WB70.   Anderson, Owen. "New Works." *Music Journal* v21 (January 1963).
   Review of W37d.

WB71.   Gottschalk, Louis Moreau. *Notes of a Pianist*, ed. Jeanne Behrend. New York: Alfred A. Knopf, 1964.
   Gottschalk mentions (p. 397) that he is working on the piece at the time of the writing (December 15, 1868).

WB72.   Hughes, Allen. "Eugene List Is Soloist with the Philharmonic." *New York Times* May 10, 1969:53.
   Review of W37h.

WB73.   Korf, William E. *The Orchestral Music of Louis Moreau Gottschalk*. Dissertation: The University of Iowa, 1974.
   Also published as *Wissenschaftliche Abhandlungen*, Vol.

28. Henryville, Pennsylvania: Institute of Mediaeval Music, 1983.

Also indexed in *Dissertation Abstracts International* 35-A/7 (January 1975), p. 4589.

WB74.   Johnson, Harriett. "List Honors Gottschalk on a Grand Scale." *New York Post* May 3, 1979:34.

A review of Eugene List's Monster Concert for the Gottschalk sesquicentennial (See: W37j).

WB75.   Horowitz, Joseph. "Concert: Gottschalk Extravaganza." *New York Times* May 4, 1979:C4.

A review of Eugene List's Monster Concert for the Gottschalk sesquicentennial (See: W37j).

WB76.   Zakariasen, Bill. "Weary Gottschalk." *New York Daily News* May 4, 1979:Friday Section, 13.

A review of Eugene List's Monster Concert for the Gottschalk sesquicentennial (See: W37j).

WB77.   Porterfield, Christopher. "Monster Rally: Pianists Celebrate Gottschalk." *Time* 113:106 (no. 20, May 14, 1979).

A review of Eugene List's Monster Concert for the Gottschalk sesquicentennial (See: W37j).

WB78.   Suttoni, Charles. "Cue Reviews: Gottschalk Monster Concert." *Cue* p36 (May 25, 1979).

A review of Eugene List's Monster Concert for the Gottschalk sesquicentennial (See: W37j).

WB79.   Anderson, William. "Speaking of Music: Monster Concert." *Stereo Review* 43:8 (July 1979).

A review of Eugene List's Monster Concert for the Gottschalk sesquicentennial (See: W37j).

WB80.   Doyle, John G. *Louis Moreau Gottschalk 1829-1869: A Bibliographical Study and Catalog of Works.* Detroit: Information Coordinators, Inc. for the College Music Society, 1983.

(See note above) Doyle (pp. 288-89) provides citations for information on various Gottschalk performances between 1864 and 1869.

WB81. Starr, S. Frederick. *Bamboula! The Life and Times of Louis Moreau Gottschalk*. New York: Oxford University Press, 1995.
(See note above)

W38. Marche (1861; unpublished; lost.)

For military orchestra.
Other indices: RO144.

Performances

W38a. April 17, 1861. Havana, Cuba. Louis Moreau Gottschalk, piano; other performers unidentified.

Bibliography

WB82. Loggins, Vernon. *Where the Word Ends: The Life of Louis Moreau Gottschalk*. Baton Rouge: Louisiana State University Press, 1958.
Loggins documents the April 17, 1861 performance of the piece in Havana. (See: W38a)

W39. Grande Marche de *Tannhauser* (c1863; unpublished; lost.)

For sixteen pianos (31 pianists) and orchestra.
Other indices: RO112.
Note: This piece is based on themes from Richard Wagner's opera *Tannhauser*.
(See also: W304)

Performances

W39a. July 11, 1863. Brooklyn, New York. Louis Moreau Gottschalk, piano; other performers unidentified.

W40. **Grande Marche de** *Faust* (c1864; unpublished; lost.)

For sixteen pianos (31 pianists) and orchestra.
Other indices: RO111.
Note: This piece is based on themes from Gounod's opera *Faust*.
(See also: W308)

Performances

W40a. October 5, 1869. Rio de Janeiro. Louis Moreau
Gottschalk, piano; other performers unidentified.

Bibliography

WB83. Lange, Francisco Curt. *Vida y muerte de Louis Moreau
Gottschalk en Rio de Janeiro, 1869.* Mendoza,
Argentina: Universidad Nacional de Cuyo, 1951.
Lange (p. 262) documents the October 1869
performance in Rio de Janeiro (See: W40a).

W41. **Symphony No. 2 ("A Montevideo")** (1865-8; New York: MCA
Music, 1969 (score and parts available on rental only).)

For orchestra.
Contents: One movement in seven sections.
Duration: 12 minutes.
Manuscript and sketches are located at the New York Public Library.
Other indices: RO257, D99.

Performances

W41a. November 1868. Montevideo.
The work's premiere.

W41b. February 25, 1969. New Orleans, Louisiana. New
Orleans Philharmonic Symphony Orchestra; Werner
Torkanowsky, conductor.
The United States premiere. (See also: WB84-88)

W41c. April 21, 1969. National Gallery of Art, Washington,
D.C. National Gallery Orchestra; Richard Cales,
conductor.

W41d.   October 6, 1969. Carnegie Hall, New York City.
             American Symphony Orchestra; Leopold Stokowski,
             conductor.
                     The New York premiere. (See also: WB89-91)

Recordings

R41a.   *A Gottschalk Festival.* Wiener Staatsopernorchester; Igor
             Buketoff, conductor. Two compact discs. Vox Box
             5009, n.d.
                     (See also: R4a, R34e, R36b, R37g, R42a, R44a,
             R191h, R220m, R228t, R258k, R298b, R302d, R305c,
             R310c)

Bibliography

WB84.   "Symphony Plans Concert in Honor of Composer." *New
             Orleans Times-Picayune* February 16, 1969.
                     A preview of W41b.

WB85.   "Rare Gottschalk Works to Be Played Tuesday." *New
             Orleans Times-Picayune* February 23, 1969.
                     A preview of W41b.

WB86.   Dufour, Charles L. "Works and Performers Glow in
             Première Here." *New Orleans States-Item* February 26,
             1969.
                     A favorable review of W41b.

WB87.   Gagnard, Frank. "Music of 100 Years Ago Heard Again
             in Concert." *New Orleans Times-Picayune* February 26,
             1969.
                     A favorable review of W41b.

WB88.   Schonberg, Harold C. "Music: Southern Original." *New
             York Times* February 27, 1969:33.
                     A favorable review of W41b.

WB89.   Keats, Sheila. "Notes on the Program." American
             Symphony Orchestra, Carnegie Hall, New York City,
             October 6, 1969.
                     Program notes for W41d.

WB90.   Schonberg, Harold C. "Stokowski Conducts the American Symphony in Unusual Program." *New York Times* October 7, 1969.
A review of W41d.

WB91.   "Yankee Doodle Dandy." *Newsweek* p130 (October 20, 1969).
A review of Stokowski and the American Symphony Orchestra's performance (See: W41d).

WB92.   Korf, William E. *The Orchestral Music of Louis Moreau Gottschalk.* Dissertation: The University of Iowa, 1974. Also published as *Wissenschaftliche Abhandlungen*, Vol. 28. Henryville, Pennsylvania: Institute of Mediaeval Music, 1983.
Also indexed in *Dissertation Abstracts International* 35-A/7 (January 1975), p. 4589.

W42.   **Variations de concert sur l'hymne portugais, Op. 91** (1865-9; New York: MCA Music, 1969.)

For piano and orchestra.
Manuscript is located at the New York Public Library.
Other indices: RO289, D157a.
(See also: W260)

Performances

W42a.   October 31, 1869. Rio de Janeiro. Louis Moreau Gottschalk, piano.

W42b.   November 13, 1869. Rio de Janerio. Louis Moreau Gottschalk, piano.

W42c.   November 15, 1869. Rio de Janeiro. Louis Moreau Gottschalk, piano.

W42d.   February 25, 1969. New Orleans, Louisiana. Eugene List, piano; New Orleans Philharmonic Orchestra; Werner Torkanowsky, conductor.
The United States premiere. (See also: WB94-98)

Recordings

R42a.   *A Gottschalk Festival.* Eugene List, piano; Wiener
          Staatsopernorchester; Igor Buketoff, conductor. Two
          compact discs. Vox Box 5009, n.d.
               (See also: R4a, R34e, R36b, R37g, R41a, R44a,
          R191h, R220m, R228t, R258k, R298b, R302d, R305c,
          R310c)

Bibliography

WB93.   Lange, Francisco Curt. *Vida y muerte de Louis Moreau
          Gottschalk en Rio de Janeiro, 1869.* Mendoza,
          Argentina: Universidad Nacional de Cuyo, 1951.
               Lange (p. 265-66) documents Gottschalk's October
          and November 1869 performances of the piece (See:
          W42a, W42b, W42c).

WB94.   "Symphony Plans Concert in Honor of Composer." *New
          Orleans Times-Picayune* February 16, 1969.
               A preview of W42d.

WB95.   "Rare Gottschalk Works to Be Played Tuesday." *New
          Orleans Times-Picayune* February 23, 1969.
               A preview of W42d.

WB96.   Dufour, Charles L. "Works and Performers Glow in
          Première Here." *New Orleans States-Item* February 26,
          1969.
               A favorable review of W42d.

WB97.   Gagnard, Frank. "Music of 100 Years Ago Heard Again
          in Concert." *New Orleans Times-Picayune* February 26,
          1969.
               A favorable review of W42d.

WB98.   Schonberg, Harold C. "Music: Southern Original." *New
          York Times* February 27, 1969:33.
               A favorable review of W42d.

WB99.   Korf, William E. *The Orchestral Music of Louis Moreau
          Gottschalk.* Dissertation: The University of Iowa, 1974.

Also published as *Wissenschaftliche Abhandlungen*, Vol. 28. Henryville, Pennsylvania: Institute of Mediaeval Music, 1983.

Also indexed in *Dissertation Abstracts International* 35-A/7 (January 1975), p. 4589.

W43.   **Solemne Marcha Triunfal a Chile** (1866; unpublished; lost.)

For orchestra.
Other indices: RO238.

W44.   **Marche solennelle (Gran Marcha Solemne)** (1866-8; New York: MCA Music, 1969, ed. Donald Hunsberger.)

For orchestra and military band.
Manuscript is located at the New York Public Library.
Other indices: RO154, D91.
Dedicated to the Emperor of Brazil.
Note: The work apparently was composed in 1866, with subsequent revisions made through 1868.
(See also: W251).

Performances

W44a.   August 16, 1866. Chile.

W44b.   November 1868. Montevideo.

W44c.   November 24, 1869. Rio de Janeiro. Festival orchestra of 650 musicians.

Recordings

R44a.   *A Gottschalk Festival.* Wiener Staatsopernorchester; Igor Buketoff, conductor. Two compact discs. Vox Box 5009, n.d.

(See also: R4a, R34e, R36b, R37g, R41a, R42a, R191h, R220m, R228t, R258k, R298b, R302d, R305c, R310c)

Bibliography

WB100.   Hensel, Octavia. *The Life and Letters of Louis Moreau Gottschalk*. Boston: Oliver Ditson & Co., 1870.
Hensel includes references to reviews of the premiere performance (See: W44a) and Gottschalk's references to the work in his letters.

WB101.   Gesualdo, Vincente. *Historia de la musica en la Argentina*. Buenos Aires: Beta, 1961.
Gesualdo documents the August 1866 performance of the march in Chile (See: W44a).

WB102.   Korf, William E. *The Orchestral Music of Louis Moreau Gottschalk*. Dissertation: The University of Iowa, 1974. Also published as *Wissenschaftliche Abhandlungen*, Vol. 28. Henryville, Pennsylvania: Institute of Mediaeval Music, 1983.
Also indexed in *Dissertation Abstracts International* 35-A/7 (January 1975), p. 4589.

W45.   **Grande Marche de *Athalia*** (1868-69; unpublished; lost.)

For thirteen pianos (25 pianists) and orchestra.
Other indices: RO110.
Note: This piece was based on themes of Felix Mendelssohn.

Performances

W45a.   November 12, 1869. Rio de Janeiro.

Bibliography

WB103.   Lange, Francisco Curt. *Vida y muerte de Louis Moreau Gottschalk en Rio de Janeiro, 1869*. Mendoza, Argentina: Universidad Nacional de Cuyo, 1951.
Lange (p. 265) documents the November 1869 performance of the piece in Rio de Janeiro (See: W45a).

W46.   **Grand March for the Sultan** (1868-69; unpublished; lost.)

For orchestra.
Other indices: RO156.

Chamber Works

W47. **Chant des oiseaux (El Canto de los pájaros)** (1857; unpublished; lost.)

For flute, soprano, and piano.
Other indices: RO50.

Performances

W47a.   January 7, 1858. Ponce, Puerto Rico. Adelina Patti, soprano; Charles Allard, flute; Louis Moreau Gottschalk, piano.

Bibliography

WB104.   Pasarell, Emilio J. "El Centenario de los conciertos de Adelina Patti y Luis Moreau Gottschalk en Puerto Rico." *Revista de Instituto de Cultura Puertorriqueña* 2:52-5 (no. 2; January-March 1959).
Pasarell (p. 53) provides information on Gottschalk, Patti, and Allard's January 7, 1858 performance in Puerto Rico (See: W47a).

WB105.   Muñoz, María Luisa. *La Musica en Puerto Rico*. Sharon, Connecticut: Troutman Press, 1966.
The author mentions several Gottschalk works, including this lost composition.

W48. **Tarantelle** (1858; unpublished; lost.)

For violin and piano. Also arranged for two violins and piano.
Other indices: RO258, D66.
Note: The work was apparently first improvised by Gottschalk and
violinist José White in Havana. It appears that it was
eventually enlarged as W37.
(See also: W247, W311, W312)

Performances

W48a.   1858. Havana. Louis Moreau Gottschalk, piano; José
White, violin.

W48b.   October 1861. Guanabacoa, Cuba. Louis Moreau
Gottschalk, piano; Anselmo Lopez, violin; José
VanderGuth, violin.

Bibliography

WB106.   Fors, Luis Ricardo. *Gottschalk*. Havana: Propagandia
Literaria, 1880.
Fors (pp. 233-34) documents the first, improvised
performance (See: W48a).

WB107.   Concert review. *Gaceta de la Habana* October 17, 1861.
Documents the October 1861 performance of the
version for two violins and piano (See: W48b)

W49. **Adieu funèbre pour violoncello et piano** (1859; unpublished; lost.)

For violoncello and piano.
Other indices: RO1.

W50. **Andante, pour violon et piano** (1859; unpublished; lost.)

For violin and piano.
Other indices: RO6.
Note: Offergeld speculates that this lost work may have been an
arrangement of the first movement of its contemporary,
Symphonie romantique (See: W34).

W51.   **Berceuse, La Même** (1861; unpublished; lost.)

For two violins and piano.
Other indices: RO29, D20b.
Note: An arrangement of *Berceuse, Op. 47* (See: W212).

W52.   **Piano Trio: Two Tarentelles** (1861; unpublished; lost.)

For violin, violoncello, and piano.
Other indices: RO201, D66.

Performances

W52a.   February 26, 1862. New York City. Louis Moreau
Gottschalk, piano; the Mollenhauer brothers, violin and
violoncello.

Bibliography

WB108.   Minor, Andrew C. *Piano Concerts in New York City
1849-1865*. Thesis: University of Michigan, 1947.
Minor (p. 354) documents the February 1862
performance of the work in New York (See: W52a).

WB109.   Loggins, Vernon. *Where the Word Ends*. Baton Rouge:
Louisiana State University Press, 1958.
Loggins (p. 188) documents the February 1862
performance of the work in New York (See: W52a).

W53.   **Romance dramatique** (1862; unpublished; lost.)

For violin and piano.
Other indices: RO230.
Note: Offergeld (p. 28) speculates that this piece, for which there is
slim evidence of being a "true" Gottschalk work, was possibly
an arrangement of Sigismund Thalberg's *Romance
dramatique, Op. 79*, which Gottschalk may have tried to pass
off as his own. No hard supporting evidence for this possible
ruse is given.

W54.   *Ballo in Maschera* **Quartet [Gran Fantasia concertante]** (1865; unpublished; lost.)

For harmonium, two violins, and piano.
Other indices: RO19.
Note: This work is based on themes from Giuseppe Verdi's 1857-8
        melodrama *Un ballo in maschera.*
(See also: W55 and W219)

Performances

W54a.   December 13, 1865. Lima, Peru. Louis Moreau
           Gottschalk, piano; other musicians unidentified.

Bibliography

WB110.   Lange, Francisco Curt. *Vida y meurte de Louis Moreau
           Gottschalk en Rio de Janeiro, 1869.* Mendoza,
           Argentina: Universidad Nacional de Cuyo, 1951.
               Lange documents the December 1865 performance in
           Lima, Peru (See: W54a).

W55.   **Piano Quintet,** *Ballo in Maschera* (1865; unpublished; lost.)

For piano, harmonium, copophone, flute, and violin.
Other indices: RO198.
Note: This work is based on themes from Giuseppe Verdi's 1857-8
        melodrama *Un ballo in maschera.*
(See also: W54 and W219)

Performances

W55a.   June 18, 1869. Rio de Janeiro. Louis Moreau Gottschalk,
           piano; other musicians unidentified.

Bibliography

WB111.   Lange, Francisco Curt. *Vida y muerte de Louis Moreau
           Gottschalk en Rio de Janeiro 1869.* Mendoza, Argentina:
           Universidad Nacional de Cuyo, 1951.
               Lange (p. 249) documents the June 1869
           performance of the work in Rio de Janeiro (See: W55a).

W56. **Grande Méditation poétique sobre *Faust* de Gounod** (c1865; unpublished; lost.)

For two violins, harmonium, and piano.
Other indices: RO113.
Note: This work is based on themes from Gounod's opera *Faust*.
(See also: W57)

Performances

W56a. December 6, 1865. Lima, Peru. Louis Moreau
Gottschalk, piano; other musicians unidentified.

Bibliography

WB112. Lange, Francisco Curt. *Vida y muerte de Louis Moreau
Gottschalk en Rio de Janeiro, 1869*. Mendoza,
Argentina: Universidad de Cuyo, 1951.
Lange (p. 283) documents the December 1865
performance in Lima, Peru (See: W56a).

W57. **Grande Méditation poétique sobre *Faust* de Gounod** (c1865; unpublished; lost.)

For piano, harmonium, copophone, flute, and violin.
Other indices: RO113.
Note: This work is based on themes from Gounod's opera *Faust*.
(See also: W56)

Performances

W57a. June 18, 1869. Rio de Janeiro. Louis Moreau Gottschalk,
piano; other musicians unidentified.

Bibliography

WB113. Lange, Francisco Curt. *Vida y muerte de Louis Moreau
Gottschalk en Rio de Janeiro, 1869*. Mendoza,
Argentina: Universidad de Cuyo, 1951.
Lange (p. 249) documents the June 1869
performance in Rio de Janeiro (See: W57a).

W58.   **Piano Septet** (1869; unpublished; lost.)

For piano and strings.

Bibliography

WB114.   Hensel, Octavia. *The Life and Letters of Louis Moreau Gottschalk.* Boston: Oliver Ditson & Co., 1870.
    Hensel (pp. 163-164) quotes from an April 14, 1869 letter of Gottschalk's in which he mentions that he had just completed a piano septet. No other contemporary evidence of the work's existence seems to exist.

W59.   **Melody** (unknown date; unpublished; lost.)

For violoncello and piano.
Other indices: RO169.

W60.   **Sonate** (unknown date.)

For violin and harp.
Contents: I. Allegro – II. Adagio espressivo – III. Rondo.
Other indices: D140.
Possibly spurious.

Performances

W60a.   1960. Zurich. Unidentified Russian performers.

W60b.   February 7, 1963. *Birmingham Festival of the Arts.* Birmingham, Alabama Sylvia Sanders, harp; Edward Lyon, violin.
    Note: Alvin E. Belden provided a lecture on the piece at the concert.

Bibliography

WB115.   Each, Patricia. "Young Musicians, Dr. Belden to Be Featured Feb. 7." *Birmingham* (Alabama) *Post-Herald* January 31, 1963: 3.
    A preview of W60b.

WB116. Belden, Alvin E. "Cultural Exchange Would Be Helpful." *Birmingham* (Alabama) *Post-Herald* February 25, 1963: Letters to the Editor.

Solo Piano Works

W61.   **Étude** (1842; unpublished; lost.)

Other indices: RO81.

W62.   **Valse de salon** (1842; printed privately; lost.)

Other indices: RO287.

W63.   **Polka de concert** (1844; unpublished; lost.)

Other indices: RO206.

W64.   **Polka de salon, Op. 1** (1844-6; Paris: A. Lafont, c1846; New York: Arno Press and *The New York Times*, 1969 (*The Piano Works of Louis Moreau Gottschalk*, vol. 4, ed. Vera Brodsky Lawrence and Richard Jackson).)

Dedication: "à Madame Céline Courtois, née Valpinçon"
Other indices: RO207, D123.
Revised as *Danse ossianique*, Op. 12 (See: W).

W65.   **Valse brillant** (1844; lost.)

Other indices: RO284.

W66.   **Souvenir des Ardennes, Mazurka de salon, Ardennes Mazurka** (1846; New York: Wm. Hall & Son, 1860. Pub. pl. no. 4585; Mainz: B. Schott's Söhne, c1875. Pub. pl. no. 22838; New York: Arno Press

& *The New York Times,* 1969 (*The Piano Works of Louis Moreau Gottschalk,* vol. 1, ed. Vera Brodsky Lawrence and Richard Jackson).)

Other indices: RO243, D143.
Manuscript is located at the New York Public Library.

W67.   Colliers d'or, deux mazurkas, Op. 6 (1846; Mainz: B. Schott's Söhne, 1851. Pub. pl. no. 11119 (*Mazuka No. 1*); Mainz: B. Schott's Söhne, 1851. Pub. pl. no. 13399 (*Mazurka No. 2*); New York: Arno Press and *The New York Times,* 1969 (*The Piano Works of Louis Moreau Gottschalk,* vol. 2, ed. Vera Brodsky Lawrence and Richard Jackson).)

Contents: two mazurkas (originally published separately)
Duration: 3 minutes.
Other indices: RO58 (Op. 6, no. 1) and RO59 (Op. 6, no. 2); D36.

Recordings

R67a.   *Gottschalk: 40 Works for Piano.* Alan Mandel, piano. Four 33-1/3 rpm phonodiscs. Desto DC 6470-73, 1969. Reissued on three compact discs, VoxBox CD3X 3033, 1995.

   For reviews of the recording, see: B360-B362, B365, B366, B369-B371, B375, B388, B396, B523, B529. (See also: R68d, R69a, R78e, R83b, R92b, R95c, R100a, R103a, R105a, R112b, R135a, R139d, R142e, R144a, R146a, R153a, R156b, R165e, R167a, R175a, R191b, R192a, R195a, R203a, R204a, R212c, R216b, R220b, R227b, R228e, R229a, R230b, R232a, R255a, R256a, R257a, R258c, R265b)

W68.   Bamboula, danse des nègres, Op. 2 (1846-8; Paris: Bureau Central de Musique, c1849. Pub. pl. no. 1112; Mainz: Schott, 1848-9. Pub. pl. no. 10301; New York: William Hall & Son, n.d. Pub. pl. no. 2395; Bryn Mawr, Pennsylvania: Theodore Presser, 1956 (*Piano Music by Louis Moreau Gottschalk,* ed. Jeanne Behrend); New York: Arno Press and *The New York Times,* 1969 (*The Piano Works of Louis Moreau Gottschalk,* vol. 1, ed. Vera Brodsky Lawrence and Richard Jackson); New York: Dover Publications, 1973 (*Piano Music of Louis Moreau Gottschalk,* selected and introduced by

Richard Jackson); Leipzig: Peters, 1973 (*Louis Moreau Gottschalk: kreolische und karibische Klavierstücke*, ed. Eberhardt Klemm); New York: Chappell, 1973 (*L.M. Gottschalk: Ten Compositions for Pianoforte*, ed. Amiram Rigai).)

Dedication: "à su Majeste Isabelle II, Reine des Espagnes."
Duration: 7 minutes.
Other indices: RO20, D13.
Note: The folk song on which this work is based is printed in WB122.

Performances

W68a.   April 17, 1849. Salle Pleyel, Paris. Louis Moreau
          Gottschalk, piano.
          This was Gottschalk's professional debut.

Recordings

R68a.   *The Banjo and Other Creole Favorites.* Eugene List,
          piano. 33-1/3 rpm phonodisc. Vanguard VRS-485, 1957.
          Reissued as part of *The World of Louis Moreau
          Gottschalk* (See: R68e). Reissued on compact disc as
          Vanguard Classics OVC 4050, 1992. Reissued as part of
          the two compact disc set *Piano Music of Louis Moreau
          Gottschalk.* Vanguard Classics 08 9143 72/08 9144-72,
          1993.
               For reviews of this recording, see: B258, B259,
          B263 and B265. (See also: R76a, R78a, R95a, R139b,
          R142a, R165a, R191a, R216a, R227a, R228b, R230a)

R68b.   *Piano Music by Louis Moreau Gottschalk.* Jeanne
          Behrend, piano. 33-1/3 rpm phonodisc. MGM E-3370,
          1957.
               For a review of this recording, see: B265. (See also:
          R78b, R88a, R139c, R142b, R156a, R165b, R212a,
          R220a, R228c)

R68c.   *Na côrte de D. Pedro II.* Various performers. *Bamboula*
          performed by Honorina Silva, piano. 33-1/3 rpm
          phonodisc. EMI Odeon SC 10.122, 1965.
               With: *Le banjo* (See: R142c) and various works by

other composers.

R68d.   *Gottschalk: 40 Works for Piano.* Alan Mandel, piano.
Four 33-1/3 rpm phonodiscs. Desto DC 6470-73, 1969.
Reissued on three compact discs, VoxBox CD3X 3033,
1995.

For reviews of this recording, see: B360-B362,
B365, B366, B369-B371, B375, B388, B396, B523,
B529. (See also: R67a, R69a, R78e, R83b, R92b, R95c,
R100a, R103a, R105a, R112b, R135a, R139d, R142e,
R144a, R146a, R153a, R156b, R165e, R167a, R175a,
R191b, R192a, R195a, R203a, R204a, R212c, R216b,
R220b, R227b, R228e, R229a, R230b, R232a, R255a,
R256a, R257a, R258c, R265b)

R68e.   *The World of Louis Moreau Gottschalk.* Various
performers. *Bamboula* performed by Eugene List, piano.
Two 33-1/3 rpm phonodiscs. Vanguard VSD-723; VSD-
724, 1973. Reissued on compact disc. Vanguard VCD
72026, 1988.

For a review of this recording, see: B417. (See also:
R34b, R37a, R76b, R78f, R95d, R139g, R142i, R165g,
R191c, R216d, R227c, R228g, R230c)

R68f.   *Louis Moreau Gottschalk, 1829-1869: American Piano
Music.* Amiram Rigai, piano. 33-1/3 rpm phonodisc.
Folkways Records FSS 37485, 1979. Reissued on
compact disc, Smithsonian Folkways 40803, 1992.
Reissued on compact disc, Smithsonian Folkways 40803,
1992.

For a review of the original recording, see: B468.
(See also: R69b, R78h, R83c, R88e, R95g, R112h,
R133a, R142m, R165k, R167e, R191d, R212e, R227e,
R228k, R249c, R275b)

R68g.   *Cakewalk.* John Arpin, piano. Compact disc. ProArte
Digital CDD515, 1990. Recorded September 25 and 27,
1989 in Toronto, Ontario, Canada.

(See also: R78j, R95h, R100d, R112e, R142n,
R165n, R191e, R204c, R212g, R227g, R228l, R257c)

R68h.   *Cervantes, Saumell, Gottschalk.* Georges Rabol, piano.

Compact disc. Opus 111 OPS 30-9001, 1990. Reissued on *Classics of the Americas: Vol. 4 Gottschalk.* Opus 111 2000, 1995.

Contains works by Manuel Saumell, Georges Rabol, and Ignatio Cervantes, in addition to several Gottschalk compositions. (See also: R76e, R78k, R165o, R191f, R228m, R249b)

R68i. *Great American Piano I. Louis Moreau Gottschalk. Vol. 7.* Leonard Pennario, piano. Compact disc. Angel Records CDM 7 64667 2, 1992. Material originally released on two 33-1/3 rpm phonodiscs as *Music of Louis Moreau Gottschalk.* Angel RL-32125, 1975.

For reviews of this recording, see: B441, B442, B446, B450, B452. (See also: R78m, R95i, R112f, R139i, R142t, R165u, R167d, R191g, R199b, R212i, R220g, R228n, R229c, R257e, R272b)

R68j. *Louis Moreau Gottschalk.* Eugene List, piano. Compact disc. Vanguard Classics OVC 4050, 1992. Contains material previously issued on 33-1/3 rpm monophonic phonodisc (See: R68a). Reissued as part of the two compact disc set *Piano Music.* Vanguard Classics 08 9143 72/08 9144-72, 1993.

(See also: R68j, R78n, R142q, R165s)

R68k. *Fascinatin' Rhythm.* Alan Feinberg, piano. Compact disc. Decca 444 457-2, 1995.

With *Columbia* (See: R178c) and various other works, primarily by American composers.

R68l. *Gottschalk: Piano Music, Vol. 3.* Philip Martin, piano. Compact disc. Hyperion CDA 66915, 1997.

For a review of this recording, see: B538. (See also: R95l, R139j, R176b, R177a, R203f, R209b, R227j, R258i, R259b)

R68m. *African-American Music.* Various performers. *Bamboula* performed by Eugene List, piano. Two compact discs. Sony Music Special Products A2 34478, 1998.

With miscellaneous other works by a wide variety of African-American composers and performers.

R68n.   *DeGaetano Plays Gottschalk.* Robert DeGaetano, piano. Compact disc. Crystonyx 1002, 1998. Recorded January-February 1989 at Denver, New York.
  (See also: R78p, R95m, R100g, R107c, R119c, R142w, R167h, R171b, R187c, R192e, R199d, R201d, R220j, R227k, R272c)

R68o.   *Louis Moreau Gottschalk: Piano Works.* Klaus Kaufmann, piano. Compact disc. Koch Schwann 360352, n.d.
  (See also: R76g, R78s, R99b, R139k, R142z, R156c, R165w, R204e, R220n, R228u)

Bibliography

WB117.   Cable, George W. "The Dance in Place Congo." *Century Magazine* 31:517-32 (February 1886).
  Cable mentions the folk song "Bamboula" and Gottschalk's use of it. According to Gottschalk biographer S. Frederick Starr (See: B524), the Cable article was probably the source of the oft-told story that Gottschalk learned African-American melodies at Congo Square, a story recounted in articles such as WB119, WB120, and WB121, and in fictionalized detail in Loggins's *Where the Word Ends* (See: B267). Starr (pp. 40-42) suggests that Cable, and later Loggins, were wrong to assume that Gottschalk learned these melodies at Congo Square and provides strong evidence to suggest that the young composer-to-be learned the tunes at home.

WB118.   Tiersot, Julien. *La Musique chez les peuples indigènes de l'Amérique du Nord.* Paris: Librarie Fischbacher, 1905-06.
  The author includes a Cuban version of the folk material Gottschalk used in *Bamboula* (See: p. 81).

WB119.   Binford, Elizabeth Harrison. "Bamboula, Danse des nègres." *Musical Monitor* 8:297-98 (March 1919).
  Binford recounts the story that Gottschalk learned the African-American melody on which the composition is based at Congo Square in New Orleans. (See also: WB117)

WB120.   Rojas, Ricardo. "El Canto Nativo." *Musica de America*
v2 (January 1921).
Similar to other references to *Bamboula* from the
general era (See: WB119 and WB121), the Rojas article
cites the second theme of the composition as an example
of African dance-influenced writing.

WB121.   Asbury, Herbert. *The French Quarter*. New York:
Knopf, 1938.
Asbury mentions *Bamboula* in his discussion of the
slave dancing at Congo Square in New Orleans (pp. 237-
53). (See also: WB117)

WB122.   *Chansons de la Louisiane*, ed. and compl. Roger
Blanchard. Paris: Heugel, 1949.
This book provides a version of the folk song (p. 15)
on which the Gottschalk work is based.

W69.   **Ossian, deux ballades, Op.** 4 (1846-7; Boston: Oliver Ditson &
Co., c1847-49. Pub. pl. no. 54900-3; Mainz: B. Schott's Söhne,
c1849. Pub. pl. no. 10684; Paris: Bureau Central de Musique, 1850.
Pub. pl. no. BC 1137; New York: Arno Press and *The New York
Times*, 1969 (*The Piano Works of Louis Moreau Gottschalk*, vol. 4,
ed. Vera Brodsky Lawrence and Richard Jackson).)

Contents: Two ballades.
Duration: 5-1/4 minutes.
Dedication: "à Mr. Camille Pleyel."
Other indices: RO187, D109.
Note: These ballades represented the start of overt Scandinavian
influence in Gottschalk's piano works.

Recordings

R69a.   *Gottschalk: 40 Works for Piano*. Alan Mandel, piano.
Four 33-1/3 rpm phonodiscs. Desto DC 6470-73, 1969.
Reissued on three compact discs, VoxBox CD3X 3033,
1995.
For reviews of this recording, see: B360-B362,
B365, B366, B369-B371, B375, B388, B396, B523,
B529. (See also: R67a, R68d, R78e, R83b, R92b, R95c,
R100a, R103a, R105a, R112b, R135a, R139d, R142e,

> R144a, R146a, R153a, R156b, R165e, R167a, R175a,
> R191b, R192a, R195a, R203a, R204a, R212c, R216b,
> R220b, R227b, R228e, R229a, R230b, R232a, R255a,
> R256a, R257a, R258c, R265b)

R69b.   *A Crazy Quilt of American Piano Music.* Leo Smit,
piano. Compact disc. Musicmasters MMD 60105M,
1986.

With: works by Irving Fine, Charles Ives, Aaron
Copland, John Cage, Virgil Thomson, Leo Smit, Pete
Johnson, Edward MacDowell, Leonard Bernstein, Harold
Shapero, George Gershwin, Louise Talma, Gail Kubik,
Samuel Barber, Arthur Farwell, and William Schuman.
Recorded April 1981 in the Great Hall, Cooper Union,
New York City. Note: Smit performs only the first of the
two ballades.

R69c.   *Louis Moreau Gottschalk. American Piano Music.*
Amiram Rigai, piano. Compact disc. Smithsonian
Folkways 40803, 1992.

For a review of the original recording, see: B468.
(See also: R68f, R78h, R83c, R88e, R95g, R112h,
R133a, R142m, R165k, R167e, R191d, R212e, R227e,
R228k, R249c, R275b)

W70.   **Marche scandinave** (1847; unpublished; lost.)

Other indices: RO153.

W71.   **Première Reflects du passé** (1847; possibly published 1857; lost.)

Other indices: RO222.

W72.   **Variations sur un theme français** (1847; unpublished; lost.)

Other indices: RO294.
Note: Offergeld speculates that the piece may have been based on
the popular French song "Partant pour la Syrie." Although
there is no direct evidence supporting this assertion, the tune
was used frequently by Gottschalk during this time period in
his improvisations.

W73. **Étude in G Major** (c1847; unpublished; lost.)

Other indices: RO86.
(See also: W74)

W74. **Grande étude de concert** (c1847; unpublished; lost.)

Other indices: RO107.
Note: Offergeld raises the possibility that this work may be related
to *Étude in G Major* (See: W73), dating from the same year.

W75. **Grande Valse de concert** (c1847; unpublished; lost.)

Other indices: RO115.

W76. **La savane, ballade crèole, Op. 3** (1847-9; Paris: Bureau Central de
Musique, 1849. Pub. pl. no. 1123; Mainz: B. Schott's Söhne, c1849.
Pub. pl. no. 10361; Philadelphia: J.E. Gould & Co., n.d. Pub. pl. no.
2190; New York: Arno Press and *The New York Times*, 1969 (*The
Piano Works of Louis Moreau Gottschalk*, ed. Vera Brodsky
Lawrence and Richard Jackson); New York: Carl Fischer, 1971
(*Gottschalk: A Compendium of Piano Music*, ed. Eugene List); New
York: Dover Publications, 1973 (*Piano Music of Louis Moreau
Gottschalk*, selected and introduced by Richard Jackson); Leipzig:
Peters, 1973 (*Louis Moreau Gottschalk: kreolische und karibische
Klavierstücke*, ed. Eberhardt Klemm); Dayton, Ohio: McAfee
Music, 1977 (*The Piano Music of Louis Moreau Gottschalk Made
Easy*, arr. David Krane).)

Duration: 6-1/2 minutes.
Dedicated to Doña Maria, Queen of Portugal.
Other indices: RO232, D135.
Note: This work is based on the Louisiana folksong "Lolotte," which
resembles the well-known song "Skip to My Lou."

Performances

W76a.   April 17, 1849. Salle Pleyel, Paris. Louis Moreau
Gottschalk, piano.
This was Gottschalk's professional debut.

W76b.　　February 17, 1853. New York City. Louis Moreau
　　　　　Gottschalk, piano.

Recordings

R76a.　　*The Banjo and Other Creole Favorites.* Eugene List,
　　　　　piano. 33-1/3 rpm phonodisc. Vanguard VRS-485, 1957.
　　　　　Reissued as part of *The World of Louis Moreau
　　　　　Gottschalk* (See: R76b). Reissued on compact disc as
　　　　　Vanguard Classics OVC 4050, 1992. Reissued as part of
　　　　　the two compact disc set *Piano Music of Louis Moreau
　　　　　Gottschalk.* Vanguard Classics 08 9143 72/08 9144-72,
　　　　　1993.
　　　　　　　For reviews of this recording, see: B258, B259,
　　　　　B263 and B265. (See also: R68a, R78a, R95a, R139b,
　　　　　R142a, R165a, R191a, R216a, R227a, R228b, R230a)

R76b.　　*The World of Louis Moreau Gottschalk.* Various
　　　　　performers. *La savane* performed by Eugene List, piano.
　　　　　Two 33-1/3 rpm phonodiscs. Vanguard VSD-723; VSD-
　　　　　724, 1973. Reissued on compact disc. Vanguard VCD
　　　　　72026, 1988.
　　　　　　　For a review of this recording, see: B417. (See also:
　　　　　R34b, R37a, R68e, R78f, R95d, R139g, R142i, R165g,
　　　　　R191c, R216d, R227c, R228g, R230c)

R76c.　　*Louis Moreau Gottschalk on Original Instruments.*
　　　　　Richard Burnett, piano. Compact disc. Amon Ra CD-
　　　　　SAR 32, 1988.
　　　　　　　All works are performed on instruments from
　　　　　Gottschalk's era. (See also: R78i, R88c, R100c, R103c,
　　　　　R107a, R112d, R165m, R187a, R199a, R201b, R204b,
　　　　　R212f, R216f, R227f, R265c, R272a)

R76d.　　*Selected Piano Music of Louis Moreau Gottschalk.*
　　　　　Lambert Orkis, piano. Compact disc. Smithsonian
　　　　　Collection of Recordings ND 033, 1988. Recorded on an
　　　　　1865 Chickering piano in Coolidge Auditorium, Library
　　　　　of Congress, Washington, D.C., May 1982.
　　　　　　　(See also: R103d, R110a, R145a, R151a, R192b,
　　　　　R220f, R234a)

R76e.   *Cervantes, Saumell, Gottschalk.* Georges Rabol, piano.
Compact disc. Opus 111 OPS 30-9001, 1990. Reissued
on *Classics of the Americas: Vol. 4 Gottschalk.* Opus
111 2000, 1995.
Contains works by Manuel Saumell, Georges Rabol,
and Ignatio Cervantes, in addition to several Gottschalk
compositions. (See also: R68h, R78k, R165o, R191f,
R228m, R249b)

R76f.   *Gottschalk: Piano Music, Vol. 2.* Philip Martin, piano.
Compact disc. Hyperion CDA 66697, 1994.
For reviews of this recording, see: B525 and B529.
(See also: R99a, R100f, R103f, R105b, R119b, R146c,
R158a, R162a, R171a, R187b, R199c, R210a, R212j,
R216h, R228o, R257f)

R76g.   *Louis Moreau Gottschalk: Piano Works.* Klaus
Kaufmann, piano. Compact disc. Koch Schwann
360352, n.d.
(See also: R68o, R78s, R99b, R139k, R142z, R156c,
R165w, R204e, R220n, R228u)

Bibliography

WB123.   Cable, George W. "Creole Slave Songs." *Century
Magazine* 31:807-28 (April 1886).
The article contains an example of the folk song
"Lolotte," utilized by Gottschalk in *La savane.*

WB124.   Minor, Andrew C. *Piano Concerts in New York City
1849-1865.* Thesis: University of Michigan, 1947.
Minor (pp. 100-102) documents Gottschalk's
February 1853 performance in New York City.

WB125.   Krehbiel, Henry Edward. *Afro-American Folksongs.*
New York: Schirmer, 1914. Reprint, New York: Unger,
1962.
Includes commentary on Gottschalk's use of the folk
song "Lolotte" in *La savane.*

W77.   **Mazurka in A minor** (1847-9; possibly published Paris: Escudier;
lost.)

Other indices: RO164.

W78.   **Le bananier, chanson nègre, Op. 5** (c1848; Paris: Bureau Central
de Musique, c1850. Pub. pl. no. 10683; Mainz: B. Schott's Söhne:
1850-51. Boston: Oliver Ditson, n.d. Pub. pl. no. 6158; New York:
William Hall & Son, n.d. Pub. pl. no. 2414; New York: The
National Society of Music, 1915, in Art of Music, vol. 14, *Musical
Examples*, ed. Henry F. Gilbert; Bryn Mawr, Pennsylvania:
Theodore Presser, 1956 (*Piano Music by Louis Moreau Gottschalk*,
ed. Jeanne Behrend); New York: Arno Press and *The New York
Times*, 1969 (*The Piano Works of Louis Moreau Gottschalk*, ed. Vera
Brodsky Lawrence and Richard Jackson); New York: Dover
Publications, 1973 (*Piano Music of Louis Moreau Gottschalk*,
selected and introduced by Richard Jackson); Leipzig: Peters, 1973
(*Louis Moreau Gottschalk: kreolische und karibische Klavierstücke*,
ed. Eberhardt Klemm); London: Peters, 1976. Edition Peters no.
7185; Dayton, Ohio: McAfee Music, 1977 (*The Piano Music of
Louis Moreau Gottschalk Made Easy*, arr. David Krane).)

Duration: 3-3/4 minutes.
Dedication: "à son ami A. Goria."
Other indices: RO21, D14.
(See also: W273)

Recordings

R78a.   *The Banjo and Other Creole Favorites*. Eugene List,
piano. 33-1/3 rpm phonodisc. Vanguard VRS-485, 1957.
Reissued as part of *The World of Louis Moreau
Gottschalk* (See: R78f). Reissued on compact disc as
Vanguard Classics OVC 4050, 1992. Reissued as part of
the two compact disc set *Piano Music*. Vanguard
Classics 08 9143 72/08 9144-72, 1993.
     For reviews of this recording, see: B258, B259,
B263 and B265. (See also: R68a, R76a, R95a, R139b,
R142a, R165a, R191a, R216a, R227a, R228b, R230a)

R78b.   *Piano Music by Louis Moreau Gottschalk*. Jeanne
Behrend, piano. 33-1/3 rpm phonodisc. MGM E-3370,
1957.
     For a review of this recording, see: B265. (See also:
R68b, R88a, R139c, R142b, R156a, R165b, R212a,

R220a, R228c)

R78c.   *American Piano Music.* Frank Glazer, piano. 33-1/3 rpm
          phonodisc. Concert Disc M-1217, 1960. Reissued as
          Everest SDBR 4217, 1972.
                 With works by Harold Shapero, Aaron Copland,
          Norman Dello Joio, and George Gershwin.

R78d.   *The Piano Music of Louis Moreau Gottschalk.* Amiram
          Rigai, piano. 33-1/3 rpm phonodisc. Decca DL 10143,
          1967. Reissued as Decca DL 710143, 1970.
                 For reviews of this recording, see: B327, B329,
          B330. (See also: R83a, R95b, R112a, R142d, R165d,
          R212b, R228d, R249a, R265a)

R78e.   *Gottschalk: 40 Works for Piano.* Alan Mandel, piano.
          Four 33-1/3 rpm phonodiscs. Desto DC 6470-73, 1969.
          Reissued on three compact discs, VoxBox CD3X 3033,
          1995.
                 For reviews of this recording, see: B360-B362,
          B365, B366, B369-B371, B375, B388, B396, B523,
          B529. (See also: R67a, R68d, R69a, R78e, R83b, R92b,
          R95c, R100a, R103a, R105a, R112b, R135a, R139d,
          R142e, R144a, R146a, R153a, R156b, R165e, R167a,
          R175a, R191b, R192a, R195a, R203a, R204a, R212c,
          R216b, R220b, R227b, R228e, R229a, R230b, R232a,
          R255a, R256a, R257a, R258c, R265b)

R78f.   *The World of Louis Moreau Gottschalk.* Various
          performers. *Le bananier* performed by Eugene List,
          piano. Two 33-1/3 rpm phonodiscs. Vanguard VSD-723;
          VSD-724, 1973. Reissued on compact disc. Vanguard
          VCD 72026, 1988.
                 For a review of this recording, see: B417. (See also:
          R34b, R37a, R68e, R76b, R95d, R139g, R142i, R165g,
          R191c, R216d, R227c, R228g, R230c)

R78g.   *The Piano Music of Louis Moreau Gottschalk.* Ivan
          Davis, piano. Simultaneously issued on 1-7/8 ips audio
          cassette, Musical Heritage Society MHC 9040 and 33-1/3
          rpm phonodisc, MHS 7040, 1975. Also issued as *Great
          Galloping Gottschalk.* 33-1/3 rpm phonodisc. London

CS-6943, 1976. Reissued on 1-7/8 ips audio cassette, 1984.

For reviews of this recording, see: B454, B455, B461. (See also: R88b, R95e, R100b, R103b, R142l, R165j, R203d, R216e, R227d, R228i, R257b)

R78h.   *Louis Moreau Gottschalk, 1829-1869: American Piano Music.* Amiram Rigai, piano. 33-1/3 rpm phonodisc. Folkways Records FSS 37485, 1979. Reissued on compact disc, Smithsonian Folkways 40803, 1992.

For a review of the original recording, see: B468. (See also: R68f, R69b, R83c, R88e, R95g, R112h, R133a, R142m, R165k, R167e, R191d, R212e, R227e, R228k, R249c, R275b)

R78i.   *Louis Moreau Gottschalk on Original Instruments.* Richard Burnett, piano. Compact disc. Amon Ra CD-SAR 32, 1988.

All works are performed on instruments from Gottschalk's era. (See also: R76c, R88c, R100c, R103c, R107a, R112d, R165m, R187a, R199a, R201b, R204b, R212f, R216f, R227f, R265c, R272a)

R78j.   *Cakewalk.* John Arpin, piano. Compact disc. ProArte Digital CDD515, 1990. Recorded September 25 and 27, 1989 in Toronto, Ontario, Canada.

(See also: R68g, R95h, R100d, R112e, R142n, R165n, R191e, R204c, R212g, R227g, R228l, R257c)

R78k.   *Cervantes, Saumell, Gottschalk.* Georges Rabol, piano. Compact disc. Opus 111 OPS 30-9001, 1990. Reissued on *Classics of the Americas: Vol. 4 Gottschalk.* Opus 111 2000, 1995.

Contains works by Manuel Saumell, Georges Rabol, and Ignatio Cervantes, in addition to several Gottschalk compositions. (See also: R68h, R76e, R165o, R191f, R228m, R249b)

R78l.   *Gottschalk: Piano Music.* Philip Martin, piano. Compact disc. Hyperion 66459, 1991.

(See also: R88d, R107b, R112g, R142p, R165p, R167i, R178d, R191i, R192d, R201c, R220l, R265d,

R272d)

R78m.   *Great American Piano 1. Louis Moreau Gottschalk. Vol.*
7. Leonard Pennario, piano. Compact disc. Angel
Records CDM 7 64667 2, 1992. Material originally
released on two 33-1/3 rpm phonodiscs as *Music of Louis*
Moreau Gottschalk. Angel RL-32125, 1975.

    For reviews of this recording, see: B441, B442,
B446, B450, B452. (See also: R68i, R95i, R112f, R139i,
R142t, R165u, R167d, R191g, R199b, R212i, R220g,
R228n, R229c, R257e, R272b)

R78n.   *Louis Moreau Gottschalk.* Eugene List, piano. Compact
disc. Vanguard Classics OVC 4050, 1992. Contains
material previously issued on 33-1/3 rpm monophonic
phonodisc (See: R78a). Reissued as part of the two
compact disc set *Piano Music.* Vanguard Classics 08
9143 72/08 9144-72, 1993.

    (See also: R68j, R142q, R165s)

R78o.   *America's Musical Landscape.* Klaus Kaufmann, piano.
1-7/8 ips audio cassette. Sony Music PT 23209, 1993.

    With: numerous works and excerpts by composers
from throughout America's musical history.

R78p.   *DeGaetano Plays Gottschalk.* Robert DeGaetano, piano.
Compact disc. Crystonyx 1002, 1998. Recorded
January-February 1989 at Denver, New York.

    (See also: R68n, R95m, R100g, R107c, R119c,
R142w, R167h, R171b, R187c, R192e, R199d, R201d,
R220j, R227k, R272c)

R78q.   *America's Musical Landscape.* Klaus Kaufmann, piano.
Two compact discs. Sony Music Special Products
ML200, 1998. Compact discs to accompany the book
America's Musical Landscape by Jean Ferris.

R78r.   *Giannina Hofmeister.* Giannina Hofmeister, piano. 33-
1/3 rpm phonodisc. Privately issued recording, n.d.

R78s.   *Louis Moreau Gottschalk: Piano Works.* Klaus
Kaufmann, piano. Compact disc. Koch Schwann

360352, n.d.
(See also: R68o, R76g, R99b, R139k, R142z, R156c,
R165w, R204e, R220n, R228u)

R78t. *Louis Moreau Gottschalk: A Night in the Tropics.*
Michael Linville, piano; Hot Springs Music Festival
Symphony Orchestra; Richard Rosenberg, conductor.
Compact disc. Naxos 8.559036, 2000.
Note: This recording was of Jack Elliott's
orchestration of the work. (See also: R16a, R34f, R37i,
R95n, R103g, R165x, R203i, R227l, R311a)

W79. **Le Sylphe** (1848; unpublished; lost.)

Other indices: RO254.

Bibliography

WB126. *The Life of Louis Moreau Gottschalk.* New York, c1863.
This pamphlet is the only known reference from
Gottschalk's time to this apparently lost work.

W80. **La mélancolie, etude caractéristique** (1848; Mainz: B. Schott's
Söhne, 1848. Pub. pl. no. 11123; Paris: Benacci-Peschier, 1852;
New York: Arno Press and *The New York Times*, 1969 (*The Piano
Works of Louis Moreau Gottschalk*, vol. 4, ed. Vera Brodsky
Lawrence and Richard Jackson).)

For solo piano.
Other indices: RO167, D95.
Note: This work is based on themes by F. Godefroid.

W81. **La moissonneuse, mazurka caractéristique, Op. 8** (1848-49; Paris:
Bureau Central de Musique, c1850. Pub. pl. no. BC 1140; Boston:
Oliver Ditson, n.d. Pub. pl. no. 8438; Mainz: B. Schott's Söhne,
c1850. Pub. pl. no. 10768; New York: Arno Press and *The New York
Times*, 1969 (*The Piano Works of Louis Moreau Gottschalk*, vol. 4,
ed. Vera Brodsky Lawrence and Richard Jackson).)

Dedication: "à son ami Alfred Jaell."
Other indices: RO173, D98.
(See also: W82)

Performances

W81a.　　March 10, 1850. Paris. Louis Moreau Gottschalk, piano.

W81b.　　February 16, 1851. Paris. Georges Bizet, piano.

W82.　**La Glaneuse, mazurka** (1848-9; unpublished; lost.)

Other indices: RO104.
Note: Offergeld suggests that this lost work might have been meant
as a companion to *La moissonneuse* (See: W81).

W83.　**La Scintilla, mazurka sentimentale (L'Étincelle), Op. 20/21**
(1848-9; New York: Firth, Pond, 1854. Pub. pl. no. 2599 (as Op.
20); Paris: Escudier, 1856 (as Op. 21). Pub. pl. no. LE 1607; Mainz:
B. Schott's Söhne, c1856. Pub. pl. no. 14794; New York: Chappell,
1973 (*L.M. Gottschalk: Ten Compositions for Pianoforte*, ed.
Amiram Rigai).)

Duration: 3 minutes.
Manuscript and sketches are located at the New York Public Library.
Dedicated to Miss Rachel C. Henriques.
Other indices: RO80, D49.
(See also: W275)

Performances

W83a.　　March 8, 1856. New York City. Louis Moreau
　　　　　Gottschalk, piano.

Recordings

R83a.　　*The Piano Music of Louis Moreau Gottschalk.* Amiram
　　　　　Rigai, piano. 33-1/3 rpm phonodisc. Decca DL 10143,
　　　　　1967. Reissued as Decca DL 710143, 1970.
　　　　　　　For reviews of this recording, see: B327, B329,
　　　　　B330. (See also: R78d, R95b, R112a, R142d, R165d,
　　　　　R212b, R228d, R249a, R265a)

R83b.　　*Gottschalk: 40 Works for Piano.* Alan Mandel, piano.
　　　　　Four 33-1/3 rpm phonodiscs. Desto DC 6470-73, 1969.

Reissued on three compact discs, VoxBox CD3X 3033, 1995.

For reviews of this recording, see: B360-B362, B365, B366, B369-B371, B375, B388, B396, B523, B529. (See also: R67a, R68d, R69a, R78e, R92b, R95c, R100a, R103a, R105a, R112b, R135a, R139d, R142e, R144a, R146a, R153a, R156b, R165e, R167a, R175a, R191b, R192a, R195a, R203a, R204a, R212c, R216b, R220b, R227b, R228e, R229a, R230b, R232a, R255a, R256a, R257a, R258c, R265b)

R83c.   *Louis Moreau Gottschalk, 1829-1869: American Piano Music.* Amiram Rigai, piano. 33-1/3 rpm phonodisc. Folkways Records FSS 37485, 1979. Reissued on compact disc, Smithsonian Folkways 40803, 1992.

For a review of the original recording, see: B468. (See also: R68f, R69b, R78h, R88e, R95g, R112h, R133a, R142m, R165k, R167e, R191d, R212e, R227e, R228k, R249c, R275b)

Bibliography

WB127.   Minor, Andrew C. *Piano Concerts in New York City 1849-1865.* Thesis: University of Michigan, 1947.
Minor documents Gottschalk's March 1856 performance of the piece. (See: W83a)

W84.   **Mazeppa, Étude dramatique** (1848-50; unpublished; lost.)

Other indices: RO162.
Dedicated to Franz Liszt.

Bibliography

WB128.   Offergeld, Robert. *The Centennial Catalogue of the Published and Unpublished Compositions of Louis Moreau Gottschalk.* New York: *Stereo Review,* 1970.
Offergeld (p. 24) provides extensive commentary on the piece, the possible circumstances surrounding Gottschalk's dedication of *Mazeppa* to Liszt, and the composer's tendency not to commit many of his works to paper.

W85. **"La chasse de jeune Henri," morceau de concert, Op. 10** (1849;
Paris: Bureau Central de Musique, 1851. Pub. pl. no. BC 1219;
Mainz: B. Schott's Söhne, 1851. Pub. pl. no. 11242; New York:
Arno Press and *The New York Times*, 1969 (*The Piano Works of
Louis Moreau Gottschalk*, vol. 2, ed. Vera Brodsky Lawrence and
Richard Jackson).)

Dedication: "à son ami Mr. Marmontel, Professeur au Conservatoire
de Paris."
Other indices: RO54, D32.
Note: This work is based on themes from Etienne-Nicolas Méhul's
opera *La chasse de jeune Henri* and is an arrangement of the
earlier, unpublished two-piano version (See: W274)

Bibliography

WB129. Suttoni, Charles R. *Piano and Opera: A Study of the
Piano Fantaisies Written on Opera Themes in the
Romantic Era.* Dissertation: New York University, 1973.

W86. **Étude in D-flat Major** (c1849; unpublished; lost.)

Other indices: RO85.

W87. **Fatma (Le Caïd)** (1849-50; unpublished; lost.)

Other indices: RO32, D52.
Based on themes from Ambroise Thomas' two-act opera *Le caïd.*

Performances

W87a. January 13, 1850. Paris. Louis Moreau Gottschalk,
piano.

W87b. August 1850. Switzerland. Louis Moreau Gottschalk,
piano.

W88. **Le mancenillier, sérénade,** (1849-50; Cleveland: S. Brainard, n.d.
Pub. pl. no. 1374-11; Paris: Bureau Central de Musique, 1851. Pub.
pl. no. BC 1209 (reprinted by A. Leduc); Mainz: B. Schott's Söhne,
c1851. Pub. pl. no. 11183; Boston: Oliver Ditson & Co., c1857. Pub.
pl. no. 3550; New York: William Hall & Son, c1857. Pub. pl. no.

3550; New York: Arno Press and *The New York Times*, 1969 (*The Piano Works of Louis Moreau Gottschalk*, vol. 3, ed. Vera Brodsky Lawrence and Richard Jackson); New York: Carl Fischer, 1971 (*Gottschalk: A Compendium of Piano Music*, ed. Eugene List); New York: Dover Publications, 1973 (*Piano Music of Louis Moreau Gottschalk*, selected and introduced by Richard Jackson).)

Dedication: "à Mennechet de Barival."
Other indices: RO142, D85.
Note: The Schott edition of *La mancenillier* contains a coda section consisting of new material. This section is missing from the 1850s American editions.

Recordings

R88a.   *Piano Music by Louis Moreau Gottschalk.* Jeanne Behrend, piano. 33-1/3 rpm phonodisc. MGM E-3370, 1957.

For a review of this recording, see: B265. (See also: R68b, R78b, R139c, R142b, R156a, R165b, R212a, R220a, R228c)

R88b.   *The Piano Music of Louis Moreau Gottschalk.* Ivan Davis, piano. Simultaneously issued on 1-7/8 ips audio cassette, Musical Heritage Society MHC 9040 and 33-1/3 rpm phonodisc, MHS 7040, 1975. Also issued as *Great Galloping Gottschalk.* 33-1/3 rpm phonodisc. London CS-6943, 1976. Reissued on 1-7/8 ips audio cassette, 1984.

For reviews of this recording, see: B454, B455, B461. (See also: R78g, R95e, R100b, R103b, R142l, R165j, R203d, R216e, R227d, R228i, R257b)

R88c.   *Louis Moreau Gottschalk on Original Instruments.* Richard Burnett, piano. Compact disc. Amon Ra CD-SAR 32, 1988.

All works are performed on instruments from Gottschalk's era. (See also: R76c, R78i, R100c, R103c, R107a, R112d, R165m, R187a, R199a, R201b, R204b, R212f, R216f, R227f, R265c, R272a)

R88d.   *Gottschalk: Piano Music.* Philip Martin, piano.

Compact disc. Hyperion 66459, 1991.
(See also: R78l, R107b, R112g, R142p, R165p,
R167i, R178d, R191i, R192d, R201c, R220l, R265d,
R272d)

R88e.   *Louis Moreau Gottschalk. American Piano Music.*
Amiram Rigai, piano. Compact disc. Smithsonian
Folkways 40803, 1992.
For a review of the original recording, see: B468.
(See also: R68f, R69b, R78h, R83c, R95g, R112h,
R133a, R142m, R165k, R167e, R191d, R212e, R227e,
R228k, R249c, R275b)

W89.   Ballades en F (1850; lost.)

Other indices: RO17.

Bibliography

WB130.   *The Life of Louis Moreau Gottschalk.* New York, 1863.
The works list in this pamphlet appears to be the
only evidence of the existence of this composition.

W90.   Le carnaval de Venice, grand caprice et variations, Op. 89 (1850;
Paris: Escudier, 1877 (ed. Nicolás Ruiz Espadero); Mainz: B.
Schott's Söhne, 1877 (ed. Nicolás Ruiz Espadero). Pub. pl. no.
22259; New York: Arno Press and *The New York Times*, 1969 (*The
Piano Works of Louis Moreau Gottschalk*, vol. 1, ed. Vera Brodsky
Lawrence and Richard Jackson).)

Other indices: RO45, D27.

Performances

W90a.   April 2, 1854. Havana. Louis Moreau Gottschalk, piano.

W91.   Danse ossianique (Danse des ombres), Op. 12 (1850, Paris:
Bureau Central de Musique, 1851. Pub. pl. no. BC 1257; Boston:
Oliver Ditson & Co., 1851. Pub. pl. no. 3002-5; Mainz: B. Schott's
Söhne, 1851. Pub. pl. no. 11592; Philadelphia: J.E. Gould, n.d. Pub.
pl. no. 2351; New York: Arno Press and *The New York Times*, 1969

(*The Piano Works of Louis Moreau Gottschalk*, vol. 2, ed. Vera Brodsky Lawrence and Richard Jackson).)

Other indices: RO63-4, D39.

Note: *Danse ossianique* is a revision of *Polka de salon, Op. 1* (See: W64). Due to the scarcity of manuscript sources for many Gottschalk compositions, some questions still exist surrounding the composition of a separate work entitled *Danse des ombres* (RO63), and the exact relationships between it, the present work, and *Polka de Salon, Op. 1.*

Performances

W91a.   September 11, 1850. Geneva. Louis Moreau Gottschalk, piano.

W91b.   February 26, 1851. Paris. Louis Moreau Gottschalk, piano.

W91c.   December 13, 1851. Madrid. Louis Moreau Gottschalk, piano.

Recordings

R91a.   *Piano Music in America.* Neely Bruce, piano. Three 33-1/3 rpm phonodiscs. Vox Box SVBX 5302, 1972.
     With: *Le banjo* (See: R142g) and miscellaneous works by other American composers. For reviews of this recording, see: B430, B432, B434.

Bibliography

WB131.   *A Manual of Music: Its History, Biography and Literature*, ed. W.M. Derthick. Chicago: Manual Publishing Co., 1888.
     This book contains the full score of *Danse ossianique*. The book also contains analyses of *Marche de nuit, The Dying Poet, Ballade sixième*, and *The Last Hope*. (See also: WB182, WB250, WB277, WB297)

W92.   God Save the Queen (America), morceau de concert, Op. 41
(1850; New York: William Hall & Son, 1860. Pub. pl. no. 4577;

Boston: Oliver Ditson. Pub. pl. no. 4577; Mainz: B. Schott's Söhne, 1862. Pub. pl. no. 16514; Paris: Escudier, 1862 (as Op. 41); New York: Arno Press and *The New York Times*, 1969 (*The Piano Works of Louis Moreau Gottschalk*, vol. 2, ed. Vera Brodsky Lawrence and Richard Jackson).)
Duration: 4-1/4 minutes.
Dedication: à Monsieur Rubinstein."
Other indices: RO106, D62.
Note: The date on the William Hall publication, "Paris 1852— Havana 1860," suggests an ongoing series of revisions.

Performances

W92a.   March 8, 1961. Willard Clapp Hall, Cleveland Institute of Music. Arthur Loesser, piano.
(See: WB132 and WB133)

Recordings

R92a.   *Music in America*. Arthur Loesser, piano. 33-1/3 rpm phonodisc. Society for the Preservation of the American Musical Heritage MIA 110, 1961.
(See also: R132a, R149a, R258b)

R92b.   *Gottschalk: 40 Works for Piano*. Alan Mandel, piano. Four 33-1/3 rpm phonodiscs. Desto DC 6470-73, 1969. Reissued on three compact discs, VoxBox CD3X 3033, 1995.
For reviews of this recording, see: B360-B362, B365, B366, B369-B371, B375, B388, B396, B523, B529. (See also: R67a, R68d, R69a, R78e, R83b, R95c, R100a, R103a, R105a, R112b, R135a, R139d, R142e, R144a, R146a, R153a, R156b, R165e, R167a, R175a, R191b, R192a, R195a, R203a, R204a, R212c, R216b, R220b, R227b, R228e, R229a, R230b, R232a, R255a, R256a, R257a, R258c, R265b)

R92c.   *The American Romantic*. Alan Feinberg, piano. Compact disc. Argo 430 330-2, 1990.
With: *La chute des feuilles* (See: R209a) and works by Amy Beach and Robert Helps.

Bibliography

WB132.   Hruby, Frank. "Loesser Salutes U.S. Composers."
 Cleveland Press March , 1961.
 A review of Loesser's Cleveland performance (See:
 W92a).

WB133.   Doyle, John G. *Louis Moreau Gottschalk, 1929-1869: A
 Bibliographical Study and Catalog of Works.* Detroit,
 Michigan: Published for the College Music Society by
 Information Coordinators, 1982.
 Doyle (p. 104) documents the Loesser performance
 of the piece (See: W92a) and provides the citation for
 Frank Hruby's review (See: WB132).

W93.   **Jerusalem, grande fantaisie triomphale, Op. 13** (1850; New York:
 Wm. Hall & Son, 1855. Pub. pl. no. 3442; Paris: Escudier, 1856.
 Pub. pl. no. LE 1581; Mainz: B. Schott's Söhne, 1859. Pub. pl. no.
 14548; New York: Arno Press and *The New York Times*, 1969 (*The
 Piano Works of Louis Moreau Gottschalk*, vol. 3, ed. Vera Brodsky
 Lawrence and Richard Jackson).)

 Dedication: "À Madame Amélie Heine."
 Other indices: RO126, D77a.
 Note: *Jerusalem* is based on theme from Guiseppi Verdi's opera *I
 lombardi.*
 (See also W276)

Bibliography

WB134.   Suttoni, Charles R. *Piano and Opera: A Study of the
 Piano Fantaisies Written on Opera Themes in the
 Romantic Era.* Dissertation: New York University, 1973.

W94.   **Le songe d'une nuit d'été, caprice élégant, Op. 9** (1850; Paris:
 Escudier, 1850; Mainz: B. Schott's Söhne, 1850. Pub. pl. no. 10863)

 Other indices: RO240, D141.
 Note: This work is based on a theme by opera composer Ambroise
 Thomas.

Performances

W94a.   February 1851. Paris. Louis Moreau Gottschalk, piano.

W95.   **Tournament Galop** (1850-54; New York: Horace Waters, 1854;
Boston: Oliver Ditson & Co., 1854; Boston: Oliver Ditson & Co.,
1882; Boston: Oliver Ditson & Co., 1897 (ed. John Orth); New
York: Arno Press and *The New York Times*, 1969 (*The Piano Works
of Louis Moreau Gottschalk*, vol. 5, ed. Vera Brodsky Lawrence and
Richard Jackson); New York: Dover Publications, 1973 (*Piano
Music of Louis Moreau Gottschalk*, selected and introduced by
Richard Jackson); New York: Chappell, 1973 (*L.M. Gottschalk:
Ten Compositions for Pianoforte*, ed. Amiram Rigai); Dayton, Ohio:
McAfee Music, 1977 (*The Piano Music of Louis Moreau Gottschalk
Made Easy*, arr. David Krane); New York: International Music Co.,
1995 (*Album of American Piano Music: From the Civil War through
World War I*, ed. David Dubal).)

Duration: 3 minutes.
Other indices: RO264, D153.
Note: The range of dates associated with the composition reflects the
evolving nature of the piece.
(See also: W293)

Performances

W95a.   April 1853. New Orleans. Louis Moreau Gottschalk,
piano.

W95b.   May 1853. New Orleans. Louis Moreau Gottschlk,
piano.

Recordings

R95a.   *The Banjo and Other Creole Favorites*. Eugene List,
piano. 33-1/3 rpm phonodisc. Vanguard VRS-485, 1957.
Reissued as part of *The World of Louis Moreau
Gottschalk* (See: D). Reissued on compact disc as
Vanguard Classics OVC 4050, 1992. Reissued as part of
the two compact disc set *Piano Music of Louis Moreau
Gottschalk*. Vanguard Classics 08 9143 72/08 9144-72,
1993.

For reviews of this recording, see: B258, B259, B263 and B265. (See also: R68a, R76a, R78a, R139b, R142a, R165a, R191a, R216a, R227a, R228b, R230a)

R95b.   *The Piano Music of Louis Moreau Gottschalk.* Amiram Rigai, piano. 33-1/3 rpm phonodisc. Decca DL 10143, 1967. Reissued as Decca DL 710143, 1970.

For reviews of this recording, see: B327, B329, B330. (See also: R78d, R83a, R112a, R142d, R165d, R212b, R228d, R249a, R265a)

R95c.   *Gottschalk: 40 Works for Piano.* Alan Mandel, piano. Four 33-1/3 rpm phonodiscs. Desto DC 6470-73, 1969. Reissued on three compact discs, VoxBox CD3X 3033, 1995.

For reviews of this recording, see: B360-B362, B365, B366, B369-B371, B375, B388, B396, B523, B529. (See also: R67a, R68d, R69a, R78e, R83b, R92b, R100a, R103a, R105a, R112b, R135a, R139d, R142e, R144a, R146a, R153a, R156b, R165e, R167a, R175a, R191b, R192a, R195a, R203a, R204a, R212c, R216b, R220b, R227b, R228e, R229a, R230b, R232a, R255a, R256a, R257a, R258c, R265b)

R95d.   *The World of Louis Moreau Gottschalk.* Various performers. *Tournament Galop* performed by Eugene List, piano. Two 33-1/3 rpm phonodiscs. Vanguard VSD-723; VSD-724, 1973. Reissued on compact disc. Vanguard VCD 72026, 1988.

For a review of this recording, see: B417. (See also: R34b, R37a, R68e, R76b, R78f, R139g, R142i, R165g, R191c, R216d, R227c, R228g, R230c)

R95e.   *The Piano Music of Louis Moreau Gottschalk.* Ivan Davis, piano. Simultaneously issued on 1-7/8 ips audio cassette, Musical Heritage Society MHC 9040 and 33-1/3 rpm phonodisc, MHS 7040, 1975. Also issued as *Great Galloping Gottschalk.* 33-1/3 rpm phonodisc. London CS-6943, 1976. Reissued on 1-7/8 ips audio cassette, 1984.

For reviews of this recording, see: B454, B455, B461. (See also: R78g, R88b, R100b, R103b, R142l,

R165j, R203d, R216e, R227d, R228i, R257b)

R95f.   *The Piano in America.* David Dubal, piano and Stanley
Waldoff, piano. *Tournament Galop* performed by David
Dubal. 33-1/3 rpm phonodisc. Musical Heritage Society
MHS 3808, 1978.

R95g.   *Louis Moreau Gottschalk, 1829-1869: American Piano
Music.* Amiram Rigai, piano. 33-1/3 rpm phonodisc.
Folkways Records FSS 37485, 1979. Reissued on
compact disc, Smithsonian Folkways 40803, 1992.
        For a review of the original recording, see: B468.
(See also: R68f, R69b, R78h, R83c, R88e, R112h,
R133a, R142m, R165k, R167e, R191d, R212e, R227e,
R228k, R249c, R275b)

R95h.   *Cakewalk.* John Arpin, piano. Compact disc. ProArte
Digital CDD515, 1990. Recorded September 25 and 27,
1989 in Toronto, Ontario, Canada.
        (See also: R68g, R78j, R100d, R112e, R142n,
R165n, R191e, R204c, R212g, R227g, R228l, R257c)

R95i.   *Great American Piano I. Louis Moreau Gottschalk. Vol.
7.* Leonard Pennario, piano. Compact disc. Angel
Records CDM 7 64667 2, 1992. Material originally
released on two 33-1/3 rpm phonodiscs as *Music of Louis
Moreau Gottschalk.* Angel RL-32125, 1975.
        For reviews of this recording, see: B441, B442,
B446, B450, B452. (See also: R68i, R78m, R112f,
R139i, R142t, R165u, R167d, R191g, R199b, R212i,
R220g, R228n, R229c, R257e, R272b)

R95j.   *Souvenirs.* Quintet of the Americas (Marco Granados,
flute; Matthew Sullivan, oboe and cor anglais;
Christopher Jepperson, clarinet; Thomas Novak, bassoon;
Barbara Oldham, horn). Simultaneously issued on 1-7/8
ips audio cassette, XLNT Music CA 18008; and compact
disc, XLNT Music CD 18008, 1992.
        The present release includes Ronald W. Tucker's
wind quintet arrangement of the Gottschalk work and was
recorded June 15-17, 1992, Skinner Auditorium, Vassar
College, Poughkeepsie, New York. With: various works

by U.S. and South American composers. (See also: R165t)

R95k.   *Pops Americana.* Joel Salsman, Yamaha Disklavier Recording Piano. 1-7/8 ips audio cassette. Joel Salsman, 1994.

Contains several Gottschalk works, as well as compositions by Joel Salsman, Zez Confrey, Scott Joplin, George Gershwin, and Nacio Herb Brown. (See also: R227i, R228q)

R95l.   *Gottschalk: Piano Music, Vol. 3.* Philip Martin, piano. Compact disc. Hyperion CDA 66915, 1997.

For a review of this recording, see: B538. (See also: R68l, R139j, R176b, R177a, R203f, R209b, R227j, R258i, R259b)

R95m.   *DeGaetano Plays Gottschalk.* Robert DeGaetano, piano. Compact disc. Crystonyx 1002, 1998. Recorded January-February 1989 at Denver, New York.

(See also: R68n, R78p, R100g, R107c, R119c, R142w, R167h, R171b, R187c, R192e, R199d, R201d, R220j, R227k, R272c)

R95n.   *Louis Moreau Gottschalk: A Night in the Tropics.* Michael Linville, piano; Hot Springs Music Festival Symphony Orchestra; Richard Rosenberg, conductor. Compact disc. Naxos 8.559036, 2000.

Note: This recording was of Jack Elliott's orchestration of the work. (See also: R16a, R34f, R37i, R78t, R103g, R165x, R203i, R227l, R311a)

R95o.   *American Classics Sampler.* Various performers. Compact disc. Naxos of America, 2001. Issued with *Gramophone* v79 (no. 942, July 2001).

W96.   Danse des sylphes, caprice de concert, Op. 86 (1850-53; Mainz: B. Schott's Söhne, 1878 (ed. Nicolás Ruiz Espadero). Pub. pl. no. 22256; New York: Arno Press and *The New York Times*, 1969 (*The Piano Works of Louis Moreau Gottschalk*, vol. 2, ed. Vera Brodsky Lawrence and Richard Jackson).)

Other indices: RO65, D40.
Note: The present work is based on Dieudonné Felix Godefroid's
popular harp composition *La Danse des sylphes.*

Performances

W96a. March 1855. New Orleans, Louisianna. Louis Moreau
Gottschalk, piano.

W96b. December 28, 1855. New York City. Louis Moreau
Gottschalk, piano.

W97. **Mazurka rustique, Op. 81** (1850-53; Boston: Oliver Ditson & Co.,
1873. Pub. pl. no. 28000; Paris: Escudier, 1873; New York: Arno
Press and *The New York Times,* 1969 (*The Piano Works of Louis
Moreau Gottschalk,* vol. 4, ed. Vera Brodsky Lawrence and Richard
Jackson).)

Manuscript is located at the New York Public Library.
Other indices: RO166, D94.
Note: The 1873 Ditson edition lists the composition date as 1857;
however, Offergeld (p. 24) calls this date "untenable" and
Doyle writes that the date probably refers to a revision (p.
302).

Bibliography

WB135. Offergeld, Robert. *The Centennial Catalogue of the
Published and Unpublished Compositions of Louis
Moreau Gottschalk.* New York: *Stereo Review,* 1970.
(See note above)

WB136. Doyle, John G. *Louis Moreau Gottschalk, 1929-1869: A
Bibliographical Study and Catalog of Works.* Detroit,
Michigan: Published for the College Music Society by
Information Coordinators, 1982.
(See note above)

W98. **Mazurka in A Major** (c1850-53; lost.)

Other indices: RO165.

W99. Scherzo Romantique, Op. 73 (1851; Boston: Oliver Ditson, 1873
(ed. Nicolás Ruiz Espadero). Pub. pl. no. 28008; Paris: Escudier,
1874 (as Op. 73); New York: Edwin F. Kalmus, n.d. Pub. pl. no.
3468 (*Album for Piano Solo*); Melville, New York: Belwin-Mills,
1976 (*Album for Piano Solo*); Miami, Florida: CPP/Belwin, 1992
(*Great American Piano Works*, ed. Dale Tucker). Pub no. EL3757.)

Dedicated to Alfredo Quesada.
Manuscript is located at the New York Public Library.
Other indices: RO233, D136.

Recordings

R99a. *Gottschalk: Piano Music, Vol. 2.* Philip Martin, piano.
Compact disc. Hyperion CDA 66697, 1994.
For reviews of this recording, see: B525 and B529.
(See also: R76f, R100f, R103f, R105b, R119b, R146c,
R158a, R162a, R171a, R187b, R199c, R210a, R212j,
R216h, R228o, R257f)

R99b. *Louis Moreau Gottschalk: Piano Works.* Klaus
Kaufmann, piano. Compact disc. Koch Schwann
360352, n.d.
(See also: R68o, R76g, R78s, R139k, R142z, R156c,
R165w, R204e, R220n, R228u)

W100. Souvenirs d'Andalousie, caprice de concert, Op. 22 (1851;
Boston: Oliver Ditson & Co., 1854. Pub. pl. no. 3443; New Orleans:
Werleins, 1855; New York: William Hall & Son, 1855. Pub. pl. no.
3443; Mainz: B. Schott's Söhne, c1855. Pub. pl. no. 14469; Paris:
Escudier, 1856; New York: Dover Publications, 1973 (*Piano Music
of Louis Moreau Gottschalk*, selected and introduced by Richard
Jackson); Dayton, Ohio: McAfee Music, 1977 (*The Piano Music of
Louis Moreau Gottschalk Made Easy*, arr. David Krane).)

Dedication: "à mon ami, Collignon."
Duration: 4-1/4 minutes.
Other indices: RO242, D148.
(See also: W106, W117, W278)

Performances

W100a. December 16, 1851. Theatre del Circo, Madrid. Louis
Moreau Gottschalk, piano.
Gottschalk reportedly improvised the basic outline of
the piece at this concert.

W100b. August 25, 1852. Palace de San Telmo, Séville. Louis
Moreau Gottschalk, piano.
This was reportedly Gottschalk's first performance of
the published version of the piece.

W100c. May 7, 1855. New Orleans. Louis Moreau Gottschalk,
piano.

W100d. December 28, 1855. New York. Louis Moreau
Gottschalk, piano.

Recordings

R100a. *Gottschalk: 40 Works for Piano.* Alan Mandel, piano.
Four 33-1/3 rpm phonodiscs. Desto DC 6470-73, 1969.
Reissued on three compact discs, VoxBox CD3X 3033,
1995.
For reviews of this recording, see: B360-B362,
B365, B366, B369-B371, B375, B388, B396, B523,
B529. (See also: R67a, R68d, R69a, R78e, R83b, R92b,
R95c, R103a, R105a, R112b, R135a, R139d, R142e,
R144a, R146a, R153a, R156b, R165e, R167a, R175a,
R191b, R192a, R195a, R203a, R204a, R212c, R216b,
R220b, R227b, R228e, R229a, R230b, R232a, R255a,
R256a, R257a, R258c, R265b)

R100b. *The Piano Music of Louis Moreau Gottschalk.* Ivan
Davis, piano. Simultaneously issued on 1-7/8 ips audio
cassette, Musical Heritage Society MHC 9040 and 33-1/3
rpm phonodisc, MHS 7040, 1975. Also issued as *Great
Galloping Gottschalk.* 33-1/3 rpm phonodisc. London
CS-6943, 1976. Reissued on 1-7/8 ips audio cassette,
1984.
For reviews of this recording, see: B454, B455,
B461. (See also: R78g, R88b, R95e, R103b, R142l,

R165j, R203d, R216e, R227d, R228i, R257b)

R100c.   *Louis Moreau Gottschalk on Original Instruments.*
Richard Burnett, piano. Compact disc. Amon Ra CD-
SAR 32, 1988.
All works are performed on instruments from
Gottschalk's era. (See also: R76c, R78i, R88c, R103c,
R107a, R112d, R165m, R187a, R199a, R201b, R204b,
R212f, R216f, R227f, R265c, R272a)

R100d.   *Cakewalk.* John Arpin, piano. Compact disc. ProArte
Digital CDD515, 1990. Recorded September 25 and 27,
1989 in Toronto, Ontario, Canada.
(See also: R68g, R78j, R95h, R112e, R142n, R165n,
R191e, R204c, R212g, R227g, R228l, R257c)

R100e.   *Louis Moreau Gottschalk.* Eugene List, piano; Joseph
Werner, piano. Compact disc. Vanguard Classics OVC
4051, 1992. Reissued as part of the two compact disc set
Piano Music. Vanguard Classics 08 9143 72/08 9144-72,
1993.
Note that this recording presents Eugene List's duet
arrangment of the piece. (See also: R34c, R37f, R220h,
R250a, R275a, R282b, R291b, R292a, R300b, R302b,
R305b, R307b, R310b)

R100f.   *Gottschalk: Piano Music, Vol. 2.* Philip Martin, piano.
Compact disc. Hyperion CDA 66697, 1994.
For reviews of this recording, see: B525 and B529.
(See also: R76f, R99a, R103f, R105b, R119b, R146c,
R158a, R162a, R171a, R187b, R199c, R210a, R212j,
R216h, R228o, R257f)

R100g.   *DeGaetano Plays Gottschalk.* Robert DeGaetano, piano.
Compact disc. Crystonyx 1002, 1998. Recorded
January-February 1989 at Denver, New York.
(See also: R68n, R78p, R95m, R107c, R119c,
R142w, R167h, R171b, R187c, R192e, R199d, R201d,
R220j, R227k, R272c)

W101. **El sitio de Zaragoza** (1851-2; unpublished; lost.)

Other indices: RO237.
Note: This was Nicolás Ruiz Espadero's transcription of W279 for
solo piano.
(See also: W102 and W105)

W102. **Marcha real española** (1851-2; unpublished; lost.)

Other indices: RO152.
Note: This work was an arrangement of part of *El sitio de Zaragoza*
(See: W101).

Performances

W102a. January 31, 1856. New York City. Louis Moreau
Gottschalk, piano.

Bibliography

WB137. Minor, Andrew C. *Piano Concerts in New York City
1849-1865.* Thesis: University of Michigan, 1947.
Minor (p. 180) documents Gottschalk's January 1856
performance of the piece. (See: W102a)

W103. **Manchega, étude de concert, Op. 38** (c1851-3; New York: Wm.
Hall & Son, 1860. Pub. pl. no. 4574 (reprinted 1888); Boston: Oliver
Ditson, 1860; Paris: Escudier, 1861; Mainz: B. Schott's Söhne,
1862. Pub. pl. no. 16348; New York: Arno Press and *The New York
Times,* 1969 (*The Piano Works of Louis Moreau Gottschalk,* vol. 3,
ed. Vera Brodsky Lawrence and Richard Jackson); New York:
Dover Publications, 1973 (*Piano Music of Louis Moreau Gottschalk,*
selected and introduced by Richard Jackson).)

Duration: 3 minutes.
Manuscript and sketches are located at the New York Public Library.
Other indices: RO143, D86.

Performances

W103a. January 31, 1856. New York City. Louis Moreau
Gottschalk, piano.

Recordings

R103a.   *Gottschalk: 40 Works for Piano*. Alan Mandel, piano.
Four 33-1/3 rpm phonodiscs. Desto DC 6470-73, 1969.
Reissued on three compact discs, VoxBox CD3X 3033,
1995.

For reviews of this recording, see: B360-B362,
B365, B366, B369-B371, B375, B388, B396, B523,
B529. (See also: R67a, R68d, R69a, R78e, R83b, R92b,
R95c, R100a, R105a, R112b, R135a, R139d, R142e,
R144a, R146a, R153a, R156b, R165e, R167a, R175a,
R191b, R192a, R195a, R203a, R204a, R212c, R216b,
R220b, R227b, R228e, R229a, R230b, R232a, R255a,
R256a, R257a, R258c, R265b)

R103b.   *The Piano Music of Louis Moreau Gottschalk*. Ivan
Davis, piano. Simultaneously issued on 1-7/8 ips audio
cassette, Musical Heritage Society MHC 9040 and 33-1/3
rpm phonodisc, MHS 7040, 1975. Also issued as *Great
Galloping Gottschalk*. 33-1/3 rpm phonodisc. London
CS-6943, 1976. Reissued on 1-7/8 ips audio cassette,
1984.

For reviews of this recording, see: B454, B455,
B461. (See also: R78g, R88b, R95e, R100b, R142l,
R165j, R203d, R216e, R227d, R228i, R257b)

R103c.   *Louis Moreau Gottschalk on Original Instruments*.
Richard Burnett, piano. Compact disc. Amon Ra CD-
SAR 32, 1988.

All works are performed on instruments from
Gottschalk's era. (See also: R76c, R78i, R88c, R100c,
R107a, R112d, R165m, R187a, R199a, R201b, R204b,
R212f, R216f, R227f, R265c, R272a)

R103d.   *Selected Piano Music of Louis Moreau Gottschalk*.
Lambert Orkis, piano. Compact disc. Smithsonian
Collection of Recordings ND 033, 1988. Recorded on an
1865 Chickering piano in Coolidge Auditorium, Library
of Congress, Washington, D.C., May 1982.

(See also: R76d, R110a, R145a, R151a, R192b,
R220f, R234a)

R103e.   *Four Piano Blues.* Michel Legrand, piano. Compact
         disc. Erato 4509-96386-2, 1994.
              With: Works by Scott Joplin, Aaron Copland, John
         Cage, Samuel Barber, Amy Cheney Beach, Morton
         Gould, Leonard Bernstein, Edward MacDowell, George
         Gershwin, and Colon Nancarrow. (See also: R142s)

R103f.   *Gottschalk: Piano Music, Vol. 2.* Philip Martin, piano.
         Compact disc. Hyperion CDA 66697, 1994.
              For reviews of this recording, see: B525 and B529.
         (See also: R76f, R99a, R100f, R105b, R119b, R146c,
         R158a, R162a, R171a, R187b, R199c, R210a, R212j,
         R216h, R228o, R257f)

R103g.   *Louis Moreau Gottschalk: A Night in the Tropics.*
         Michael Linville, piano; Hot Springs Music Festival
         Symphony Orchestra; Richard Rosenberg, conductor.
         Compact disc. Naxos 8.559036, 2000.
              Note: This recording was of Jack Elliott's
         orchestration of the work. (See also: R16a, R34f, R37i,
         R78t, R95n, R165x, R203i, R227l, R311a)

Bibliography

WB138.   Minor, Andrew C. *Piano Concerts in New York City
         1849-1865.* Thesis: University of Michigan, 1947.
              Minor (p. 180) documents Gottschalk's 1856
         performance of the piece in New York City (See:
         W103a).

W104.   **The Water Sprite (La naïde), polka de salon, Op. 27** (1851-3;
        Philadelphia: J. E. Gould, 1853. Pub. pl. no. 1664; Paris: Escudier,
        1857. Pub. pl. no. LE 1701; Mainz: B. Schott's Söhne, c1859. Pub.
        pl. no. 15119; Boston: Oliver Ditson & Co., 1888. Pub. pl. no.
        1664.)

Dedicated to Miss Mary J. Smith of Philadelphia.
Other indices: RO296, D159.

Performances

W104a.   March 20, 1856. New York City. Louis Moreau

Gottschalk, piano.

Bibliography

WB139.   Minor, Andrew C. *Piano Concerts in New York City 1849-1865.* Thesis: University of Michigan, 1947.
Minor (p. 188) documents Gottschalk's March 1856 performance of the piece in New York City (See: W104a).

W105.   **La jota aragonesa, caprice espagnol, Op. 14** (1851-3; New York: William Hall & Son, 1855. Pub. pl. no. 3445; New Orleans: Werlein, 1855; Paris: Escudier, 1856. Pub. pl. no. LE 1580; Mainz: B. Schott's Söhne, 1859; New York: Arno Press and *The New York Times,* 1969 (*The Piano Works of Louis Moreau Gottschalk,* vol. 3, ed. Vera Brodsky Lawrence and Richard Jackson); New York: Dover Publications, 1973 (*Piano Music of Louis Moreau Gottschalk,* selected and introduced by Richard Jackson).)

Manuscript is located at the New York Public Library.
Dedication: "à mon vieux maitre et ami Monsieur Letellier, Témoignage d'affection et de reconnaissance." (François Letellier was Gottschalk's friend and his first teacher.)
Duration: 4 minutes.
An excerpt from *El sitio de Zaragoza* (See: W101), arranged by Nicolás Ruiz Espadero.
Other indices: RO130, D79.
(See also: W282)

Performances

W105a.   April 29, 1853. New Orleans. Louis Moreau Gottschalk, piano.

Recordings

R105a.   *Gottschalk: 40 Works for Piano.* Alan Mandel, piano. Four 33-1/3 rpm phonodiscs. Desto DC 6470-73, 1969. Reissued on three compact discs, VoxBox CD3X 3033, 1995.
For reviews of this recording, see: B360-B362, B365, B366, B369-B371, B375, B388, B396, B523,

B529. (See also: R67a, R68d, R69a, R78e, R83b, R92b, R95c, R100a, R103a, R112b, R135a, R139d, R142e, R144a, R146a, R153a, R156b, R165e, R167a, R175a, R191b, R192a, R195a, R203a, R204a, R212c, R216b, R220b, R227b, R228e, R229a, R230b, R232a, R255a, R256a, R257a, R258c, R265b)

R105b.   *Gottschalk: Piano Music, Vol. 2.* Philip Martin, piano. Compact disc. Hyperion CDA 66697, 1994.
    For reviews of this recording, see: B525 and B529. (See also: R76f, R99a, R100f, R103f, R119b, R146c, R158a, R162a, R171a, R187b, R199c, R210a, R212j, R216h, R228o, R257f)

Bibliography

WB140.   Ribera y Tarrago, Julian. *La Musica de la jota aragonesa.* Madrid: Instituto de Valencia de Don Juan, 1928.
    A source, cited by Doyle (p. 138), which provides musical examples of the traditional material used by Gottschalk.

WB141.   Gonzalez Valle, Jose Vincente. "La jota aragonesa en la musica romantica mas alla de nuestras fronteras." *Aragon del mundo* pp353-363 (1988).
    The author deals with the differences and similarities between the traditional popular jotas and those written as concert pieces by the likes of Gottschalk, Massenet, Chabrier, Glinka, and others.

W106.   **La Caña, chanson andalouse** (1852; unpublished; lost.)

Other indices: RO33.
Note: Offergeld suggests that the piece may have been an
    arrangement of part of *Souvenirs d'Andalousie* (See: W100).

W107.   **Chanson du gitano (Canto del gitano)** (c1852; New York: New York Public Library; Sole agent, A. Broude, 1976 (*The Little Book of Louis Moreau Gottschalk*, ed. Richard Jackson and Neil Ratliff).)

Manuscript is located at the New York Public Library.

Other indices: RO70 (*Danza in C minor*), RO274 (*Untitled piece
No. 5 in C minor*), RO35 (*Canto del gitano*); D28.
Note: Doyle (See: WB142) suggests that *Chanson du gitano* is
Offergeld's RO70 and RO274. Lowens and Starr (See:
WB143) suggest that *Chanson du gitano* is in fact Offergeld's
RO35 (*Canto del gitano*) and RO274.

Recordings

R107a.   *Louis Moreau Gottschalk on Original Instruments.*
Richard Burnett, piano. Compact disc. Amon Ra CD-
SAR 32, 1988.
All works are performed on instruments from
Gottschalk's era. (See also: R76c, R78i, R88c, R100c,
R103c, R112d, R165m, R187a, R199a, R201b, R204b,
R212f, R216f, R227f, R265c, R272a)

R107b.   *Gottschalk: Piano Music.* Philip Martin, piano.
Compact disc. Hyperion 66459, 1991.
(See also: R78l, R88d, R112g, R142p, R165p,
R167i, R178d, R191i, R192d, R201c, R220l, R265d,
R272d)

R107c.   *DeGaetano Plays Gottschalk.* Robert DeGaetano, piano.
Compact disc. Crystonyx 1002, 1998. Recorded
January-February 1989 at Denver, New York.
(See also: R68n, R78p, R95m, R100g, R119c,
R142w, R167h, R171b, R187c, R192e, R199d, R201d,
R220j, R227k, R272c)

Bibliography

WB142.   Doyle, John G. *Louis Moreau Gottschalk, 1929-1869: A
Bibliographical Study and Catalog of Works.* Detroit,
Michigan: Published for the College Music Society by
Information Coordinators, 1982.
(See note above)

WB143.   Lowens, Irving and S. Frederick Starr. *The New Grove
Dictionary of Music and Musicians*, 2nd ed. s.v.
"Gottschalk, Louis Moreau." London: Macmillan, 2000.
(See note above)

W108. **Polka caracteristica sobre Le mancenillier** (c1852; Madrid: Casimiro Martin, c1852. Pub. pl. no. C.M. 200.)

Other indices: D122.
Dedicated to Leopold Poulet.

W109. **Le réveil de l'aigle** (c1852; unpublished.)

Manuscript is located at the New York Public Library.
Dedication: "His Imperial Majesty, Napoleon III."
Other indices: D132.
Note: Gottschalk used the pseudonym Paul Ernest for this work.
Note: Although the manuscript was fully edited for publication, no evidence of publication exists.

W110. **[Second/Deuxième] Banjo, Op. 82** (1852-4; Boston: Oliver Ditson Company, 1873. Pub. pl. no. 28004; Paris: Escudier, c1873 (ed. Nicolás Ruiz Espadero); New York: Arno Press and *The New York Times*, 1969 (*The Piano Works of Louis Moreau Gottschalk*, vol. 1, ed. Vera Brodsky Lawrence and Richard Jackson).)

Other indices: RO24, RO36, D16.
Duration: 4-3/4 minutes.
Note: Although the title of this work is often given as the *Second Banjo* to distinguish it from the better-known *Le banjo, Op. 15* (See: W142), it is highly likely that *Banjo, Op. 82* was the first to be composed; the publication order was reversed.
Note: There is some evidence that *Banjo, Op. 82* is also the same as RO36 (*Première Caprice américain*), based upon Gottschalk's known performances and the absence of *Banjo* from *The Life of Louis Moreau Gottschalk* (See: B61).

Performances

W110a.   February 1854. New Orleans. Louis Moreau Gottschalk, piano.

Recordings

R110a.   *Selected Piano Music of Louis Moreau Gottschalk.* Lambert Orkis, piano. Compact disc. Smithsonian Collection of Recordings ND 033, 1988. Recorded on an

1865 Chickering piano in Coolidge Auditorium, Library of Congress, Washington, D.C., May 1982.
(See also: R76d, R103d, R145a, R151a, R192b, R220f, R234a)

Bibliography

WB144.   Concert announcement. *Courrier de la Louisiane* February 1, 1854.
Previews Gottschalk's performance of the piece (See: W110a).

W111.   **Pensée poétique, nocturne, Op. 18** (1852-3; Paris: Chabal, c1856. Pub. pl. no. 1034; Paris: Choudens, n.d. Pub. pl. no. 1034.)

Other indices: D116.

W112.   **Minuit à Séville, caprice, Op. 30** (1852-6; New York: William Hall & Son, 1859. Pub. pl. no. 4167; Paris: Escudier, 1859; Mainz: B. Schott's Söhne, 1859. Pub. pl. no. 15462; New York: Arno Press and *The New York Times*, 1969 (*The Piano Works of Louis Moreau Gottschalk*, vol. 4, ed. Vera Brodsky Lawrence and Richard Jackson); New York: Carl Fischer, 1971 (*Gottschalk: A Compendium of Piano Music*, ed. Eugene List); New York: Dover Publications, 1973 (*Piano Music of Louis Moreau Gottschalk*, selected and introduced by Richard Jackson); New York: Chappell, 1973 (*L.M. Gottschalk: Ten Compositions for Pianoforte*, ed. Amiram Rigai).)

Dedication: "à mon cher ami Nicholas Ruiz y Espadero de la Havane."
Manuscript is located at the New York Public Library.
Duration: 5 minutes.
Other indices: RO170, D96.
Note: Although Doyle and Offergeld give the New York publication date as 1858, the 1859 copyright date on the William Hall & Son title page suggests publication one year later.

Performances

W112a.   March 1856. New York City. Louis Moreau Gottschalk, piano.

W112b.   December 17, 1969. *Louis Moreau Gottschalk Centennial Concert*. Alan Mandel, piano.
(See also: R112c)

Recordings

R112a.   *The Piano Music of Louis Moreau Gottschalk*. Amiram Rigai, piano. 33-1/3 rpm phonodisc. Decca DL 10143, 1967. Reissued as Decca DL 710143, 1970.
For reviews of this recording, see: B327, B329, B330. (See also: R78d, R83a, R95b, R142d, R165d, R212b, R228d, R249a, R265a)

R112b.   *Gottschalk: 40 Works for Piano*. Alan Mandel, piano. Four 33-1/3 rpm phonodiscs. Desto DC 6470-73, 1969. Reissued on three compact discs, VoxBox CD3X 3033, 1995.
For reviews of this recording, see: B360-B362, B365, B366, B369-B371, B375, B388, B396, B523, B529. (See also: R67a, R68d, R69a, R78e, R83b, R92b, R95c, R100a, R103a, R105a, R135a, R139d, R142e, R144a, R146a, R153a, R156b, R165e, R167a, R175a, R191b, R192a, R195a, R203a, R204a, R212c, R216b, R220b, R227b, R228e, R229a, R230b, R232a, R255a, R256a, R257a, R258c, R265b)

R112c.   *Louis Moreau Gottschalk: A Centennial Concert*. Various pianists. *Minuit à Séville* performed by Alan Mandel. 33-1/3 rpm phonodisc. Turnabout TV-S 34426, 1971. Recorded live December 17, 1969.
For reviews of this recording, see: B415 and B440. (See also: R135b, R139e, R142f, R165f, R167b, R203b, R212d, R216c, R229b, R258d)

R112d.   *Louis Moreau Gottschalk on Original Instruments*. Richard Burnett, piano. Compact disc. Amon Ra CD-SAR 32, 1988.
All works are performed on instruments from Gottschalk's era. (See also: R76c, R78i, R88c, R100c, R103c, R107a, R165m, R187a, R199a, R201b, R204b, R212f, R216f, R227f, R265c, R272a)

R112e.   *Cakewalk.* John Arpin, piano. Compact disc. ProArte
Digital CDD515, 1990. Recorded September 25 and 27,
1989 in Toronto, Ontario, Canada.
   (See also: R68g, R78j, R95h, R100d, R142n, R165n,
R191e, R204c, R212g, R227g, R228l, R257c)

R112f.   *Great American Piano I. Louis Moreau Gottschalk. Vol.
7.* Leonard Pennario, piano. Compact disc. Angel
Records CDM 7 64667 2, 1992. Material originally
released on two 33-1/3 rpm phonodiscs as *Music of Louis
Moreau Gottschalk.* Angel RL-32125, 1975.
   For reviews of this recording, see: B441, B442,
B446, B450, B452. (See also: R68i, R78m, R95i, R139i,
R142t, R165u, R167d, R191g, R199b, R212i, R220g,
R228n, R229c, R257e, R272b)

R112g.   *Gottschalk: Piano Music.* Philip Martin, piano.
Compact disc. Hyperion 66459, 1991.
   (See also: R78l, R88d, R107b, R142p, R165p,
R167i, R178d, R191i, R192d, R201c, R220l, R265d,
R272d)

R112h.   *Louis Moreau Gottschalk. American Piano Music.*
Amiram Rigai, piano. Compact disc. Smithsonian
Folkways 40803, 1992.
   For a review of the original recording, see: B468.
(See also: R68f, R69b, R78h, R83c, R88e, R95g, R133a,
R142m, R165k, R167e, R191d, R212e, R227e, R228k,
R249c, R275b)

Bibliography

WB145.   Minor, Andrew C. *Piano Concerts in New York City
1849-1865.* Thesis: University of Michigan, 1947.
   Minor (p. 189) documents Gottschalk's March 1856
performance in New York (See: W112a).

W113.   **Valse de concert in G** (before 1853; unpublished; lost.)

Other indices: RO285.

W114.   **Valse en A flat** (before 1853; unpublished; lost.)

Other indices: RO279.

W115.   **Le bengali au réveil, bluette en form d'étude** (before 1853; Paris: Brandus, 1853; lost.)

Other indices: D19.

W116.   **Moripont** (1853; unpublished; lost.)

Bibliography

WB146.   Starr, S. Frederick. *Bamboula! The Life and Times of Louis Moreau Gottschalk.* New York: Oxford University Press, 1995.
Starr (p. 143) cites newspaper evidence of this work, which is listed by no previous biographer or bibliography.

W117.   **Fandango** (1853; unpublished; lost.)

Other indices: RO92.
Note: Offergeld suggests that this work may be a separate arrangement of the "Fandango" from *Souvenirs d'Andalousie* (See: W100).

Performances

W117a.   May 1853. Théâtre d'Orléans, New Orleans. Louis Moreau Gottschalk, piano.

W118.   **Autrefrois, ballade** (1853; lost.)

Other indices: RO9.

W119.   **Ballade (in A-flat Major)** (1853; New York, 1876; New York: New York Public Library; Sole agent, A. Broude, 1976 (*The Little Book of Louis Moreau Gottschalk,* ed. Richard Jackson and Neil Ratliff).)

Manuscript is located at the New York Public Library.
Other indices: RO271, D9.
(See also: W120)

Recordings

R119a.   *Great American Piano II. Gottschalk, Joplin, Gershwin. Vol. 8.* Leonard Pennario, piano. Compact disc. Angel Records CDM 7 64668 2, 1992. Gottschalk material originally released on two 33-1/3 rpm phonodiscs as *Music of Louis Moreau Gottschalk.* Angel RL-32125, 1975.

Contains several Gottschalk compositions, as well as works by George Gershwin and Scott Joplin performed by Leonard Pennario and Joshua Rifkin (Joplin works only). (See also: R178b, R203c, R204d, R216g, R244a)

R119b.   *Gottschalk: Piano Music, Vol. 2.* Philip Martin, piano. Compact disc. Hyperion CDA 66697, 1994.

For reviews of this recording, see: B525 and B529. (See also: R76f, R99a, R100f, R103f, R105b, R146c, R158a, R162a, R171a, R187b, R199c, R210a, R212j, R216h, R228o, R257f)

R119c.   *DeGaetano Plays Gottschalk.* Robert DeGaetano, piano. Compact disc. Crystonyx 1002, 1998. Recorded January-February 1989 at Denver, New York.

(See also: R68n, R78p, R95m, R100g, R107c, R142w, R167h, R171b, R187c, R192e, R199d, R201d, R220j, R227k, R272c)

W120.   Caprice en A-flat (1853; unpublished; lost.)

Other indices: RO39.
Note: While *The Life of Louis Moreau Gottschalk* (See: B61) lists *Caprice en A-flat* as an 1853 composition, Offergeld raises the possibility that the piece may in fact be the same work as the separately listed c1853 *Danse des Sylphes* (See: W96). Given the unpublished and lost nature of the work, it is impossible to determine if this is the case; another possible explanation would be that *Caprice en A-flat* was a companion to the A-flat major *Ballade* (See: W119), also written in 1853.

W121.   Bunker's Hill (American Reminiscences, National Glory), fantaisie triomphale (1853; unpublished; lost.)

Other indices: RO31.

Note: This work incorporated American national airs, as well as the Stephen Foster melodies "Oh! Susanna" and "Old Folks at Home."

(See also: W285)

Performances

W121a.　March 3, 1853. Philadelphia. Louis Moreau Gottschalk, piano.

W121b.　March 19, 1853. Louisville, Kentucky. Louis Moreau Gottschalk, piano.

W121c.　April 6, 1853. New Orleans. Louis Moreau Gottschalk, piano.

W121d.　October 13, 1853. New York. Louis Moreau Gottschalk, piano.

W122.　**Forest Glade Polka, polka brillante, Op. 25** (1853; Philadelphia: J.E. Gould, 1853. Pub. pl. no. 1756; Paris: Escudier, 1857. Pub. pl. no. 1756; Mainz: B. Schott's Söhne, c1859. Pub. pl. no. 15021; Rio de Janeiro: Narciso y Napoleão, n.d.; Boston: Oliver Ditson Company, 1888. Pub. pl. no. 1756; New York: Arno Press and *The New York Times*, 1969 (*The Piano Works of Louis Moreau Gottschalk*, vol. 2, ed. Vera Brodsky Lawrence and Richard Jackson).)

Manuscript is located at the New York Public Library.
Other indices: RO98, D58.
(See also: W284)

Performances

W122a.　February 1, 1854. New Orleans. Louis Moreau Gottschalk, piano.

Bibliography

WB147.　Doyle, John G. *Louis Moreau Gottschalk, 1929-1869: A Bibliographical Study and Catalog of Works*. Detroit,

Michigan: Published for the College Music Society by Information Coordinators, 1982.

Doyle (p. 285) cites an article in *The Bee* (New Orleans) announcing Gottschalk's New Orleans performance (See: W122a).

W123.   *Lucrezia Borgia,* **Transcription du Final** (1853; unpublished; lost.)

Other indices: RO139.

Note: This work is a transcription of the finale from Donizetti's opera *Lucrezia Borgia*.

(See also: W238 and W240)

Performances

W123a.   January 25, 1856. New York City. Louis Moreau Gottschalk, piano.

Bibliography

WB148.   Minor, Andrew C. *Piano Concerts in New York City 1849-1865*. Thesis: University of Michigan, 1947.
Minor documents Gottschalk's January 1856 performance of the work (See: W123a).

WB149.   Suttoni, Charles R. *Piano and Opera: A Study of the Piano Fantaisies Written on Opera Themes in the Romantic Era*. Dissertation: New York University, 1973.

W124.   **Valse en E flat** (1853; unpublished; lost.)

Other indices: RO281.

W125.   **I'll Pray for Thee** (1853; Philadelphia: J.E. Gould, 1853; lost.)

Other indices: D73.

Note: *I'll Pray for Thee* is a transcription of Donizetti's aria "Quando rapito in estasi" from the opera *Lucia di Lammermoor*.

(See also: W126)

W126. **Prière** (1853; unpublished; lost.)

Other indices: RO213.
Note: The existence of two similarly titled works (W125 and W126) dating from the same year, raises the possibility that the lost *Prière* may in fact be an alternate title for *I'll Pray for Thee*.

Performances

W126a. March 13, 1856. New York City. Louis Moreau Gottschalk, piano.

W126b. March 18, 1856. New York City. Louis Moreau Gottschalk, piano.

W126c. March 20, 1856. New York City. Louis Moreau Gottschalk, piano.

W126d. April 10, 1856. New York City. Louis Moreau Gottschalk, piano.

Bibliography

WB150. Minor, Andrew C. *Piano Concerts in New York City 1849-1865*. Thesis: University of Michigan, 1947.
Minor documents Gottschalk's March and April 1856 performances of the work (See: W126a-d).

W127. **Étude en A-flat** (c1853; unpublished; lost.)

Other indices: RO83.

Bibliography

WB151. *Life of Louis Moreau Gottschalk*. New York, c1863.
The works list in this pamphlet is the source for this the otherwise undocumented *Étude en A-flat*.

W128. **Polka poétique** (c1853; unpublished; lost.)

Other indices: RO209 (possibly the same work as RO204).

W129.   **Italian Glories** (c1853.)

Contents: four transcriptions.
Manuscripts are located at the New York Public Library.
Other indices: D76.
Note: Gottschalk used the pseudonym Oscar Litti on the manuscript
of *Italian Glories*.
Note: *Italian Glories* uses themes from Donizetti's operas *Don
Pasquale*, *La fille du regiment*, and *Lucrezia Borgia*. The
work is of a considerably less technically challenging nature
than other Gottschalk transcriptions, suggesting that the work
was designed for mass sales, rather than as a representation of
what Gottschalk typically played in concert.

Bibliography

WB152.   Suttoni, Charles R. *Piano and Opera: A Study of the
Piano Fantaisies Written on Opera Themes in the
Romantic Era.* Dissertation: New York University, 1973.

WB153.   Doyle, John G. *Louis Moreau Gottschalk 1829-1869: A
Bibliographical Study and Catalog of Works.* Detroit:
Information Coordinators, Inc. for the College Music
Society, 1983.

W130.   **Caprice cubain** (c1853; unpublished; lost.)

Other indices: RO37.

W131.   **Nocturne** (c1853; unpublished; lost.)

Other indices: RO178.

Performances

W131a.   April 16, 1863. New York City. Louis Moreau
Gottschalk, piano.

Bibliography

WB154.   Minor, Andrew C. *Piano Concerts in New York City*

1849-1865. Thesis: University of Michigan, 1947.
Minor (p. 386) documents Gottschalk's April 1863
performance of the piece (See: W131a).

W132.   **Marche funèbre, Op. 61** (1853-4; Boston: Oliver Ditson & Co.,
1870; New York: Wm. Hall & Son, 1870. Pub. pl. no. 6519
(reprinted 1898); Mainz: B. Schott's Söhne, c1870. Pub. pl. no.
20536 (as Op. 61); New York: Arno Press and *The New York Times*,
1969 (*The Piano Works of Louis Moreau Gottschalk*, vol. 4, ed. Vera
Brodsky Lawrence and Richard Jackson).)

Other indices: RO147, D90a.
Note: Doyle raises the possibility that Gottschalk sent this version of
the *Marche funèbre* to his publisher without the knowledge of
Espadero (who edited the version of the piece listed here as
W133).
(See also: W133 and W286)

Recordings

R132a.   *Music in America*. Arthur Loesser, piano. 33-1/3 rpm
phonodisc. Society for the Preservation of the American
Musical Heritage MIA 110, 1961.
(See also: R92a, R149a, R258b)

W133.   **Marche funèbre, Op. 64** (1853-4; Paris: Escudier, c1874 (ed.
Nicolás Ruiz Espadero). Pub. pl. no. 3345; New York: Chappell,
1973 (*L.M. Gottschalk: Ten Compositions for Pianoforte*, ed.
Amiram Rigai).

Other indices: RO148, D90b.
Note: *Marche funèbre, Op. 64* apparently was a revision of *Marche
funèbre, Op. 61* (See: W132), superceding it, although see the
note in the listing for the Op. 61 version.
(See also: W286)

Recordings

R133a.   *Louis Moreau Gottschalk, 1829-1869: American Piano
Music*. Amiram Rigai, piano. 33-1/3 rpm phonodisc.
Folkways Records FSS 37485, 1979. Reissued on
compact disc, Smithsonian Folkways 40803, 1992.

For a review of the original recording, see: B468.
(See also: R68f, R69b, R78h, R83c, R88e, R95g, R112h,
R142m, R165k, R167e, R191d, R212e, R227e, R228k,
R249c, R275b)

W134.   **Variations on "Old Folks at Home"** (c1853-4; unpublished; lost.)

Other indices: RO292.
Note: This lost piece was based on the Stephen Foster song "Old
Folks at Home."

Performances

W134a.   March 13, 1854. Havana. Louis Moreau Gottschalk,
piano.

Bibliography

WB155.   Loggins, Vernon. *Where the Word Ends*. Baton Rouge:
Louisiana State University Press, 1958.
Loggins (p. 144) documents Gottschalk's March
1854 performance of the piece in Havana (See: W134a).

W135.   **El cocoyé, grand caprice cubain de bravura, Op. 80** (1854;
Boston: Oliver Ditson & Co., c1861; Paris: Escudier, c1861;
Boston: Oliver Ditson & Co., 1873 (ed. Nicolás Ruiz Espadero).
Pub. pl. no. 28006; Paris: Escudier, 1874 (as Op. 80); New York:
Arno Press and *The New York Times*, 1969 (*The Piano Works of
Louis Moreau Gottschalk*, vol. 2, ed. Vera Brodsky Lawrence and
Richard Jackson).)

Duration: 6-1/4 minutes.
Dedication: "To Monsieur Adolphe Quesada."
Other indices: RO57, D35.
Note: The 1873 Ditson publication contains fairly extensive remarks
by Nicolás Ruiz Espadero about Gottschalk and his piano
playing and composing.

Performances

W135a.   April 2, 1854. Havana. Louis Moreau Gottschalk, piano.

W135b.   March 27, 1855. New Orleans Louis Moreau Gottschalk, piano.
The United States premiere.

W135c.   December 17, 1969. *Louis Moreau Gottschalk Centennial Concert.* John Kirkpatrick, piano.
(See also: R135b)

Recordings

R135a.   *Gottschalk: 40 Works for Piano.* Alan Mandel, piano.
Four 33-1/3 rpm phonodiscs. Desto DC 6470-73, 1969.
Reissued on three compact discs, VoxBox CD3X 3033, 1995.
For reviews of this recording, see: B360-B362, B365, B366, B369-B371, B375, B388, B396, B523, B529. (See also: R67a, R68d, R69a, R78e, R83b, R92b, R95c, R100a, R103a, R105a, R112b, R139d, R142e, R144a, R146a, R153a, R156b, R165e, R167a, R175a, R191b, R192a, R195a, R203a, R204a, R212c, R216b, R220b, R227b, R228e, R229a, R230b, R232a, R255a, R256a, R257a, R258c, R265b)

R135b.   *Louis Moreau Gottschalk: A Centennial Concert.*
Various pianists. *El Cocoyé* performed by John Kirkpatrick. 33-1/3 rpm phonodisc. Turnabout TV-S 34426, 1971. Recorded live December 17, 1969.
For reviews of this recording, see: B415 and B440.
(See also: R112c, R139e, R142f, R165f, R167b, R203b, R212d, R216c, R229b, R258d)

R135c.   *A Gottschalk Gala.* Various artists. Compact disc.
Premiere Recordings PRCD 1063, 1998.

Bibliography

WB156.   Carpentier, Alejo. *La música en Cuba.* Mexico: Fondo de Cultura Económica, 1946.
Carpentier discusses the origins of the Cuban material upon which Gottschalk based this work.

WB157.   Borbolla, Carlos. "El Cocoyé, un canto omtarsero qua

origino un potpourri con zabe historico." Havana:
manuscipt, Museo de la Música, 1954.

WB158. Doyle, John G. *Louis Moreau Gottschalk, 1929-1869: A
Bibliographical Study and Catalog of Works*. Detroit,
Michigan: Published for the College Music Society by
Information Coordinators, 1982.
Doyle cites newspaper evidence of Gottschalk's
United States premiere (See: W135b).

WB159. Béhague, Gerard and Carlos Borbolla. *The New Grove
Dictionary of Music and Musicians*, ed. Stanley Sadie.
s.v. "Cuba. I. Art Music. Folk Music." London:
Macmillan, 1980.
The authors deal with the origins of the folk sources
utilized by Gottschalk in *El Cocoyé*.

W136.   **Maria la O (Maria la Ho)** (1854; unpublished; lost.)

Other indices: RO159.

Performances

W136a.   April 2, 1854. Havana. Louis Moreau Gottschalk, piano.

W136b.   March 23, 1855. New Orleans. Louis Moreau
Gottschalk, piano.

W136c.   January 31, 1856. New York City. Louis Moreau
Gottschalk, piano.

Bibliography

WB160. Carpentier, Alejo. *La música en Cuba*. Mexico: Fondo
de Cultura Económica, 1946.
Carpentier provides information (pp. 104-105) on the
Cuban influences in this work.

WB161. Minor, Andrew C. *Piano Concerts in New York City
1849-1865*. Thesis: University of Michigan, 1947.
Minor documents Gottschalk's January 1856
performance of the work (See: W136c).

W137.   **Camagüay Fantasy** (1854; unpublished; lost.)

Performances

W137a.   December 4, 1854. Puerto Príncipe, Cuba. Louis Moreau Gottschalk, piano.

W137b.   December 11, 1854. Puerto Príncipe, Cuba. Louis Moreau Gottschalk, piano.

Bibliography

WB162.   Starr, S. Frederick. *Bamboula! The Life and Times of Louis Moreau Gottschalk.* New York: Oxford University Press, 1995. Paperback edition: Urbana: University of Illinois Press, 2000.
  Starr (p. 192) cites evidence from Cuban news clippings in the New York Public Library's Gottschalk collection of Gottschalk's Cuban performances of this piece (See: W137a and W137b).

W138.   **Caprichos sobre danses de Puerto Principe** (1854; unpublished; lost.)

Other indices: RO43.

Performances

W138a.   December 4, 1854. Puerto Príncipe, Cuba. Louis Moreau Gottschalk, piano.

W138b.   December 11, 1854. Puerto Príncipe, Cuba. Louis Moreau Gottschalk, piano.

W138c.   January 31, 1856. New York City. Louis Moreau Gottschalk, piano.

Bibliography

WB163.   Minor, Andrew C. Piano Concerts in New York City 1849-1865. Thesis: University of Michigan, 1947.

Minor (p. 180) documents Gottschalk's January 1856 New York performance (See: W138c).

WB164.   Starr, S. Frederick. *Bamboula! The Life and Times of Louis Moreau Gottschalk*. New York: Oxford University Press, 1995. Paperback edition: Urbana: University of Illinois Press, 2000.

Starr (p. 192) cites evidence from Cuban news clippings in the New York Public Library's Gottschalk collection of Gottschalk's Cuban performances of this piece (See: W138a and W138b). Some indices date the piece from 1855. This later date is contradicted by the evidence cited by Starr.

W139.   **The Last Hope, Religious Meditation, Op. 16** (1854; Firth, Pond & Co., 1854. Pub. pl. no. 3005; New York: Wm. Hall & Son, 1856. Pub. pl. no. 3515; Mainz: B. Schott's Söhne, 1859. Pub. pl. no. 14468; Boston: Oliver Ditson & Co. after 1884; New York: G. Schirmer, 1899. Pub. pl. no. 14383 (edited and fingered by Louis Oesterle); Saint Louis: Art Publication Society, 1913; New York: Century, n.d. (available Carlstadt, New Jersey: Teachers Music Service, Century Edition no. 636); New York: Carl Fischer, 1943 (*Advanced Classics for the Piano*); Bryn Mawr, Pennsylvania: Theodore Presser, 1956 (*Piano Music by Louis Moreau Gottschalk*, ed. Jeanne Behrend); New York: Arno Press and *The New York Times*, 1969 (*The Piano Works of Louis Moreau Gottschalk*, ed. Vera Brodsky Lawrence and Richard Jackson); New York: Dover Publications, 1973 (*Piano Music of Louis Moreau Gottschalk*, selected and introduced by Richard Jackson).)

Duration: 6 minutes.
Manuscript and sketches are located at the New York Public Library.
Dedicated to Miss Annie Myers of Philadelphia (Gottschalk's cousin).
Other indices: RO133, D80.
Note: The post-1884 Oliver Ditson & Co. publication is billed as the "new and only correct edition."
(See also: W288)

Performances

W139a.   March 13, 1855. New Orleans. Louis Moreau

Gottschalk, piano.

W139b.   December 17, 1969. *Louis Moreau Gottschalk*
         Centennial Concert. Alan Mandel, piano.
         (See also: R139e)

Recordings

R139a.   *The Last Hope.* Ferdinand Himmelreich, piano. 10-inch,
         78 rpm phonodisc. Victor 17100-B, 1913.

R139b.   *The Banjo and Other Creole Favorites.* Eugene List,
         piano. 33-1/3 rpm phonodisc. Vanguard VRS-485, 1957.
         Reissued as part of *The World of Louis Moreau*
         Gottschalk (See: R139g). Reissued on compact disc as
         Vanguard Classics OVC 4050, 1992. Reissued as part of
         the two compact disc set *Piano Music.* Vanguard Classics
         08 9143 72/08 9144-72, 1993.
                For reviews of this recording, see: B258, B259,
         B263 and B265. (See also: R68a, R76a, R78a, R95a,
         R142a, R165a, R191a, R216a, R227a, R228b, R230a)

R139c.   *Piano Music by Louis Moreau Gottschalk.* Jeanne
         Behrend, piano. 33-1/3 rpm phonodisc. MGM E-3370,
         1957.
                For a review of this recording, see: B265. (See also:
         R68b, R78b, R88a, R142b, R156a, R165b, R212a, R220a,
         R228c)

R139d.   *Gottschalk: 40 Works for Piano.* Alan Mandel, piano.
         Four 33-1/3 rpm phonodiscs. Desto DC 6470-73, 1969.
         Reissued on three compact discs, VoxBox CD3X 3033,
         1995.
                For reviews of this recording, see: B360-B362,
         B365, B366, B369-B371, B375, B388, B396, B523,
         B529. (See also: R67a, R68d, R69a, R78e, R83b, R92b,
         R95c, R100a, R103a, R105a, R112b, R135a, R142e,
         R144a, R146a, R153a, R156b, R165e, R167a, R175a,
         R191b, R192a, R195a, R203a, R204a, R212c, R216b,
         R220b, R227b, R228e, R229a, R230b, R232a, R255a,
         R256a, R257a, R258c, R265b)

R139e. *Louis Moreau Gottschalk: A Centennial Concert.*
Various pianists. *The Last Hope* performed by Alan
Mandel. 33-1/3 rpm phonodisc. Turnabout TV-S 34426,
1971. Recorded live December 17, 1969.
  For reviews of this recording, see: B415 and B440.
(See also: R112c, R135b, R142f, R165f, R167b, R203b,
R212d, R216c, R229b, R258d)

R139f. *A Festival of Americana: The Romantic Era in American
Music.* Various performers. *The Last Hope* performed by
Yasuo Watanabe, piano. 1-7/8 ips audio cassette. New
England Conservatory of Music, 1972.
  (See also: R228f)

R139g. *The World of Louis Moreau Gottschalk.* Various
performers. *The Last Hope* performed by Eugene List,
piano. Two 33-1/3 rpm phonodiscs. Vanguard VSD-723;
VSD-724, 1973. Reissued on compact disc. Vanguard
VCD 72026, 1988.
  For a review of this recording, see: B417. (See also:
R34b, R37a, R68e, R76b, R78f, R95d, R142i, R165g,
R191c, R216d, R227c, R228g, R230c)

R139h. *Organ Music.* 33-1/3 rpm phonodisc. The Friends of
Hildene, 1982.
  With: a variety of organ works, primarily by
American composers. *The Last Hope* was recorded from
an organ roll on the organ at Robert Todd Lincoln's
Hildene.

R139i. *Great American Piano I. Louis Moreau Gottschalk. Vol.
7.* Leonard Pennario, piano. Compact disc. Angel
Records CDM 7 64667 2, 1992. Material originally
released on two 33-1/3 rpm phonodiscs as *Music of Louis
Moreau Gottschalk.* Angel RL-32125, 1975.
  For reviews of this recording, see: B441, B442,
B446, B450, B452. (See also: R68i, R78m, R95i, R112f,
R142t, R165u, R167d, R191g, R199b, R212i, R220g,
R228n, R229c, R257e, R272b)

R139j. *Gottschalk: Piano Music, Vol. 3.* Philip Martin, piano.
Compact disc. Hyperion CDA 66915, 1997.

For a review of this recording, see: B538. (See also: R68l, R95l, R176b, R177a, R203f, R209b, R227j, R258i, R259b)

R139k.   *Louis Moreau Gottschalk: Piano Works.* Klaus Kaufmann, piano. Compact disc. Koch Schwann 360352, n.d.
        (See also: R68o, R76g, R78s, R99b, R142z, R156c, R165w, R204e, R220n, R228u)

Bibliography

WB165.   Chouquet, Gustave. "The Last Hope." *La France musicale* 1856.
        Chouquet's description of *The Last Hope*, excerpted from his writings in *La France musicale*, is included as front matter in some editions of the piece. This fanciful story of how Gottschalk came to write the piece during his 1854-55 tour of Cuba was told to Chouquet by the composer in a letter.

WB166.   "The Origin of Gottschalk's *Last Hope*." *Current Literature* 23:249 (March 1898).
        (See also: WB167 and WB168)

WB167.   Hawes, William L. "The Origin of Gottschalk's *Last Hope*." *New Orleans Times-Democrat* April 30, 1899. Reprinted in *Music* 16:309-10 (July 1899).
        A comparison of the original 1854 publication of the work with the revised, now standard version. (See also: WB168 and WB170)

WB168.   Hawes, William L. "The Original *Last Hope*." *Musical Record* p1 (July 1899).
        (See also: WB167 and WB170)

WB169.   Harwood, Bertha. "Reminiscences of Louis Moreau Gottschalk." *Musical Courier* 56:39-40 (May 13, 1908).
        Although the article is of a general nature, it does contain a reproduction of the manuscript of *The Last Hope*.

WB170.   Hawes, William L. "Gottschalk's *Last Hope*." *Musician* 13:440 (October 1908).
(See also: WB167 and WB168)

WB171.   Hamilton, Anna Heuermann. *Program of American Music from Mayflower Days to the Present*. St. Louis: Art Publication Society, 1923.
Contains notes on *The Last Hope*, as well as *Berceuse* and *Marche de nuit*. (See also: WB184 and WB236)

WB172.   Offergeld, Robert. "More on the Gottschalk-Ives Connection." *ISAM Newsletter* 15:1+ (no. 2, May 1986).
Offergeld deals with Ives's quotation of the main theme of *The Last Hope* in his *Psalm 90* setting. Ives probably knew the tune as the hymn tune *Gottschalk* (later known as *Mercy*). The author maintains that the text wedded to the Gottschalk theme alludes to Gottschalk's private life.

WB173.   Starr, S. Frederick. *Bamboula! The Life and Times of Louis Moreau Gottschalk*. New York: Oxford University Press, 1995. Paperback edition: Urbana: University of Illinois Press, 2000.
Starr (pp. 195-205) discusses the merits of *The Last Hope* and Gottschalk's other sentimental solo piano works.

W140.   Souvenir de la Louisiane (1854; unpublished; lost.)

Other indices: RO248.

Performances

W140a.   March 29, 1854. Havana. Louis Moreau Gottschalk, piano.

Bibliography

WB174.   Loggins, Vernon. *Where the Word Ends*. Baton Rouge: Louisiana State University Press, 1958.
Loggins (p. 145) documents Gottschalk's March

1854 performance, possibly the premiere, of the work in
Havana (See: W140a).

W141.   **Adiós à Cuba** (1854; lost.)

Other indices: RO2.
Note: Offergeld raises the possibility that this work may in fact be
Souvenir de Cuba (See: W198).

Performances

W141a.   July 1854. Cienfuegas, Cuba. Louis Moreau Gottschalk,
piano.

Bibliography

WB175.   Loggins, Vernon. *Where the Word Ends: The Life of
Louis Moreau Gottschalk.* Baton Rouge: Louisiana State
University Press, 1958.
Loggins notes Gottschalk's July 1854 Cuban
performance (See: W141a).

W142.   **Le banjo, grotesque fantaisie, esquisse américaine (An American
Sketch), Op. 15** (1854-5; New York, William Hall & Son, 1855.
Pub. pl. no. 3345; Boston: Oliver Ditson, c1855. Pub. pl. no. 3345;
Mainz: B. Schott's Söhne, n.d. Pub. pl. no. 14471; Paris: Escudier,
1856. Pub. pl. no. LE 1600; New York: Century, n.d. (available
Carlstadt, New Jersey: Teachers Music Service, Century Edition no.
4482); Bryn Mawr, Pennsylvania: Theodore Presser, 1956 (*Piano
Music by Louis Moreau Gottschalk*, ed. Jeanne Behrend); New York:
Edwin F. Kalmus, n.d. Pub. pl. no. 3468 (*Album for Piano Solo*);
New York: Arno Press and *The New York Times*, 1969 (*The Piano
Works of Louis Moreau Gottschalk*, ed. Vera Brodsky Lawrence and
Richard Jackson); New York: Carl Fischer, 1971 (*Gottschalk: A
Compendium of Piano Music*, ed. Eugene List); New York: Dover
Publications, 1973 (*Piano Music of Louis Moreau Gottschalk*,
selected and introduced by Richard Jackson); Leipzig: Peters, 1973
(*Louis Moreau Gottschalk: kreolische und karibische Klavierstücke*,
ed. Eberhardt Klemm); New York: Chappell, 1973 (*L.M.
Gottschalk: Ten Compositions for Pianoforte*, ed. Amiram Rigai);
Melville, New York: Belwin-Mills, 1976 (*Album for Piano Solo*);
New York: Dover Publications, 1978 (*Nineteenth-Century American*

Piano Music, ed. John Gillespie); New York: G. Schirmer, 1985
(*Encores*). Pub. no. ED 3561; New York: G. Schirmer, 1997
(*American Classic Masters*, ed. Lawrence Rosen). Pub. pl. no. ED
3981.)

Dedication: "To Richard Hoffman."
Duration: 3-3/4 minutes.
Manuscript is located at the New York Public Library.
Other indices: RO22, D15.
Note: *Le banjo* uses themes from Stephen Foster's "Camptown
      Races" and the spiritual "Roll, Jordan, Roll!"
(See also: W290)

Performances

W142a.   1854-1869. Performances in North America, the
           Caribbean, and South America. Louis Moreau
           Gottschalk, piano.
                Easily Gottschalk's best-known composition during
           his lifetime, he performed the piece at countless concerts.

W142b.   December 17, 1969. *Louis Moreau Gottschalk
           Centennial Concert*. Robert Pritchard, piano.
                (See also: R142f)

W142c.   February 1973. Philadelphia, Pennsylvania. Natalie
           Hinderas, piano.

W142d.   1973. Heeren Recital Hall, Southern Baptist Theological
           Seminary. Maurice Hinson, piano.

W142e.   September 27, 1998. The Boston Conservatory, Boston,
           Massachussetts. Michael Lewin, piano.

Recordings

R142a.   *The Banjo and Other Creole Favorites*. Eugene List,
           piano. 33-1/3 rpm phonodisc. Vanguard VRS-485, 1957.
           Reissued as part of *The World of Louis Moreau
           Gottschalk* (See: R142i). Reissued on compact disc as
           Piano Music of Louis Moreau Gottschalk. Vanguard
           Classics OVC 4050, 1992.

For reviews of this recording, see: B258, B259, B263 and B265. (See also: R68a, R76a, R78a, R95a, R139b, R165a, R191a, R216a, R227a, R228b, R230a)

R142b. *Piano Music by Louis Moreau Gottschalk.* Jeanne Behrend, piano. 33-1/3 rpm phonodisc. MGM E-3370, 1957.

For a review of this recording, see: B265. (See also: R68b, R78b, R88a, R139c, R156a, R165b, R212a, R220a, R228c)

R142c. *Na côrte de D. Pedro II.* Various performers. *Le banjo* performed by Honorina Silva, piano. 33-1/3 rpm phonodisc. EMI Odeon SC 10.122, 1965.

With: *Bamboula* (See: R68c) and various works by other composers.

R142d. *The Piano Music of Louis Moreau Gottschalk.* Amiram Rigai, piano. 33-1/3 rpm phonodisc. Decca DL 10143, 1967. Reissued as Decca DL 710143, 1970.

For reviews of this recording, see: B327, B329, B330. (See also: R78d, R83a, R95b, R112a, R165d, R212b, R228d, R249a, R265a)

R142e. *Gottschalk: 40 Works for Piano.* Alan Mandel, piano. Four 33-1/3 rpm phonodiscs. Desto DC 6470-73, 1969. Reissued on three compact discs, VoxBox CD3X 3033, 1995.

For reviews of this recording, see: B360-B362, B365, B366, B369-B371, B375, B388, B396, B523, B529. (See also: R67a, R68d, R69a, R78e, R83b, R92b, R95c, R100a, R103a, R105a, R112b, R135a, R139d, R144a, R146a, R153a, R156b, R165e, R167a, R175a, R191b, R192a, R195a, R203a, R204a, R212c, R216b, R220b, R227b, R228e, R229a, R230b, R232a, R255a, R256a, R257a, R258c, R265b)

R142f. *Louis Moreau Gottschalk: A Centennial Concert.* Various pianists. *Le banjo* performed by Robert Pritchard. 33-1/3 rpm phonodisc. Turnabout TV-S 34426, 1971. Recorded live December 17, 1969.

For reviews of this recording, see: B415 and B440.

(See also: R112c, R135b, R139e, R165f, R167b, R203b, R212d, R216c, R229b, R258d)

R142g.   *Piano Music in America.* Neely Bruce, piano. Three 33-1/3 rpm phonodiscs. Vox Box SVBX 5302, 1972.
With: *Danse ossianique* (See: R91a) and miscellaneous works by other American composers. For reviews of this recording, see: B430, B432, B434.

R142h.   *Legendary Pianists of the Romantic Era: Concert I.* Arthur Friedheim, piano. 33-1/3 rpm phonodisc. Klavier Records KS 114, 1973.
Recorded from the early twentieth-century Duo-Art reproducing piano.

R142i.   *The World of Louis Moreau Gottschalk.* Various performers. *Le banjo* performed by Eugene List, piano. Two 33-1/3 rpm phonodiscs. Vanguard VSD-723; VSD-724, 1973. Reissued on compact disc. Vanguard VCD 72026, 1988.
For a review of this recording, see: B417. (See also: R34b, R37a, R68e, R76b, R78f, R95d, R139g, R165g, R191c, R216d, R227c, R228g, R230c)

R142j.   *Louis Moreau Gottschalk: Piano Music.* Edward Gold, piano. 33-1/3 rpm phonodisc. Musical Heritage Society MHS 1629, 1974.
(See also: R165h, R167c, R176c, R178a, R228h, R254a, R259a)

R142k.   *Festival of American Music.* Seymour Bernstein, piano. National Federation of Music Clubs NFMC 302, 1975.
With: *Souvenir de Porto Rico* (See: R165i) and works by miscellaneous other American composers.

R142l.   *The Piano Music of Louis Moreau Gottschalk.* Ivan Davis, piano. Simultaneously issued on 1-7/8 ips audio cassette, Musical Heritage Society MHC 9040 and 33-1/3 rpm phonodisc, MHS 7040, 1975. Also issued as *Great Galloping Gottschalk.* 33-1/3 rpm phonodisc. London CS-6943, 1976. Reissued on 1-7/8 ips audio cassette, 1984.

For reviews of this recording, see: B454, B455, B461. (See also: R78g, R88b, R95e, R100b, R103b, R165j, R203d, R216e, R227d, R228i, R257b)

R142m.   *Louis Moreau Gottschalk, 1829-1869: American Piano Music.* Amiram Rigai, piano. 33-1/3 rpm phonodisc. Folkways Records FSS 37485, 1979. Reissued on compact disc, Smithsonian Folkways 40803, 1992.
For a review of the original recording, see: B468. (See also: R68f, R69b, R78h, R83c, R88e, R95g, R112h, R133a, R165k, R167e, R191d, R212e, R227e, R228k, R249c, R275b)

R142n.   *Cakewalk.* John Arpin, piano. Compact disc. ProArte Digital CDD515, 1990. Recorded September 25 and 27, 1989 in Toronto, Ontario, Canada.
(See also: R68g, R78j, R95h, R100d, R112e, R165n, R191e, R204c, R212g, R227g, R228l, R257c)

R142o.   *From Rags to Rich's.* Rich Ridenour, piano. Compact disc. B&R Recordings BANDR1, 1991. Recorded in DeVos Hall, Grand Rapids, Michigan, September 14, 1991.
With various works by Scott Joplin, William Bolcom, George Gershwin, and Zez Confrey.

R142p.   *Gottschalk: Piano Music.* Philip Martin, piano. Compact disc. Hyperion 66459, 1991.
(See also: R78l, R88d, R107b, R112g, R165p, R167i, R178d, R191i, R192d, R201c, R220l, R265d, R272d)

R142q.   *Louis Moreau Gottschalk.* Eugene List, piano. Compact disc. Vanguard Classics OVC 4050, 1992. Contains material previously issued on 33-1/3 rpm monophonic phonodisc (See: R142a). Reissued as part of the two compact disc set *Piano Music.* Vanguard Classics 08 9143 72/08 9144-72, 1993.
(See also: R68j, R78n, R165s)

R142r.   *An American Portrait.* Richard Allen Crosby, piano. Compact disc. Richard A. Crosby RAC-001, 1994.

With: Works by Charles Tomlinson Griffes, Amy
Beach, Lee Hoiby, William Grant Still, David Guion, and
George Gershwin.

R142s.   *Four Piano Blues.* Michel Legrand, piano. Compact
disc. Erato 4509-96386-2, 1994.
With: Works by Scott Joplin, Aaron Copland, John
Cage, Samuel Barber, Amy Cheney Beach, Morton
Gould, Leonard Bernstein, Edward MacDowell, George
Gershwin, and Colon Nancarrow. (See also: R103e)

R142t.   *Great American Piano I. Louis Moreau Gottschalk. Vol.
7.* Leonard Pennario, piano. Compact disc. Angel
Records CDM 7 64667 2, 1992. Material originally
released on two 33-1/3 rpm phonodiscs as *Music of Louis
Moreau Gottschalk.* Angel RL-32125, 1975.
For reviews of this recording, see: B441, B442,
B446, B450, B452. (See also: R68i, R78m, R95i, R112f,
R139i, R165u, R167d, R191g, R199b, R212i, R220g,
R228n, R229c, R257e, R272b)

R142u.   *Piano Portraits from Nineteenth-Century America.* Noël
Lester, piano. Compact disc. Centaur CRC 2250, 1995.
With: *Sospiro* (See: R152a); *L'Union* (See: R220i);
Pasquinade (See: R228r); and various works by
Benjamin Carr, Arthur Clifton, Stephen Collins Foster,
William Mason, Richard Hoffman, John Knowles Paine,
and Edward MacDowell. For a review of this recording,
see: B533.

R142v.   *Sophisticated Innocence: American Novelty Piano Solos.*
Lincoln Mayorga, piano. Compact disc. Town Hall 35,
1995.
With various piano works by a variety of composers.

R142w.   *DeGaetano Plays Gottschalk.* Robert DeGaetano, piano.
Compact disc. Crystonyx 1002, 1998. Recorded
January-February 1989 at Denver, New York.
(See also: R68n, R78p, R95m, R100g, R107c,
R119c, R167h, R171b, R187c, R192e, R199d, R201d,
R220j, R227k, R272c)

R142x.   *Arthur Friedheim Plays Liszt/Rosenthal/Gottschalk.*
Arthur Friedheim, piano. Compact disc. Nimbus 8815,
n.d.

R142y.   *Great Pianists of the Golden Era.* Arthur Friedheim,
piano. Compact disc. Fone 9007, n.d.
With miscellaneous works by Schubert, Liszt,
Lyadov, and Johann Sebastian Bach. Note: The
recording of *Le banjo* is taken from a piano roll.

R142z.   *Louis Moreau Gottschalk: Piano Works.* Klaus
Kaufmann, piano. Compact disc. Koch Schwann
360352, n.d.
(See also: R68o, R76g, R78s, R99b, R139k, R156c,
R165w, R204e, R220n, R228u)

Bibliography

WB176.   Cockrell, Findlay and Daniel Nimetz. *Keyboard Masters.*
Albany, New York: State University of New York, 1968.
Page 129 of this book contains study materials on *Le
banjo.*

WB177.   Nazzaro, William J. "Hinderas Gives First Piano Recital
in 17 Years." *Philadelphia Evening Bulletin* February 26,
1973:26.
A review of W142b.

WB178.   Smith, Paul Ely. "Gottshalk's *The Banjo, Op. 15,* and the
Banjo in the Nineteenth Century." *Current Musicology*
n50:47-61 (1992).
Smith describes the Gottschalk work as the most
detailed surviving record of early nineteenth-century
African-American banjo technique. *The Banjo, Op. 15*
provides evidence of a link between performance
practices on the African lute and the African-American
banjo.

W143.   **Recuerdo de la Vuelta de Abajo** (c1854-5; lost, except for a
fragment of "Le Zapateado.")

Contents: I. "Le Zapateado cubano"; II. "Tengue terengue"; III. "Bembo como ta."

Manuscript fragment of "Le Zapateado" is located at the New York Public Library.

Other indices: RO221.

Performances

W143a. January 31, 1856. New York City. Louis Moreau Gottschalk, piano.

Bibliography

WB179. Minor, Andrew C. *Piano Concerts in New York City, 1849-1865.* Thesis: University of Michigan, 1947. Minor documents Gottschalk's January 1856 performance of the piece (See: W143a).

W144. **Chant du soldat, grand caprice de concert, Op. 23** (1854-6; New York: Wm. Hall & Son, 1857. Pub. pl. no. 4033; Mainz: B. Schott's Söhne, 1857. Pub. pl. no. 14959; Paris: Escudier, 1857. Pub. pl. no. LE 1622; New York: Arno Press and *The New York Times*, 1969 (*The Piano Works of Louis Moreau Gottschalk*, vol. 2, ed. Vera Brodsky Lawrence and Richard Jackson).)

Duration: 8-1/4 minutes.
Dedication: "À mon ami Georges Henriques, Esq. de New York."
Manuscript is located at the New York Public Library.
Other indices: RO51, D31.

Performances

W144a. February 14, 1856. New York City. Louis Moreau Gottschalk, piano.

Recordings

R144a. *Gottschalk: 40 Works for Piano.* Alan Mandel, piano. Four 33-1/3 rpm phonodiscs. Desto DC 6470-73, 1969. Reissued on three compact discs, VoxBox CD3X 3033, 1995.
For reviews of this recording, see: B360-B362,

B365, B366, B369-B371, B375, B388, B396, B523, B529. (See also: R67a, R68d, R69a, R78e, R83b, R92b, R95c, R100a, R103a, R105a, R112b, R135a, R139d, R142e, R146a, R153a, R156b, R165e, R167a, R175a, R191b, R192a, R195a, R203a, R204a, R212c, R216b, R220b, R227b, R228e, R229a, R230b, R232a, R255a, R256a, R257a, R258c, R265b)

Bibliography

WB180.   Minor, Andrew C. *Piano Concerts in New York City 1849-1865*. Thesis: University of Michigan, 1947.
Minor (p. 182) provides information on Gottschalk's 1856 performance (See: W144a).

W145.   **Le chant du martyr (The Martyr's Song), grand caprice religieux** (1854-9; Boston: Oliver Ditson, 1864. Pub. pl. no. 22460; Mainz: B. Schott's Söhne, 1878. Pub. pl. no. 22834; Paris: Escudier, 1879; New York: Arno Press and *The New York Times*, 1969 (*The Piano Works of Louis Moreau Gottschalk*, vol. 1, ed. Vera Brodsky Lawrence and Richard Jackson).)

Manuscript is located at the New York Public Library.
Other indices: RO49, D30.
Dedicated to Maurice Strakosh.
Duration: 6-1/4 minutes.
Note: Gottschalk used the pseudonym Seven Octaves for the initial publication of this piece.

Recordings

R145a.   *Selected Piano Music of Louis Moreau Gottschalk.*
Lambert Orkis, piano. Compact disc. Smithsonian Collection of Recordings ND 033, 1988. Recorded on an 1865 Chickering piano in Coolidge Auditorium, Library of Congress, Washington, D.C., May 1982.
(See also: R76d, R103d, R110a, R151a, R192b, R220f, R234a)

W146.   **Marche de nuit, Op. 17** (1855; Boston: Oliver Ditson & Co., 1856; New York: William Hall & Son, 1856. Pub. pl. no. 3528; Paris: Escudier, 1856. Pub. pl. no. LE 1602; Mainz: B. Schott's Söhne,

1856. Pub. pl. no. 14470; St. Louis: Art Publication Society, 1913 (*Advanced Classics for the Piano*); New York: Carl Fischer, 1943 (*Advanced Classics for the Piano*); New York: Arno Press and *The New York Times*, 1969 (*The Piano Works of Louis Moreau Gottschalk*, vol. 3, ed. Vera Brodsky Lawrence and Richard Jackson).)

Duration: 4-3/4 minutes.
Dedication: "Au Général Don José Paez, ex-President de la Republique de Venezuela."
Other indices: RO151, D89.
Note: *Marche de nuit* was also arranged for concert band by John Phillip Sousa and for guitar by Douglas Back: Pacific, Missouri: Mel Bay Publications, 1997 (*Great American Marches, Polkas, and Grand Concert Walzes for Acoustic Guitar*).
(See also: W291)

Performances

W146a.   December 20, 1855. New York City. Louis Moreau Gottschalk, piano.

Recordings

R146a.   *Gottschalk: 40 Works for Piano.* Alan Mandel, piano. Four 33-1/3 rpm phonodiscs. Desto DC 6470-73, 1969. Reissued on three compact discs, VoxBox CD3X 3033, 1995.
     For reviews of this recording, see: B360-B362, B365, B366, B369-B371, B375, B388, B396, B523, B529. (See also: R67a, R68d, R69a, R78e, R83b, R92b, R95c, R100a, R103a, R105a, R112b, R135a, R139d, R142e, R144a, R153a, R156b, R165e, R167a, R175a, R191b, R192a, R195a, R203a, R204a, R212c, R216b, R220b, R227b, R228e, R229a, R230b, R232a, R255a, R256a, R257a, R258c, R265b)

R146b.   *From Dowland to Gottschalk.* Olav Chris Henricksen, guitar. Digital audio tape. The Boston Conservatory, 1993. Recorded at The Boston Conservatory, January 28, 1993.

Note: The present recording is of a guitar
arrangement of the Gottschalk work.

R146c. *Gottschalk: Piano Music, Vol. 2.* Philip Martin, piano.
Compact disc. Hyperion CDA 66697, 1994.
For reviews of this recording, see: B525 and B529.
(See also: R76f, R99a, R100f, R103f, R105b, R119b,
R158a, R162a, R171a, R187b, R199c, R210a, R212j,
R216h, R228o, R257f)

Bibliography

WB181. Chouquet, Gustave. "Marche de nuit." *La France
musicale* n.d.
Chouquet's description of *Marche de nuit*, excerpted
from his writings in *La France musicale*, is included as
front matter in some editions of the piece.

WB182. *A Manual of Music: Its History, Biography and
Literature*, ed. W.M. Derthick. Chicago: Manual
Publishing Co., 1888.
This book contains analyses of *Marche de nuit*, *The
Dying Poet*, *Sixième Ballade*, and *The Last Hope*. The
full score of *Danse ossianique* is also included. (See also:
WB131, WB250, WB277, WB297)

WB183. Minor, Andrew C. *Piano Concerts in New York City
1849-1865.* Thesis: University of Michigan, 1947.
Minor (p. 174) documents Gottschalk's December
1855 performance of the piece (See: W146a).

WB184. Hamilton, Anna Heuermann. *Program of American
Music from Mayflower Days to the Present.* St. Louis:
Art Publication Society, 1923.
Contains notes on *Marche de nuit*, as well as
Berceuse and *The Last Hope*. (See also: WB171 and
WB236).

W147. **Fantaisie sur *Lucia* (1855; unpublished; lost.)**

Other indices: RO136.
Note: This piece is based on themes from Donizetti's opera *Lucia di*

Lammermoor.

Performances

W147a.   December 20, 1855. New York City. Louis Moreau
Gottschalk, piano.

W147b.   March 8, 1856. New York City. Louis Moreau
Gottschalk, piano.

W147c.   November 25, 1865. Lima, Peru. Louis Moreau
Gottschalk, piano.

Bibliography

WB185.   Minor, Andrew C. *Piano Concerts in New York City
1849-1865.* Thesis: University of Michigan, 1947.
        Minor documents Gottschalk's performances of
"fragments" of this work (pp. 174 and 187). (See:
W147a and W147b).

WB186.   Offergeld, Robert. *The Centennial Catalogue of the
Published and Unpublished Compositions of Louis
Moreau Gottschalk.* New York: Stereo Review, 1970.
        Offergeld (p. 22) cites several earlier references to
this apparently lost, unpublished work.

WB187.   Suttoni, Charles R. *Piano and Opera: A Study of the
Piano Fantaisies Written on Opera Themes in the
Romantic Era.* Dissertation: New York University, 1973.

W148.   **Fantaisie sur *Fille du Regiment*** (1855; unpublished; lost.)

Other indices: RO96.
Note: This work is based on themes by Gaetano Donizetti.

Performances

W148a.   December 20, 1855. New York City. Louis Moreau
Gottschalk, piano.

W148b.   February 28, 1856. New York City. Louis Moreau
Gottschalk, piano.

W148c.   June 21, 1869. Rio de Janeiro. Louis Moreau Gottschalk,
piano.

Bibliography

WB188.   Minor, Andrew C. *Piano Concerts in New York City
1849-1865*. Thesis: University of Michigan, 1947.
Minor (p. 174 and 184) documents Gottschalk's New
York City performances of the piece (See: W148a and
W148b).

WB189.   Lange, Francisco Curt. *Vida y muerte de Louis Moreau
Gottschalk en Rio de Janeiro, 1869*. Mendoza,
Argentina: Universidad Nacional de Cuyo, 1951.
Lange (p. 249) documents Gottschalk's performance
of the piece in Rio de Janeiro (See: W148c).

WB190.   Suttoni, Charles R. *Piano and Opera: A Study of the
Piano Fantaisies Written on Opera Themes in the
Romantic Era*. Dissertation: New York University, 1973.

W149.   Printemps d'amour, mazurka, caprice de concert, Op. 40 (1855;
New York, William Hall & Son, 1860. Pub. pl. no. 4578; Paris:
Escudier, 1861; Mainz: B. Schott's Söhne, 1862. Pub. pl. no. 16444;
New York: Arno Press and *The New York Times*, 1969 (*The Piano
Works of Louis Moreau Gottschalk*, vol. 4, ed. Vera Brodsky
Lawrence and Richard Jackson).)

Dedication: "à Mon Ami Isidore Van Montenacken (d'Anvers)."
Manuscript is located at the New York Public Library.
Other indices: RO214, D125.
(See also: W292)

Recordings

R149a.   *Music in America*. Arthur Loesser, piano. 33-1/3 rpm
phonodisc. Society for the Preservation of the American
Musical Heritage MIA 110, 1961.
(See also: R92a, R132a, R258b)

W150.   **Rayons d'azur, polka de salon, Op. 77** (1855; Boston: Oliver Ditson & Co., 1873. Pub. pl. no. 28007; Paris: Escudier, 1874 (ed. Clara Gottschalk).)

Dedicated to Celestine and Clara Gottschalk (the composer's sisters). Other indices: RO220, D128.

Performances

W150a.   February 14, 1856. New York City. Louis Moreau Gottschalk, piano.

Bibliography

WB191.   Apthorp, William Foster. "New Music." *Atlantic Monthly* 33:256 (February 1874).
          A review of *Rayons d'azur* and several other posthumous Gottschalk publications.

WB192.   Minor, Andrew C. *Piano Concerts in New York City 1849-1865*. Thesis: University of Michigan, 1947.
          Minor (p. 183) documents Gottschalk's February 1856 performance of the work (See: W150a).

W151.   **Solitude, Op. 65** (1855; Boston: Oliver Ditson & Co., 1871. Pub. pl. no. 6560; New York: William Hall & Son, 1871 (with no opus number); Mainz: B. Schott's Söhne, c1871 (as Op. 65). Pub. pl. no. 20653; Paris: Escudier, 1873 (as Op. 65).)

Manuscript is located at the New York Public Library. Other indices: RO239, D139. Duration: 4 minutes.

Performances

W151a.   January 25, 1856. New York City. Louis Moreau Gottschalk, piano.

Recordings

R151a.   *Selected Piano Music of Louis Moreau Gottschalk*. Lambert Orkis, piano. Compact disc. Smithsonian

Collection of Recordings ND 033, 1988. Recorded on an
1865 Chickering piano in Coolidge Auditorium, Library
of Congress, Washington, D.C., May 1982.
(See also: R76d, R103d, R110a, R145a, R192b,
R220f, R234a)

Bibliography

WB193.   Concert preview. *Le Courrier des Étas-Unis* January 24,
1856.
Gottschalk's upcoming New York performance of
the piece (See: W151a) is mentioned.

WB194.   Minor, Andrew C. *Piano Concerts in New York City
1849-1865.* Thesis: University of Michigan, 1947.
Minor (p. 178) documents Gottschalk's January 1856
performance of the piece, said to be the premiere (See:
W151a).

W152.   **Sospiro, valse poétique, Op. 24** (1855; New York: William Hall &
Son, 1857. Pub. pl. no. 4110; Paris: Escudier, 1857; Mainz: B.
Schott's Söhne, c1859; New York: Edwin F. Kalmus, n.d. Pub. pl.
no. 3468 (*Album for Piano Solo*); Melville, New York, 1976 (*Album
for Piano Solo*).)

Other indices: RO241, D142.
Dedicated to Madame Taylor of Baltimore.
(See also: W31)

Performances

W152a.   January 25, 1856. New York City. Louis Moreau
Gottschalk, piano.

W152b.   May 1856. New York City. Louis Moreau Gottschalk,
piano.

Recordings

R152a.   *Piano Portraits from Nineteenth-Century America.* Noël
Lester, piano. Compact disc. Centaur CRC 2250, 1995.
With: *Le banjo* (See: R142u); *L'Union* (See:

R220i); *Pasquinade* (See: R228r); and various works by
Benjamin Carr, Arthur Clifton, Stephen Collins Foster,
William Mason, Richard Hoffman, John Knowles Paine,
and Edward MacDowell. For a review of this recording,
see: B533.

Bibliography

WB195.   Minor, Andrew C. *Piano Concerts in New York City
1849-1865.* Thesis: University of Michigan, 1947.
Minor (pp. 179 and 198) documents Gottschalk's
New York performances of the piece (See: W152a and
W152b).

W153.   **Pensée poétique (L'extase), Op. 61 (62)** (1855-6; Rio de Janerio:
Napoleão, 1869; New York: Wm. Hall & Son, 1870. Pub. pl. no.
6520; Boston: Oliver Ditson & Co., 1870. Pub. pl. no. 6520; Mainz:
B. Schott's Söhne, c1870. Pub. pl. no. 20537; New York: Arno Press
and *The New York Times*, 1969 (*The Piano Works of Louis Moreau
Gottschalk*, vol. 4, ed. Vera Brodsky Lawrence and Richard
Jackson).)

Dedication: "À Mlle. Cara de la Montagnie Hall de New York."
Duration: 3-1/2 minutes.
Manuscript is privately held.
Other indices: RO194, D117.

Recordings

R153a.   *Gottschalk: 40 Works for Piano.* Alan Mandel, piano.
Four 33-1/3 rpm phonodiscs. Desto DC 6470-73, 1969.
Reissued on three compact discs, VoxBox CD3X 3033,
1995.
For reviews of this recording, see: B360-B362,
B365, B366, B369-B371, B375, B388, B396, B523,
B529. (See also: R67a, R68d, R69a, R78e, R83b, R92b,
R95c, R100a, R103a, R105a, R112b, R135a, R139d,
R142e, R144a, R146a, R156b, R165e, R167a, R175a,
R191b, R192a, R195a, R203a, R204a, R212c, R216b,
R220b, R227b, R228e, R229a, R230b, R232a, R255a,
R256a, R257a, R258c, R265b)

W154.   **Prelude** (1855-6; unpublished; lost.)

Other indices: RO212.

Performances

W154a.   January 17, 1856. New York City. Louis Moreau
Gottschalk, piano.

Bibliography

WB196.   Minor, Andrew C. *Piano Concerts in New York City
1849-1865.* Thesis: University of Michigan, 1947.
Minor (p. 178) documents Gottschalk's January 1856
performance of this work (See: W154a). Interestingly,
the piece is not included in any of the works lists from
Gottschalk's lifetime, raising the possibility that the
Prelude performed on the documented concert may have
been an alternate title for some other Gottschalk
composition.

WB197.   Lowens, Irving and S. Frederick Starr. *The New Grove
Dictionary of Music and Musicians,* 2nd ed. s.v.
"Gottschalk, Louis Moreau." London: Macmillan, 2000.

W155.   **La Gaselle: Andante elegant** (1855-6; unpublished; lost.)

Other indices: RO102.

Performances

W155a.   February 28, 1856. New York City. Louis Moreau
Gottschalk, piano.

Bibliography

WB198.   Minor, Andrew C. *Piano Concerts in New York City
1849-1865.* Thesis: University of Michigan, 1947.
Minor (p. 184) documents Gottschalk's New York
City performance (See: W155a) of the piece.

W156.   **Ricordati (Yearning), nocturne, méditation, romance, Op. 26**
(1855-6; New York: William Hall & Son, 1857. Pub. pl. no. 4113;
Boston: Oliver Ditson & Co., 1857; Paris: Escudier, 1857 (as Op.
26); Mainz: B. Schott's Söhne, 1859 (as Op. 26). Pub. pl. no. 15110;
New York: G. Schirmer, 1901. Pub. pl. no. 15275; St. Louis:
Kunkel, 1907 (simplified version); Bryn Mawr, Pennsylvania:
Theodore Presser, 1956 (*Piano Music by Louis Moreau Gottschalk*,
ed. Jeanne Behrend).)

Duration: 4 minutes.
Dedicated to Baron de Trobriand.
Other indices: RO227, D133.

Performances

W156a.   May 5, 1862. New York City. Louis Moreau Gottschalk,
piano.

W156b.   1972. *A Festival of Americana: The Romantic Era in
American Music.* New England Conservatory of Music,
Boston. Kathy Hulstrand, piano.

Recordings

R156a.   *Piano Music by Louis Moreau Gottschalk.* Jeanne
Behrend, piano. 33-1/3 rpm phonodisc. MGM E-3370,
1957.
    For a review of this recording, see: B265. (See also:
R68b, R78b, R88a, R139c, R142b, R165b, R212a, R220a,
R228c)

R156b.   *Gottschalk: 40 Works for Piano.* Alan Mandel, piano.
Four 33-1/3 rpm phonodiscs. Desto DC 6470-73, 1969.
Reissued on three compact discs, VoxBox CD3X 3033,
1995.
    For reviews of this recording, see: B360-B362,
B365, B366, B369-B371, B375, B388, B396, B523,
B529. (See also: R67a, R68d, R69a, R78e, R83b, R92b,
R95c, R100a, R103a, R105a, R112b, R135a, R139d,
R142e, R144a, R146a, R153a, R165e, R167a, R175a,
R191b, R192a, R195a, R203a, R204a, R212c, R216b,

R220b, R227b, R228e, R229a, R230b, R232a, R255a,
R256a, R257a, R258c, R265b)

R156c.   *Louis Moreau Gottschalk: Piano Works*. Klaus
Kaufmann, piano. Compact disc. Koch Schwann
360352, n.d.
(See also: R68o, R76g, R78s, R99b, R139k, R142z,
R165w, R204e, R220n, R228u)

Bibliography

WB199.   Minor, Andrew C. *Piano Concerts in New York City
1849-1865*. Thesis: University of Michigan, 1947.
Minor mentions Gottschalk's May 1862 performance
of the piece (See: W156a.).

W157.   **Apothéose, grande marche solennelle, Op. 29** (1855-6; (?) Boston:
Oliver Ditson & Co., 1857. Pub. pl. no. 4137; New York: Wm. Hall
& Son, 1858. Pub. pl. no. 4137; Paris: Escudier, 1859; Mainz: B.
Schott's Söhne, c1859-60 (as op. 29). Pub. pl. no. 15164;; New
York: Arno Press & *The New York Times*, 1969 (*The Piano Works of
Louis Moreau Gottschalk*, vol. 1, ed. Vera Brodsky Lawrence and
Richard Jackson).)

Other indices: RO8, D5.
Dedicated to King Leopold I of Belgium.

Performances

W157a.   October 14, 1856. Brooklyn Athenaeum, Brooklyn, New
York. Louis Moreau Gottschalk, piano.

Bibliography

WB200.   Doyle, John G. *Louis Moreau Gottschalk, 1929-1869: A
Bibliographical Study and Catalog of Works*. Detroit,
Michigan: Published for the College Music Society by
Information Coordinators, 1982.
Doyle takes the lead (p. 262) in speculating that the
Grande marche solennelle performed at the October 14,
1856 Brooklyn Athenaeum concert (See: W157a) was
Apothéose; later Gottschalk researchers concur.

W158. **Caprice-polka, Op. 79** (1856; Boston: Oliver Ditson & Co., 1873
(ed. Nicolás Ruiz Espadero). Pub. pl. no. 28005; Paris: Escudier,
1874; New York: Arno Press and *The New York Times,* 1969 (*The
Piano Works of Louis Moreau Gottschalk*, vol. 1, ed. Vera Brodsky
Lawrence and Richard Jackson).)

Manuscript and sketches are located at the New York Public Library.
Dedication: "à son ami Nicolás Ruiz Espadero de la Havane."
Other indices: RO44, D26.

Recordings

R158a. *Gottschalk: Piano Music, Vol. 2.* Philip Martin, piano.
Compact disc. Hyperion CDA 66697, 1994.
    For reviews of this recording, see: B525 and B529.
(See also: R76f, R99a, R100f, R103f, R105b, R119b,
R146c, R162a, R171a, R187b, R199c, R210a, R212j,
R216h, R228o, R257f)

W159. *Il Trovatore,* **Grand Duo di bravura** (c1856; unpublished; lost.)

Other indices: RO267.
Note: Offergeld discusses the apparent confusion over the
    authorship and the very existence of this work. (See also:
    WB201)
Note: The piece was based on themes from Verdi's opera *Il
    Trovatore* and may have been arranged for two pianos (See:
    W294).

Bibliography

WB201. Hoffman, Richard. *Some Musical Recollections of Fifty
    Years.* New York: Scribner's,1910. Reprinted with new
    introductory material by Frank E. Kirby and John G.
    Doyle. Detroit: Information Coordinators, 1976.
        Although Hoffman's book deals relatively little with
    Gottschalk, it does suggest that the *Grand Duo di bravura*
    was jointly composed by Gottschalk and Sigismund
    Thalberg.

WB202. Offergeld, Robert. *The Centennial Catalogue of the
    Published and Unpublished Compositions of Louis*

Moreau Gottschalk. New York: Stereo Review, 1970. Offergeld offers extensive commentary on the confusion over the authorship of the work. (See note above)

WB203.   Suttoni, Charles R. *Piano and Opera: A Study of the Piano Fantaisies Written on Opera Themes in the Romantic Era*. Dissertation: New York University, 1973.

W160.   **Esquisse** (c1856; unpublished; lost.)

Other indices: RO78.

Performances

W160a.   April 5, 1856. New York City. Louis Moreau Gottschalk, piano.

Bibliography

WB204.   Minor, Andrew C. *Piano Concerts in New York City 1849-1865*. Thesis: University of Michigan, 1947.
Minor (p. 191) provides mention of Gottschalk's April 5, 1856 performance (See: W160a).

W161.   **[Deuxième] Relects du passé, Op. 28** (1856; Boston: Oliver Ditson & Co., 1857. Pub. pl. no. 4136; New York: William Hall & Son, 1857. Pub. pl. no. 4136; Mainz: B. Schott's Söhne, 1857. Pub. pl. no. 15111.)

Other indices: RO223, D129.

W162.   **Miserere du *Trovatore*, paraphrase de concert, Op. 52** (1856-7; New York: Wm. Hall & Son, 1864. Pub. pl. no. 5964; Boston: Oliver Ditson & Co., 1864. Pub. pl. no. 5964; Mainz: B. Schott's Söhne, 1865; Paris: Escudier, 1866; New York: Arno Press and *The New York Times*, 1969 (*The Piano Works of Louis Moreau Gottschalk*, vol. 4, ed. Vera Brodsky Lawrence and Richard Jackson).)

Dedication: "To George Wm. Warren."
Sketches are located at the New York Public Library

Other indices: RO171, D97.

Note: This work is based on themes from Guiseppe Verdi's opera *Il Trovatore*.

(See also: W295)

Recordings

R162a.   *Gottschalk: Piano Music, Vol. 2.* Philip Martin, piano. Compact disc. Hyperion CDA 66697, 1994.

For reviews of this recording, see: B525 and B529. (See also: R76f, R99a, R100f, R103f, R105b, R119b, R146c, R158a, R171a, R187b, R199c, R210a, R212j, R216h, R228o, R257f)

Bibliography

WB205.   Suttoni, Charles R. *Piano and Opera: A Study of the Piano Fantaisies Written on Opera Themes in the Romantic Era.* Dissertation: New York University, 1973.

W163.   Tennessee (1857; unpublished; lost.)

Other indices: RO263.

Note: Offergeld speculates that this piece may be named after a ship named the Tennessee, although it is unclear whether it was the Tennessee constructed in the 1840s or a vessel on its maiden voyage at the time of this composition's writing.

Performances

W163a.   Late 1857. Ponce, Puerto Rico. Louis Moreau Gottschalk, piano.

Bibliography

WB206.   Pasarell, Emilio J. "El Centenario de los conciertos de Adelina Patti y Luis Moreau Gottschalk en Puerto Rico." *Revista del Instituto de Cultura Puertorriqueña* 2:52-55 (January-March 1959).

Pasarell (pp. 52-53) provides documentation of Gottschalk's performance of work by this title in late

1857 in Ponce, Puerto Rico (See: W163a).

WB207.   Offergeld, Robert. *The Centennial Catalogue of the
         Published and Unpublished Compositions of Louis
         Moreau Gottschalk.* New York: Stereo Review, 1970.
         Offergeld (p. 30) discusses the mystery surrounding
         the naming of this piece.

W164.   Chant des Caraïbes (1857; unpublished; lost.)

Other indices: RO47.
Note: *The Life of Louis Moreau Gottschalk* (See: B61) provides the
      date of this piece. Apparently no other documentation exists.
      Offergeld provides some information on the Indians whose
      melodies Gottschalk may have incorporated in the work.

W165.   Souvenir de Porto Rico, Marche des Gibaros, Op. 31 (1857-8;
         Mainz: B Schott's Söhne, c1860. Pub. pl. no. 15773; Paris:
         Escudier, c1860; New York: Wm. A. Pond, n.d. Pub. pl. no. 4868;
         New York: Music Press, 1947 (ed. John Kirkpatrick); New York:
         Carl Fischer, 1971 (*Gottschalk: A Compendium of Piano Music*, ed.
         Eugene List); New York: Dover Publications, 1973 (*Piano Music of
         Louis Moreau Gottschalk*, selected and introduced by Richard
         Jackson); Leipzig: Peters, 1973 (*Louis Moreau Gottschalk:
         kreolische und karibische Klavierstücke*, ed. Eberhardt Klemm);
         Dayton, Ohio: McAfee Music, 1977 (*The Piano Music of Louis
         Moreau Gottschalk Made Easy*, arr. David Krane).)

Duration: 5-1/2 minutes.
Dedication: "À Mr. Ernest Lubeck."
Other indices: RO250, D147.

Performances

W165a.   Late 1857. Puerto Rico. Louis Moreau Gottschalk,
         piano.

W165b.   January 7, 1858. Ponce, Puerto Rico. Adelina Patti,
         piano.

W165c.   December 22, 1859. Havana. Louis Moreau Gottschalk,
         piano.

W165d. January 28, 1936. Town Hall, New York City. John Kirkpatrick, piano.

W165e. December 17, 1969. *Louis Moreau Gottschalk Centennial Concert*. Robert Pritchard, piano.
(See also: R165f)

W165f. February 9, 1993. *An American Music Sampler*. Heeren Recital Hall, Southern Baptist Theological Seminary. Sandra Chucalo Turner, piano.

W165g. September 8, 1998. *Faculty Gala Recital*. Alumni Memorial Chapel, Southern Baptist Theological Seminary. Sandra Chucalo Turner, piano.

W165h. September 27, 1998. The Boston Conservatory, Boston, Massachussetts. Michael Lewin, piano.

Recordings

R165a. *The Banjo and Other Creole Favorites*. Eugene List, piano. 33-1/3 rpm phonodisc. Vanguard VRS-485, 1957. Reissued as part of *The World of Louis Moreau Gottschalk* (See: R165g). Reissued on compact disc as Vanguard Classics OVC 4050, 1992. Reissued as part of the two compact disc set *Piano Music of Louis Moreau Gottschalk*. Vanguard Classics 08 9143 72/08 9144-72, 1993.
For reviews of this recording, see: see: B258, B259, B263 and B265. (See also: R68a, R76a, R78a, R95a, R139b, R142a, R191a, R216a, R227a, R228b, R230a)

R165b. *Piano Music by Louis Moreau Gottschalk*. Jeanne Behrend, piano. 33-1/3 rpm phonodisc. MGM E-3370, 1957.
For a review of this recording, see: B265. (See also: R68b, R78b, R88a, R139c, R142b, R156a, R212a, R220a, R228c)

R165c. *American Piano Music*. Jeanne Behrend, piano. 33-1/3 rpm phonodisc. Allegro ALG 3024, 1962.
With a variety of other American works.

R165d.   *The Piano Music of Louis Moreau Gottschalk.* Amiram
          Rigai, piano. 33-1/3 rpm phonodisc. Decca DL 10143,
          1967. Reissued as Decca DL 710143, 1970.
              For reviews of this recording, see: B327, B329,
          B330. (See also: R78d, R83a, R95b, R112a, R142d,
          R212b, R228d, R249a, R265a)

R165e.   *Gottschalk: 40 Works for Piano.* Alan Mandel, piano.
          Four 33-1/3 rpm phonodiscs. Desto DC 6470-73, 1969.
          Reissued on three compact discs, VoxBox CD3X 3033,
          1995.
              For reviews of this recording, see: B360-B362,
          B365, B366, B369-B371, B375, B388, B396, B523,
          B529. (See also: R67a, R68d, R69a, R78e, R83b, R92b,
          R95c, R100a, R103a, R105a, R112b, R135a, R139d,
          R142e, R144a, R146a, R153a, R156b, R167a, R175a,
          R191b, R192a, R195a, R203a, R204a, R212c, R216b,
          R220b, R227b, R228e, R229a, R230b, R232a, R255a,
          R256a, R257a, R258c, R265b)

R165f.   *Louis Moreau Gottschalk: A Centennial Concert.*
          Various pianists. *Souvenir de Porto Rico* performed by
          Robert Pritchard. 33-1/3 rpm phonodisc. Turnabout TV-
          S 34426, 1971. Recorded live December 17, 1969.
              For reviews of this recording, see: B415 and B440.
          (See also: R112c, R135b, R139e, R142f, R167b, R203b,
          R212d, R216c, R229b, R258d)

R165g.   *The World of Louis Moreau Gottschalk.* Various
          performers. *Souvenir de Porto Rico* performed by
          Eugene List, piano. Two 33-1/3 rpm phonodiscs.
          Vanguard VSD-723; VSD-724, 1973. Reissued on
          compact disc. Vanguard VCD 72026, 1988.
              For a review of this recording, see: B417. (See also:
          R34b, R37a, R68e, R76b, R78f, R95d, R139g, R142i,
          R191c, R216d, R227c, R228g, R230c)

R165h.   *Louis Moreau Gottschalk: Piano Music.* Edward Gold,
          piano. 33-1/3 rpm phonodisc. Musical Heritage Society
          MHS 1629, 1974.
              (See also: R142j, R167c, R176c, R178a, R228h,
          R254a, R259a)

R165i.   *Festival of American Music.* Seymour Bernstein, piano. National Federation of Music Clubs NFMC 302, 1975.
          With: *Le banjo* (See: R142k) and works by miscellaneous other American composers.

R165j.   *The Piano Music of Louis Moreau Gottschalk.* Ivan Davis, piano. Simultaneously issued on 1-7/8 ips audio cassette, Musical Heritage Society MHC 9040 and 33-1/3 rpm phonodisc, MHS 7040, 1975. Also issued as *Great Galloping Gottschalk.* 33-1/3 rpm phonodisc. London CS-6943, 1976. Reissued on 1-7/8 ips audio cassette, 1984.
          For reviews of this recording, see: B454, B455, B461. (See also: R78g, R88b, R95e, R100b, R103b, R142l, R203d, R216e, R227d, R228i, R257b)

R165k.   *Louis Moreau Gottschalk, 1829-1869: American Piano Music.* Amiram Rigai, piano. 33-1/3 rpm phonodisc. Folkways Records FSS 37485, 1979. Reissued on compact disc, Smithsonian Folkways 40803, 1992.
          For a review of the original recording, see: B468. (See also: R68f, R69b, R78h, R83c, R88e, R95g, R112h, R133a, R142m, R167e, R191d, R212e, R227e, R228k, R249c, R275b)

R165l.   *American Encores.* Grant Johannesen, piano. 33-1/3 rpm phonodisc. Golden Crest CR 4065, n.d. (before 1983).
          With works by George Gershwin, John Alden Carpenter, and Arthur Farwell.

R165m.   *Louis Moreau Gottschalk on Original Instruments.* Richard Burnett, piano. Compact disc. Amon Ra CD-SAR 32, 1988.
          All works are performed on instruments from Gottschalk's era. (See also: R76c, R78i, R88c, R100c, R103c, R107a, R112d, R187a, R199a, R201b, R204b, R212f, R216f, R227f, R265c, R272a)

R165n.   *Cakewalk.* John Arpin, piano. Compact disc. ProArte Digital CDD515, 1990. Recorded September 25 and 27, 1989 in Toronto, Ontario, Canada.
          (See also: R68g, R78j, R95h, R100d, R112e, R142n,

R191e, R204c, R212g, R227g, R228l, R257c)

R165o. *Cervantes, Saumell, Gottschalk.* Georges Rabol, piano.
Compact disc. Opus 111 OPS 30-9001, 1990. Reissued
on *Classics of the Americas: Vol. 4 Gottschalk.* Opus
111 2000, 1995.
Contains works by Manuel Saumell, Georges Rabol,
and Ignatio Cervantes, in addition to several Gottschalk
compositions. (See also: R68h, R76e, R78k, R191f,
R228m, R249b)

R165p. *Gottschalk: Piano Music.* Philip Martin, piano.
Compact disc. Hyperion 66459, 1991.
(See also: R78l, R88d, R107b, R112g, R142p,
R167i, R178d, R191i, R192d, R201c, R220l, R265d,
R272d)

R165q. *Musique américaine pour piano.* Noël Lee, piano.
Compact disc. Chant du monde LCD 278-1067, 1991.
With: *The Dying Poet* (See: R227h); *Grand scherzo,
Op. 57* (See: R257d); and works by Edward MacDowell,
Aaron Copland, John Cage, and Elliott Carter.

R165r. *Thar They Blow.* Nuclear Whales Saxophone Orchestra.
Compact disc. Whaleco 102, 1991. Reissued on 1-7/8
ips audio cassette, 2000.
With a wide variety of concert and jazz compositions
arranged for saxophone ensemble with accompanying
instruments.

R165s. *Louis Moreau Gottschalk.* Eugene List, piano. Compact
disc. Vanguard Classics OVC 4050, 1992. Contains
material previously issued on 33-1/3 rpm monophonic
phonodisc (See: R165a). Reissued as part of the two
compact disc set *Piano Music.* Vanguard Classics 08
9143 72/08 9144-72, 1993.
(See also: R68j, R78n, R142q)

R165t. *Souvenirs.* Quintet of the Americas (Marco Granados,
flute; Matthew Sullivan, oboe and cor anglais;
Christopher Jepperson, clarinet; Thomas Novak, bassoon;
Barbara Oldham, horn). Simultaneously issued on 1-7/8

ips audio cassette, XLNT Music CA 18008; and compact disc, XLNT Music CD 18008, 1992.

The present release includes a wind quintet arrangement (by Ronald W. Tucker) of the Gottschalk work and was recorded June 15-17, 1992, Skinner Auditorium, Vassar College, Poughkeepsie, New York. With: various works by U.S. and South American composers. (See also: R95j)

R165u.   *Great American Piano I. Louis Moreau Gottschalk. Vol. 7.* Leonard Pennario, piano. Compact disc. Angel Records CDM 7 64667 2, 1992. Material originally released on two 33-1/3 rpm phonodiscs as *Music of Louis Moreau Gottschalk*. Angel RL-32125, 1975.

For reviews of this recording, see: B441, B442, B446, B450, B452. (See also: R68i, R78m, R95i, R112f, R139i, R142t, R167d, R191g, R199b, R212i, R220g, R228n, R229c, R257e, R272b)

R165v.   *Caribbean Souvenires.* William Kanengiser, guitar. Compact disc. GSP Productions GSP 1008CD, 1998. Recorded July 20-22, 1997.

With: *Souvenir de la Havane* (See: R192c), *Caprice, Op. 44* (See: R203g);, and miscellaneous Caribbean and Caribbean-influenced works. Note: The Gottschalk works are all performed in Kanengiser's arrangements for guitar.

R165w.   *Louis Moreau Gottschalk: Piano Works.* Klaus Kaufmann, piano. Compact disc. Koch Schwann 360352, n.d.

(See also: R68o, R76g, R78s, R99b, R139k, R142z, R156c, R204e, R220n, R228u)

R165x.   *Louis Moreau Gottschalk: A Night in the Tropics.* Michael Linville, piano; Hot Springs Music Festival Symphony Orchestra; Richard Rosenberg, conductor. Compact disc. Naxos 8.559036, 2000.

Note: This recording is of Jack Elliott's orchestration of the work. (See also: R16a, R34f, R37i, R78t, R95n, R103g, R203i, R227l, R311a)

Bibliography

WB208.   Concert review. *Gaceta de la Habana* December 24, 1859.
A review, cited by Doyle (See: B484), of Gottschalk's December 1859 performance in Havana (See: W165c).

WB209.   *The Life of Louis Moreau Gottschalk*. New York, c1863.
The works list in this pamphlet gives the composition date as 1858; however, some researchers have cited evidence of an earlier date (See: WB212).

WB210.   S., I. "John Kirkpatrick's Recital." *New York Times* January 29, 1936:15.
A review of W165d.

WB211.   Deliz, Monserrate. *Renadio del cantar folklórico de Puerto Rico*. Madrid: El Instituto de Literatura de Puerto Rico, 1952.
The book contains (p. 243) an *aguinaldo* resembling the one used by Gottschalk in *Souvenir de Porto Rico*.

WB212.   Parasell, Emilio J. "El Centenario de lost conciertos de Andelina Patti y Luis Moreau Gottschalk en Puerto Rico." *Revista del Instituto de Cultura Puertorriqueña* 2:52-55 (January-March 1959).
Parasell documents Gottschalk's performance of the piece in Puerto Rico, late 1857 (See: W165a). (See also: WB209)

WB213.   Sahr, Hadassah Gallup. *Performance and Analytical Study of Selected Piano Music by American Composers*. Dissertation: Columbia University, 1969.
The author devotes a chapter to *Souvenir de Porto Rico*. Also indexed in *Dissertation Abstracts International* 30-A/9 (March 1970), p. 3976

W166.   **Caprice sur la danse créole** (c1857-8; unpublished; lost.)

Other indices: RO41.

W167.   **Danza, Op. 33** (1857-9; Mainz: B. Schott's Söhne, c1859. Pub. pl.
no. 15921; Philadelphia: G. André & Cie, c1859. Pub. pl. no. 15921;
New York: Schargenberg and Luis, c1859. Pub. pl. no. 15921; New
York: Arno Press and *The New York Times*, 1969 (*The Piano Works
of Louis Moreau Gottschalk*, vol. 2, ed. Vera Brodsky Lawrence and
Richard Jackson); New York: Carl Fischer, 1971 (*Gottschalk: A
Compendium of Piano Music*, ed. Eugene List); New York: Dover
Publications, 1973 (*Piano Music of Louis Moreau Gottschalk*,
selected and introduced by Richard Jackson); Bedford Hills, New
York: Ekay Music (*The Piano Duet Book*).)

Duration: 6 minutes.
Dedication: "À mon vieil ami Edouard Verger de Saint Pierre,
Martinique."
Other indices: RO66, D41.
Note: The Schott edition is dated "Porto-Rico Novembre 1857."
    Some sources list the completion dates variously between
    1857 and 1859.

Performances

W167a.   December 17, 1969. *Louis Moreau Gottschalk
    Centennial Concert.* John Kirkpatrick, piano.
    (See also: R167b)

Recordings

R167a.   *Gottschalk: 40 Works for Piano.* Alan Mandel, piano.
    Four 33-1/3 rpm phonodiscs. Desto DC 6470-73, 1969.
    Reissued on three compact discs, VoxBox CD3X 3033,
    1995.
        For reviews of this recording, see: B360-B362,
    B365, B366, B369-B371, B375, B388, B396, B523,
    B529. (See also: R67a, R68d, R69a, R78e, R83b, R92b,
    R95c, R100a, R103a, R105a, R112b, R135a, R139d,
    R142e, R144a, R146a, R153a, R156b, R165e, R175a,
    R191b, R192a, R195a, R203a, R204a, R212c, R216b,
    R220b, R227b, R228e, R229a, R230b, R232a, R255a,
    R256a, R257a, R258c, R265b)

R167b.   *Louis Moreau Gottschalk: A Centennial Concert.*
    Various pianists. *Danza, Op. 33* performed by John

Kirkpatrick. 33-1/3 rpm phonodisc. Turnabout TV-S
34426, 1971. Recorded live December 17, 1969.
For reviews of this recording, see: B415 and B440.
(See also: R112c, R135b, R139e, R142f, R165f, R203b,
R212d, R216c, R229b, R258d)

R167c.   *Louis Moreau Gottschalk: Piano Music.* Edward Gold,
piano. 33-1/3 rpm phonodisc. Musical Heritage Society
MHS 1629, 1974.
(See also: R142j, R165h, R176c, R178a, R228h,
R254a, R259a)

R167d.   *Great American Piano I. Louis Moreau Gottschalk. Vol.
7.* Leonard Pennario, piano. Compact disc. Angel
Records CDM 7 64667 2, 1992. Material originally
released on two 33-1/3 rpm phonodiscs as *Music of Louis
Moreau Gottschalk.* Angel RL-32125, 1975.
For reviews of this recording, see: B441, B442,
B446, B450, B452. (See also: R68i, R78m, R95i, R112f,
R139i, R142t, R165u, R191g, R199b, R212i, R220g,
R228n, R229c, R257e, R272b)

R167e.   *Louis Moreau Gottschalk. American Piano Music.*
Amiram Rigai, piano. Compact disc. Smithsonian
Folkways 40803, 1992.
For a review of the original recording, see: B468.
(See also: R68f, R69b, R78h, R83c, R88e, R95g, R112h,
R133a, R142m, R165k, R191d, R212e, R227e, R228k,
R249c, R275b)

R167f.   *Three Stories.* Van Dyke Parks, piano. 1-7/8 ips audio
cassette. Children's Book-of-the-Month Club, 1994.
This recording consistes of three children's stories
written by Eric Carle and read by Madeline Kahn. The
Van Dyke Parks recording of the Gottschalk work is a
"bonus instrumental."

R167g.   *Fantasy for Wizards!* Wizards! (double reed ensemble).
Compact disc. Crystal Records CD872, 1997.
The Gottschalk work is arranged for double reed
ensemble. With various other arrangements and original
works for the ensemble.

R167h.   *DeGaetano Plays Gottschalk.* Robert DeGaetano, piano. Compact disc. Crystonyx 1002, 1998. Recorded January-February 1989 at Denver, New York.
(See also: R68n, R78p, R95m, R100g, R107c, R119c, R142w, R171b, R187c, R192e, R199d, R201d, R220j, R227k, R272c)

R167i.   *Gottschalk: Piano Music.* Philip Martin, piano. Compact disc. Hyperion 66459, 1991.
(See also: R78l, R88d, R107b, R112g, R142p, R165p, R178d, R191i, R192d, R201c, R220l, R265d, R272d)

W168.   La gitanella, caprice caractéristique, Op. 35 (1857-9; Paris: Escudier, 1862. Pub. pl. no. 4636; Mainz: B. Schott's Söhne, c1862. Pub. pl. no. 16265; New York: William Hall & Son, n.d.; New York: Arno Press and *The New York Times*, 1969 (*The Piano Works of Louis Moreau Gottschalk*, vol. 2, ed. Vera Brodsky Lawrence and Richard Jackson).)

Dedication: "à Mr. Jules Fontana."
Other indices: RO103, D61.

Performances

W168a.   Late 1857. Puerto Rico. Louis Moreau Gottschalk, piano.

Bibliography

WB214.   Fors, Luis Ricardo. *Gottschalk.* Havana: Propagandia Literaria, 1880.
Fors reports the date (p. 66) of the work's composition as 1858. (See also: WB215)

WB215.   Pasarell, Emilio J. "El Centenario de los conciertos de Adelina Patti y Luis Moreau Gottschalk en Puerto Rico." *Revista del Instituto de Cultura Puertorriqueña* 2:52-55 (no. 2; January-March 1959).
Pasarell documents Gottschalk's late 1857 performance of a piece of this title in Puerto Rico (See: W168a). Note the conflict between the completion date

given by Fors (See: WB214) and this reputed performance. Other sources list dates ranging from 1857 to 1860.

W169. **Chant de guerre, Op. 78** (1857-9; Boston: Oliver Ditson & Co., 1873 (ed. Nicolás Ruiz Espadero). Pub. pl. no. 27999; Paris: Escudier, 1874; New York: Arno Press and *The New York Times*, 1969 (*The Piano Works of Louis Moreau Gottschalk*, vol. 1, ed. Vera Brodsky Lawrence and Richard Jackson).)

Manuscript is located at the New York Public Library.
Other indices: RO48, D29.

W170. **Las patitas de mi sobrina, danza** (1857-61; unpublished.)

Manuscript is located at the New York Public Library.
Other indices: D115.

W171. **Ynés, danza in E-flat Major** (1857-61; New York: New York Public Library; Sole agent, A. Broude, 1976 (*The Little Book of Louis Moreau Gottschalk*, ed. Richard Jackson and Neil Ratliff).)

Manuscript is located at the New York Public Library.
Dedication: "Danza compuesta por L.M. Gottschalk y dedicata a su bella discipula."
Other indices: RO277; D161.

Recordings

R171a.   *Gottschalk: Piano Music, Vol. 2.* Philip Martin, piano. Compact disc. Hyperion CDA 66697, 1994.
     For reviews of this recording, see: B525 and B529.
     (See also: R76f, R99a, R100f, R103f, R105b, R119b, R146c, R158a, R162a, R187b, R199c, R210a, R212j, R216h, R228o, R257f)

R171b.   *DeGaetano Plays Gottschalk.* Robert DeGaetano, piano. Compact disc. Crystonyx 1002, 1998. Recorded January-February 1989 at Denver, New York.
     (See also: R68n, R78p, R95m, R100g, R107c, R119c, R142w, R167h, R187c, R192e, R199d, R201d, R220j, R227k, R272c)

W172.   El silvido, contradanza (1857-62; unpublished.)

Manuscript is located at the New York Public Library.
Other indices: D138.

W173.   Marlborough, s'en va t'en guerre (1858; unpublished; lost.)

Other indices: RO160.
Note: Sources cited in Offergeld document performances by the
      composer over the course of several years; *Marlborough*
      seems to have stayed in Gottschalk's repertoire longer than
      many of his works.

Performances

W173a.   May 5, 1862. New York City. Louis Moreau Gottschalk,
          piano.

W173b.   October 2, 1862. New York City. Louis Moreau
          Gottschalk, piano.

W173c.   October 15, 1862. Boston. Louis Moreau Gottschalk,
          piano.

W173d.   1863. Irving Hall, New York City. Louis Moreau
          Gottschalk, piano.

W173e.   November 25, 1865. Lima, Peru. Louis Moreau
          Gottschalk, piano.

W173f.   October 10, 1869. Rio de Janeiro. Louis Moreau
          Gottschalk, piano.

W174.   Fantaisie sur des airs martiniquais (1858; unpublished; lost.)

Other indices: RO93.
Note: As Offergeld suggests, Gottschalk was not known to have
      been in Martinique until February 1859; however, *The Life of
      Louis Moreau Gottschalk* (See: B61) gives 1858 as the
      composition date. If Gottschalk based the piece on melodies
      he heard on his travels, the date given in *The Life of Louis
      Moreau Gottschalk* may be off by a year; however, it is

possible that the composer wrote the piece in anticipation of performances in Martinique and did so in 1858.

W175. **Love and Chivalry (Amour chevaleresque, caprice élégant en forme de schottisch), Op.** 97 (1858-9; Boston: Oliver Ditson, 1859. Pub. pl. no. 22048; Mainz: B Schott's Söhne, n.d. Pub. pl. no. 22836 and Pub. pl. no. 22966; New York: Arno Press & *The New York Times*, 1969 (*The Piano Works of Louis Moreau Gottschalk*, vol. 1, ed. Vera Brodsky Lawrence and Richard Jackson).)

Duration: 4-3/4 minutes.
Dedicated to Miss Medora Henriques.
Other indices: RO135, D82.
Sketches are located the New York Public Library.
Note: This piece originally was published under Gottschalk's pseudonym Seven Octaves.

Recordings

R175a. *Gottschalk: 40 Works for Piano.* Alan Mandel, piano. Four 33-1/3 rpm phonodiscs. Desto DC 6470-73, 1969. Reissued on three compact discs, VoxBox CD3X 3033, 1995.

For reviews of this recording, see: B360-B362, B365, B366, B369-B371, B375, B388, B396, B523, B529. (See also: R67a, R68d, R69a, R78e, R83b, R92b, R95c, R100a, R103a, R105a, R112b, R135a, R139d, R142e, R144a, R146a, R153a, R156b, R165e, R167a, R191b, R192a, R195a, R203a, R204a, R212c, R216b, R220b, R227b, R228e, R229a, R230b, R232a, R255a, R256a, R257a, R258c, R265b)

W176. **Murmures éoliens, Op.** 46 (1858-9; New York: William Hall & Son, 1862. Pub. pl. no. 4688; Boston: Oliver Ditson & Co., 1862. Pub. pl. no. 4688; Paris: Escudier, 1862; Mainz: B. Schott's Söhne, 1863. Pub. pl. no. 17064; Rio de Janeiro: Narciso y Napoleão, n.d.; New York: Arno Press and *The New York Times*, 1969 (*The Piano Works of Louis Moreau Gottschalk*, vol. 4, ed. Vera Brodsky Lawrence and Richard Jackson).)

Dedication: "À mon ami Albert H. Wood."
Other indices: RO176, D102.

Performances

W176a. December 22, 1859. Havana. Louis Moreau Gottschalk, piano.

Recordings

R176a. *Louis Moreau Gottschalk: Piano Music.* Edward Gold, piano. 33-1/3 rpm phonodisc. Musical Heritage Society MHS 1629, 1974.
   (See also: R142j, R165h, R167c, R178a, R228h, R254a, R259a)

R176b. *Gottschalk: Piano Music, Vol. 3.* Philip Martin, piano. Compact disc. Hyperion CDA 66915, 1997.
   For a review of this recording, see: B538. (See also: R681, R951, R139j, R177a, R203f, R209b, R227j, R258i, R259b)

Bibliography

WB216. Doyle, John G. *Louis Moreau Gottschalk, 1929-1869: A Bibliographical Study and Catalog of Works.* Detroit, Michigan: Published for the College Music Society by Information Coordinators, 1982.
   Doyle (p. 305) cites a Havana newspaper notice that documents Gottschalk's December 1859 performance (See: W176a).

W177.   Andante de la symphonie romantique (Andante from Symphony No. 1) ("La nuit des tropiques") (1858-9; Rio de Janeiro: Narciso y Napoleão, c1880; Mainz: B. Schott's Söhne, 1880. Pub. pl. no. 22839; New York: Arno Press and *The New York Times*, 1969 (*The Piano Works of Louis Moreau Gottschalk*, vol. 4, ed. Vera Brodsky Lawrence and Richard Jackson).)

Note: This work was an arrangement by Arthur Napoleão of the first movement of W34. Gottschalk's letters contain evidence that he performed excerpts from the symphony in a solo piano version as early as 1859, but no evidence has surfaced that he intended the 1859 performance to represent a new, standalone composition.

Other indices: RO5, D4.

Performances

W177a.   1866. Santiago, Chile. Louis Moreau Gottschalk, piano.

W177b.   November 24, 1869. Rio de Janeiro. Louis Moreau
Gottschalk, piano.

Recordings

R177a.   *Gottschalk: Piano Music, Vol. 3.* Philip Martin, piano.
Compact disc. Hyperion CDA 66915, 1997.
For a review of this recording, see: B538. (See also:
R681, R951, R139j, R176b, R203f, R209b, R227j, R258i,
R259b)

Bibliography

WB217.   Stevenson, Robert. "Gottschalk in Western South
America." *Inter-American Music Bulletin* 74:7-16
(November 1969).
Stevenson (p. 11) documents Gottschalk's 1866
performance in Santiago, Chile (See: W177a).

WB218.   Lange, Francisco Curt. *Vida y muerte de Louis Moreau
Gottschalk en Rio de Janeiro, 1869.* Mendoza,
Argentina: Universidad Nacional de Cuyo, 1951.
Lange (pp. 267-69) documents Gottschalk's
performance of the "Andante" at his November 24, 1869
Rio de Janeiro concert (See: W177b).

W178.   **Columbia, caprice américain, Op. 34** (1859; New York: Firth,
Pond & Co., 1860. Pub. pl. no. 4939; Paris: Escudier, c1860; Mainz:
B. Schott's Söhne, c1860. Pub. pl. no. 16010; New York: Wm. A.
Pond & Co., 1888. Pub. pl. no. 4939; New York: Arno Press and
The New York Times, 1969 (*The Piano Works of Louis Moreau
Gottschalk*, vol. 2, ed. Vera Brodsky Lawrence and Richard
Jackson).)

Duration: 6-3/4 minutes.
Other indices: RO61, D38.

Note: *Columbia* is based in part on Stephen Foster's "My Old Kentucky Home."

Recordings

R178a.   *Louis Moreau Gottschalk: Piano Music.* Edward Gold, piano. 33-1/3 rpm phonodisc. Musical Heritage Society MHS 1629, 1974.
(See also: R142j, R165h, R167c, R176c, R228h, R254a, R259a)

R178b.   *Great American Piano II. Gottschalk, Joplin, Gershwin. Vol. 8.* Leonard Pennario, piano. Compact disc. Angel Records CDM 7 64668 2, 1992. Gottschalk material originally released on two 33-1/3 rpm phonodiscs as *Music of Louis Moreau Gottschalk.* Angel RL-32125, 1975.
Contains several Gottschalk compositions, as well as works by George Gershwin and Scott Joplin performed by Leonard Pennario and Joshua Rifkin (Joplin works only).
(See also: R119a, R203c, R204d, R216g, R244a)

R178c.   *Fascinatin' Rhythm.* Alan Feinberg, piano. Compact disc. Decca 444 457-2, 1995.
With *Bamboula* (See: R68k) and various other works, primarily by American composers.

R178d.   *Gottschalk: Piano Music.* Philip Martin, piano. Compact disc. Hyperion 66459, 1991.
(See also: R78l, R88d, R107b, R112g, R142p, R165p, R167i, R191i, R192d, R201c, R220l, R265d, R272d)

W179.   **Danza en E** (1859; unpublished; lost.)

Other indices: RO71.

W180.   **Danza en F** (1859; unpublished; lost.)

Other indices: RO72.

W181.   **Étude pour un main** (1859; unpublished; lost.)

Other indices: RO87.

W182.   **Rome, étude** (1859; unpublished; lost.)

Other indices: RO231.

W183.   **Fairy Land (Dans les nuages), schottische de concert** (1859;
Boston: Oliver Ditson Company, 1863. Pub. pl. no. 21874; Mainz:
B. Schott's Söhne, c1863. Pub. pl. no. 22835; New York: Arno Press
and *The New York Times*, 1969 (*The Piano Works of Louis Moreau
Gottschalk*, vol. 2, ed. Vera Brodsky Lawrence and Richard
Jackson).)
Manuscript is located at the New York Public Library.
Dedication: "To my friend L.M. Gottschalk by Seven Octaves."
        (See note below)
Other indices: RO91, D50.
Note: This piece was published using Gottschalk's pseudonym
        Seven Octaves.

W184.   **Jeune Fille aux yeaux noirs** (1859; unpublished; lost.)

Other indices: RO128.

W185.   **Pastorella e cavalliere, Op. 32** (1859; Boston: Oliver Ditson & Co.,
1860. Pub. pl. no. 4683; New York: William Hall & Son, 1862. Pub.
pl. no. 4683; Mainz: B. Schott's Söhne, c1862. Pub. pl. no. 15892;
New York: Edwin F. Kalmus, n.d. Pub. pl. no. 3468 (*Album for
Piano Solo*); Melville, New York: Belwin-Mills, 1976 (*Album for
Piano Solo*).)

Other indices: RO190, D114.
Note: The 1862 William Hall & Son edition contains a twenty-eight-
        measure introduction not found in other contemporary
        editions.
(See also: W23)

Performances

W185a.   December 22, 1859. Havana. Louis Moreau Gottschalk,
          piano.

W185b.   February 1, 1862. New York. Louis Moreau Gottschalk, piano.

Recordings

R185a.   *A Gottschalk Gala.* Various artists. Compact disc. Premiere Recordings PRCD 1063, 1998.

Bibliography

WB219.   Minor, Andrew C. *Piano Concerts in New York City 1849-1865.* Thesis: University of Michigan, 1947.
Minor lists Gottschalk's February 1862 New York performance of the piece (See: W185b).

WB220.   Concert Review. *Gaceta de la Habana* December 24, 1859.
Doyle cites this review of Gottschalk's December 22, 1859 perfomance of the piece in Havana (See: W185a).

WB221.   Jackson, Richard. Notes to *The Complete Published Songs of Louis Moreau Gottschalk, with a Selection of Other Songs of Mid-Nineteenth-Century America.* Newton Centre, Massachusetts: Margun Music, 1992.
Jackson compares the piano and voice arrangement with the piano version.

W186.   **Hurrah Galop, pas redoublé de concert** (1859; Boston: Oliver Ditson & Co., 1863. Pub. pl. no. 22047; Mainz: B. Schott's Söhne, c1879. Pub. pl. no. 22967; Boston: Oliver Ditson & Co., 1891. Pub. pl. no. 22047; New York: Arno Press and *The New York Times,* 1969 (*The Piano Works of Louis Moreau Gottschalk,* vol. 3, ed. Vera Brodsky Lawrence and Richard Jackson).)

Manuscript and sketches are located at the New York Public Library.
Dedication: "Au General Grant."
Other indices: RO118, D70.
Note: This piece originally was published under Gottschalk's pseudonym Seven Octaves.
Note: Offergeld suggests that the dedication to General U.S. Grant may have been added by the publisher, as Gottschalk "seems to have taken a sympathetic view of Grant's rival General

[George B.] McClellan as late as June, 1863" (See: B378, p. 21). Starr (See: B524, p. 354) suggests that the dedication may have come from Gottschalk, but only because he was not aware of Grant's anti-Semitic views.

W187. **Polka in A-flat Major** (1859; New York: New York Public Library and Continuo Music Press, 1976 (*The Little Book of Louis Moreau Gottschalk*, ed. Richard Jackson and Neil Ratliff).)

Manuscript is located at the New York Public Library.
Other indices: RO275 (RO203), D120.
Note: There is a possibility that this may be one of the lost *Danzas in A-flat Major* (See: W188and W189)

Recordings

R187a. *Louis Moreau Gottschalk on Original Instruments.* Richard Burnett, piano. Compact disc. Amon Ra CD-SAR 32, 1988.

All works are performed on instruments from Gottschalk's era. (See also: R76c, R78i, R88c, R100c, R103c, R107a, R112d, R165m, R199a, R201b, R204b, R212f, R216f, R227f, R265c, R272a)

R187b. *Gottschalk: Piano Music, Vol. 2.* Philip Martin, piano. Compact disc. Hyperion CDA 66697, 1994.

For reviews of this recording, see: B525 and B529. (See also: R76f, R99a, R100f, R103f, R105b, R119b, R146c, R158a, R162a, R171a, R199c, R210a, R212j, R216h, R228o, R257f)

R187c. *DeGaetano Plays Gottschalk.* Robert DeGaetano, piano. Compact disc. Crystonyx 1002, 1998. Recorded January-February 1989 at Denver, New York.

(See also: R68n, R78p, R95m, R100g, R107c, R119c, R142w, R167h, R171b, R192e, R199d, R201d, R220j, R227k, R272c)

W188. **Danza en A-flat, No. 1** (1859; unpublished; lost.)

Other indices: RO68.
(See also: W187)

Bibliography

WB222.   *Life of Louis Moreau Gottschalk.* New York, c1863.
The works list (p. 11) seems to be the sole reference from Gottschalk's lifetime to the present piece.

W189.   Danza en A-flat, No. 2 (1859; unpublished; lost.)

Other indices: RO69.
(See also: W187)

Bibliography

WB223.   *Life of Louis Moreau Gottschalk.* New York, c1863.
The works list (p. 11) seems to be the sole reference from Gottschalk's lifetime to the present piece.

W190.   Polonia, grande caprice de concert, Op. 35 (43) (1859; New York: Wm. Hall & Son, 1861 (as Op. 35). Pub. pl. no. 4638; Mainz: B. Schott's Söhne, 1862 (as Op. 43). Pub. pl. no. 16613; New York: Arno Press and *The New York Times*, 1969 (*The Piano Works of Louis Moreau Gottschalk*, vol. 4, ed. Vera Brodsky Lawrence and Richard Jackson).)

Dedication: "à Mademoiselle Louise Clayssen."
Other indices: RO210, D124.

Performances

W190a.   March 18, 1862. New York City. Louis Moreau Gottschalk, piano.

Bibliography

WB224.   Minor, Andrew C. *Piano Concerts in New York City 1849-1865.* Thesis: University of Michigan, 1947.
Minor (p. 355) lists Gottschalk's March 1862 New York performance (See: W190a).

W191.   Ojos criollos (Les yeux créoles), danse cubaine, caprice brillant, contradanza, Op. 37 (1859; Havana: Edelmann, 1860; New York: William Hall & Son, 1864. Pub. pl. no. 5963; Paris: Escudier, 1865;

Mainz: chez les fils de B. Schott, 1865. Pub. pl. no. 16278.18008; New York: G. Schirmer, 1907. Pub. pl. no. 19462; New York: Arno Press and *The New York Times*, 1969 (*The Piano Works of Louis Moreau Gottschalk*, vol. 4, ed. Vera Brodsky Lawrence and Richard Jackson); New York: Carl Fischer, 1971 (*Gottschalk: A Compendium of Piano Music*, ed. Eugene List); New York: Dover Publications, 1973 (*Piano Music of Louis Moreau Gottschalk*, selected and introduced by Richard Jackson); Leipzig: Peters, 1973 (*Louis Moreau Gottschalk: kreolische und karibische Klavierstücke*, ed. Eberhardt Klemm).)

Duration: 2 minutes.
Other indices: RO185, D105a.
A solo piano arrangement of W298.

Recordings

R191a.   *The Banjo and Other Creole Favorites*. Eugene List, piano. 33-1/3 rpm phonodisc. Vanguard VRS-485, 1957. Reissued as part of *The World of Louis Moreau Gottschalk* (See: D). Reissued on compact disc as Vanguard Classics OVC 4050, 1992. Reissued as part of the two compact disc set *Piano Music of Louis Moreau Gottschalk*. Vanguard Classics 08 9143 72/08 9144-72, 1993.
　　　For reviews of this recording, see: B258, B259, B263 and B265. (See also: R68a, R76a, R78a, R95a, R139b, R142a, R165a, R216a, R227a, R228b, R230a)

R191b.   *Gottschalk: 40 Works for Piano*. Alan Mandel, piano. Four 33-1/3 rpm phonodiscs. Desto DC 6470-73, 1969. Reissued on three compact discs, VoxBox CD3X 3033, 1995.
　　　For reviews of this recording, see: B360-B362, B365, B366, B369-B371, B375, B388, B396, B523, B529. (See also: R67a, R68d, R69a, R78e, R83b, R92b, R95c, R100a, R103a, R105a, R112b, R135a, R139d, R142e, R144a, R146a, R153a, R156b, R165e, R167a, R175a, R192a, R195a, R203a, R204a, R212c, R216b, R220b, R227b, R228e, R229a, R230b, R232a, R255a, R256a, R257a, R258c, R265b)

R191c.   *The World of Louis Moreau Gottschalk.* Various
performers. *Ojos criollos* performed by Eugene List,
piano. Two 33-1/3 rpm phonodiscs. Vanguard VSD-723;
VSD-724, 1973. Reissued on compact disc. Vanguard
VCD 72026, 1988.

For a review of this recording, see: B417. (See also:
R34b, R37a, R68e, R76b, R78f, R95d, R139g, R142i,
R165g, R216d, R227c, R228g, R230c)

R191d.   *Louis Moreau Gottschalk, 1829-1869: American Piano
Music.* Amiram Rigai, piano. 33-1/3 rpm phonodisc.
Folkways Records FSS 37485, 1979. Reissued on
compact disc, Smithsonian Folkways 40803, 1992.

For a review of the original recording, see: B468.
(See also: R68f, R69b, R78h, R83c, R88e, R95g, R112h,
R133a, R142m, R165k, R167e, R212e, R227e, R228k,
R249c, R275b)

R191e.   *Cakewalk.* John Arpin, piano. Compact disc. ProArte
Digital CDD515, 1990. Recorded September 25 and 27,
1989 in Toronto, Ontario, Canada.

(See also: R68g, R78j, R95h, R100d, R112e, R142n,
R165n, R204c, R212g, R227g, R228l, R257c)

R191f.   *Cervantes, Saumell, Gottschalk.* Georges Rabol, piano.
Compact disc. Opus 111 OPS 30-9001, 1990. Reissued
on *Classics of the Americas: Vol. 4 Gottschalk.* Opus
111 2000, 1995.

Contains works by Manuel Saumell, Georges Rabol,
and Ignatio Cervantes, in addition to several Gottschalk
compositions. (See also: R68h, R76e, R78k, R165o,
R228m, R249b)

R191g.   *Great American Piano I. Louis Moreau Gottschalk. Vol.
7.* Leonard Pennario, piano. Compact disc. Angel
Records CDM 7 64667 2, 1992. Material originally
released on two 33-1/3 rpm phonodiscs as *Music of Louis
Moreau Gottschalk.* Angel RL-32125, 1975.

For reviews of this recording, see: B441, B442,
B446, B450, B452. (See also: R68i, R78m, R95i, R112f,
R139i, R142t, R165u, R167d, R199b, R212i, R220g,
R228n, R229c, R257e, R272b)

R191h.   *A Gottschalk Festival.* Eugene List, piano. Two compact
discs. Vox Box 5009.
   (See also: R4a, R34e, R36b, R37g, R41a, R42a,
R44a, R220m, R228t, R258k, R298b, R302d, R305c,
R310c)

R191i.   *Gottschalk: Piano Music.* Philip Martin, piano.
Compact disc. Hyperion 66459, 1991.
   (See also: R78l, R88d, R107b, R112g, R142p,
R165p, R167i, R178d, R192d, R201c, R220l, R265d,
R272d)

Bibliography

WB225.   Hinson, Maurice. *Masters of American Piano Music.*
Van Nuys, California: Alfred Publishing, 1992.
   Hinson's book contains his edition of the Gottschalk
composition and also includes suggestions on the work's
interpretation.

W192.   **Souvenir de la Havane (Recuerdos de la Habana), grande caprice
de concert, Op. 39** (1859; Havana: Union Musical Española, 1860
(as Op. 39); New York: Wm. Hall & Son, 1860. Pub. pl. no. 4593;
Boston: Oliver Ditson & Co., 1860. Pub. pl. no. 4593; B. Schott's
Söhne, c1860. Pub. pl. no. 16367; New York: Dover Publications,
1973 (*Piano Music of Louis Moreau Gottschalk*, selected and
introduced by Richard Jackson); Leipzig: Peters, 1973 (*Louis
Moreau Gottschalk: kreolische und karibische Klavierstücke*, ed.
Eberhardt Klemm); Dayton, Ohio: McAfee Music, 1977 (*The Piano
Music of Louis Moreau Gottschalk Made Easy*, arr. David Krane).)

Manuscript is located at the New York Public Library.
Dedication: "À Mademoiselle Marie Luisa del Rio Noguerida y de
   Sedano (de la Havane)."
Duration: 6 minutes.
Other indices: RO246, D145.

Performances

W192a.   April 27, 1860. Havana. Louis Moreau Gottschalk,
piano.

Recordings

R192a.   *Gottschalk: 40 Works for Piano.* Alan Mandel, piano.
Four 33-1/3 rpm phonodiscs. Desto DC 6470-73, 1969.
Reissued on three compact discs, VoxBox CD3X 3033,
1995.
For reviews of this recording, see: B360-B362,
B365, B366, B369-B371, B375, B388, B396, B523,
B529. (See also: R67a, R68d, R69a, R78e, R83b, R92b,
R95c, R100a, R103a, R105a, R112b, R135a, R139d,
R142e, R144a, R146a, R153a, R156b, R165e, R167a,
R175a, R191b, R195a, R203a, R204a, R212c, R216b,
R220b, R227b, R228e, R229a, R230b, R232a, R255a,
R256a, R257a, R258c, R265b)

R192b.   *Selected Piano Music of Louis Moreau Gottschalk.*
Lambert Orkis, piano. Compact disc. Smithsonian
Collection of Recordings ND 033, 1988. Recorded on an
1865 Chickering piano in Coolidge Auditorium, Library
of Congress, Washington, D.C., May 1982.
(See also: R76d, R103d, R110a, R145a, R151a,
R220f, R234a)

R192c.   *Caribbean Souvenires.* William Kanengiser, guitar.
Compact disc. GSP Productions GSP 1008CD, 1998.
Recorded July 20-22, 1997.
With: *Souvenir de Porto Rico* (See: R165v),
Caprice, Op. 44 (See: R203g), and miscellaneous
Caribbean and Caribbean-influenced works. Note: The
Gottschalk works are all performed in Kanengiser's
arrangements for guitar.

R192d.   *Gottschalk: Piano Music.* Philip Martin, piano.
Compact disc. Hyperion 66459, 1991.
(See also: R78l, R88d, R107b, R112g, R142p,
R165p, R167i, R178d, R191i, R201c, R220l, R265d,
R272d)

R192e.   *DeGaetano Plays Gottschalk.* Robert DeGaetano, piano.
Compact disc. Crystonyx 1002, 1998. Recorded
January-February 1989 at Denver, New York.
(See also: R68n, R78p, R95m, R100g, R107c,

R119c, R142w, R167h, R171b, R187c, R199d, R201d,
R220j, R227k, R272c)

W193. **Réponds-moi, danse cubaine, caprice brillant, Op. 50** (1859;
Mainz: B. Schott's Söhne, 1869 (as Op. 50). Pub. pl. no. 19606;
Boston: Oliver Ditson, 1888.)

Other indices: RO226, D131a.
Note: The published version is a solo piano arrangement of W300 by
C. Wachtmann. There is evidence, however, that Gottschalk
performed a solo version probably of his own arrangement
(See: W193a, below).
Note: While Offergeld (See: B378) mentions this solo arrangement
of W300, he does not assign the arrangement a separate index
number.

Performances

W193a. November 29, 1861. Havana. Louis Moreau Gottschalk,
piano.

Bibliography

WB226. Rubin, Libby Antarsh. *Gottschalk in Cuba.* Dissertation:
Columbia University, 1974.
Rubin (pp. 199 and 203) suggests that Gottschalk
performed the solo piano version of the work in Havana
in November 1861 (See: W193a).

W194. *La favorita,* **grand fantaisie triomphale, Op. 68** (1859; New York:
Wm. Hall & Son, 1871 (with no opus number). Pub. pl. no. 6568;
Boston: Oliver Ditson, 1871. Pub. pl. no. 6568; Rio de Janeiro:
Napoleão, c1871; Mainz: B. Schott's Söhne, c1877 (as Op. 68);
New York: Arno Press and *The New York Times,* 1969 (*The Piano
Works of Louis Moreau Gottschalk,* vol. 2, ed. Vera Brodsky
Lawrence and Richard Jackson).)

Other indices: RO95, D54.
Note: This piece is based on themes from Donizetti's opera *La
favorita.*
(See also: W299)

Performances

W194a. February 12, 1862. New York City. Louis Moreau Gottschalk, piano.

W194b. November 21, 1865. Lima, Peru. Louis Moreau Gottschalk, piano.

W194c. October 5, 1869. Rio de Janeiro. Louis Moreau Gottschalk, piano.

Bibliography

WB227. Minor, Andrew C. *Piano Concerts in New York City 1849-1865*. Thesis: University of Michigan, 1947.
Minor (p. 250) lists Gottschalk's New York performance (See: W194a) of the piece.

WB228. Lange, Francisco Curt. *Vida y muerte de Louis Moreau Gottschalk en Rio de Janeiro, 1869*. Mendoza, Argentina: Universidad Nacional de Cuyo, 1951.
Lange (pp. 262, 281) documents Gottschalk's performance of the piece in Lima, Peru (See: W194b), as well as the composer's Rio de Janeiro performance (See: W194c).

WB229. Suttoni, Charles R. *Piano and Opera: A Study of the Piano Fantaisies Written on Opera Themes in the Romantic Era*. Dissertation: New York University, 1973.

W195.   Jeunesse, mazurka brillante, Op. 70 (1859; New York: Wm. Hall & Son, 1860. Pub. pl. no. 4576; Mainz: B. Schott's Söhne, 1871. Pub. pl. no. 20697; Paris: Escudier, 1873; Boston: Oliver Ditson, n.d. Pub. pl. no. 4-104-64598-8, ed. John Orth; New York: Arno Press and *The New York Times*, 1969 (*The Piano Works of Louis Moreau Gottschalk*, vol. 3, ed. Vera Brodsky Lawrence and Richard Jackson).)

Duration: 2 minutes.
Other indices: RO129, D78.

Recordings

R195a.   *Gottschalk: 40 Works for Piano*. Alan Mandel, piano.
Four 33-1/3 rpm phonodiscs. Desto DC 6470-73, 1969.
Reissued on three compact discs, VoxBox CD3X 3033,
1995.

For reviews of this recording, see: B360-B362,
B365, B366, B369-B371, B375, B388, B396, B523,
B529. (See also: R67a, R68d, R69a, R78e, R83b, R92b,
R95c, R100a, R103a, R105a, R112b, R135a, R139d,
R142e, R144a, R146a, R153a, R156b, R165e, R167a,
R175a, R191b, R192a, R203a, R204a, R212c, R216b,
R220b, R227b, R228e, R229a, R230b, R232a, R255a,
R256a, R257a, R258c, R265b)

W196.   **Études de concert** (1859; unpublished; lost.)

Other indices: RO88.

W197.   **Tres Romanzas** (1859; unpublished; lost.)

Other indices: RO266.

W198.   **Souvenir de Cuba, mazurka, Op. 75** (1859; Boston: Oliver Ditson
& Co., 1873. Pub. pl. no. 28003; Paris: Escudier, 1874.)

Manuscript is located at the New York Public Library.
Other indices: RO245, D144.
Note: Offergeld raises the possibility that this work may be the same
as *Adiós à Cuba* (See: W141) although Doyle dismisses the
notion.

W199.   **Polka in B-flat Major** (c1859; New York: New York Public
Library and Continuo Music Press; Sole agent, A. Broude, 1976 (*The
Little Book of Louis Moreau Gottschalk*, ed. Richard Jackson and
Neil Ratliff).)

Manuscript is located at the New York Public Library.
Other indices: RO273, D121.

Recordings

R199a.   *Louis Moreau Gottschalk on Original Instruments.*
Richard Burnett, piano. Compact disc. Amon Ra CD-
SAR 32, 1988.
All works are performed on instruments from
Gottschalk's era. (See also: R76c, R78i, R88c, R100c,
R103c, R107a, R112d, R165m, R187a, R201b, R204b,
R212f, R216f, R227f, R265c, R272a)

R199b.   *Great American Piano I. Louis Moreau Gottschalk. Vol.
7.* Leonard Pennario, piano. Compact disc. Angel
Records CDM 7 64667 2, 1992. Material originally
released on two 33-1/3 rpm phonodiscs as *Music of Louis
Moreau Gottschalk.* Angel RL-32125, 1975.
For reviews of this recording, see: B441, B442,
B446, B450, B452. (See also: R68i, R78m, R95i, R112f,
R139i, R142t, R165u, R167d, R191g, R212i, R220g,
R228n, R229c, R257e, R272b)

R199c.   *Gottschalk: Piano Music, Vol. 2.* Philip Martin, piano.
Compact disc. Hyperion CDA 66697, 1994.
For reviews of this recording, see: B525 and B529.
(See also: R76f, R99a, R100f, R103f, R105b, R119b,
R146c, R158a, R162a, R171a, R187b, R210a, R212j,
R216h, R228o, R257f)

R199d.   *DeGaetano Plays Gottschalk.* Robert DeGaetano, piano.
Compact disc. Crystonyx 1002, 1998. Recorded
January-February 1989 at Denver, New York.
(See also: R68n, R78p, R95m, R100g, R107c,
R119c, R142w, R167h, R171b, R187c, R192e, R201d,
R220j, R227k, R272c)

W200.   **Fantôme de bonheur, illusions perdues, caprice, Op. 36** (c1859;
Paris: Escudier, 1861; Boston: Oliver Ditson & Co., 1864. Pub. pl.
no. 5948; New York: Wm. Hall & Son, 1864. Pub. pl. no. 5948;
Mainz: B Schott's Söhne, c1864; New York: Arno Press and *The
New York Times*, 1969 (*The Piano Works of Louis Moreau
Gottschalk*, vol. 3, ed. Vera Brodsky Lawrence and Richard
Jackson).)

Dedication: "À Monsieur Fontana."
Other indices: RO94, D51.
Note: The Schott edition does not include the 32-measure
introduction found in the Ditson and Hall publications.

Performances

W200a.   May 2, 1862. New York City. Louis Moreau Gottschalk,
piano.

Bibliography

WB230.   Minor, Andrew C. *Piano Concerts in New York City
1849-1865.* Thesis: University of Michigan, 1947.
Minor lists Gottschalk's May 1862 New York
performance of the piece (See: W200a).

W201.   **Romance in E-flat Major** (c1859; New York: New York Public
Library & Continuo Music Press; Sole agent, A. Broude, 1976 (*The
Little Book of Louis Moreau Gottschalk*, ed. Richard Jackson and
Neil Ratliff).)

Manuscript is located at the New York Public Library.
Other indices: RO270, D134.
Note: This appears to be the work Offergeld lists as an untitled piece
in E-flat.

Recordings

R201a.   *The Wind Demon.* Ivan Davis, piano. 33-1/3 rpm
phonodisc. New World Records NW 257, 1976.
Reissued on compact disc. New World Records 80257-2,
1995.

R201b.   *Louis Moreau Gottschalk on Original Instruments.*
Richard Burnett, piano. Compact disc. Amon Ra CD-
SAR 32, 1988.
All works are performed on instruments from
Gottschalk's era. (See also: R76c, R78i, R88c, R100c,
R103c, R107a, R112d, R165m, R187a, R199a, R204b,
R212f, R216f, R227f, R265c, R272a)

R201c.   *Gottschalk: Piano Music.* Philip Martin, piano.
Compact disc. Hyperion 66459, 1991.
(See also: R78l, R88d, R107b, R112g, R142p,
R165p, R167i, R178d, R191i, R192d, R220l, R265d,
R272d)

R201d.   *DeGaetano Plays Gottschalk.* Robert DeGaetano, piano.
Compact disc. Crystonyx 1002, 1998. Recorded
January-February 1989 at Denver, New York.
(See also: R68n, R78p, R95m, R100g, R107c,
R119c, R142w, R167h, R171b, R187c, R192e, R199d,
R220j, R227k, R272c)

W202.   **El festival, danza** (c1859-60; Havana: Edelmann, 1860; lost)

Other indices: D55.

W203.   **O, Ma charmante, épargnez-moi!, caprice (O, My Charmer,
Spare Me), Op. 44** (c1859-61; Boston: Oliver Ditson & Co., 1862.
Pub. pl. no. 4684; New York: William Hall & Son, 1862. Pub. pl.
no. 4684; Paris: Escudier, 1862; Mainz: B. Schott's Söhne, 1862.
Pub. pl. no. 17062; New York: Arno Press and *The New York Times*,
1969 (*The Piano Works of Louis Moreau Gottschalk*, vol. 4, ed. Vera
Brodsky Lawrence and Richard Jackson); New York: Dover
Publications, 1973 (*Piano Music of Louis Moreau Gottschalk*,
selected and introduced by Richard Jackson).)

Duration: 2-1/4 minutes.
Other indices: RO182, D107.
Note: The 1862 William Hall & Son publication contains
Gottschalk's notes on the nature of rubato, warning on its
overuse. These notes are dated "New York 21 Juin 1862."
Note: The title is frequently given as "O! Ma charmante..." The
title page and the first page of the 1862 William Hall
publication use a period rather than the exclamation mark. I
have opted for the probably more appropriate comma, as used
in the 1973 Dover edition.

Performances

W203a.   February 18, 1862. New York City. Louis Moreau
Gottschalk, piano.

W203b.   December 17, 1969. *Louis Moreau Gottschalk Centennial Concert.* John Kirkpatrick, piano. (See also: R203b)

Recordings

R203a.   *Gottschalk: 40 Works for Piano.* Alan Mandel, piano. Four 33-1/3 rpm phonodiscs. Desto DC 6470-73, 1969. Reissued on three compact discs, VoxBox CD3X 3033, 1995.

For reviews of this recording, see: B360-B362, B365, B366, B369-B371, B375, B388, B396, B523, B529. (See also: R67a, R68d, R69a, R78e, R83b, R92b, R95c, R100a, R103a, R105a, R112b, R135a, R139d, R142e, R144a, R146a, R153a, R156b, R165e, R167a, R175a, R191b, R192a, R195a, R204a, R212c, R216b, R220b, R227b, R228e, R229a, R230b, R232a, R255a, R256a, R257a, R258c, R265b)

R203b.   *Louis Moreau Gottschalk: A Centennial Concert.* Various pianists. *O ma charmante* performed by John Kirkpatrick. 33-1/3 rpm phonodisc. Turnabout TV-S 34426, 1971. Recorded live December 17, 1969.

For reviews of this recording, see: B415 and B440. (See also: R112c, R135b, R139e, R142f, R165f, R167b, R212d, R216c, R229b, R258d)

R203c.   *Great American Piano II. Gottschalk, Joplin, Gershwin. Vol. 8.* Leonard Pennario, piano. Compact disc. Angel Records CDM 7 64668 2, 1992. Gottschalk material originally released on two 33-1/3 rpm phonodiscs as *Music of Louis Moreau Gottschalk.* Angel RL-32125, 1975.

Contains several Gottschalk compositions, as well as works by George Gershwin and Scott Joplin performed by Leonard Pennario and Joshua Rifkin (Joplin works only). (See also: R119a, R178b, R204d, R216g, R244a)

R203d.   *The Piano Music of Louis Moreau Gottschalk.* Ivan Davis, piano. Simultaneously issued on 1-7/8 ips audio cassette, Musical Heritage Society MHC 9040 and 33-1/3 rpm phonodisc, MHS 7040, 1975. Also issued as *Great*

Galloping Gottschalk. 33-1/3 rpm phonodisc. London CS-6943, 1976. Reissued on 1-7/8 ips audio cassette, 1984.

For reviews of this recording, see: B454, B455, B461. (See also: R78g, R88b, R95e, R100b, R103b, R142l, R165j, R216e, R227d, R228i, R257b)

R203e.   *Cuba Piano.* Luiz de Moura Castro, piano. Compact disc. Discos Ensayo ENY-CD-9722, 1991. Recorded May 1991, St. Martin's Church, East Woodhay, England. Reissued in 1997.

With various works by Cuban composers or influenced by Cuban music.

R203f.   *Gottschalk: Piano Music, Vol. 3.* Philip Martin, piano. Compact disc. Hyperion CDA 66915, 1997.

For a review of this recording, see: B538. (See also: R68l, R95l, R139j, R176b, R177a, R209b, R227j, R258i, R259b)

R203g.   *Caribbean Souvenires.* William Kanengiser, guitar. Compact disc. GSP Productions, 1998. Recorded July 20-22, 1997.

With: *Souvenir de Porto Rico* (See: R165v), *Souvenir de la Havane* (See: R192c), and miscellaneous Caribbean and Caribbean-influenced works. Note: The Gottschalk works are all performed in Kanengiser's arrangements for guitar.

R203h.   *A Gottschalk Gala.* Various artists. Compact disc. Premiere Recordings PRCD 1063, 1998.

R203i.   *Louis Moreau Gottschalk: A Night in the Tropics.* Michael Linville, piano; Hot Springs Music Festival Symphony Orchestra; Richard Rosenberg, conductor. Compact disc. Naxos 8.559036, 2000.

Note: This recording was of Jack Elliott's orchestration of the piece. (See also: R16a, R34f, R37i, R78t, R95n, R103g, R165x, R227l, R311a)

Bibliography

WB231.   Minor, Andrew C. *Piano Concerts in New York City 1849-1865*. Thesis: University of Michigan, 1947.
Minor (p. 353) documents Gottschalk's February 1862 performance of the piece (See: W203a).

WB232.   Sandner, Wolfgang. "*Oh meine Liebe, verschonen Sie mich*, Opus 44. Ein Portrat des Komponisten und ersten Klaviervirtuosen Amerikas: Louis Moreau Gottschalk." *HiFi—Stereophonie* 20:354-56 (no. 4, 1981).

WB233.   Hinson, Maurice. *Masters of Piano Program Music: A Guide to Style and Interpretation*. Van Nuys, California: Alfred Publishing, 1990.
Hinson's book contains his edition of the Gottschalk composition, including suggestions on the piece's interpretation.

W204.   La Gallina (The Hen), danse cubaine, Op. 53 (1859-63; New York: William Hall & Son, 1864. Pub. pl. no. 6436; Mainz: B. Schott's Söhne, c1868. Pub. pl. no. 19607; New York: William Hall & Son, 1869. Pub. pl. no. 6436; Boston: Oliver Ditson & Co., 1869. Pub. pl. no. 6436; New York: Arno Press and *The New York Times*, 1969 (*The Piano Works of Louis Moreau Gottschalk*, vol. 2, ed. Vera Brodsky Lawrence and Richard Jackson); New York: Dover Publications, 1973 (*Piano Music of Louis Moreau Gottschalk*, selected and introduced by Richard Jackson).)

Duration: 3 minutes.
Dedication: "à Mlle. Augusta Reichel."
Other indices: RO101, D60a.
An arrangement by C. Wachtmann of W302.

Performances

W204a.   September 1, 1976. Heeren Recital Hall, Southern Baptist Theological Seminary. Maurice Hinson, piano.

Recordings

R204a.   *Gottschalk: 40 Works for Piano*. Alan Mandel, piano.

Four 33-1/3 rpm phonodiscs. Desto DC 6470-73, 1969. Reissued on three compact discs, VoxBox CD3X 3033, 1995.

For reviews of this recording, see: B360-B362, B365, B366, B369-B371, B375, B388, B396, B523, B529. (See also: R67a, R68d, R69a, R78e, R83b, R92b, R95c, R100a, R103a, R105a, R112b, R135a, R139d, R142e, R144a, R146a, R153a, R156b, R165e, R167a, R175a, R191b, R192a, R195a, R203a, R212c, R216b, R220b, R227b, R228e, R229a, R230b, R232a, R255a, R256a, R257a, R258c, R265b)

R204b. *Louis Moreau Gottschalk on Original Instruments.* Richard Burnett, piano. Compact disc. Amon Ra CD-SAR 32, 1988.

All works are performed on instruments from Gottschalk's era. (See also: R76c, R78i, R88c, R100c, R103c, R107a, R112d, R165m, R187a, R199a, R201b, R212f, R216f, R227f, R265c, R272a)

R204c. *Cakewalk.* John Arpin, piano. Compact disc. ProArte Digital CDD515, 1990. Recorded September 25 and 27, 1989 in Toronto, Ontario, Canada.

(See also: R68g, R78j, R95h, R100d, R112e, R142n, R165n, R191e, R212g, R227g, R228l, R257c)

R204d. *Great American Piano II. Gottschalk, Joplin, Gershwin. Vol. 8.* Leonard Pennario, piano. Compact disc. Angel Records CDM 7 64668 2, 1992. Gottschalk material originally released on two 33-1/3 rpm phonodiscs as *Music of Louis Moreau Gottschalk.* Angel RL-32125, 1975.

Contains several Gottschalk compositions, as well as works by George Gershwin and Scott Joplin performed by Leonard Pennario and Joshua Rifkin (Joplin works only). (See also: R119a, R178b, R203c, R216g, R244a)

R204e. *Louis Moreau Gottschalk: Piano Works.* Klaus Kaufmann, piano. Compact disc. Koch Schwann 360352, n.d.

(See also: R68o, R76g, R78s, R99b, R139k, R142z, R156c, R165w, R220n, R228u)

W205. **Valse en D minor** (1860; unpublished; lost.)

Other indices: RO280.

W206. **Fantaisie sur *I Puritani*** (1860; unpublished; lost.)

Other indices: RO216.
Note: This work is based on themes from Bellini's opera *I Puritani*.

W207. **Fantaisie sur *La Norma*** (1860; unpublished; lost.)

Other indices: RO179.
Note: This work is based on themes from Bellini's opera *Norma*.

Performances

W207a. January 2, 1866. Lima, Peru. Louis Moreau Gottschalk, piano.

Bibliography

WB234. Lange, Francisco Curt. *Vida y muerte de Louis Moreau Gottschalk en Rio de Janeiro, 1869.* Mendoza, Argentina: Universidad Nacional de Cuyo, 1951.
Lange (p. 283) documents Gottschalk's January 1866 performance of the piece (See: W207a).

W208. **Ay! Lunarcitos!, contradanza** (1860; Havana: Edelmann, c1862.)

Other indices: D7.
Dedicated to Isabel de Sarachaga.
Sketches are located at the New York Public Library.

W209. **La chute des feuilles (Mélodie de Nicolás Ruiz Espadero de la Havane), nocturne, Op. 42** (1860; New York: Wm. Hall & Son, 1860. Pub. pl. no. 4591; Mainz: B. Schott's Söhne, 1862. Pub. pl. no. 16515; Paris: Escudier, 1862; New York: Schirmer, 1904. Pub. pl. no. 17018; New York: Arno Press and *The New York Times*, 1969 (*The Piano Works of Louis Moreau Gottschalk*, vol. 2, ed. Vera Brodsky Lawrence and Richard Jackson).)

Manuscript is located at the New York Public Library.
Dedication: "à Monsieur Ambroise Thomas (de l'Institut)."
Other indices: RO55, D34.
Note: The melody for this piece was composed by Nicolás Ruiz
Espadero.

Performances

W209a.   February 1, 1959. New York City, Hunter Playhouse.
Unidentified pianist.
This performance was the premiere of Katherine
Litz's ballet *The Fall of the Leaf,* based on the Gottschalk
piano piece.

Recordings

R209a.   *The American Romantic.* Alan Feinberg, piano. Compact
disc. Argo 430 330-2, 1990.
With: *God Save the Queen* (See: R92c) and works
by Amy Beach and Robert Helps.

R209b.   *Gottschalk: Piano Music, Vol. 3.* Philip Martin, piano.
Compact disc. Hyperion CDA 66915, 1997.
(See also: R68l, R95l, R139j, R176b, R177a, R203f,
R227j, R258i, R259b)

W210.   **Souvenir de Lima, mazurka, Op. 74** (1860; Boston: Oliver Ditson
& Co., 1873. Pub. pl. no. 28002; Paris: Escudier, 1874 (as Op. 74).)

Manuscript is located at the New York Public Library.
Dedicated to Charles G. Pond.
Other indices: RO247, D146.

Recordings

R210a.   *Gottschalk: Piano Music, Vol. 2.* Philip Martin, piano.
Compact disc. Hyperion CDA 66697, 1994.
For reviews of this recording, see: B525 and B529.
(See also: R76f, R99a, R100f, R103f, R105b, R119b,
R146c, R158a, R162a, R171a, R187b, R199c, R212j,
R216h, R228o, R257f)

W211. **Étude de force en B Major** (c1860; unpublished; lost.)

Other indices: RO82.

Bibliography

WB235. *Life of Louis Moreau Gottschalk.* New York, c1863.
The works list in this pamphlet is the only known
reference from Gottschalk's lifetime to this composition.

W212. **Berceuse (Cradle Song), Op. 47** (c1860-61; New York: William
Hall & Son, 1862. Pub. pl. no. 4746 (Hall also issued an edition with
no plate number earlier in 1862); Boston: Oliver Ditson & Co., after
1862; Paris: Escudier, after 1862; Bryn Mawr, Pennsylvania:
Theodore Presser, 1956 (*Piano Music by Louis Moreau Gottschalk*,,
ed. Jeanne Behrend); New York: Arno Press and *The New York
Times*, 1969 (*The Piano Works of Louis Moreau Gottschalk*, vol. 1,
ed. Vera Brodsky Lawrence and Richard Jackson); New York:
Dover Publications, 1973 (*Piano Music of Louis Moreau Gottschalk*,
selected and introduced by Richard Jackson); New York: Dover
Publications, 1978 (*Nineteenth-Century American Piano Music*, ed.
John Gillespie).)

Duration: 6-1/2 minutes.
Dedication: "à Mlle. Marie Damainville."
Other indices: RO27, D20.
Note: The work is based on the French folk lullaby "Fais dodo."
(See also: W51)

Performances

W212a. December 17, 1969. *Louis Moreau Gottschalk
Centennial Concert.* Robert Pritchard, piano.
(See also: R212d)

W212b. 1973. Heeren Recital Hall, Southern Baptist Theological
Seminary. Maurice Hinson, piano.

Recordings

R212a. *Piano Music by Louis Moreau Gottschalk.* Jeanne
Behrend, piano. 33-1/3 rpm phonodisc. MGM E-3370,

1957.
> For a review of this recording, see: B265. (See also: R68b, R78b, R88a, R139c, R142b, R156a, R165b, R220a, R228c)

R212b.   *The Piano Music of Louis Moreau Gottschalk.* Amiram Rigai, piano. 33-1/3 rpm phonodisc. Decca DL 10143, 1967. Reissued as Decca DL 710143, 1970.
> For reviews of this recording, see: B327, B329, B330. (See also: R78d, R83a, R95b, R112a, R142d, R165d, R228d, R249a, R265a)

R212c.   *Gottschalk: 40 Works for Piano.* Alan Mandel, piano. Four 33-1/3 rpm phonodiscs. Desto DC 6470-73, 1969. Reissued on three compact discs, VoxBox CD3X 3033, 1995.
> For reviews of this recording, see: B360-B362, B365, B366, B369-B371, B375, B388, B396, B523, B529. (See also: R67a, R68d, R69a, R78e, R83b, R92b, R95c, R100a, R103a, R105a, R112b, R135a, R139d, R142e, R144a, R146a, R153a, R156b, R165e, R167a, R175a, R191b, R192a, R195a, R203a, R204a, R216b, R220b, R227b, R228e, R229a, R230b, R232a, R255a, R256a, R257a, R258c, R265b)

R212d.   *Louis Moreau Gottschalk: A Centennial Concert.* Various pianists. *Berceuse* performed by Robert Pritchard. 33-1/3 rpm phonodisc. Turnabout TV-S 34426, 1971. Recorded live December 17, 1969.
> For reviews of this recording, see: B415 and B440. (See also: R112c, R135b, R139e, R142f, R165f, R167b, R203b, R216c, R229b, R258d)

R212e.   *Louis Moreau Gottschalk, 1829-1869: American Piano Music.* Amiram Rigai, piano. 33-1/3 rpm phonodisc. Folkways Records FSS 37485, 1979. Reissued on compact disc, Smithsonian Folkways 40803, 1992.
> For a review of the original recording, see: B468. (See also: R68f, R69b, R78h, R83c, R88e, R95g, R112h, R133a, R142m, R165k, R167e, R191d, R227e, R228k, R249c, R275b)

R212f. *Louis Moreau Gottschalk on Original Instruments.* Richard Burnett, piano. Compact disc. Amon Ra CD-SAR 32, 1988.

All works are performed on instruments from Gottschalk's era. (See also: R76c, R78i, R88c, R100c, R103c, R107a, R112d, R165m, R187a, R199a, R201b, R204b, R216f, R227f, R265c, R272a)

R212g. *Cakewalk.* John Arpin, piano. Compact disc. ProArte Digital CDD515, 1990. Recorded September 25 and 27, 1989 in Toronto, Ontario, Canada.

(See also: R68g, R78j, R95h, R100d, R112e, R142n, R165n, R191e, R204c, R227g, R228l, R257c)

R212h. *Silks & Rags.* The Great American Main St. Band. Compact disc. Angel 54131, 1991.

With various works by other American composers arranged for small concert band.

R212i. *Great American Piano I. Louis Moreau Gottschalk. Vol. 7.* Leonard Pennario, piano. Compact disc. Angel Records CDM 7 64667 2, 1992. Gottschalk material originally released on two 33-1/3 rpm phonodiscs as *Music of Louis Moreau Gottschalk.* Angel RL-32125, 1975.

For reviews of this recording, see: B441, B442, B446, B450, B452. (See also: R68i, R78m, R95i, R112f, R139i, R142t, R165u, R167d, R191g, R199b, R220g, R228n, R229c, R257e, R272b)

R212j. *Gottschalk: Piano Music, Vol. 2.* Philip Martin, piano. Compact disc. Hyperion CDA 66697, 1994.

For reviews of this recording, see: B525 and B529. (See also: R76f, R99a, R100f, R103f, R105b, R119b, R146c, R158a, R162a, R171a, R187b, R199c, R210a, R216h, R228o, R257f)

R212k. *A Gottschalk Gala.* Various artists. Compact disc. Premiere Recordings PRCD 1063, 1998.

Bibliography

WB236.   Hamilton, Anna Heuermann. *Program of American
Music from Mayflower Days to the Present.* St. Louis:
Art Publication Society, 1923.
   Contains notes on *Berceuse*, as well as *The Last
Hope* and *Marche de nuit.* (See also: WB171 and
WB184)

WB237.   Whitfield, Irene Therese. *Louisiana French Folksongs.*
Baton Rouge: Louisiana State University Press, 1937.
   Cited by Doyle (p. 158) as containing a folk melody
resembling the main theme of *Berceuse.*

WB238.   Widor, Charles Marie. *Vielles chansons.* Paris: Plon-
Nourrit, n.d.
   Cited by Doyle (p. 158) as containing the French
folksong "Dodo, l'enfant do," a melody similar to the
main theme of *Berceuse.*

WB239.   Gallo, Sergio Robert. *The "Berceuse" for Piano: An
Overview of the Genre.* Dissertation: University of
California, Santa Barbara, 1998.
   Also indexed in *Dissertation Abstracts International*
60-A/3 (September 1999), p. 586.

W213.   **Ay pimpillo, no me mates!, contradanza** (c1860-61; Havana:
Edelmann, 1861; lost.)

Other indices: RO11, D8.

Performances

W213a.   April 17, 1861. Havana, Cuba. Louis Moreau
Gottschalk, piano; 38 other pianists.

Bibliography

WB240.   Loggins, Vernon. *Where the Word Ends: The Life of
Louis Moreau Gottschalk.* Baton Rouge, Louisiana:
Louisiana State University Press, 1958.
   Loggins makes note of Gottschalk's April 1861

performance (See: W213a).

W214. **Variations on "Dixie's Land"** (1860-62; unpublished; lost.)

Other indices: RO291.
Note: This composition was based on the song "I Wish I Was in Dixie's Land" by Daniel Decatur Emmett.

W215. **Polka militaire** (c1861; unpublished; lost.)

Other indices: RO208.

W216. **Suis-moi! (Follow Me!) (Vamos a la azotea), contradanza, caprice, Op. 45** (c1861; Havana: Edelmann, 1861; Havana: Wagner y Levien, 1861. Pub. pl. no. 117; Boston: Oliver Ditson & Co., 1862. Pub. pl. no. 4689; New York: Wm. Hall & Son, 1862; Paris: Escudier, 1862; Mainz: B. Schott's Söhne, 1862. Pub. pl. no. 17063; New York: Dover Publications, 1973 (*Piano Music of Louis Moreau Gottschalk*, selected and introduced by Richard Jackson).)

Duration: 3 minutes.
Manuscript and sketches are located at the New York Public Library.
Dedication: "À mon ami Charles Fradel."
Other indices: RO253 (RO288), D150.
Note: The Wagner y Levien edition is a simplified version of the piece.
Note: The 1862 Wm. Hall & Son publication contains Gottschalk's notes on the nature of rubato, warning on its overuse. These notes are dated "New York 21 Juin 1862."
Note: Doyle 1960 considers *Vamos a la azotea* (Offergeld's RO288) to be an abridged version of *Suis-moi!*

Performances

W216a. February 18, 1862. New York City. Louis Moreau Gottschalk, piano.

W216b. December 17, 1969. *Louis Moreau Gottschalk Centennial Concert.* John Kirkpatrick, piano.
(See also: R216c)

Recordings

R216a. *The Banjo and Other Creole Favorites.* Eugene List, piano. 33-1/3 rpm phonodisc. Vanguard VRS-485, 1957. Reissued as part of *The World of Louis Moreau Gottschalk* (See: D). Reissued on compact disc as Vanguard Classics OVC 4050, 1992. Reissued as part of the two compact disc set *Piano Music of Louis Moreau Gottschalk.* Vanguard Classics 08 9143 72/08 9144-72, 1993.

     For reviews of this recording, see: B258, B259, B263 and B265. (See also: R68a, R76a, R78a, R95a, R139b, R142a, R165a, R191a, R227a, R228b, R230a)

R216b. *Gottschalk: 40 Works for Piano.* Alan Mandel, piano. Four 33-1/3 rpm phonodiscs. Desto DC 6470-73, 1969. Reissued on three compact discs, VoxBox CD3X 3033, 1995.

     For reviews of this recording, see: B360-B362, B365, B366, B369-B371, B375, B388, B396, B523, B529. (See also: R67a, R68d, R69a, R78e, R83b, R92b, R95c, R100a, R103a, R105a, R112b, R135a, R139d, R142e, R144a, R146a, R153a, R156b, R165e, R167a, R175a, R191b, R192a, R195a, R203a, R204a, R212c, R220b, R227b, R228e, R229a, R230b, R232a, R255a, R256a, R257a, R258c, R265b)

R216c. *Louis Moreau Gottschalk: A Centennial Concert.* Various pianists. *Suis-moi!* performed by John Kirkpatrick. 33-1/3 rpm phonodisc. Turnabout TV-S 34426, 1971. Recorded live December 17, 1969.

     For reviews of this recording, see: B415 and B440. (See also: R112c, R135b, R139e, R142f, R165f, R167b, R203b, R212d, R229b, R258d)

R216d. *The World of Louis Moreau Gottschalk.* Various performers. *Suis-moi!* performed by Eugene List, piano. Two 33-1/3 rpm phonodiscs. Vanguard VSD-723; VSD-724, 1973. Reissued on compact disc. Vanguard VCD 72026, 1988.

     For a review of this recording, see: B417. (See also: R34b, R37a, R68e, R76b, R78f, R95d, R139g, R142i,

R165g, R191c, R227c, R228g, R230c)

R216e.   *The Piano Music of Louis Moreau Gottschalk.* Ivan
Davis, piano. Simultaneously issued on 1-7/8 ips audio
cassette, Musical Heritage Society MHC 9040 and 33-1/3
rpm phonodisc, MHS 7040, 1975. Also issued as *Great
Galloping Gottschalk.* 33-1/3 rpm phonodisc. London
CS-6943, 1976. Reissued on 1-7/8 ips audio cassette,
1984.
    For reviews of this recording, see: B454, B455,
B461. (See also: R78g, R88b, R95e, R100b, R103b,
R142l, R165j, R203d, R227d, R228i, R257b)

R216f.   *Louis Moreau Gottschalk on Original Instruments.*
Richard Burnett, piano. Compact disc. Amon Ra CD-
SAR 32, 1988.
    All works are performed on instruments from
Gottschalk's era. (See also: R76c, R78i, R88c, R100c,
R103c, R107a, R112d, R165m, R187a, R199a, R201b,
R204b, R212f, R227f, R265c, R272a)

R216g.   *Great American Piano II. Gottschalk, Joplin, Gershwin.
Vol. 8.* Leonard Pennario, piano. Compact disc. Angel
Records CDM 7 64668 2, 1992. Gottschalk material
originally released on two 33-1/3 rpm phonodiscs as
Music of Louis Moreau Gottschalk. Angel RL-32125,
1975.
    Contains several Gottschalk compositions, as well as
works by George Gershwin and Scott Joplin performed by
Leonard Pennario and Joshua Rifkin (Joplin works only).
(See also: R119a, R178b, R203c, R204d, R244a)

R216h.   *Gottschalk: Piano Music, Vol. 2.* Philip Martin, piano.
Compact disc. Hyperion CDA 66697, 1994.
    For reviews of this recording, see: B525 and B529.
(See also: R76f, R99a, R100f, R103f, R105b, R119b,
R146c, R158a, R162a, R171a, R187b, R199c, R210a,
R212j, R228o, R257f)

Bibliography

WB241.   Minor, Andrew C. *Piano Concerts in New York City*

1849-1865. Thesis: University of Michigan, 1947.
   Minor (p. 353) reports Gottschalk's February 1862 performance of the piece (See: W216a).

WB242.   Doyle, John Godfrey. *The Piano Music of Louis Moreau Gottschalk, 1829-1869*. Dissertation: New York University, 1960.
   Contains a fair amount of discussion of the piece.

W217.   **Drums and Cannon, military polka** (c1861-2; New York: Wm. A. Pond & Co., 1863. Pub. pl. no. 5509; New York: Arno Press and *The New York Times*, 1969 (*The Piano Works of Louis Moreau Gottschalk*, vol. 2, ed. Vera Brodsky Lawrence and Richard Jackson).)

Other indices: RO74, D44.
Note: This piece was published under Gottschalk's pseudonym Oscar Litti.

W218.   *Rigoletto* **Quartet, transcription de bravura** (1861-2; unpublished; lost.)

Other indices: RO228.
Note: The work in based on themes from Giuseppe Verdi's opera *Rigoletto*.

Performances

W218a.   February 11, 1862. New York City. Louis Moreau Gottschalk, piano.

W219.   *La Ballo in Maschera,* **fantaisie triomphale** (1862; lost.)

Other indices: RO18.
Note: The work in based on themes from the 1857-8 Giuseppe Verdi melodrama *Un ballo in maschera*.
(See also: W54 and W55)

Performances

W219a.   May 24, 1862. New York City. Louis Moreau Gottschalk, piano.

W220. **L'Union, paraphrase de concert, Op. 48** (1862; New York: Wm. Hall & Son, 1863. Pub. pl. no. 4756; Boston: Oliver Ditson & Co., 1863. Pub. pl. no. 4756; Paris: Escudier, 1863; Mainz: B. Schott's Söhne, 1863. Pub. pl. no. 17443; Bryn Mawr, Pennsylvania: Theodore Presser, 1956 (*Piano Music by Louis Moreau Gottschalk*, ed. Jeanne Behrend); New York: Dover Publications, 1973 (*Piano Music of Louis Moreau Gottschalk*, selected and introduced by Richard Jackson); New York: Dover Publications, 1978 (*Nineteenth-Century American Piano Music*, ed. John Gillespie).)

Dedication: "To Major General Geo. B. McClellan."
Duration: 6-3/4 minutes.
Other indices: RO269, D156.
Note: This work includes melodic material from "The Star-Spangled Banner," "Yankee Doodle," and "Hail Columbia."
Note: While the work is in part based on the 1851-2 *El sitio de Zaragoza* (See: W101, etc.), evidence Doyle (See: WB245) cites evidence of an 1862 completion of *L'Union* in its final form. Some sources, such as Lowens and Starr (See: WB246) give the composition date as 1852-62. I have placed *L'Union* in 1862 as Gottschalk seems not to have transformed the piece over time, but to have revived and rewritten the work (with American tunes substituted for Spanish tunes) at the later date.

Performances

W220a. February 22, 1862. Niblo's Garden and Saloon, New York City. Louis Moreau Gottschalk, piano.

W220b. February 26, 1862. New York City. Louis Moreau Gottschalk, piano.

W220c. March 24, 1864. Washington, D.C. Louis Moreau Gottschalk, piano.
   Gottschalk's two March 1864 Washington performances were attended by President and Mrs. Lincoln and General U.S. Grant.

W220d. March 26, 1864. Washington, D.C. Louis Moreau Gottschalk, piano.
   Gottschalk's two March 1864 Washington performances were attended by President and Mrs.

Lincoln and General U.S. Grant.

W220e.   January 12, 1995. Hubbard Recital Hall, Manhattan
School of Music. Jamorn Supapol, piano.

W220f.   May 6, 1996. Kilbourn Hall, Eastman School of Music,
Rochester, New York. Joel Schoenhals, piano.

Recordings

R220a.   *Piano Music by Louis Moreau Gottschalk.* Jeanne
Behrend, piano. 33-1/3 rpm phonodisc. MGM E-3370,
1957.
  For a review of this recording, see: B265. (See also:
R68b, R78b, R88a, R139c, R142b, R156a, R165b, R212a,
R228c)

R220b.   *Gottschalk: 40 Works for Piano.* Alan Mandel, piano.
Four 33-1/3 rpm phonodiscs. Desto DC 6470-73, 1969.
Reissued on three compact discs, VoxBox CD3X 3033,
1995.
  For reviews of this recording, see: B360-B362,
B365, B366, B369-B371, B375, B388, B396, B523,
B529. (See also: R67a, R68d, R69a, R78e, R83b, R92b,
R95c, R100a, R103a, R105a, R112b, R135a, R139d,
R142e, R144a, R146a, R153a, R156b, R165e, R167a,
R175a, R191b, R192a, R195a, R203a, R204a, R212c,
R216b, R227b, R228e, R229a, R230b, R232a, R255a,
R256a, R257a, R258c, R265b)

R220c.   *Mansfield State College Symphonic and Mountie Bands.*
William M. Goode, piano (on the Gottschalk work). 33-
1/3 rpm phonodisc. Stith Custom Records, 1975.

R220d.   *Wie einst in schönern Taen: Salonmusik der Gründerzeit.*
Various performers. *L'Union* performed by Bruno
Canino, piano. Two 33-1/3 rpm phonodiscs. EMI
Electrola 1C 187 30682, 1976.
  With: various nineteenth-century works for various
combinations of piano, soprano, flute, and violoncello.

R220e.   *The Best of Louis Moreau Gottschalk.* Eugene List, piano; Vienna State Opera Orchestra; Igor Buketoff, conductor. 33-1/3 rpm phonodisc. Turnabout TV-S 34449, c1979.

Note: This performance is of an orchestration of the work for piano and orchestra by Samuel Adler. (See also: R36a, R37b, R258e)

R220f.   *Selected Piano Music of Louis Moreau Gottschalk.* Lambert Orkis, piano. Compact disc. Smithsonian Collection of Recordings ND 033, 1988. Recorded on an 1865 Chickering piano in Coolidge Auditorium, Library of Congress, Washington, D.C., May 1982.

(See also: R76d, R103d, R110a, R145a, R151a, R192b, R234a)

R220g.   *Great American Piano I. Louis Moreau Gottschalk. Vol. 7.* Leonard Pennario, piano. Compact disc. Angel Records CDM 7 64667 2, 1992. Material originally released on two 33-1/3 rpm phonodiscs as *Music of Louis Moreau Gottschalk.* Angel RL-32125, 1975.

For reviews of this recording, see: B441, B442, B446, B450, B452. (See also: R68i, R78m, R95i, R112f, R139i, R142t, R165u, R167d, R191g, R199b, R212i, R228n, R229c, R257e, R272b)

R220h.   *Louis Moreau Gottschalk.* Eugene List, piano; Cary Lewis, piano. Compact disc. Vanguard Classics OVC 4051, 1992. Reissued as part of the two compact disc set *Piano Music.* Vanguard Classics 08 9143 72/08 9144-72, 1993.

Note: This recording is of Eugene List's arrangement of the work for two pianos. (See also: R34c, R37f, R100e, R250a, R275a, R282b, R291b, R292a, R300b, R302b, R305b, R307b, R310b)

R220i.   *Piano Portraits from Nineteenth-Century America.* Noël Lester, piano. Compact disc. Centaur CRC 2250, 1995.

With: *Le banjo* (See: R142u); *Sospiro* (See: R152a); *Pasquinade* (See: R228r); and various works by Benjamin Carr, Arthur Clifton, Stephen Collins Foster, William Mason, Richard Hoffman, John Knowles Paine, and Edward A. MacDowell. For a review of this recording, see: B533.

R220j.   *DeGaetano Plays Gottschalk.* Robert DeGaetano, piano. Compact disc. Crystonyx 1002, 1998. Recorded January-February 1989 at Denver, New York.

(See also: R68n, R78p, R95m, R100g, R107c, R119c, R142w, R167h, R171b, R187c, R192e, R199d, R201d, R227k, R272c)

R220k.   *Stars and Stripes Forever: The Great American Piano.* Paul Bisaccia, piano. Compact disc. Towerhill TH-71992, 2000.

With various works by other American composers. Note: The recordings were made for a PBS Television special.

R220l.   *Gottschalk: Piano Music.* Philip Martin, piano. Compact disc. Hyperion 66459, 1991.

(See also: R78l, R88d, R107b, R112g, R142p, R165p, R167i, R178d, R191i, R192d, R201c, R265d, R272d)

R220m.   *A Gottschalk Festival.* Eugene List, piano. Two compact discs. Vox Box 5009, n.d.

(See also: R4a, R34e, R36b, R37g, R41a, R42a, R44a, R191h, R228t, R258k, R298b, R302d, R305c, R310c)

R220n.   *Louis Moreau Gottschalk: Piano Works.* Klaus Kaufmann, piano. Compact disc. Koch Schwann 360352, n.d.

(See also: R68o, R76g, R78s, R99b, R139k, R142z, R156c, R165w, R204e, R228u)

Bibliography

WB243.   Minor, Andrew C. *Piano Concerts in New York City 1849-1865.* Thesis: University of Michigan, 1947.

Minor (p. 353) reports Gottschalk's February 26, 1862 performance of the piece (See: W220b).

WB244. Loggins, Vernon. *Where the Word Ends.* Baton Rouge: Louisiana State University Press, 1958.

Loggins (p. 188) documents Gottschalk's February 22, 1862 performance of the piece (See: W220a).

WB245. Doyle, John G. *Louis Moreau Gottschalk, 1929-1869: A Bibliographical Study and Catalog of Works.* Detroit, Michigan: Published for the College Music Society by Information Coordinators, 1982.

(See note above)

WB246. Lowens, Irving and S. Frederick Starr. *The New Grove Dictionary of Music and Musicians*, 2nd ed. s.v. "Gottschalk, Louis Moreau." London: Macmillan, 2000.

(See note above)

W221. Home, Sweet Home (Charme du foyer), caprice, Op. 51 (c1862; New York: Wm. Hall & Son, 1864. Pub. pl. no. 5980; Boston: Oliver Ditson & Co., 1864; Pub. .pl. no. 5980; Mainz: B. Schott's Söhne, 1865. Pub. pl. no. 18161; Paris: Escudier, 1865; New York: Arno Press and *The New York Times*, 1969 (*The Piano Works of Louis Moreau Gottschalk*, vol. 3, ed. Vera Brodsky Lawrence and Richard Jackson).)

Sketches are located at the New York Public Library.
Dedication: "à Madame Mary Eugénie Martin (Née Curlett) (de Baltimore)."
Other indices: RO117, D69.
Note: This work is based on Henry Bishop's song "Home, Sweet Home," popular during Gottschalk's day.

Performances

W221a. October 1862. New York City. Louis Moreau Gottschalk, piano.

W221b. June 15, 1869. Rio de Janeiro. Louis Moreau Gottschalk, piano.

Bibliography

WB247. Minor, Andrew C. *Piano Concerts in New York City*

1849-1865. Thesis: University of Michigan, 1947.
Minor (p. 375) documents Gottschalk's October 1862
New York performance (See: W221a).

WB248.   Lange, Francisco Curt. *Vida y muerte de Louis Moreau
Gottschalk en Rio de Janeiro, 1869*. Mendoza,
Argentina: Universidad de Cuyo, 1951.
Lange (p. 259) documents Gottschalk's June 1869
performance in Rio de Janeiro (See: W221b).

W222.   **Polka di bravura** (c1862; unpublished; lost.)

Other indices: RO205.

Performances

W222a.   March 18, 1862. New York City. Louis Moreau
Gottschalk, piano.

Bibliography

WB249.   Minor, Andrew C. *Piano Concerts in New York City
1849-1865*. Thesis: University of Michigan, 1947.
Minor documents Gottschalk's March 1862
performance of the work (See: 224a). Unfortunately, the
evidence that Gottschalk performed a work of his own
composition with this title given on the printed program
seems to be the only evidence of the existence of the
piece; *Polka di bravura* could have been an alternative
title of another Gottschalk composition.

W223.   **Valse de** *Faust* (c1862-3; New York: Beer & Schirmer, 1863.)

Manuscript is located at the New York Public Library.
Other indices: D53.
Dedication: "a son ami, L.M. Gottschalk."
Note: This piece was published under Gottschalk's pseudonym
Oscar Litti.
Note: *Valse de "Faust"* is based on themes from Gounod's *Faust*.

W224. **Bailemos, Creole Dance** (c1862-3; possibly published; lost.)

Other indices: RO12.

W225. **Pensive, polka-rédowa, Op. 68** (c1862-3; Boston: Oliver Ditson & Co., 1864; Mainz: B. Schott's Söhne, c1872. Pub. pl. no. 20699; Paris: Escudier, 1873 (as Op. 68); New York: Arno Press and *The New York Times*, 1969 (*The Piano Works of Louis Moreau Gottschalk*, vol. 4, ed. Vera Brodsky Lawrence and Richard Jackson).)

Other indices: RO196, D119.
Note: This piece was published under Gottschalk's pseudonym Seven Octaves.

W226. **La colombe (The Dove), petite polka, Op. 49** (1863; Boston: Oliver Ditson & Co., 1864. Pub. pl. no. 5965; New York: William Hall & Son, 1864. Pub. pl. no. 5965; Mainz: B Schott's Söhne, c1864. Pub. pl. no. 18033; New York: Arno Press and *The New York Times*, 1969 (*The Piano Works of Louis Moreau Gottschalk*, vol. 2, ed. Vera Brodsky Lawrence and Richard Jackson).)

Manuscript and sketches are located at the New York Public Library.
Dedication: "À mon ami F.G. Hill, de Boston."
Other indices: RO60, D37.

Performances

W226a. April 24, 1863. Philadelphia. Louis Moreau Gottschalk, piano.

Recordings

R226a. *A Gottschalk Gala*. Various artists. Compact disc. Premiere Recordings PRCD 1063, 1998.

W227. **The Dying Poet (Le poète mourant), Meditation** (c1863; Boston: Oliver Ditson & Co., 1864. Pub. pl. no. 22291 [See note below]; Mainz: B. Schott's Söhne, c1877. Pub. pl. no. 22833; Boston: Oliver Ditson & Co., 1883; New York: G. Schirmer, 1907. Pub. pl. no. 19466; New York: Arno Press and *The New York Times*, 1969 (*The Piano Works of Louis Moreau Gottschalk*, vol. 2, ed. Vera

Brodsky Lawrence and Richard Jackson); New York: Dover
Publications, 1973 (*Piano Music of Louis Moreau Gottschalk*,
selected and introduced by Richard Jackson); Dayton, Ohio: McAfee
Music, 1977 (*The Piano Music of Louis Moreau Gottschalk Made
Easy*, arr. David Krane).)

Duration: 5-1/2 minutes.
Dedication: "To Mrs. Geo. Henriques. N. York."
Other indices: RO75, D45.
Note: This piece originally was published under Gottschalk's
     pseudonym Seven Octaves; a later, undated Oliver Ditson
     reprint credits the piece to Gottschalk, with the pseudonym
     given parenthetically.
Note: Although the initial Oliver Ditson printing does not include a
     plate number, later reprints by the company do.

Performances

W227a.   December 6, 1865. Lima, Peru. Louis Moreau
         Gottschalk, piano.

Recordings

R227a.   *The Banjo and Other Creole Favorites*. Eugene List,
         piano. 33-1/3 rpm phonodisc. Vanguard VRS-485, 1957.
         Reissued as part of *The World of Louis Moreau
         Gottschalk* (See: D). Reissued on compact disc as
         Vanguard Classics OVC 4050, 1992. Reissued as part of
         the two compact disc set *Piano Music of Louis Moreau
         Gottschalk*. Vanguard Classics 08 9143 72/08 9144-72,
         1993.
            For reviews of this recording, see: see: B258, B259,
         B263 and B265. (See also: R68a, R76a, R78a, R95a,
         R139b, R142a, R165a, R191a, R216a, R228b, R230a)

R227b.   *Gottschalk: 40 Works for Piano*. Alan Mandel, piano.
         Four 33-1/3 rpm phonodiscs. Desto DC 6470-73, 1969.
         Reissued on three compact discs, VoxBox CD3X 3033,
         1995.
            For reviews of this recording, see: B360-B362,
         B365, B366, B369-B371, B375, B388, B396, B523,
         B529. (See also: R67a, R68d, R69a, R78e, R83b, R92b,

R95c, R100a, R103a, R105a, R112b, R135a, R139d,
R142e, R144a, R146a, R153a, R156b, R165e, R167a,
R175a, R191b, R192a, R195a, R203a, R204a, R212c,
R216b, R220b, R228e, R229a, R230b, R232a, R255a,
R256a, R257a, R258c, R265b)

R227c. *The World of Louis Moreau Gottschalk.* Various
performers. *The Dying Poet* performed by Eugene List,
piano. Two 33-1/3 rpm phonodiscs. Vanguard VSD-723;
VSD-724, 1973. Reissued on compact disc. Vanguard
VCD 72026, 1988.

For a review of this recording, see: B417. (See also:
R34b, R37a, R68e, R76b, R78f, R95d, R139g, R142i,
R165g, R191c, R216d, R228g, R230c)

R227d. *The Piano Music of Louis Moreau Gottschalk.* Ivan
Davis, piano. Simultaneously issued on 1-7/8 ips audio
cassette, Musical Heritage Society MHC 9040 and 33-1/3
rpm phonodisc, MHS 7040, 1975. Also issued as *Great
Galloping Gottschalk.* 33-1/3 rpm phonodisc. London
CS-6943, 1976. Reissued on 1-7/8 ips audio cassette,
1984.

For reviews of this recording, see: B454, B455,
B461. (See also: R78g, R88b, R95e, R100b, R103b,
R142l, R165j, R203d, R216e, R228i, R257b)

R227e. *Louis Moreau Gottschalk, 1829-1869: American Piano
Music.* Amiram Rigai, piano. 33-1/3 rpm phonodisc.
Folkways Records FSS 37485, 1979. Reissued on
compact disc, Smithsonian Folkways 40803, 1992.

For a review of the original recording, see: B468.
(See also: R68f, R69b, R78h, R83c, R88e, R95g, R112h,
R133a, R142m, R165k, R167e, R191d, R212e, R228k,
R249c, R275b)

R227f. *Louis Moreau Gottschalk on Original Instruments.*
Richard Burnett, piano. Compact disc. Amon Ra CD-
SAR 32, 1988.

All works are performed on instruments from
Gottschalk's era. (See also: R76c, R78i, R88c, R100c,
R103c, R107a, R112d, R165m, R187a, R199a, R201b,
R204b, R212f, R216f, R265c, R272a)

R227g.   *Cakewalk*. John Arpin, piano. Compact disc. ProArte Digital CDD515, 1990. Recorded September 25 and 27, 1989 in Toronto, Ontario, Canada.

   (See also: R68g, R78j, R95h, R100d, R112e, R142n, R165n, R191e, R204c, R212g, R228l, R257c)

R227h.   *Musique américaine pour piano*. Noël Lee, piano. Compact disc. Chant du monde LCD 278-1067, 1991.

   With: *Souvenir de Porto Rico* (See: R165q); *Grand scherzo, Op. 57* (See: R257d); and works by Edward MacDowell, Aaron Copland, John Cage, and Elliott Carter.

R227i.   *Pops Americana*. Joel Salsman, Yamaha Disklavier Recording Piano. 1-7/8 ips audio cassette. Joel Salsman, 1994.

   Contains several Gottschalk works, as well as compositions by Joel Salsman, Zez Confrey, Scott Joplin, George Gershwin, and Nacio Herb Brown. (See also: R95k, R228q)

R227j.   *Gottschalk: Piano Music, Vol. 3*. Philip Martin, piano. Compact disc. Hyperion CDA 66915, 1997.

   For a review of this recording, see: B538. (See also: R68l, R95l, R139j, R176b, R177a, R203f, R209b, R258i, R259b)

R227k.   *DeGaetano Plays Gottschalk*. Robert DeGaetano, piano. Compact disc. Crystonyx 1002, 1998. Recorded January-February 1989 at Denver, New York.

   (See also: R68n, R78p, R95m, R100g, R107c, R119c, R142w, R167h, R171b, R187c, R192e, R199d, R201d, R220j, R272c)

R227l.   *Louis Moreau Gottschalk: A Night in the Tropics*. Yi-Chun Sunny Kuo, piano; Hot Springs Music Festival Symphony Orchestra; Richard Rosenberg, conductor. Compact disc. Naxos 8.559036, 2000.

   Note: This is a recording of Jack Elliott's orchestration of the piece. (See also: R16a, R34f, R37i, R78t, R95n, R103g, R165x, R203i, R311a)

Bibliography

WB250. *A Manual of Music: Its History, Biography and Literature*, ed. W.M. Derthick. Chicago: Manual Publishing Co., 1888.

This book contains analyses of *The Dying Poet, Marche de nuit, Sixième Ballade*, and *The Last Hope*. The full score of *Danse ossianique* is also included. (See also: WB131, WB182, WB277, WB297)

WB251. Stevenson, Robert. "Gottschalk in Western South America." *Inter-American Music Bulletin* 74:7-16 (November 1969).

Stevenson (p. 10) documents Gottschalk's performance in Lima, Peru (See: W227a).

W228. **Pasquinade, caprice, Op. 59** (c1863; New York: Wm. Hall & Son, 1870. Pub. pl. no. 6542; Paris: Escudier, 1870; Mainz: B. Schott's Söhne, 1870. Pub. pl. no. 20226; Boston: Oliver Ditson & Co., after 1870. Pub. pl. no. 4-29-60947-9; Bryn Mawr, Pennsylvania: Theodore Presser, 1956 (*Piano Music by Louis Moreau Gottschalk*, ed. Jeanne Behrend); New York: Arno Press and *The New York Times*, 1969 (*The Piano Works of Louis Moreau Gottschalk*, vol. 4, ed. Vera Brodsky Lawrence and Richard Jackson); New York: Edwin F. Kalmus, n.d. Pub. pl. no. 3468 (*Album for Piano Solo*); New York: Dover Publications, 1973 (*Piano Music of Louis Moreau Gottschalk*, selected and introduced by Richard Jackson); Leipzig: Peters, 1973 (*Louis Moreau Gottschalk: kreolische und karibische Klavierstücke*, ed. Eberhardt Klemm); New York: Chappell, 1973 (*L.M. Gottschalk: Ten Compositions for Pianoforte*, ed. Amiram Rigai); Melville, New York: Belwin-Mills, 1976 (*Album for Piano Solo*).)

Duration: 4 minutes.
Dedication: "À Mlle. Katherine Sandford (New York)."
Manuscript is located at the New York Public Library.
Other indices: RO189, D113.

Performances

W228a. October 28, 1863. Musical Fund Hall, Philadelphia. Louis Moreau Gottschalk, piano.

W228b.   September 27, 1998. The Boston Conservatory, Boston,
Massachussetts. Michael Lewin, piano.

Recordings

R228a.   *Pasquinade*. Frank La Forge, piano. 10-inch, 78 rpm
phonodisc. Victor 45060, 1913.

R228b.   *The Banjo and Other Creole Favorites*. Eugene List,
piano. 33-1/3 rpm phonodisc. Vanguard VRS-485, 1957.
Reissued as part of *The World of Louis Moreau
Gottschalk* (See: D). Reissued on compact disc as
Vanguard Classics OVC 4050, 1992. Reissued as part of
the two compact disc set *Piano Music of Louis Moreau
Gottschalk*. Vanguard Classics 08 9143 72/08 9144-72,
1993.
        For reviews of this recording, see: see: B258, B259,
B263 and B265. (See also: R68a, R76a, R78a, R95a,
R139b, R142a, R165a, R191a, R216a, R227a, R230a)

R228c.   *Piano Music by Louis Moreau Gottschalk*. Jeanne
Behrend, piano. 33-1/3 rpm phonodisc. MGM E-3370,
1957.
        For a review of this recording, see: B265. (See also:
R68b, R78b, R88a, R139c, R142b, R156a, R165b, R212a,
R220a)

R228d.   *The Piano Music of Louis Moreau Gottschalk*. Amiram
Rigai, piano. 33-1/3 rpm phonodisc. Decca DL 10143,
1967. Reissued as Decca DL 710143, 1970.
        For reviews of this recording, see: B327, B329,
B330. (See also: R78d, R83a, R95b, R112a, R142d,
R165d, R212b, R249a, R265a)

R228e.   *Gottschalk: 40 Works for Piano*. Alan Mandel, piano.
Four 33-1/3 rpm phonodiscs. Desto DC 6470-73, 1969.
Reissued on three compact discs, VoxBox CD3X 3033,
1995.
        For reviews of this recording, see: B360-B362,
B365, B366, B369-B371, B375, B388, B396, B523,
B529. (See also: R67a, R68d, R69a, R78e, R83b, R92b,
R95c, R100a, R103a, R105a, R112b, R135a, R139d,

R142e, R144a, R146a, R153a, R156b, R165e, R167a,
R175a, R191b, R192a, R195a, R203a, R204a, R212c,
R216b, R220b, R227b, R229a, R230b, R232a, R255a,
R256a, R257a, R258c, R265b)

R228f.   *A Festival of Americana: The Romantic Era in American
Music*. Various performers. *Pasquinade* performed by
James Winn, piano. 1-7/8 ips audio cassette. New
England Conservatory of Music, 1972.
   (See also: R139f)

R228g.   *The World of Louis Moreau Gottschalk*. Various
performers. *Pasquinade* performed by Eugene List,
piano. Two 33-1/3 rpm phonodiscs. Vanguard VSD-723;
VSD-724, 1973. Reissued on compact disc. Vanguard
VCD 72026, 1988.
   For a review of this recording, see: B417. (See also:
R34b, R37a, R68e, R76b, R78f, R95d, R139g, R142i,
R165g, R191c, R216d, R227c, R230c)

R228h.   *Louis Moreau Gottschalk: Piano Music*. Edward Gold,
piano. 33-1/3 rpm phonodisc. Musical Heritage Society
MHS 1629, 1974.
   (See also: R142j, R165h, R167c, R176c, R178a,
R254a, R259a)

R228i.   *The Piano Music of Louis Moreau Gottschalk*. Ivan
Davis, piano. Simultaneously issued on 1-7/8 ips audio
cassette, Musical Heritage Society MHC 9040 and 33-1/3
rpm phonodisc, MHS 7040, 1975. Also issued as *Great
Galloping Gottschalk*. 33-1/3 rpm phonodisc. London
CS-6943, 1976. Reissued on 1-7/8 ips audio cassette,
1984.
   For reviews of this recording, see: B454, B455,
B461. (See also: R78g, R88b, R95e, R100b, R103b,
R142l, R165j, R203d, R216e, R227d, R257b)

R228j.   *Music of the Romantic Pianist-Composer*. David Dubal,
piano; Stanley Waldoff, piano. 33-1/ rpm phonodisc.
Musical Heritage Society MHS 3681F, 1978.
   With works by Chopin, Thalberg, and other
nineteenth-century composers.

R228k. *Louis Moreau Gottschalk, 1829-1869: American Piano Music*. Amiram Rigai, piano. 33-1/3 rpm phonodisc. Folkways Records FSS 37485, 1979. Reissued on compact disc, Smithsonian Folkways 40803, 1992.

For a review of the original recording, see: B468. (See also: R68f, R69b, R78h, R83c, R88e, R95g, R112h, R133a, R142m, R165k, R167e, R191d, R212e, R227e, R249c, R275b)

R228l. *Cakewalk*. John Arpin, piano. Compact disc. ProArte Digital CDD515, 1990. Recorded September 25 and 27, 1989 in Toronto, Ontario, Canada.

(See also: R68g, R78j, R95h, R100d, R112e, R142n, R165n, R191e, R204c, R212g, R227g, R257c)

R228m. *Cervantes, Saumell, Gottschalk*. Georges Rabol, piano. Compact disc. Opus 111 OPS 30-9001, 1990. Reissued on *Classics of the Americas: Vol. 4 Gottschalk*. Opus 111 2000, 1995.

Contains works by Manuel Saumell, Georges Rabol, and Ignatio Cervantes, in addition to several Gottschalk compositions. (See also: R68h, R76e, R78k, R165o, R191f, R249b)

R228n. *Great American Piano I. Louis Moreau Gottschalk. Vol. 7*. Leonard Pennario, piano. Compact disc. Angel Records CDM 7 64667 2, 1992. Material originally released on two 33-1/3 rpm phonodiscs as *Music of Louis Moreau Gottschalk*. Angel RL-32125, 1975.

For reviews of this recording, see: B441, B442, B446, B450, B452. (See also: R68i, R78m, R95i, R112f, R139i, R142t, R165u, R167d, R191g, R199b, R212i, R220g, R229c, R257e, R272b)

R228o. *Gottschalk: Piano Music, Vol. 2*. Philip Martin, piano. Compact disc. Hyperion CDA 66697, 1994.

For reviews of this recording, see: B525 and B529. (See also: R76f, R99a, R100f, R103f, R105b, R119b, R146c, R158a, R162a, R171a, R187b, R199c, R210a, R212j, R216h, R257f)

R228p. *David Helfgott*. David Helfgott, piano. Compact disc.

RAP Productions RAPCD 190547-1, 1994.
With various works by Chopin, Beethoven, and
Mussorgsky.

R228q.   *Pops Americana.* Joel Salsman, Yamaha Disklavier
Recording Piano. 1-7/8 ips audio cassette. Joel Salsman,
1994.
Contains several Gottschalk works, as well as
compositions by Joel Salsman, Zez Confrey, Scott Joplin,
George Gershwin, and Nacio Herb Brown. (See also:
R95k, R227i)

R228r.   *Piano Portraits from Nineteenth-Century America.* Noël
Lester, piano. Compact disc. Centaur CRC 2250, 1995.
With: *Le banjo* (See: R142u); *Sospiro* (See:
R152a); *L'Union* (See: R220i); and various works by
Benjamin Carr, Arthur Clifton, Stephen Collins Foster,
William Mason, Richard Hoffman, John Knowles Paine,
and Edward A. MacDowell. For a review of this
recording, see: B533.

R228s.   *Courtly Dances.* United States Marine Band; John R.
Bourgeois, conductor. Simultaneously issued on 1-7/8 ips
audio cassette and compact disc. United States Marine
Band, 1996. Recorded at the Center for the Arts, George
Mason University, May 23-27, 1994.
Note: The Gottschalk work was orchestrated by Erik
Leidzén.

R228t.   *A Gottschalk Festival.* Eugene List, piano. Two compact
discs. Vox Box 5009, n.d.
(See also: R4a, R34e, R36b, R37g, R41a, R42a,
R44a, R191h, R220m, R258k, R298b, R302d, R305c,
R310c)

R228u.   *Louis Moreau Gottschalk: Piano Works.* Klaus
Kaufmann, piano. Compact disc. Koch Schwann
360352, n.d.
(See also: R68o, R76g, R78s, R99b, R139k, R142z,
R156c, R165w, R204e, R220n)

W229.   **Battle Cry of Freedom (Le Cri de délivrance), grand caprice de concert, Op. 55** (1863-4; Chicago: Root & Cady, 1865. Pub. pl. no. 440-20; Paris: Escudier, 1865; B. Schott's Söhne, 1865. Pub. pl. no. 20005; New York: Arno Press and *The New York Times*, 1969 (*The Piano Works of Louis Moreau Gottschalk*, vol. 1, ed. Vera Brodsky Lawrence and Richard Jackson).)

Duration: 5-1/2 minutes.
Manuscript and sketches are located at the New York Public Library.
Dedication: "To my friend George F. Root, Esq."
Other indices: RO62, D18.
Note: This work consists of variations based on the song "The Battle Cry of Freedom" by George F. Root.

Performances

W229a.   1864 and 1865. Numerous venues. Louis Moreau Gottschalk, piano.

W229b.   December 17, 1969. *Louis Moreau Gottschalk Centennial Concert*. Alan Mandel, piano.
(See also: R229b)

Recordings

R229a.   *Gottschalk: 40 Works for Piano*. Alan Mandel, piano. Four 33-1/3 rpm phonodiscs. Desto DC 6470-73, 1969. Reissued on three compact discs, VoxBox CD3X 3033, 1995.

For reviews of this recording, see: B360-B362, B365, B366, B369-B371, B375, B388, B396, B523, B529. (See also: R67a, R68d, R69a, R78e, R83b, R92b, R95c, R100a, R103a, R105a, R112b, R135a, R139d, R142e, R144a, R146a, R153a, R156b, R165e, R167a, R175a, R191b, R192a, R195a, R203a, R204a, R212c, R216b, R220b, R227b, R228e, R230b, R232a, R255a, R256a, R257a, R258c, R265b)

R229b.   *Louis Moreau Gottschalk: A Centennial Concert*. Various pianists. *Battle Cry of Freedom* performed by Alan Mandel. 33-1/3 rpm phonodisc. Turnabout TV-S 34426, 1971. Recorded live December 17, 1969.

For reviews of this recording, see: B415 and B440.
(See also: R112c, R135b, R139e, R142f, R165f, R167b,
R203b, R212d, R216c, R258d)

R229c.   *Great American Piano I. Louis Moreau Gottschalk. Vol.
7*. Leonard Pennario, piano. Compact disc. Angel
Records CDM 7 64667 2, 1992. Material originally
released on two 33-1/3 rpm phonodiscs as *Music of Louis
Moreau Gottschalk*. Angel RL-32125, 1975.
For reviews of this recording, see: B441, B442,
B446, B450, B452. (See also: R68i, R78m, R95i, R112f,
R139i, R142t, R165u, R167d, R191g, R199b, R212i,
R220g, R228n, R257e, R272b)

R229d.   *A Gottschalk Gala*. Various artists. Compact disc.
Premiere Recordings PRCD 1063, 1998.

W230.   **The Maiden's Blush (Le sourire d'une jeune fille), Grande valse
de concert, Op. 106** (c1863-4; Boston: Oliver Ditson, 1865. Pub. pl.
no. 23014; Mainz: B. Schott's Söhne, c1878. Pub. pl. no. 22837.)

Duration: 3-1/4 minutes.
Dedication: "à son ami de Ham de Pittsburgh."
Other indices: RO141, D84.
Note: This piece originally was published under Gottschalk's
pseudonym Seven Octaves.

Recordings

R230a.   *The Banjo and Other Creole Favorites*. Eugene List,
piano. 33-1/3 rpm phonodisc. Vanguard VRS-485, 1957.
Reissued as part of *The World of Louis Moreau
Gottschalk* (See: 230c). Reissued on compact disc as
Vanguard Classics OVC 4050, 1992. Reissued as part of
the two compact disc set *Piano Music of Louis Moreau
Gottschalk*. Vanguard Classics 08 9143 72/08 9144-72,
1993.
For reviews of this recording, see: B258, B259,
B263 and B265. (See also: R68a, R76a, R78a, R95a,
R139b, R142a, R165a, R191a, R216a, R227a, R228b)

R230b.   *Gottschalk: 40 Works for Piano*. Alan Mandel, piano.

Four 33-1/3 rpm phonodiscs. Desto DC 6470-73, 1969.
Reissued on three compact discs, VoxBox CD3X 3033,
1995.

For reviews of this recording, see: B360-B362,
B365, B366, B369-B371, B375, B388, B396, B523,
B529. (See also: R67a, R68d, R69a, R78e, R83b, R92b,
R95c, R100a, R103a, R105a, R112b, R135a, R139d,
R142e, R144a, R146a, R153a, R156b, R165e, R167a,
R175a, R191b, R192a, R195a, R203a, R204a, R212c,
R216b, R220b, R227b, R228e, R229a, R232a, R255a,
R256a, R257a, R258c, R265b)

R230c.   *The World of Louis Moreau Gottschalk.* Various
performers. *The Maiden's Blush* performed by Eugene
List, piano. Two 33-1/3 rpm phonodiscs. Vanguard
VSD-723; VSD-724, 1973. Reissued on compact disc.
Vanguard VCD 72026, 1988.

For a review of this recording, see: B417. (See also:
R34b, R37a, R68e, R76b, R78f, R95d, R139g, R142i,
R165g, R191c, R216d, R227c, R228g)

Bibliography

WB252.   Selden, Margery Stomne. "Gottschalk, Ochs, and
Glinka's *Last Rose of Summer.*" *Piano Quarterly* 87:25-
30 (fall 1974).

The article discusses *The Maiden's Blush*, Siegfried
Ochs's humorous variations on a German folk song and
Glinka's variations on the Scottish tune "The Last Rose of
Summer."

W231.   Orfa, grande polka, Op. 71 (c1863-4; Boston: Oliver Ditson &
Co., 1864. Pub. pl. no. 22491; Mainz: B. Schott's Söhne, 1872 (as
Op. 71); Paris: Escudier, 1873 (as Op. 71); New York: Arno Press
and *The New York Times*, 1969 (*The Piano Works of Louis Moreau
Gottschalk*, vol. 4, ed. Vera Brodsky Lawrence and Richard
Jackson).)

Manuscript is located at the New York Public Library.
Dedication: "To my friend Blodgett, of Buffalo, N.Y."
Other indices: RO186, D108.
Note: This piece was originally published using Gottschalk's

pseudonym Seven Octaves.
(See also: W307)

Bibliography

WB253. Orem, Preston Ware. "Study Notes on *Etude* Music."
        Etude 32:426 (June 1914).
        Orem provides suggestions on the performance of
        Orfa; the score is also reproduced.

W232. **Radieuse, grande valse de concert, Op. 72 (Op. 116)** (c1863-4;
        Mainz: B. Schott's Söhne, 1874. Pub. pl. no. 21230; Boston: Oliver
        Ditson, 1878 (arr. and ed. Henry Maylath); New York: Arno Press
        and *The New York Times*, 1969 (*The Piano Works of Louis Moreau
        Gottschalk*, vol. 4, ed. Vera Brodsky Lawrence and Richard
        Jackson).)

Other indices: RO218, D127c.
Duration: 5-1/2 minutes.
(See also: W305)

Recordings

R232a. *Gottschalk: 40 Works for Piano*. Alan Mandel, piano.
        Four 33-1/3 rpm phonodiscs. Desto DC 6470-73, 1969.
        Reissued on three compact discs, VoxBox CD3X 3033,
        1995.
        For reviews of this recording, see: B360-B362,
        B365, B366, B369-B371, B375, B388, B396, B523,
        B529. (See also: R67a, R68d, R69a, R78e, R83b, R92b,
        R95c, R100a, R103a, R105a, R112b, R135a, R139d,
        R142e, R144a, R146a, R153a, R156b, R165e, R167a,
        R175a, R191b, R192a, R195a, R203a, R204a, R212c,
        R216b, R220b, R227b, R228e, R229a, R230b, R255a,
        R256a, R257a, R258c, R265b)

W233. **Unadilla Waltz** (c1863-5; Washington, D.C., n.d., lost.)

Other indices: D155.

W234. **La brise (The Breeze), valse de concert** (1865; New York: C.M.
        Cady, 1878; New York: Arno Press and *The New York Times*, 1969

(*The Piano Works of Louis Moreau Gottschalk*, vol. 1, ed. Vera Brodsky Lawrence and Richard Jackson).)

Dedication: "Respectfully Dedicated to Mrs. Kate Sanger."
Other indices: RO30, D23.
Duration: 4 minutes.

Recordings

R234a.   *Selected Piano Music of Louis Moreau Gottschalk.* Lambert Orkis, piano. Compact disc. Smithsonian Collection of Recordings ND 033, 1988. Recorded on an 1865 Chickering piano in Coolidge Auditorium, Library of Congress, Washington, D.C., May 1982.
    (See also: R76d, R103d, R110a, R145a, R151a, R192b, R220f)

W235.   **Caprice on Peruvian Airs (Variaciones de aires nacionales del Perú) (1865; unpublished; lost.)**

Other indices: RO40.

Performances

W235a.   Late 1865. Callao, Peru. Louis Moreau Gottschalk, piano.

W235b.   December 22, 1865. Lima, Peru. Louis Moreau Gottschalk, piano.

Bibliography

WB254.   Lange, Francisco Curt. *Vida y muerte de Louis Moreau Gottschalk en Rio de Janeiro.* Mendoza, Argentina: Universidad Nacional de Cuyo, 1951.
    Lange (p. 284) documents the Gottschalk's December 1865 performance in Lima (See: W235b).

WB255.   Starr, S. Frederick. *Bamboula! The Life and Times of Louis Moreau Gottschalk.* New York: Oxford University Press, 1995.
    Starr (p. 388) discusses Gottschalk's 1865

performance in Callao, Peru (See: W235a).

W236. **Variations on "Auld Lang Syne"** (1865; unpublished; lost.)

Note: The lack of inclusion of this piece in previous indices suggests a central problem in indexing Gottschalk's compositions. Although Starr (See: WB256) has traced evidence that Gottschalk performed the piece, there seems to be no evidence that it was ever written down.

Performances

W236a. Late 1865. Callao, Peru. Louis Moreau Gottschalk, piano.

Bibliography

WB256. Starr, S. Frederick. *Bamboula! The Life and Times of Louis Moreau Gottschalk.* New York: Oxford University Press, 1995.
Starr (p. 388) mentions Gottschalk's 1865 performance of the work in Peru (See: W236a).

W237. **Ses yeux, polka de concert, Op. 66** (1865; Rio de Janerio: Narciso y Napoleão, c1870; Mainz, B. Schott's Söhne, c1872. Pub. pl. no. 20696; Paris: Escudier, c1874. Pub. pl. no. L.E. 3368; New York: Dover Publications, 1973 (*Piano Music of Louis Moreau Gottschalk,* selected and introduced by Richard Jackson).)

Other indices: RO235, D137a.
Note: This was a solo piano arrangement of W309 by Arthur Napoleão.
(See also: W310)

W238. **Fantasia sobre la *Lucrezia Borgia*** (c1865; unpublished; lost.)

Other indices: RO138.
Note: This work is based on themes from Donizetti's opera *Lucrezia Borgia.*
(See also: W123 and W240)

Performances

W238a.   December 13, 1865. Lima, Peru. Louis Moreau Gottschalk, piano.

Bibliography

WB257.   Lange, Francisco Curt. *Vida y muerte de Louis Moreau Gottschalk en Rio de Janeiro, 1869.* Mendoza, Argentina: Universidad Nacional de Cuyo, 1951.
Lange (p. 283) documents the work's December 1865 performance in Lima(See: W238a).

W239.   **Ultima rosa (The Last Rose of Summer)** (1865-69; unpublished; lost.)

Other indices: RO268.

Performances

W239a.   June 21, 1869. Rio de Janeiro. Louis Moreau Gottschalk, piano.

Bibliography

WB258.   Lange, Francisco Curt. *Vida y muerte de Louis Moreau Gottschalk en Rio de Janeiro.* Mendoza, Argentina: Universidad Nacional de Cuyo, 1951.
Lange (p. 249) documents the June 1869 Rio de Janeiro performance by Gottschalk (See: W239a).

W240.   **Souvenir de *Lucrezia Borgia*** (1865-1869; unpublished; lost.)

Other indices: RO249.
Note: The work may be related to Gottschalk's two other works based on themes from Donezzeti's opera *Lucrezia Borgia* (See: W123 and W238)

Performances

W240a.   October 10, 1869. Rio de Janeiro. Louis Moreau Gottschalk, piano.

Bibliography

WB259. Lange, Francisco Curt. *Vida y muerte de Louis Moreau Gottschalk en Rio de Janeiro, 1869.* Mendoza, Argentina: Universidad Nacional de Cuyo, 1951.
Lange documents Gottschalk's October 1869 performance of the piece in Rio de Janeiro (See: W240a).

W241. **Marche in E-flat Major** (before 1866; unpublished.)

Manuscript is located at the New York Public Library.
Other indices: D88.

W242. **Grande phantasie sobre** *Martha* (after 1865; unpublished; lost.)

Other indices: RO161.
Note: This work was based on themes from Flotow's opera *Martha*.

Performances

W242a. June 18, 1869. Rio de Janeiro. Louis Moreau Gottschalk, piano.

W242b. September 5, 1869. São Paulo, Brazil. Louis Moreau Gottschalk, piano.

Bibliography

WB260. Lange, Francisco Curt. *Vida y muerte de Louis Moreau Gottschalk en Rio de Janeiro, 1869.* Mendoza, Argentina: Universidad Nacional de Cuyo, 1951.
Lange documents Gottschalk's 1869 performances of the piece in Rio de Janeiro and São Paulo (See: W242a and W242b).

W243. **L'Alianza** (1866; unpublished; lost.)

Performances

W243a. June 3, 1866. Santiago, Chile. Louis Moreau Gottschalk, piano.

Bibliography

WB261. Starr, S. Frederick. *Bamboula! The Life and Times of Louis Moreau Gottschalk*. New York: Oxford University Press, 1995.
  Starr (p. 393) describes the piece and Gottschalk's performance in Santiago (See: W243a).

W244. **Marguerite, grande valse brillante, valse sentimentale, Op. 76** (c1866; Boston: Oliver Ditson & Co., 1873 (ed. Clara Gottschalk). Pub. pl. no. 28001; Paris: Escudier, 1874; New York: Arno Press and *The New York Times*, 1969 (*The Piano Works of Louis Moreau Gottschalk*, vol. 4, ed. Vera Brodsky Lawrence and Richard Jackson).)

Dedicated to Madam Ernest Dupeyroni.
Other indices: RO158, D92.
Note: The 1873 Ditson publication includes commentary by Espadero about Gottschalk and his compositional style.
(See also: W24)

Recordings

R244a. *Great American Piano II. Gottschalk, Joplin, Gershwin. Vol. 8.* Various performers. *Marguerite* performed by Leonard Pennario, piano. Compact disc. Angel Records CDM 7 64668 2, 1992. Gottschalk material originally released on two 33-1/3 rpm phonodiscs as *Music of Louis Moreau Gottschalk*. Angel RL-32125, 1975.
  Contains several Gottschalk compositions, as well as works by George Gershwin and Scott Joplin performed by Leonard Pennario and Joshua Rifkin (Joplin works only). (See also: R119a, R178b, R203c, R204d, R216g)

W245. **Bataille, étude de concert, Op. 63 (64)** (c1867-8; Boston: Oliver Ditson Company, 1870. Pub. pl. no. 6522; New York: William Hall & Son, 1870; Paris: Escudier, c1870 (as Op. 63); Mainz: B Schott's Söhne, 1871 (as Op. 64). Pub. pl. no. 20539; New York: Arno Press and *The New York Times*, 1969 (*The Piano Works of Louis Moreau Gottschalk*, vol. 1, ed. Vera Brodsky Lawrence and Richard Jackson).)

Dedication: "À mon ami Sig. A. Cortada de Brooklyn."
Other indices: RO25, D17.

Performances

W245a.   June 9, 1869. Rio de Janeiro. Louis Moreau Gottschalk, piano.

Bibliography

WB262.   Lange, Francisco Curt. *Vida y muerte de Louis Moreau Gottschalk en Rio de Janeiro 1869*. Mendoza, Argentina: Universidad Nacional de Cuyo, 1951.
Lange (p. 258) documents Gottschalk's June 9, 1869 performance of the work in Rio de Janeiro (See: W245a).

W246.   **Dernier amour, étude de concert, Op. 62 (63)** (1867-9; Boston: Oliver Ditson & Co.,1870. Pub. pl. no. 6521; New York: Wm. Hall & Son, 1870. Pub. pl. no. 6521; Paris: Escudier, 1871 (as Op. 62); Mainz: B. Schott's Söhne, 1871 (as Op. 63). Pub. pl. no. 20538; New York: Arno Press and *The New York Times*, 1969 (*The Piano Works of Louis Moreau Gottschalk*, vol. 2, ed. Vera Brodsky Lawrence and Richard Jackson).)

Dedication: "à mon ami Charles G. Pond de New York."
Other indices: RO73, D43 (Doyle lists an organ adaptation by L.O. Emerson as D43a.).

Performances

W246a.   June 18, 1869. Rio de Janeiro. Louis Moreau Gottschalk, piano.

Bibliography

WB263.   Lange, Francisco Curt. *Vida y muerte de Louis Moreau Gottschalk en Rio de Janeiro 1869*. Mendoza, Argentina: Universidad Nacional de Cuyo, 1951.
Lange (p. 249) documents Gottschalk's June 18, 1869 performance of the work in Rio de Janeiro (See: W246a).

W247.   **Grande tarantelle, Op. 67** (1868; Mainz: B. Schott's Söhne, 1873.
Pub. pl. no. 20822; Paris: Escudier, 1874 (ed. N.R. Espadero). Pub.
pl. no. LE 3370; Boston: Oliver Ditson, 1874 (ed. N.R. Espadero).
Pub. pl. no. 28384; Rio de Janeiro: Narciso and Napoleão, n.d.;
Paris: Mackar & Nöel, 1890; New York: Arno Press and *The New
York Times*, 1969 (*The Piano Works of Louis Moreau Gottschalk*,
vol. 3, ed. Vera Brodsky Lawrence and Richard Jackson).)

Other indices: RO262, D67.
Note: An arrangement of W37. Note that many of the editions vary
    considerably; aside from the editions credited to Espadero, it
    is unclear who is responsible for many of the editions, as well
    as how closely they might adhere to Gottschalk's own solo
    piano performances of the piece.
(See also: W37, W48, W311, W312)

W248.   **La flor que ella me envia** (c1868; Buenos Aires, 1869; lost.)

Other indices: D57.
Note: While there is clear evidence that Gottschalk wrote a vocal
    work with this title (See: W26), this solo piano listing is
    speculative.

W249.   **Morte!! (She Is Dead), Lamentation, Op. 60 (55)** (c1868; Boston:
Oliver Ditson & Co., 1869. Pub. pl. no. 6498; New York: Wm. Hall
& Son, 1869. Pub. pl. no. 6498; Mainz: B. Schott's Söhne, 1870.
Pub. pl. no. 20228; Paris: Escudier, 1870; Rio de Janeiro: Narciso y
Napoleão, n.d.; New York: Arno Press and *The New York Times*,
1969 (*The Piano Works of Louis Moreau Gottschalk*, vol. 4, ed. Vera
Brodsky Lawrence and Richard Jackson); New York: Dover
Publications, 1973 (*Piano Music of Louis Moreau Gottschalk*,
selected and introduced by Richard Jackson); New York: Chappell,
1973 (*L.M. Gottschalk: Ten Compositions for Pianoforte*, ed.
Amiram Rigai).)
Dedication: "À mon ami Monsieur le Comte Jioannini, Minister de
    la Majesté le Roi d'Italie."
Other indices: RO174, D100.
Note: The 1869 William Hall & Son edition is incorrectly
    designated Op. 55; other contemporaneous publications give
    Op. 60.

Performances

W249a.   November 25, 1869. Rio de Janeiro. Louis Moreau
Gottschalk, piano.
This was Gottschalk's last performance.

Recordings

R249a.   *The Piano Music of Louis Moreau Gottschalk.* Amiram
Rigai, piano. 33-1/3 rpm phonodisc. Decca DL 10143,
1967. Reissued as Decca DL 710143, 1970.
For reviews of this recording, see: B327, B329,
B330. (See also: R78d, R83a, R95b, R112a, R142d,
R165d, R212b, R228d, R265a)

R249b.   *Cervantes, Saumell, Gottschalk.* Georges Rabol, piano.
Compact disc. Opus 111 OPS 30-9001, 1990. Reissued
on *Classics of the Americas: Vol. 4 Gottschalk.* Opus
111 2000, 1995.
Contains works by Manuel Saumell, Georges Rabol,
and Ignatio Cervantes, in addition to several Gottschalk
compositions. (See also: R68h, R76e, R78k, R165o,
R191f, R228m)

R249c.   *Louis Moreau Gottschalk. American Piano Music.*
Amiram Rigai, piano. Compact disc. Smithsonian
Folkways 40803, 1992.
For a review of the original recording, see: B468.
(See also: R68f, R69b, R78h, R83c, R88e, R95g, R112h,
R133a, R142m, R165k, R167e, R191d, R212e, R227e,
R228k, R275b)

Bibliography

WB264.   Brockett, Clyde W. "Louis Moreau Gottschalk and His
Morte!! (She Is Dead): Lamentation. American Music
8:29-53 (no. 1, spring 1990).
Brockett reconstructs Gottschalk's writing of *Morte!!*
and his subsequent performances in Buenos Aires,
Montevideo, and Rio de Janeiro based on Fors's
biography (See: B112) and contemporary South
American newspaper accounts.

W250.   **Tremelo, grande étude de concert, Op. 58** (c1868; Rio de Janeiro: Narciso y Napoleão, 1869; Paris: Escudier, 1870; New York: William Hall & Son, 1871; Boston: Oliver Ditson & Co., 1871. Pub. pl. no. 6591; Mainz: B. Schott's Söhne, 1873. Pub. pl. no. 20227; New York: Edwin F. Kalmus, n.d. Pub. pl. no. 3468 (*Album for Piano Solo*); Melville, New York: Belwin-Mills, 1976 (*Album for Piano Solo*).)

Other indices: RO265, D154.

Performances

W250a.   June 18, 1869. Rio de Janeiro. Louis Moreau Gottschalk, piano.

W250b.   November 25, 1869. Theatro Lyrico Fluminense, Rio de Janeiro. Louis Moreau Gottschalk, piano.
Although Gottschalk reportedly performed *Tremelo* at least five times in Rio de Janeiro in 1869, this quickly became the most famous; this was the last piece he played at his last ever performance. The musician collapsed during the opening measures and had to be carried from the stage.

Recordings

R250a.   *Louis Moreau Gottschalk*. Eugene List, piano. Compact disc. Vanguard Classics OVC 4051, 1992. Reissued as part of the two compact disc set *Piano Music*. Vanguard Classics 08 9143 72/08 9144-72, 1993.
(See also: R34c, R37f, R100e, R220h, R275a, R282b, R291b, R292a, R300b, R302b, R305b, R307b, R310b)

Bibliography

WB265.   Lange, Francisco Curt. *Vida y muerte de Louis Moreau Gottschalk en Rio de Janeiro, 1869*. Mendoza, Argentina: Universidad Nacional de Cuyo, 1951.
Lange (p. 249) provides evidence of Gottschalk's June 1869 performance of the piece in Rio de Janeiro (See: W250a).

W251.   **Gran marcha solemne (Marche solennelle)** (1868; Rio de Janeiro: Narciso and Napoleão, c1870 (arr. Arthur Napoleão). Pub. pl. no. 1620.)

Other indices: RO155, D64.

Note: Although the arrangement of this work from W44 is generally attributed to Arthur Napoleão, Lange (See: WB266, p. 96) claims that Gottschalk had performed the work in its solo piano version; therefore it is possible that Napoleão recreated Gottschalk's arrangment after the composer's death.

Bibliography

WB266.   Lange, Francisco Curt. *Vida y muerte de Louis Moreau Gottschalk en Rio de Janeiro, 1869.* Mendoza, Argentina: Universidad Nacional de Cuyo, 1951.

W252.   **Caprice élégiaque, Op. 56** (c1868-9; Mainz: B. Schott's Söhne, 1870. Pub. pl. no. 20033; Paris: Escudier, 1870; New York: Arno Press and *The New York Times*, 1969 (*The Piano Works of Louis Moreau Gottschalk*, vol. 1, ed. Vera Brodsky Lawrence and Richard Jackson).)
Dedication: "à mon ami Joseph Green."
Other indices: RO38, D25.

Performances

W252a.   September 21, 1869. Rio de Janeiro. Louis Moreau Gottschalk, piano.

Bibliography

WB267.   Lange, Francisco Curt. *Vida y muerte de Louis Moreau Gottschalk en Rio de Janeiro.* Mendoza, Argentina: Universidad Nacional de Cuyo, 1951.
Lange (p. 261) documents Gottschalk's September 1869 performance (See: W252a).

W253.   **Vision, étude** (1868-9; Rio de Janeiro: Narciso y Napoleão, c1870. Pub. pl. no. 1932; New York: Arno Press and *The New York Times*,

1969 (*The Piano Works of Louis Moreau Gottschalk*, vol. 5, ed. Vera Brodsky Lawrence and Richard Jackson).)

Other indices: RO295, D158.

W254. **The Dying Swan, romance poétique, Op. 100** (c1868-9; St. Louis: Kunkel Brothers, 1870. Pub. pl. no. 131-5; New York: Arno Press and *The New York Times*, 1969 (*The Piano Works of Louis Moreau Gottschalk*, vol. 2, ed. Vera Brodsky Lawrence and Richard Jackson); Dayton, Ohio: McAfee Music Corp., 1975 (*The Bicentennial Collection of American Keyboard Music*, ed. Edward Gold).)

Dedicated to Miss Eva Waldence Hedge of Chicago.
Other indices: RO76, D46.

Recordings

R254a.   *Louis Moreau Gottschalk: Piano Music.* Edward Gold, piano. 33-1/3 rpm phonodisc. Musical Heritage Society MHS 1629, 1974.
          (See also: R142j, R165h, R167c, R176c, R178a, R228h, R259a)

W255. **Forget Me Not (Ne m'oubliez pas), mazurka caprice** (c1868-9; St. Louis: Kunkel Brothers, 1870. Pub. pl. no. 142-7; St. Louis: Kunkel Brothers, 1905. Pub. pl. no. 811-5; New York: Arno Press and *The New York Times*, 1969 (*The Piano Works of Louis Moreau Gottschalk*, vol. 2, ed. Vera Brodsky Lawrence and Richard Jackson).)

Duration: 3 minutes.
Dedication: "To the Ladies of the United States."
Other indices: RO99, D59.
Note: The Kunkel Brothers edition includes the description "Gottschalk's Last Composition" on the title page.

Recordings

R255a.   *Gottschalk: 40 Works for Piano.* Alan Mandel, piano. Four 33-1/3 rpm phonodiscs. Desto DC 6470-73, 1969.

Reissued on three compact discs, VoxBox CD3X 3033, 1995.

For reviews of this recording, see: B360-B362, B365, B366, B369-B371, B375, B388, B396, B523, B529. (See also: R67a, R68d, R69a, R78e, R83b, R92b, R95c, R100a, R103a, R105a, R112b, R135a, R139d, R142e, R144a, R146a, R153a, R156b, R165e, R167a, R175a, R191b, R192a, R195a, R203a, R204a, R212c, R216b, R220b, R227b, R228e, R229a, R230b, R232a, R256a, R257a, R258c, R265b)

W256. **Impromptu, Op. 54** (1869; New York: Wm. Hall & Son, 1869. Pub. pl. no. 6499; Boston: Oliver Ditson, 1869. Pub. pl. no. 6499; Mainz: B. Schott's Söhne, 1870 (as Op. 54). Pub. pl. no. 20004; Paris: Escudier, 1870 (as Op. 54); New York: Arno Press and *The New York Times*, 1969 (*The Piano Works of Louis Moreau Gottschalk*, vol. 3, ed. Vera Brodsky Lawrence and Richard Jackson).)

Duration: 5 minutes.
Dedication: "à mon amie Madame Elise D'Aubigny (de Montevideo)."
Other indices: RO122, D74.

Performances

W256a. September 21, 1869. Rio de Janeiro. Louis Moreau Gottschalk, piano.

Recordings

R256a. *Gottschalk: 40 Works for Piano*. Alan Mandel, piano. Four 33-1/3 rpm phonodiscs. Desto DC 6470-73, 1969. Reissued on three compact discs, VoxBox CD3X 3033, 1995.

For reviews of this recording, see: B360-B362, B365, B366, B369-B371, B375, B388, B396, B523, B529. (See also: R67a, R68d, R69a, R78e, R83b, R92b, R95c, R100a, R103a, R105a, R112b, R135a, R139d, R142e, R144a, R146a, R153a, R156b, R165e, R167a, R175a, R191b, R192a, R195a, R203a, R204a, R212c,

R216b, R220b, R227b, R228e, R229a, R230b, R232a,
R255a, R257a, R258c, R265b)

Bibliography

WB268.   Lange, Francisco Curt. *Vida y muerte de Louis Moreau
Gottschalk en Rio de Janeiro, 1869.* Mendoza,
Argentina: Universidad Nacional de Cuyo, 1951.
Lange (p. 261) documents Gottschalk's September
1869 performance of the piece in Rio de Janeiro (See:
W256a).

W257.   Grand scherzo, Op. 57 (1869; Mainz: B. Schott's Söhne, 1870 (as
Op. 57). Pub. pl. no. 20034; New York: Wm. Hall & Son, 1870.
Pub. pl. no. 6540; Boston: Oliver Ditson, 1870. Pub. pl. no. 6540;
Paris: Escudier, 1870 (as Op. 57); Bryn Mawr, Pennsylvania:
Theodore Presser, 1956 (*Piano Music by Louis Moreau Gottschalk*,
ed. Jeanne Behrend); New York: Arno Press and *The New York
Times*, 1969 (*The Piano Works of Louis Moreau Gottschalk*, vol. 3,
ed. Vera Brodsky Lawrence and Richard Jackson); New York:
Dover Publications, 1973 (*Piano Music of Louis Moreau Gottschalk*,
selected and introduced by Richard Jackson).)

Duration: 5 minutes.
Dedication: "à mon ami G. Nessler" (1870 Schott edition); "À
Mdlle. Anna Edckardt (de New York)" (1870 Hall edition).
Manuscript is located at the New York Public Library.
Other indices: RO114, D65.

Recordings

R257a.   *Gottschalk: 40 Works for Piano.* Alan Mandel, piano.
Four 33-1/3 rpm phonodiscs. Desto DC 6470-73, 1969.
Reissued on three compact discs, VoxBox CD3X 3033,
1995.
For reviews of this recording, see: B360-B362,
B365, B366, B369-B371, B375, B388, B396, B523,
B529. (See also: R67a, R68d, R69a, R78e, R83b, R92b,
R95c, R100a, R103a, R105a, R112b, R135a, R139d,
R142e, R144a, R146a, R153a, R156b, R165e, R167a,
R175a, R191b, R192a, R195a, R203a, R204a, R212c,

R216b, R220b, R227b, R228e, R229a, R230b, R232a,
R255a, R256a, R258c, R265b)

R257b.   *The Piano Music of Louis Moreau Gottschalk.* Ivan
Davis, piano. Simultaneously issued on 1-7/8 ips audio
cassette, Musical Heritage Society MHC 9040 and 33-1/3
rpm phonodisc, MHS 7040, 1975. Also issued as *Great
Galloping Gottschalk.* 33-1/3 rpm phonodisc. London
CS-6943, 1976. Reissued on 1-7/8 ips audio cassette,
1984.
    For reviews of this recording, see: B454, B455,
B461. (See also: R78g, R88b, R95e, R100b, R103b,
R142l, R165j, R203d, R216e, R227d, R228i)

R257c.   *Cakewalk.* John Arpin, piano. Compact disc. ProArte
Digital CDD515, 1990. Recorded September 25 and 27,
1989 in Toronto, Ontario, Canada.
    (See also: R68g, R78j, R95h, R100d, R112e, R142n,
R165n, R191e, R204c, R212g, R227g, R228l)

R257d.   *Musique américaine pour piano.* Noël Lee, piano.
Compact disc. Chant du monde LCD 278-1067, 1991.
    With: *Souvenir de Porto Rico* (See: R165q); *The
Dying Poet* (See: R227h); and works by Edward
MacDowell, Aaron Copland, John Cage, and Elliott
Carter.

R257e.   *Great American Piano I. Louis Moreau Gottschalk. Vol.
7.* Leonard Pennario, piano. Compact disc. Angel
Records CDM 7 64667 2, 1992. Material originally
released on two 33-1/3 rpm phonodiscs as *Music of Louis
Moreau Gottschalk.* Angel RL-32125, 1975.
    For reviews of this recording, see: B441, B442,
B446, B450, B452. (See also: R68i, R78m, R95i, R112f,
R139i, R142t, R165u, R167d, R191g, R199b, R212i,
R220g, R228n, R229c, R272b)

R257f.   *Gottschalk: Piano Music, Vol. 2.* Philip Martin, piano.
Compact disc. Hyperion CDA 66697, 1994.
    For reviews of this recording, see: B525 and B529.
(See also: R76f, R99a, R100f, R103f, R105b, R119b,

R146c, R158a, R162a, R171a, R187b, R199c, R210a,
R212j, R216h, R228o)

W258.   **Grande fantaisie triomphale sur l'hymne national brésilien, Op.
69** (1869; Rio de Janeiro: Napoleão, 1869; Mainz: B. Schott's
Söhne, c1873. Pub. pl. no. 20850; Paris: Escudier, 1873; New York:
Arno Press and *The New York Times,* 1969 (*The Piano Works of
Louis Moreau Gottschalk,* vol. 2, ed. Vera Brodsky Lawrence and
Richard Jackson).)

Duration: 9-1/4 minutes.
Dedication: "à Son Altesse Imperiale Madame la Comtesse d'Eu."
Manuscript is located at the New York Public Library.
Other indices: RO108, D63.

Performances

W258a.   1869. Various Rio de Janeiro concert venues. Louis
Moreau Gottschalk, piano.

W258b.   April 1968. Philadelphia. Eunice Katunda, piano.

W258c.   December 13, 1969. Hunter College Assembly Hall, New
York City. Guiomar Novaës, piano.

W258d.   December 17, 1969. *Louis Moreau Gottschalk
Centennial Concert.* Guiomar Novaës, piano.
(See also: R258d)

W258e.   October 3, 1970. New York City. Guiomar Novaës,
piano.
(See also: R258g)

W258f.   1971. Carnegie Hall, New York City. Christina Ortiz,
piano.

Recordings

R258a.   Guiomar Novaës, piano. Two, single-face 78-rpm
phonodiscs. RCA Victor 74675/74825, 1919-24.
Reissued as Victor 6372. Reissued on *Guiomar Novaës.*
Compact disc. Music & Arts CD 702, 1991.

R258b.   *Music in America.* Arthur Loesser, piano. 33-1/3 rpm
phonodisc. Society for the Preservation of the American
Musical Heritage MIA 110, 1961.
(See also: R92a, R132a, R149a)

R258c.   *Gottschalk: 40 Works for Piano.* Alan Mandel, piano.
Four 33-1/3 rpm phonodiscs. Desto DC 6470-73, 1969.
Reissued on three compact discs, VoxBox CD3X 3033,
1995.

For reviews of this recording, see: B360-B362,
B365, B366, B369-B371, B375, B388, B396, B523,
B529. (See also: R67a, R68d, R69a, R78e, R83b, R92b,
R95c, R100a, R103a, R105a, R112b, R135a, R139d,
R142e, R144a, R146a, R153a, R156b, R165e, R167a,
R175a, R191b, R192a, R195a, R203a, R204a, R212c,
R216b, R220b, R227b, R228e, R229a, R230b, R232a,
R255a, R256a, R257a, R265b)

R258d.   *Louis Moreau Gottschalk: A Centennial Concert.*
Various pianists. *Grande fantaisie* performed by
Guiomar Novaës. 33-1/3 rpm phonodisc. Turnabout TV-
S 34426, 1971. Recorded live December 17, 1969.

For reviews of this recording, see: B415 and B440.
(See also: R112c, R135b, R139e, R142f, R165f, R167b,
R203b, R212d, R216c, R229b)

R258e.   *The Best of Louis Moreau Gottschalk.* Eugene List,
piano; Berlin Symphony Orchestra; Samuel Adler,
conductor. 33-1/3 rpm phonodisc. Turnabout TV-S
34449, c1979.

Note: This performance is of an arrangement
orchestration of the work for piano and orchestra by
Samuel Adler. (See also: R36a, R37b, R220e)

R258f.   *Rhapsody in Blue.* Cristina Ortiz, piano; Royal
Philharmonic Orchestra; Moshe Atzmon, conductor.
Compact disc. London 430 726-2, 1991.

With other works for piano(s) and orchestra by
George Gershwin, Henry Litolff, Richard Addinsell, and
Franz Liszt, performed by various soloists and various
orchestras. Note that the Gottschalk work is orchestrated
by Chris Hazell.

R258g.   *The International Piano Library Benefit Concert.*
Guiomar Novaës, piano. 33-1/3 rpm phonodisc.
International Piano Library IPL 5005-6, 1970.
   Recorded live in New York City, October 3, 1970
(See: W258e).

R258h.   *Este Brasil que tanto amo!* Eudóxia de Barros, piano.
Compact disc. Paulinas COMEP CD 6673-7, c1996.
   With various dance-based works by Brazilian
composers.

R258i.   *Gottschalk: Piano Music, Vol. 3.* Philip Martin, piano.
Compact disc. Hyperion CDA 66915, 1997.
   For a review of this recording, see: B538. (See also:
R681, R951, R139j, R176b, R177a, R203f, R209b, R227j,
R259b)

R258j.   *Hino nacional brasileiro.* Various performers. *Grande
fantaisie triomphale sur l'hymne national brésilien*
performed by Arthur Moreira Lima, piano. Compact disc.
RioArte Digital RD 019, 1998.
   With miscellaneous other patriotic Brazilian works.

R258k.   *A Gottschalk Festival.* Eugene List, piano; Wiener
Staatsopernorchester; Igor Buketoff, conductor. Two
compact discs. Vox Box 5009, n.d.
   (See also: R4a, R34e, R36b, R37g, R41a, R42a,
R44a, R191h, R220m, R228t, R298b, R302d, R305c,
R310c)

Bibliography

WB269.   Hensel, Octavia. *Life and Letters of Louis Moreau
Gottschalk.* Boston: Oliver Ditson & Co., 1870.
   Hensel (p. 171) includes a letter from Gottschalk in
which the composer states that the piece "pleased the
emperor" of Brazil.

WB270.   d'Or. "O grande compositor norteamericano Gottschalk e
o hymno nacional brasileiro." In *Brazil-Estados Unidos:
Diario de noticias.* Rio de Janeiro, 1939:297-298.
   According to Doyle (See: B484, p. 130), this article

concerns Gottschalk and his composition of the *Grande fantaisie triomphale.*

WB271.　Singer, Samuel L. "Brazilian Pianist Presented."
Philadelphia Inquirer April 23, 1968.
A review of W258b.

WB272.　Davis, Peter G. "Guiomar Novaës Interprets Beethoven."
New York Times December 15, 1969:63.
A review of W258c.

WB273.　Ericson, Raymond. "Recital on Piano by Christina
Ortiz." *Piano Guild Notes* 21:7-8 (no. 2, September-
October 1971).
A report on W258e.

WB274.　Eureka, Leonard. "Christina Stunning at Carnegie Hall."
Piano Guild Notes 21:8 (no. 2, September-October 1971).
Reprinted from *Ft. Worth Star-Telegram.*
A review of W258e.

W259.　**Hercule, grande étude de concert, Op. 88** (1869; Mainz: B.
Schott's Söhne, 1877 (ed. Nicolás Ruiz Espadero). Pub. pl. no.
22258; New York: Arno Press and *The New York Times*, 1969 (*The
Piano Works of Louis Moreau Gottschalk*, vol. 3, ed. Vera Brodsky
Lawrence and Richard Jackson).)

Dedication: "à N.R. Espadero (Souvenir d'affection)."
Other indices: RO116, D68.

Recordings

R259a.　*Louis Moreau Gottschalk: Piano Music.* Edward Gold,
piano. 33-1/3 rpm phonodisc. Musical Heritage Society
MHS 1629, 1974.
(See also: R142j, R165h, R167c, R176c, R178a,
R228h, R254a)

R259b.　*Gottschalk: Piano Music, Vol. 3.* Philip Martin, piano.
Compact disc. Hyperion CDA 66915, 1997.
For a review of this recording, see: B538. (See also:
R68l, R95l, R139j, R176b, R177a, R203f, R209b, R227j,

R258i)

W260.   **Variations de concert sur l'hymne portugais, Op.** 91 (1869; Rio de Janeiro: Narciso y Napoleão, 1869; Mainz: B. Schott's Söhne, 1881 (arr. Arthur Napoleão). Pub. pl. no. 23264; New York: Arno Press and *The New York Times*, 1969 (*The Piano Works of Louis Moreau Gottschalk*, vol. 3, ed. Vera Brodsky Lawrence and Richard Jackson).)

Other indices: RO290, D157.
(See also: W42)

Performances

W260a.   June 18, 1869. Rio de Janeiro. Louis Moreau Gottschalk, piano.
The premiere of the work.

W260b.   August 8, 1869. Imperial Palace, Rio de Janeiro. Louis Moreau Gottschalk, piano.

W261.   **Regarde moi, idylle** (c1869; Rio de Janeiro: Narciso and Napoleão, c1870; lost.)

Other indices: RO224, D130.

W262.   **Variations sur le dernière pensée de Weber** (c1869; unpublished; lost.)

Other indices: RO293.
Note: The title suggests that this piece was based on a theme by Carl Maria von Weber.

Performances

W262a.   June 15, 1869. Rio de Janeiro. Louis Moreau Gottschalk, piano.

Bibliography

WB275.   Lange, Francisco Curt. *Vida y muerte de Louis Moreau*

Gottschalk en Rio de Janeiro, 1869. Mendoza,
Argentina: Universidad Nacional de Cuyo, 1951.
Lange (p. 259) documents Gottschalk's June 1869
performance of the piece in Rio de Janeiro (See: W262a).

W263.   **Spirito gentil** (c1869; unpublished; lost.)

Other indices: RO251.
Note: This work is based on a theme from Donizetti's opera *La
Favorita.*

Performances

W263a.   June 2, 1869. Rio de Janeiro. Louis Moreau Gottschalk,
piano.

W263b.   June 9, 1869. Rio de Janeiro. Louis Moreau Gottschalk,
piano.

Bibliography

WB276.   Lange, Francisco Curt. *Vida y muerte de Louis Moreau
Gottschalk en Rio de Janeiro, 1869.* Mendoza,
Argentina: Universidad Nacional de Cuyo, 1951.
Lange (pp. 249 and 258) documents Gottschalk's
June 1869 performances of the piece in Rio de Janeiro
(See: W263a and W263b).

W264.   **Madeleine, étude** (c1869; Rio de Janeiro: Narciso y Napoleão,
1870. Pub. pl. no. 110; New York: Arno Press and *The New York
Times,* 1969 (*The Piano Works of Louis Moreau Gottschalk,* vol. 3,
ed. Vera Brodsky Lawrence and Richard Jackson).)

Dedication: "Pour l'album de mon vieil ami et compagnon de Paris
Achilee Arnaud souvenir affectueux."
Other indices: RO140, D83.
Note: A publisher's note suggests that this may have been
Gottschalk's last composition.

W265.   **Sixième Ballade, Op. 83 (85)** (unknown date; Boston, after 1869 (as
Op. 83); Paris: Escudier, after 1869 (as Op. 83); Mainz: B. Schott's
Söhne, 1877 (as Op. 85). Pub. pl. no. 22255 (ed. Nicolás Ruiz

Espadero); New York: J.F. Fischer, 1909, transcribed for organ by
Henry B. Vincent; New York: Arno Press & *The New York Times*,
1969 (*The Piano Works of Louis Moreau Gottschalk*, vol. 1, ed. Vera
Brodsky Lawrence and Richard Jackson); New York: Dover
Publications, 1973 (*Piano Music of Louis Moreau Gottschalk*,
selected and introduced by Richard Jackson); New York: Chappell,
1973 (*L.M. Gottschalk: Ten Compositions for Pianoforte*, ed.
Amiram Rigai); Dayton, Ohio: McAfee Music, 1977 (*The Piano
Music of Louis Moreau Gottschalk Made Easy*, arr. David Krane).)

Duration: 7-1/4 minutes.
Manuscript fragment is located at the Americana Collection, Lincoln
Center Library and Museum of the Performing Arts, New
York.
Other indices: RO14, D10.

Recordings

R265a.   *The Piano Music of Louis Moreau Gottschalk.* Amiram
          Rigai, piano. 33-1/3 rpm phonodisc. Decca DL 10143,
          1967. Reissued as Decca DL 710143, 1970.
          For reviews of this recording, see: B327, B329,
          B330. (See also: R78d, R83a, R95b, R112a, R142d,
          R165d, R212b, R228d, R249a)

R265b.   *Gottschalk: 40 Works for Piano.* Alan Mandel, piano.
          Four 33-1/3 rpm phonodiscs. Desto DC 6470-73, 1969.
          Reissued on three compact discs, VoxBox CD3X 3033,
          1995.
          For reviews of this recording, see: B360-B362,
          B365, B366, B369-B371, B375, B388, B396, B523,
          B529. (See also: R67a, R68d, R69a, R78e, R83b, R92b,
          R95c, R100a, R103a, R105a, R112b, R135a, R139d,
          R142e, R144a, R146a, R153a, R156b, R165e, R167a,
          R175a, R191b, R192a, R195a, R203a, R204a, R212c,
          R216b, R220b, R227b, R228e, R229a, R230b, R232a,
          R255a, R256a, R257a, R258c)

R265c.   *Louis Moreau Gottschalk on Original Instruments.*
          Richard Burnett, piano. Compact disc. Amon Ra CD-
          SAR 32, 1988.
          All works are performed on instruments from

Gottschalk's era. (See also: R76c, R78i, R88c, R100c, R103c, R107a, R112d, R165m, R187a, R199a, R201b, R204b, R212f, R216f, R227f, R272a)

R265d.   *Gottschalk: Piano Music*. Philip Martin, piano. Compact disc. Hyperion 66459, 1991.
　　　　(See also: R78l, R88d, R107b, R112g, R142p, R165p, R167i, R178d, R191i, R192d, R201c, R220l, R272d)

Bibliography

WB277.   *A Manual of Music: Its History, Biography and Literature*, ed. W.M. Derthick. Chicago: Manual Publishing Co., 1888.
　　　　This book contains analyses of *Sixième Ballade*, *Marche de nuit*, *The Dying Poet*, and *The Last Hope*. The full score of *Danse ossianique* is also included. (See also: WB131, WB182, WB250, WB297)

W266.   **Septième Ballade, Op. 87** (unknown date; Paris: Escudier, after 1869; Mainz: B Schott's Söhne, 1877. Pub. pl. no. 22257 (ed. Nicolás Ruiz Espadero); New York: Arno Press & *The New York Times*, 1969 (*The Piano Works of Louis Moreau Gottschalk*, vol. 1, ed. Vera Brodsky Lawrence and Richard Jackson).)

Other indices: RO15, D11.

W267.   **Huitième Ballade, Op. 90** (unknown date; Paris: Escudier, after 1869; Mainz: Les Fils de B. Schott, 1877. Pub. pl. no. 22260 (ed. Nicolás Ruiz Espadero); New York: Arno Press & *The New York Times*, 1969 (*The Piano Works of Louis Moreau Gottschalk*, vol. 1, ed. Vera Brodsky Lawrence and Richard Jackson).)

Other indices: RO16, D12.

W268.   **Esquisses créoles** (unknown date; lost.)

Other indices: RO79.

W269.   **Fleur de lys, gallop brillante** (unknown date.)

Manuscript is located at the New York Public Library.
Note: This piece was written under Gottschalk's pseudonym Paul
  Ernest.
(See also: W315)

W270.   **Innocence, grand valse de concert** (unknown date; Brussels: Schott
Freres, n.d.; lost.)

Other indices: D75.
Note: Doyle (See: WB278, p. 293) raises the possibility that this
  was an alternate title for *The Maiden's Blush* (See: W230).

Bibliography

WB278.   Doyle, John G. *Louis Moreau Gottschalk 1829-1869: A*
      Bibliographical Study and Catalog of Works. Detroit:
      Information Coordinators, Inc. for the College Music
      Society, 1983.
         See note above.

W271.   **Étude in C-sharp minor** (unknown date; unpublished.)

Manuscript fragment is located at the New York Public Library.
Other indices: RO84.

W272.   **Mazurk in F-sharp minor** (unknown date; New York: New York
Public Library & Continuo Music Press, 1976 (*The Little Book of
Louis Moreau Gottschalk*, ed. Richard Jackson and Neil Ratliff).)

Manuscript is located at the New York Public Library.
Other indices: RO276 (as *Untitled piece No. 7 in F-sharp minor*),
  D93.

Recordings

R272a.   *Louis Moreau Gottschalk on Original Instruments.*
      Richard Burnett, piano. Compact disc. Amon Ra CD-
      SAR 32, 1988.
         All works are performed on instruments from
      Gottschalk's era. (See also: R76c, R78i, R88c, R100c,
      R103c, R107a, R112d, R165m, R187a, R199a, R201b,
      R204b, R212f, R216f, R227f, R265c)

R272b. *Great American Piano I. Louis Moreau Gottschalk. Vol. 7.* Leonard Pennario, piano. Compact disc. Angel Records CDM 7 64667 2, 1992. Material originally released on two 33-1/3 rpm phonodiscs as *Music of Louis Moreau Gottschalk.* Angel RL-32125, 1975.

For reviews of this recording, see: B441, B442, B446, B450, B452. (See also: R68i, R78m, R95i, R112f, R139i, R142t, R165u, R167d, R191g, R199b, R212i, R220g, R228n, R229c, R257e)

R272c. *DeGaetano Plays Gottschalk.* Robert DeGaetano, piano. Compact disc. Crystonyx 1002, 1998. Recorded January-February 1989 at Denver, New York.

(See also: R68n, R78p, R95m, R100g, R107c, R119c, R142w, R167h, R171b, R187c, R192e, R199d, R201d, R220j, R227k)

R272d. *Gottschalk: Piano Music.* Philip Martin, piano. Compact disc. Hyperion 66459, 1991.

(See also: R78l, R88d, R107b, R112g, R142p, R165p, R167i, R178d, R191i, R192d, R201c, R220l, R265d)

Works for Multiple Pianists

W273. **Le bananier, chanson nègre, Op. 5** (c1848; Paris: Leduc, 1855, arr. Ch. Czerny; Mainz: B. Schott's Söhne, n.d.; Rio de Janeiro: Narciso y Napoleão, c1869-70; New York: Peer-Southern, 1983 (*Gottschalk: Piano Duets*, vol. 2, ed. Eugene List).)

For piano, four hands.
Other indices: D14a.
(See also: W78)

Recordings

R273a.   *Louis Moreau Gottschalk: Music for Piano, Four-Hands.* David Apter, piano; Deborah Apter, piano. 33-1/3 rpm phonodisc. Musical Heritage Society MHS 3430, n.d. (before 1983).
      (See also: R277b, R282a, R291a, R300a, R302a, R305a, R310a)

R273b.   *The Monster Concert in Celebration of Louis Moreau Gottschalk.* Various performers. *Le bananier* performed by Joseph Werner, piano; Wade Peeples, piano. 33-1/3 rpm phonodisc. Musicmasters MM 20061, 1983. Reissued as Musical Heritage Society MHS 4924, 1984.
      Contains a number of Gottschalk compositions and other works from the era. (See also: R37d, R279a, R297b, R307a)

W274.   **"La chasse de jeune Henri"** (1849; unpublished.)

For two pianos.
Manuscript fragments and sketches are located at the New York
   Public Library.
Other indices: RO53, D32a.
Note: This work is based on themes from Etienne-Nicolas Méhul's
   opera *La chasse de jeune Henri*.
See also: W85)

Performances

W274a.   December 1849. Paris. Louis Moreau Gottschalk, piano;
   Neuman, piano.

W274b.   February 1850. Paris. Louis Moreau Gottschalk, piano;
   Alexandre Edouard Goria, piano. Several subsequent
   performances with Goria.

Bibliography

WB279.   Concert Review. *La France musicale* December 16,
   1849.
   This review documents the first Paris performance
   (See: W274a) and is cited by Doyle (See: B484, p. 274).

W275.   **La Scintilla, mazurka sentimentale (L'Étincelle), Op. 20/21**
   (1848-9; Boston: Oliver Ditson & Co., 1854; New York: Peer-
   Southern, 1983 (*Gottschalk: Piano Duets,* vol. 2, ed. Eugene List).)

For two pianos.
Duration: 3 minutes.
Other indices: RO80, D49a
Note: This is an arrangement of a work originally written for solo
   piano (See: W83).

Recordings

R275a.   *Louis Moreau Gottschalk.* Eugene List, piano; Joseph
   Werner, piano. Compact disc. Vanguard Classics OVC
   4051, 1992. Reissued as part of the two compact disc set
   Piano Music. Vanguard Classics 08 9143 72/08 9144-72,

1993. Contains material originally issued as *Louis Moreau Gottschalk: Music for Piano, Four Hands and Two Pianos*. 33-1/3 rpm phonodisc. Vanguard VSD 71218, 1977.

For reviews of this recording, see: B462 and B463. (See also: R34c, R37f, R100e, R220h, R250a, R282b, R291b, R292a, R300b, R302b, R305b, R307b, R310b)

R275b.   *Louis Moreau Gottschalk. American Piano Music.* Amiram Rigai, piano. Compact disc. Smithsonian Folkways 40803, 1992.

For a review of the original recording, see: B468. (See also: R68f, R69b, R78h, R83c, R88e, R95g, R112h, R133a, R142m, R165k, R167e, R191d, R212e, R227e, R228k, R249c)

W276.   **Jerusalem, grande fantaisie triomphale, Op. 84** (1850-51; Paris: Escudier, 1875.)

For two pianos.
Other indices: RO127, D77.
Manuscript sketches are located at the New York Public Library.
Note: *Jerusalem* is based on themes from Verdi's opera *I lombardi* and was originally written for solo piano (See: W93).

Performances

W276a.   July 1851. Bordeaux, France. Louis Moreau Gottschalk, piano; unidentified second pianist.
The premiere of the composition.

W276b.   February 11, 1853. New York City. Louis Moreau Gottschalk, piano; Richard Hoffman, piano.
This concert was Gottschalk's New York debut.

W277.   **Overture de *Guillaume Tell*, grande morceau de concert** (1850-54; New York: Wm. Hall & Son, 1864. Pub. pl. no. 6000; Boston: Oliver Ditson & Co., 1864. Pub. pl. no. 6000; New York: Arno Press and *The New York Times*, 1969 (*The Piano Works of Louis Moreau Gottschalk*, vol. 3, ed. Vera Brodsky Lawrence and Richard Jackson).)

For piano, four hands (also various combinations of multiple pianists).

Dedication: "To my friend Frederic E. Church."

Other indices: RO297, D160.

Note: This work is based on the overture to Rossini's opera *Guillaume Tell.*

Note: The published work evolved over time, apparently beginning as a January 1850, near improvisation by Gottschalk and violinist Henri Max-Mayer on themes from the Rossini work.

Performances

W277a. November 7, 1857. Ponce, Puerto Rico. Louis Moreau Gottschalk, piano; unidentified second pianist.

W277b. February 11, 1862. New York City. Louis Moreau Gottschalk, piano; unidentified second pianist.

W277c. April 5, 1864. Scranton, Pennsylvania. Louis Moreau Gottschalk, piano; unidentified second pianist.

W277d. March 2, 1973. Radio City Music Hall, New York City. Eugene List, Frank Glazer, Barry Snyder, Maria Luisa Faini, Nancy Bachus, Gregory Butler, Blair Cosman, Edward Easley, Wallace Gray, Michael Guiltinan, Neal Larrabee, Gladys Leventon, Elizabeth Riepe, Mary Jo Santuccio, Kimberly Schmidt, Joe Stuesy, Joseph Werner, pianos; Samuel Adler, conductor.

    Note: Recordings from the concert were also issued (See: R277a).

W277e. September 10, 1995. Gateways Music Festival, Eastman Theatre, Rochester, New York. Jennifer Blyth, Roy Eaton, Richard Fields, Raymond Jackson, Barbara Lister-Sink, Jerome Lowenthal, Kevin Sharpe, Barry Snyder, Nelita True, Karen Walwyn, pianos; Awadagin Pratt, conductor.

Recordings

R277a. *Monster Concert: Ten Pianos, Sixteen Pianists.* Eugene List, Frank Glazer, Barry Snyder, Maria Luisa Faini,

Nancy Bachus, Gregory Butler, Blair Cosman, Edward
Easley, Wallace Gray, Michael Guiltinan, Neal Larrabee,
Gladys Leventon, Elizabeth Riepe, Mary Jo Santuccio,
Kimberly Schmidt, Joe Stuessy, and Joseph Werner,
piano; Samuel Adler, conductor. 33-1/3 rpm phonodisc.
Columbia M/MQ 31726, 1973.

For reviews of this recording, see: B426, B427,
B429, B433, B458. With: *Ojos criollos* (See: R298a);
and works by miscellaneous other composers. (See also:
W277d)

R277b.   *Louis Moreau Gottschalk: Music for Piano, Four-Hands.*
David Apter, piano; Deborah Apter, piano. 33-1/3 rpm
phonodisc. Musical Heritage Society MHS 3430, n.d.
(before 1983).

(See also: R273a, R282a, R291a, R300a, R302a,
R305a, R310a)

R277c.   *Salon Classics for Piano.* Paul Hersh, piano; David
Montgomery, piano. 33-1/3 rpm phonodisc. Orion ORS
76247, n.d. (before 1983).

Bibliography

WB280.   Hensel, Octavia. The Life and Letters of Louis Moreau
Gottschalk. Boston: Oliver Ditson & Co., 1870.

Hensel (p. 194) quotes Chicago critic George
Upton's 1870 obituary of Gottschalk in which he refers to
the "splendid instrumentation" of the piece; the term
"instrumentation" being used at that time to mean
"arrangement."

WB281.   Minor, Andrew C. *Piano Concerts in New York City
1849-1865.* Thesis: University of Michigan, 1947.

Minor (p. 349) documents the February 1862
performance of the piece in New York City (See: 279b).

W278.   **Souvenirs d'Andalouise, Caprice de concert, Op. 22** (1851;
Mainz: B. Schott's Söhne, n.d.)

For piano, four hands.
Other indices: D148a.

Note: This was an arrangement of a work originally written for solo
piano (See: W100).

W279.   **El sitio de Zaragoza** (1851-2; unpublished; lost.)

For ten pianos.
Other indices: RO236.
Note: Although the ten piano parts are lost, parts of *El sitio de
Zaragoza* found their way in to *La jota aragonesa, caprice
espagnol* (See: W282) and *L'Union* (See: W220).
Sketches are located at the New York Public Library.
(See also: W101)

Performances

W279a.   May 2, 1979. Carnegie Hall, New York City. Victor
Savant and Cary Lewis, pianos.
Part of Eugene List's Monster Concert in celebration
of the Gottschalk Sesquicentennial. The performance was
of Savant's reconstruction of the piece. (See also:
R279a)

Recordings

R279a.   *The Monster Concert in Celebration of Louis Moreau
Gottschalk.* Various performers. *El sitio de Zaragoza*
performed by Victor Savant, piano; Cary Lewis, piano.
33-1/3 rpm phonodisc. Musicmasters MM 20061, 1983.
Reissued as Musical Heritage Society MHS 4924, 1984.
Contains a number of Gottschalk compositions and
other works from the era. The present recording is of
Victor Savant's two-piano arrangment of the present
work. (See also: R37d, R273b, R297b, R307a)

Bibliography

WB282.   Johnson, Harriett. "List Honors Gottschalk on a Grand
Scale." *New York Post* May 3, 1979:34.
A review of Eugene List's Monster Concert for the
Gottschalk sesquicentennial (See: W279a).

WB283.   Horowitz, Joseph. "Concert: Gottschalk Extravaganza."

New York Times May 4, 1979:C4.
A review of Eugene List's Monster Concert for the Gottschalk sesquicentennial (See: W279a).

WB284. Zakariasen, Bill. "Weary Gottschalk." *New York Daily News* May 4, 1979:Friday Section, 13.
A review of Eugene List's Monster Concert for the Gottschalk sesquicentennial (See: W279a).

WB285. Porterfield, Christopher. "Monster Rally: Pianists Celebrate Gottschalk." *Time* 113:106 (no. 20, May 14, 1979).
A review of Eugene List's Monster Concert for the Gottschalk sesquicentennial (See: W279a).

WB286. Suttoni, Charles. "*Cue* Reviews: Gottschalk Monster Concert." *Cue* p36 (May 25, 1979).
A review of Eugene List's Monster Concert for the Gottschalk sesquicentennial (See: W279a).

WB287. Anderson, William. "Speaking of Music: Monster Concert." *Stereo Review* 43:8 (July 1979).
A review of Eugene List's Monster Concert for the Gottschalk sesquicentennial (See: W279a).

WB288. Brockett, Clyde W. "Gottschalk in Madrid: A Tale of Ten Pianos." *Musical Quarterly* 75:279-315 (no. 3, fall 1991).
El sitio de Zaragoza played a prominent role in the success Gottschalk enjoyed in Spain in 1851 and 1852. The author also deals with Gottschalk's role as a sort of musical diplomat.

WB289. Brockett, Clyde W. "The Madrilene and Vallisolitan Composition of L.M. Gottschalk." *Revista de musicologia* 16:3554-3567 (no. 6, 1993).
Gottschalk's use of Spanish folk material is detailed.

W280. **La Vallisoletana** (1852; unpublished; lost.)

For two pianos.

Performances

W280a.   1852. Teatro del Principe, Madrid, Spain. Louis Moreau
Gottschalk, piano; J.G. Miralles, piano.
The premiere performance.

Bibliography

WB290.   Brockett, Clyde W. "The Madrilene and Vallisolitan
Composition of L.M. Gottschalk." *Revista de
musicologia* 16:3554-3567 (no. 6, 1993).
Gottschalk's use of Spanish folk material is detailed.

W281.   Valse di bravura (1852; unpublished; lost.)

For two pianos.
Other indices: RO282.

Bibliography

WB291.   Hensel, Octavia. *The Life and Letters of Louis Moreau
Gottschalk.* Boston: Oliver Ditson, 1870.
Hensel (p. 47) provides commentary on Gottschalk's
composition of this work, a task that reportedly took only
four hours.

W282.   La jota aragonesa, caprice espagnol, Op. 14 (1852; Mainz, B.
Schott's Söhne, 1876. Pub. pl. no. 21804; New York: Arno Press
and *The New York Times*, 1969 (*The Piano Works of Louis Moreau
Gottschalk*, vol. 3, ed. Vera Brodsky Lawrence and Richard
Jackson); New York: Peer-Southern, 1982 (*Gottschalk: Piano
Duets*, vol. 1, ed. Eugene List).)

For piano, four hands.
Duration: 3 minutes.
Other indices: RO131, D79a.
Derived from *El sitio de Zaragoza* (See: W279)
(See also: W105)

Recordings

R282a.   *Louis Moreau Gottschalk: Music for Piano, Four-Hands.*

David Apter, piano; Deborah Apter, piano. 33-1/3 rpm phonodisc. Musical Heritage Society MHS 3430, n.d. (before 1983).
(See also: R273a, R277b, R291a, R300a, R302a, R305a, R310a)

R282b.   *Louis Moreau Gottschalk.* Eugene List, piano; Cary Lewis, piano. Compact disc. Vanguard Classics OVC 4051, 1992. Reissued as part of the two compact disc set *Piano Music.* Vanguard Classics 08 9143 72/08 9144-72, 1993. Contains material originally issued as *Louis Moreau Gottschalk: Music for Piano, Four Hands and Two Pianos.* 33-1/3 rpm phonodisc. Vanguard VSD 71218, 1977.
For reviews of this recording, see: B462 and B463.
(See also: R34c, R37f, R100e, R220h, R250a, R275a, R291b, R292a, R300b, R302b, R305b, R307b, R310b)

Bibliography

WB292.   Campbell, Mary. "10 Pianists Join in Performing Gottschalk's Work." *Star-Gazette* (Elmira, New York) September 25, 1969:38.

WB293.   Henahan, Daniel. "16 Pianists Tuning Up for Saragossa." *New York Times* September 24, 1969:50.

WB294.   "Bulletin Board: The Siege of Saragossa." *Music Educators Journal* 56:67 (December 1969).

W283.   **Souvenirs de Bellini (Fantaisie sur *La Sonnambula*)** (1852; unpublished; lost.)

For two pianos?
Other indices: RO244.
Note: This work was based on themes from Bellini's opera *La Sonnambula.*
(See also: W289)

Performances

W283a.   June 13, 1852. Madrid, Spain. Louis Moreau Gottschalk, piano; possible other performers unidentified.

W283b.   November 21, 1865. Lima, Peru. Louis Moreau
Gottschalk, piano; possible other performers unidentified.

Bibliography

WB295.   Lange, Francisco Curt. *Vida y muerte de Louis Moreau
Gottschalk en Rio de Janeiro, 1869.* Mendoza,
Argentina: Universidad Nacional de Cuyo, 1951.
Lange (p. 281) documents the November 1865
performance of the work in Lima, Peru (See: W283b).

W284.   **Forest Glade Polka, polka brillante, Op. 25** (1853; Philadelphia:
J.E. Gould, 1853.)

For piano, four hands.
Other indices: D58a.
Note: This was an arrangement by J.C. Viereck on a work originally
composed for solo piano (See: W122).

W285.   **Grand National Symphony for Ten Pianos, Bunker's Hill** (1853-
4; unpublished and lost.)

For ten pianos.
Other indices: RO31.
Note: *Bunker's Hill* was apparently a revision of *El sitio de
Zaragoza* (See: W279), with American national airs and the
Stephen Foster melodies "Oh! Susanna" and "Old Folks at
Home" substituted for the earlier Spanish themes.
(See also: W121)

Performances

W285a.   February 1854. New Orleans. Louis Moreau Gottschalk,
piano; nine other pianists.

W286.   **Marche funèbre, Op. 61** (1853-4; Mainz: B Schott's Söhne, 1875;
New York: Peer-Southern, 1982 (*Gottschalk: Piano Duets*, vol. 2,
ed. Eugene List).)

For piano, four hands.
Other indices: RO149, D90c.

Note: The present is the four-hand arrangement of the piano solo
Marche funèbre, Op. 61 (See: W132)
(See also: W133)

W287. **Recuerdos de Puerto-Príncipe** (1854; unpublished; lost.)

For six pianos.

Performances

W287a. December 4, 1854. Puerto Príncipe, Cuba. Louis Moreau
Gottschalk, piano; other performers unidentified.

W287b. December 11, 1854. Puerto Príncipe, Cuba. Louis
Moreau Gottschalk, piano; other performers unidentified.

Bibliography

WB296. Starr, S. Frederick. *Bamboula! The Life and Times of
Louis Moreau Gottschalk.* New York: Oxford University
Press, 1995. Paperback edition: Urbana: University of
Illinois Press, 2000.
      Starr (p. 192) cites evidence from Cuban news
clippings in the New York Public Library's Gottschalk
collection of Gottschalk's Cuban performances of this
piece (See: W287a and W287b).

W288. **The Last Hope, Religious Meditation** (1854; New York: William
Hall & Son, 1856. Pub. pl. no. 3515; Boston: Oliver Ditson & Co.,
1904. Pub. pl. no. 6743; New York: Arno Press and *The New York
Times*, 1969 (*The Piano Works of Louis Moreau Gottschalk*, vol. 3,
ed. Vera Brodsky Lawrence and Richard Jackson).)

For piano, four hands.
Duration: 6 minutes.
Other indices: RO134, D80a.
(See also: W139)

Bibliography

WB297. *A Manual of Music: Its History, Biography and
Literature*, ed. W.M. Derthick. Chicago: Manual

Publishing Co., 1888.

This book contains analyses of *The Last Hope*, *Marche de nuit*, *The Dying Poet*, and *Sixième Ballade*. The full score of *Danse ossianique* is also included. (See also: WB131, WB182, WB250, WB277)

W289.   Gloires italiennes (1854; unpublished; lost.)

For two pianos.
Other indices: RO105.
Note: This lost work might be related to *Souvenirs de Bellini* (See: W283).

Performances

W289a.   December 20, 1855. New York City. Louis Moreau Gottschalk, piano; Karl Wels, piano.

W289b.   December 28, 1855. New York City. Louis Moreau Gottschalk, piano; Karl Wels, piano.

W289c.   June 21, 1869. Rio de Janeiro. Louis Moreau Gottschalk, piano; second pianist unidentified.

W290.   Le banjo, grotesque fantaisie, esquisse américaine (An American Sketch), Op. 15 (1854-5; New York: J. Fischer and Bro., 1935, arr. Jerome Moross.)

For two pianos.
Duration: 3-3/4 minutes.
Other indices: RO23, D15.
(See also: W142)
Note: *Le banjo* uses themes from Stephen Foster's "Camptown Races" and the spiritual "Roll, Jordan, Roll!"

W291.   Marche de nuit, Op. 17 (1855; Mainz, B. Schott's Söhne, 1873; New York: Thos. J. Hall, 1876; Boston: Ditson, 1904; New York: Peer-Southern, 1982 (*Gottschalk: Piano Duets*, vol. 1, ed. Eugene List).)

For piano, four hands.
Other indices: RO151, D89a.

Note: Although Offergeld suggests the existence of this four-hand arrangment of *Marche de nuit*, he does not provide the work with a separate index number.
(See also: W146)

Recordings

R291a.   *Louis Moreau Gottschalk: Music for Piano, Four-Hands.* David Apter, piano; Deborah Apter, piano. 33-1/3 rpm phonodisc. Musical Heritage Society MHS 3430, n.d. (before 1983).
    (See also: R273a, R277b, R282a, R300a, R302a, R305a, R310a)

R291b.   *Louis Moreau Gottschalk.* Eugene List, piano; Joseph Werner, piano. Compact disc. Vanguard Classics OVC 4051, 1992. Reissued as part of the two compact disc set *Piano Music.* Vanguard Classics 08 9143 72/08 9144-72, 1993. Contains material originally issued as *Louis Moreau Gottschalk: Music for Piano, Four Hands and Two Pianos.* 33-1/3 rpm phonodisc. Vanguard VSD 71218, 1977.
    For reviews of this recording, see: B462 and B463.
    (See also: R34c, R37f, R100e, R220h, R250a, R275a, R282b, R292a, R300b, R302b, R305b, R307b, R310b)

W292.   Printemps d'amour, mazurka, caprice de concert, Op. 40 (1855; Boston: Oliver Ditson & Co., c1873; Mainz: B. Schott's Söhne, n.d.)

For piano, four hands.
Other indices: RO214, D125a.
Note: Although Offergeld mentions the existence of this arrangment of the piano solo *Printemps d'amour* (See: W149), he does not provide the arrangment with a separate index number.

Recordings

R292a.   *Louis Moreau Gottschalk.* Eugene List, piano; Cary Lewis, piano. Compact disc. Vanguard Classics OVC 4051, 1992. Reissued as part of the two compact disc set *Piano Music.* Vanguard Classics 08 9143 72/08 9144-72,

1993. Contains material originally issued as *Louis Moreau Gottschalk: Music for Piano, Four Hands and Two Pianos*. 33-1/3 rpm phonodisc. Vanguard VSD 71218, 1977.

For reviews of this recording, see: B462 and B463. (See also: R34c, R37f, R100e, R220h, R250a, R275a, R282b, R291b, R300b, R302b, R305b, R307b, R310b)

W293.   Gran Galopada según Quidant (c1855-56; unpublished; lost.)

For two pianos.
Other indices: RO109, D103a.
Note: Offergeld and Doyle suggest that this piece may have been closely related to *Tournament Galop* (See: W95).

Performances

W293a.   May 20, 1856. New York City. Louis Moreau Gottschalk, piano; unidentified second pianist.

W293b.   January 29, 1860. Havana. Louis Moreau Gottschalk, piano; Nicolás Ruiz Espadero, piano.

Bibliography

WB298.   Fors, Luis Ricardo. *Gottschalk*. Havana: La Propaganda Literaria; New York: "La Razalatina," 1880. English translation by J. Peter Heinrich. Rochester, New York, 1973.

Fors suggests that, contrary to the title, this piece was not so much of a transcription of an A. Quidant galop as it was an original composition.

WB299.   Minor, Andrew C. *Piano Concerts in New York City, 1849-1865*. Thesis: University of Michigan, 1947.

Minor (p. 188) documents Gottschalk's May 1856 performance in New York City (See: W293a).

W294.   *Il Trovatore*, Grand Duo di bravura (c1856; unpublished; lost.)

For two pianos?
Other indices: RO267.

Note: Offergeld (See: WB301) discusses the apparent confusion over the authorship and the very existence of this work. (See also: WB300)

Note: The piece was based on themes from Verdi's opera *Il Trovatore* and may have been arranged for either one or two pianos.

(See also: W159)

Bibliography

WB300. Hoffman, Richard. *Some Musical Recollections of Fifty Years.* New York: Scribner's,1910. Reprinted with new introductory material by Frank E. Kirby and John G. Doyle. Detroit: Information Coordinators, 1976.

Although Hoffman's book deals relatively little with Gottschalk, it does suggest that the *Grand Duo di bravura* was jointly composed by Gottschalk and Sigismund Thalberg.

WB301. Offergeld, Robert. *The Centennial Catalogue of the Published and Unpublished Compositions of Louis Moreau Gottschalk.* New York: Stereo Review, 1970.

Offergeld offers extensive commentary on the confusion over the authorship of the work. (See note above)

WB302. Suttoni, Charles R. *Piano and Opera: A Study of the Piano Fantaisies Written on Opera Themes in the Romantic Era.* Dissertation: New York University, 1973.

W295. **Miserere du *Trovatore*, paraphrase de concert, Op. 52** (1856-57; New York: William Hall & Son, 1864(?); Pub. pl. no. 54253-14; Boston: Oliver Ditson & Co., 1864(?). Pub. pl. no. 54253-14; Mainz: B. Schott's Söhne, 1878.)

For piano, four hands.
Other indices: RO172, D97a.
Note: This work is based on themes from Guiseppe Verdi's opera *Il Trovatore.*
Note: Copies of all of the published editions of this piece seem to have vanished.
(See also: W162)

Performances

W295a.   December 26, 1856. New York City. Louis Moreau
Gottschalk, piano; Sigismond Thalberg, piano.
(See also: WB303)

Bibliography

WB303.   Hoffman, Richard. *Some Musical Recollections of Fifty
Years.* New York: Scribner's, 1910. Reprinted with new
introduction by Frank E. Kirby and John G. Doyle.
Detroit: Information Coordinators, 1976.
Hoffman (reprint pp. 130-131) documented
Gottschalk and Thalberg's performance of piece (See:
W295a), writing that "a remarkable double shake which
Thalberg played in the middle of the piano, while
Gottschalk was flying all over the keyboard in the 'Anvil
Chorus,' produced the most prodigious volume of tone I
ever heard from the piano."

WB304.   Schonberg, Harold C. "Facts and Fantaisies About
Pianists in Pairs." *New York Times* February 13, 1977:II,
21.

W296.   **Overture d'*Oberon*, Op. 83** (1857; Boston: Oliver Ditson & Co.,
1873, ed. C. Gottschalk Peterson. Pub. pl. no. 28009; Paris:
Escudier, 1875; New York: Arno Press and *The New York Times*,
1969 (*The Piano Works of Louis Moreau Gottschalk*, vol. 4, ed. Vera
Brodsky Lawrence and Richard Jackson).)

For piano, four hands.
Other indices: RO183, D110.
Note: This work is a transcription of the overture of Carl Maria von
Weber's opera *Oberon*.

Performances

W296a.   March 5, 1864. New York City. Louis Moreau
Gottschalk, piano; Eugénie Barnetche, piano.

W296b.   1865. San Franciso. Louis Moreau Gottschalk, piano;
unidentified second pianist.

W296c.   November 18, 1869.   Rio de Janeiro.   Louis Moreau
         Gottschalk, piano; unidentified second pianist.

Bibliography

WB305.   Lange, Francisco Curt. *Vida y muerte de Louis Moreau
         Gottschalk en Rio de Janeiro, 1869*.   Mendoza,
         Argentina: Universidad Nacional de Cuyo, 1951.
              Lange documents Gottschalk's 1869 Rio de Janeiro
         performance of the piece (See: W296c).

WB306.   Gottschalk, Louis Moreau. *Notes of a Pianist*, ed. Jeanne
         Behrend.   New York: Alfred A. Knopf, 1964.
              Behrend (p. 315) mentions the 1865 San Francisco
         performance (See: W296b).

**W297.   Symphonie romantique [Symphony No. 1] ("La nuit des
          tropiques") (1858-9; unpublished.)**

For two pianos.
Contents: I. Andante ("Noche en los Tropicos"), II. Allegro
     moderato ("Festa Criolla").
Other indices: RO256.
Note: Two arrangements exist: (1) by Nicolás Ruiz Espadero; and
     (2) a 1948 arrangement based on the manuscript of the
     symphony and the Espadero version by John Kirkpatrick.
(See: W34)

Performances

W297a.   December 22, 1948.   John Kirkpatrick, piano; Arthur
         Loesser, piano.

Recordings

R297a.   *Night in the Tropics and The Ornithological Combat of
         Kings*.   Anthony Paratore, piano; Joseph Paratore, piano.
         33-1/3 rpm phonodisc.   New World Records NW 208,
         1978.
              With Anthony Philip Heinrich's *The Ornithological
         Combat of Kings*.   For a review of this recording, see:
         B469.

R297b.   *The Monster Concert in Celebration of Louis Moreau Gottschalk.* Various performers. The second movement of *Symphony No. 1* performed by ten pianists; Eugene List, director. 33-1/3 rpm phonodisc. Musicmasters MM 20061, 1983. Reissued as Musical Heritage Society MHS 4924, 1984.

Contains a number of Gottschalk compositions and other works from the era. (See also: R37d, R273b, R279a, R307a)

W298.   Ojos criollos (Les yeux créoles), danse cubaine, caprice brillant, contradanza, Op. 37 (1859; New York: Wm. Hall & Son, 1860. Pub. pl. no. 4592; New York: Arno Press and *The New York Times,* 1969 (*The Piano Works of Louis Moreau Gottschalk,* vol. 4, ed. Vera Brodsky Lawrence and Richard Jackson).)

For piano, four hands.
Duration: 2 minutes.
Other indices: RO184, D105.
(See also: W191)

Performances

W298a.   April 17, 1862. Havana. Thirty-nine pianists under the leadership of Louis Moreau Gottschalk.

W298b.   March 2, 1973. Radio City Music Hall, New York City. Eugene List, Frank Glazer, Barry Snyder, Maria Luisa Faini, Nancy Bachus, Gregory Butler, Blair Cosman, Edward Easley, Wallace Gray, Michael Guiltinan, Neal Larrabee, Gladys Leventon, Elizabeth Riepe, Mary Jo Santuccio, Kimberly Schmidt, Joe Stuesy, Joseph Werner, pianos; Samuel Adler, conductor.

Note: Recordings from the concert were also issued (See: R298a).

W298c.   September 10, 1995. Gateways Music Festival, Eastman Theatre, Rochester, New York. Jennifer Blyth, Roy Eaton, Richard Fields, Raymond Jackson, Barbara Lister-Sink, Jerome Lowenthal, Kevin Sharpe, Barry Snyder, Nelita True, Karen Walwyn, pianos; Awadagin Pratt, conductor.

Recordings

R298a.   *Monster Concert: Ten Pianos, Sixteen Pianists.* Eugene
List, Frank Glazer, Barry Snyder, Maria Luisa Faini,
Nancy Bachus, Gregory Butler, Blair Cosman, Edward
Easley, Wallace Gray, Michael Guiltinan, Neal Larrabee,
Gladys Leventon, Elizabeth Riepe, Mary Jo Santuccio,
Kimberly Schmidt, Joe Stuessy, and Joseph Werner,
piano; Samuel Adler, conductor. 33-1/3 rpm phonodisc.
Columbia M/MQ 31726, 1973.

    For reviews of this recording, see: B426, B427,
B429, B433, B458. With: *Overture de "Guillaume Tell"*
(See: R277e) and works by miscellaneous other
composers.

R298b.   *A Gottschalk Festival.* Eugene List, piano; Cary Lewis or
Brady Millican, piano; Wiener Staatsopernorchester; Igor
Buketoff, conductor. Two compact discs. Vox Box
5009, n.d.

    (See also: R4a, R34e, R36b, R37g, R41a, R42a,
R44a, R191h, R220m, R228t, R258k, R302d, R305c,
R310c)

Bibliography

WB307.   Loggins, Vernon. *Where the Word Ends.* Baton Rouge:
Louisiana State University Press, 1958.

    Loggins documents the April 1862 performance in
Havana (See: W298a).

WB308.   McGraw, Cameron. "A Selected List of 4-Hand Music."
Piano Quarterly n91:17-27 (Fall 1975).

    The author praises this work, along with *La Gallina*
and *Réponds-moi.* (See also: WB310 and WB312)

W299.   **La favorita, grand fantaisie triomphale, Op. 68** (1859; Mainz: B.
Schott's Söhne, c1878. Pub. pl. no. 22404.)

For piano, four hands.
Other indices: D54a.
Note: This is an arrangment by H. Rupp of a composition originally
     for piano, two hands, and is based on themes from Donizetti's

opera *La favorita*.
(See also: W194)

W300.   **Réponds-moi (Dì que sì), danse cubaine, caprice brillant, Op. 50**
(1859; Havana: Edelmann, 1861; New York: William Hall & Son,
1864. Pub. pl. no. 5966; Mainz: B. Schott's Söhne, 1865 (as Op. 50);
Paris: Escudier, 1869 (as Op. 50); Boston: Oliver Ditson & Co.,
c1888. Pub. pl. no. 52963-6; New York: Peer-Southern, 1982
(*Gottschalk: Piano Duets*, vol. 1, ed. Eugene List).)

For piano, four hands.
Dedicated to Ernesto Saporta (Edelmann edition).
Dedicated to Madame F. Chickering (William Hall edition).
Other indices: RO225, D131.
(See also: W193)

Performances

W300a.   October 3, 1861. Guanabacoa, Cuba.Louis Moreau
Gottschalk, piano; unidentified second pianist.

W300b.   April 30, 1862. New York City. Louis Moreau
Gottschalk, piano; unidentified second pianist.

Recordings

R300a.   *Louis Moreau Gottschalk: Music for Piano, Four-Hands.*
David Apter, piano; Deborah Apter, piano. 33-1/3 rpm
phonodisc. Musical Heritage Society MHS 3430, n.d.
(before 1983).
(See also: R273a, R277b, R282a, R291a, R302a,
R305a, R310a)

R300b.   *Louis Moreau Gottschalk.* Eugene List, piano; Cary
Lewis, piano. Compact disc. Vanguard Classics OVC
4051, 1992. Reissued as part of the two compact disc set
Piano Music. Vanguard Classics 08 9143 72/08 9144-72,
1993. Contains material originally issued as *Louis
Moreau Gottschalk: Music for Piano, Four Hands and
Two Pianos.* 33-1/3 rpm phonodisc. Vanguard VSD
71218, 1977.
For reviews of this recording, see: B462 and B463.

(See also: R34c, R37f, R100e, R220h, R250a, R275a,
R282b, R291b, R292a, R302b, R305b, R307b, R310b)

Bibliography

WB309.   Concert Preview. *Gaceta de la Habana* October 2, 1861.
This preview, cited by Doyle, mentions Gottschalk's
October 3, 1861 performance of the piece in Havana (See:
W300a).

WB310.   Minor, Andrew C. *Piano Concerts in New York City,
1849-1865.* Thesis: University of Michigan, 1947.
Minor (p. 183) documents Gottschalk's April 1862
performance in New York City (See: W300b).

WB311.   McGraw, Cameron.   "A Selected List of 4-Hand Music."
Piano Quarterly n91:17-27 (Fall 1975).
The author praises this work, along with *Ojos criollos*
and *La Gallina*.   (See also: WB308 and WB312)

W301.   **Adiós a la Habana** (c1859-61; unpublished?)

For piano, four hands.
Manuscript sketches are located at the New York Public Library.
Other indices: D1.
Note: Doyle places the composition date between 1859 and 1861
based on Gottschalk's thematic borrowing during the period.
Offergeld does not list the work.

W302.   **La Gallina (The Hen), danse cubaine, Op. 53** (1859-63; New
York: William Hall & Son, 1865. Pub. pl. no. 5992; Boston: Oliver
Ditson & Co., 1865; Paris: Escudier, c1866 (as Op. 53); Mainz: B.
Schott's Söhne, c1866 (as Op. 53); New York: Arno Press and *The
New York Times*, 1969 (*The Piano Works of Louis Moreau
Gottschalk*, vol. 2, ed. Vera Brodsky Lawrence and Richard
Jackson); Chapel Hill, North Carolina: Hinshaw Music, 1975 (*Piano
Music in Nineteenth-Century America*, vol. 2, ed. Maurice Hinson);
New York: Peer-Southern, 1982 (*Gottschalk: Piano Duets*, vol. 1,
ed. Eugene List).)

For piano, four hands.
Dedication: "A las señoritas de Galarraga (de la Habana)."

Other indices: RO100, D60.
Duration: 3 minutes.
Sketches are located at the New York Public Library.
(See also: W204)

Performances

W302a.   October 29, 1864. Academy of Music, Philadelphia.
Louis Moreau Gottschalk, piano; Lassere, piano.

W302b.   March 2, 1973. Radio City Music Hall, New York City.
Eugene List, Frank Glazer, Barry Snyder, Maria Luisa
Faini, Nancy Bachus, Gregory Butler, Blair Cosman,
Edward Easley, Wallace Gray, Michael Guiltinan, Neal
Larrabee, Gladys Leventon, Elizabeth Riepe, Mary Jo
Santuccio, Kimberly Schmidt, Joe Stuesy, Joseph Werner,
pianos; Samuel Adler, conductor.

W302c.   September 14, 1976. Heeren Recital Hall, Southern
Baptist Theological Seminary. Maurice Hinson, piano;
Ron Boud, piano.

Recordings

R302a.   *Louis Moreau Gottschalk: Music for Piano, Four-Hands.*
David Apter, piano; Deborah Apter, piano. 33-1/3 rpm
phonodisc. Musical Heritage Society MHS 3430, n.d.
(before 1983).
        (See also: R273a, R277b, R282a, R291a, R300a,
R305a, R310a)

R302b.   *Louis Moreau Gottschalk.* Eugene List, piano; Joseph
Werner, piano. Compact disc. Vanguard Classics OVC
4051, 1992. Reissued as part of the two compact disc set
Piano Music. Vanguard Classics 08 9143 72/08 9144-72,
1993. Contains material originally issued as *Louis
Moreau Gottschalk: Music for Piano, Four Hands and
Two Pianos.* 33-1/3 rpm phonodisc. Vanguard VSD
71218, 1977.
        For reviews of this recording, see: B462 and B463.
(See also: R34c, R37f, R100e, R220h, R250a, R275a,
R282b, R291b, R292a, R300b, R305b, R307b, R310b)

R302c.   *Creole Music.* Frank French, piano; Scott Kirby, piano. Compact disc. VRD 2006, 1997.

R302d.   *A Gottschalk Festival.* Eugene List, piano; Cary Lewis or Brady Millican, piano. Two compact discs. Vox Box 5009, n.d.

        (See also: R4a, R34e, R36b, R37g, R41a, R42a, R44a, R191h, R220m, R228t, R258k, R298b, R305c, R310c)

Bibliography

WB312.   McGraw, Cameron. "A Selected List of 4-Hand Music." *Piano Quarterly* n91:17-27 (Fall 1975).

        The author praises this work, along with *Ojos criollos* and *Réponds-moi.* (See also: WB308 and WB311)

W303.   *La Ballo in Maschera,* **fantaisie triomphale** (1862; lost.)

For two pianos.
Other indices: RO18.
Note: Based on themes from the 1857-8 Giuseppe Verdi melodrama *Un ballo in maschera.*
(See also: W54 and W219)

Performances

W303a.   July 1863. New York City. Louis Moreau Gottschalk, piano; Harry Sanderson, piano.

W304.   **Marche de** *Tannhäuser* (c1863; unpublished.)

For multiple pianos.
Manuscript fragment is located at the New York Public Library.
Other indices: D152.
Note: Thematic material is based on Richard Wagner's *Tannhäuser.*
(See also: W39)

Performances

W304a.   April 20, 1863. Irving Hall, New York City. Louis Moreau Gottschalk, piano; three unidentified pianists.

W305.   **Radieuse, grande valse de concert, Op.** 72 (c1863-4; Boston: Oliver Ditson & Co., 1865; Paris: Escudier, 1873 (as Op. 72); Mainz: B. Schott's Söhne, c1873; New York: Arno Press and *The New York Times*, 1969 (*The Piano Works of Louis Moreau Gottschalk*, vol. 4, ed. Vera Brodsky Lawrence and Richard Jackson); New York: Peer-Southern, 1982 (*Gottschalk: Piano Duets*, vol. 1, ed. Eugene List).)

For piano, four hands.
Duration: 5-1/2 minutes.
Dedicated to Sarah and Hattie Monteath, Albany, N.Y.
Other indices: RO217, D127.
Note: This piece originally was published under Gottschalk's pseudonym Seven Octaves.
(See also: W232)

Recordings

R305a.   *Louis Moreau Gottschalk: Music for Piano, Four-Hands.* David Apter, piano; Deborah Apter, piano. 33-1/3 rpm phonodisc. Musical Heritage Society MHS 3430, n.d. (before 1983).
　　　(See also: R273a, R277b, R282a, R291a, R300a, R302a, R310a)

R305b.   *Louis Moreau Gottschalk.* Eugene List, piano; Joseph Werner, piano. Compact disc. Vanguard Classics OVC 4051, 1992. Reissued as part of the two compact disc set *Piano Music.* Vanguard Classics 08 9143 72/08 9144-72, 1993. Contains material originally issued as *Louis Moreau Gottschalk: Music for Piano, Four Hands and Two Pianos.* 33-1/3 rpm phonodisc. Vanguard VSD 71218, 1977.
　　　For reviews of this recording, see: B462 and B463.
(See also: R34c, R37f, R100e, R220h, R250a, R275a, R282b, R291b, R292a, R300b, R302b, R307b, R310b)

R305c.   *A Gottschalk Festival.* Eugene List, piano; Cary Lewis or Brady Millican, piano. Two compact discs. Vox Box 5009, n.d.
　　　(See also: R4a, R34e, R36b, R37g, R41a, R42a, R44a, R191h, R220m, R228t, R258k, R298b, R302d,

R310c)

W306. **Im Hochland** (c1863-4; unpublished; lost.)

For two pianos.
Other indices: RO121.
Note: This piece is based on themes from Niels Gade's *Scotch Symphony*.

Performances

W306a. Early 1864. Philadelphia. Louis Moreau Gottschalk, piano; Carl Wolfsohn, piano.

Bibliography

WB313. Hensel, Octavia. *Life and Letters of Louis Moreau Gottschalk*. Boston: Oliver Ditson & Co., 1870.
Hensel (p. 108) documents Gottschalk's 1864 performance in Philadelphia (See: W306a).

W307. **Orfa, grande polka, Op. 71** (c1863-4; Mainz: B. Schott's Söhne, 1876; New York: Peer-Southern, 1982 (*Gottschalk: Piano Duets*, vol. 1, ed. Eugene List).)

For piano, four hands.
Other indices: RO186, D108a.
(See also: W231)

Recordings

R307a. *The Monster Concert in Celebration of Louis Moreau Gottschalk*. Various performers. *Orfa, grande polka* performed by Kimberly Schmidt, piano; James Anagnoson, piano. 33-1/3 rpm phonodisc. Musicmasters MM 20061, 1983. Reissued as Musical Heritage Society MHS 4924, 1984.
Contains a number of Gottschalk compositions and other works from the era. (See also: R37d, R273b, R279a, R297b)

R307b. *Louis Moreau Gottschalk*. Eugene List, piano; Cary Lewis, piano. Compact disc. Vanguard Classics OVC

4051, 1992. Reissued as part of the two compact disc set
Piano Music. Vanguard Classics 08 9143 72/08 9144-72,
1993. Contains material originally issued as *Louis
Moreau Gottschalk: Music for Piano, Four Hands and
Two Pianos.* 33-1/3 rpm phonodisc. Vanguard VSD
71218, 1977.
    For reviews of this recording, see: B462 and B463.
(See also: R34c, R37f, R100e, R220h, R250a, R275a,
R282b, R291b, R292a, R300b, R302b, R305b, R310b)

W308.   **Grande Marche de** *Faust* (c1864; unpublished; lost.)

For four pianos.
Other indices: RO111.
Note: This piece is based on themes from Gounod's opera *Faust*.
(See also: W40)

Performances

W308a.   April 17, 1864. Newburgh, New York. Louis Moreau
    Gottschalk, piano; other unidentified pianists.

Bibliography

WB314.   Gottschalk, Louis Moreau. *Notes of a Pianist*, ed. Jeanne
    Behrend. New York: Alfred A. Knopf, 1964.
        Gottschalk (p. 190) mentions the April 1864
    performance of the piece (See: W308a).

W309.   **Ses yeux, polka de concert, Op. 66** (1865; New York: Thomas J.
Hall, 1875. Pub. pl. no. 6670; New York: Peer-Southern, 1983
(*Gottschalk: Piano Duets*, vol. 2, ed. Eugene List).)

For piano, four hands.
Dedicated to Marietta and Hattie Littlefield of New York.
Other indices: D137.
(See also: W237 and W310)

W310.   **Ses yeux, polka de concert, Op. 66** (1865-69; Rio de Janeiro:
Narciso y Napoleão, c1870; Mainz: B. Schott's Söhne, c1873. Pub.
pl. no. 21119.)

For two pianos.
Other indices: RO234, D137.
Note: This was apparently a revision of W309 for two pianos.
(See also: W237)

Performances

W310a.   November 21, 1865. Lima, Peru. Louis Moreau
           Gottschalk, piano; unidentified second pianist.

W310b.   December 22, 1865. Lima, Peru. Louis Moreau
           Gottschalk, piano; unidentified second pianist.

W310c.   June 15, 1869. Rio de Janeiro. Louis Moreau Gottschalk,
           piano; unidentified second pianist.

Recordings

R310a.   *Louis Moreau Gottschalk: Music for Piano, Four-Hands.*
           David Apter, piano; Deborah Apter, piano. 33-1/3 rpm
           phonodisc. Musical Heritage Society MHS 3430, n.d.
           (before 1983).
               (See also: R273a, R277b, R282a, R291a, R300a,
           R302a, R305a)

R310b.   *Louis Moreau Gottschalk.* Eugene List, piano; Joseph
           Werner, piano. Compact disc. Vanguard Classics OVC
           4051, 1992. Reissued as part of the two compact disc set
           Piano Music. Vanguard Classics 08 9143 72/08 9144-72,
           1993. Contains material originally issued as *Louis
           Moreau Gottschalk: Music for Piano, Four Hands and
           Two Pianos.* 33-1/3 rpm phonodisc. Vanguard VSD
           71218, 1977.
               For reviews of this recording, see: B462 and B463.
           (See also: R34c, R37f, R100e, R220h, R250a, R275a,
           R282b, R291b, R292a, R300b, R302b, R305b, R307b)

R310c.   *A Gottschalk Festival.* Eugene List, piano; Cary Lewis or
           Brady Millican, piano. Two compact discs. Vox Box
           5009.

(See also: R4a, R34e, R36b, R37g, R41a, R42a, R44a, R191h, R220m, R228t, R258k, R298b, R302d, R305c)

Bibliography

WB315.   Lange, Franciso Curt. *Vida y muerte de Louis Moreau Gottschalk en Rio de Janeiro 1869.* Mendoza, Argentina: Universidad Nacional de Cuyo, 1951.
    Lange (pp. 281, 284, 259) documents the above three South American performances of the piece (See: W310a, W310b, and W310c).

W311.   **Grande tarantelle (Célèbre tarentelle), Op.** 67 (1868; Paris: Escudier, 1874 (arr. Nicolás Ruiz Espadero). Pub. pl. no. L.E. 3378; New York: Arno Press and *The New York Times*, 1969 (*The Piano Works of Louis Moreau Gottschalk*, vol. 3, ed. Vera Brodsky Lawrence and Richard Jackson) [Contains first piano part only].)

For two pianos.
Dedication: M.M. Kowalski et Bachmann.
Other indices: RO260, D67a.
Note: An arrangement by Espadero of W37.
(See also: W48, W24, W311, W312)

Recordings

R311a.   *Louis Moreau Gottschalk: A Night in the Tropics.* Gary Hammond, piano; Sakiko Ohashi, piano. Compact disc. Naxos 8.559036, 2000.
    Note: This recording was of Sidney Lambert's 1890 arrangement of the work for two pianos. (See also: R16a, R34f, R37i, R78t, R95n, R103g, R165x, R203i, R227l)

Bibliography

WB316.   Landaluze, Victor P. de. "*Célèbre Tarantella* de Gottschalk y obras postumas de este artista." *Diario de la Marina* (Havana) (1874).
    Reprinted in Fors (See: B112, pp. 284-90).

WB317. Apthorp, William Foster. "Recent Music." *Atlantic Monthly* 35:380-81 (March 1875).
A review of several of Gottschalk's posthumously published works, including the *Grand tarantelle*.

W312. **Grand tarantelle (Célèbre tarentelle), Op. 67** (1868; Mainz: B. Schott's Söhne, 1874. Pub. pl. no. 21013; Paris: A. O'Kelly, 1883; Paris: Mackar & Nöel, 1891; New York: Arno Press and *The New York Times*, 1969 (*The Piano Works of Louis Moreau Gottschalk*, vol. 3, ed. Vera Brodsky Lawrence and Richard Jackson).)

For piano, four hands.
Other indices: RO261, D67d.
Note: An arrangment by Maurice Decourcelle.
(See also: W37, W48, W247, W311)

Bibliography

WB318. Apthorp, William Foster. "Recent Music." *Atlantic Monthly* 35:380-81 (March 1875).
A review of several of Gottschalk's posthumously published works, including the duet arrangement of *Grand tarantelle*.

W313. **Grande Phantasia sobre motives de *Norma*** (1869; unpublished; lost.)

For two pianos.
Other indices: RO180.
Note: This piece is based on themes from Bellini's opera *Norma*.
Performances

W313a. June 5, 1869. Rio de Janeiro. Louis Moreau Gottschalk, piano; unidentified second pianist.

W313b. September 5, 1869. São Paulo, Brazil. Louis Moreau Gottschalk, piano; unidentified second pianist.

Bibliography

WB319. Lange, Francisco Curt. *Vida y muerte de Louis Moreau Gottschalk en Rio de Janeiro, 1869.* Mendoza,

Argentina: Universidad Nacional de Cuyo, 1951.
Lange (p. 258) documents Gottschalk's June 1869
performance of the piece (See: W313a).

W314.   Grande Fantaisie de *Lucia* (1869; unpublished; lost.)

For two pianos.
Other indices: RO137.
Note: This piece is based on themes from Donizetti's opera *Lucia di
Lammermoor.*

Performances

W314a.   November 12, 1869. Rio de Janeiro. Louis Moreau
Gottschalk, piano; unidentified second pianist.

Bibliography

WB320.   Lange, Francisco Curt. *Vida y muerte de Louis Moreau
Gottschalk en Rio de Janeiro, 1869.* Mendoza,
Argentina: Universidad Nacional de Cuyo, 1951.
Lange (p. 265) documents the November 1869
performance of the work in Rio de Janeiro (See: W314a).

W315.   Fleur de lys, gallop brillante à 4 mains (unknown date.)

For piano, four hands.
Manuscript is located at the New York Public Library.
Other indices: D56.
Note: This piece was written under Gottschalk's pseudonym Paul
Ernest.
(See also: W269)

Miscellaneous Works

W316. **The Andes** (George William Warren)

For piano; also arranged for two pianos.
Other indices: RO7.
Note: Offergeld (See: WB321) speculates that Gottschalk may have had a hand in the composition or arrangement of this George W. Warren piece.

Bibliography

WB321. Offergeld, Robert. *The Centennial Catalogue of the Published and Unpublished Compositions of Louis Moreau Gottschalk.* New York: Stereo Review, 1970.

W317. **Quadrille créole** (Arr. Émile Waldteufel; Paris: Leduc, 1860.)

For orchestra.
Other indices: D126.
Note: This work is an arrangment and orchestration by Waldteufel including themes from several of Gottschalk's Creole works.

W318. **Workbook**

Other indices: RO298.
Manuscript is located at the New York Public Library.
Note: The Gottschalk *Workbook* contains sketches, manuscripts, and copyists' copies of a number of published and unpublished pieces and fragments.

W319.   **Cakewalk: Ballet** (Hershy Kay)

For orchestra.
Duration: 35 minutes.
Note: A composition by Hershy Kay using primarily the themes of
Louis Moreau Gottschalk.

Recordings

R319a.   *Suite from the Ballet "Stars and Stripes."* Boston Pops
Orchestra; Arthur Fiedler, conductor. 33-1/3 rpm
phonodisc. RCA Victor LM 2240, 1958.
With: Hershy Kay's *Stars and Stripes: After Music
by John Philip Sousa.* (See also: R319c)

R319b.   *Cakewalk.* Louisville Orchestra; Akira Endo, conductor.
33-1/3 rpm phonodisc. Louisville Orchestra LS782,
1983. Reissued on compact disc, Albany TROY016-2,
1989.
With: *The Incredible Flutist* by Walter Piston
(compact disc). The Hershy Kay work was recorded May
26, 1982 in the Macauley Theatre, Louisville, Kentucky.

R319c.   *Stars and Stripes – Cakewalk.* Boston Pops Orchestra;
Arthur Fiedler, conductor. Compact disc. RCA Victor
09026-61501-2, 1993. Also issued as Musical Heritage
Society 514357X.
With: works by Morton Gould, Hershy Kay,
Leonard Bernstein, John Philip Sousa, and Aaron
Copland. A digitally remastered reissue of a 1958
recording (See: R319a).

R319d.   *American Jubilee.* Cincinnati Pops Orchestra; Erich
Kunzel, conductor. Simultaneously issued on 1-7/8 ips
audio cassette and compact disc, Telarc 80144, 1988.
Contains the "Grand Walkaround," "Wallflower
Waltz," and "Gala Cakewalk" movements. With: works
by Charles Ives, George Whitefield Chadwick, Daniel
Decatur Emmett, Aaron Copland, John Williams, George
M. Cohan, Morton Gould, Samuel Ward, Irving Berlin
and John Philip Sousa.

R319e.   *American Composers.* Boston Pops Orchestra; Arthur
Fiedler, conductor. Compact disc. Time-Life Music
TCD-763 R832-14, 1997.
With: works by George Gershwin, George M.
Cohan, Aaron Copland, and Charles Ives.

Bibliography

WB322.   Martin, John. "City Ballet Gives New Work by Boris."
New York Times June 14, 1951.

WB323.   Terry, Walter. "The Ballet." *New York Herald-Tribune*
September 6, 1951.

WB324.   Balanchine, George. *Complete Stories of the Great
Ballets.* New York: Doubleday, 1954.
The noted choreographer discusses the ballet
Cakewalk on pp. 62 and 562.

WB325.   Bagar, Robert. "New Works Given by Joffrey Ballet."
Villager September 15, 1956.
A review of a performance of *Cakewalk.*

WB326.   Barnes, Clive. "Cakewalk." *New York Times* March 12,
1958.

WB327.   Barnes, Clive. "Bouncy Creole Tunes Get New Setting."
New York Times September 9, 1966.

WB328.   Barnes, Clive. "Struggling Higher." *New York Times*
September 20, 1966.

WB329.   Kay, Hershy. *Interview with Hershy Kay.* 1-7/8 ips audio
cassette. New York Public Library, 1968.
Kay, interviewed by Marian Horosko for radio
station WBAI, New York City, discusses, among other
things, his work in reconstructing the music of Gottschalk
for *Cakewalk.*

Filmography and Videography

F1.   *American Ballet Theatre in San Francisco.* VHS-format videocassette and 12 inch videodisc. 105 minutes. Produced by Robin Scott. Choreography of "Great Galloping Gottschalk" by Lynn Taylor-Corbett. Chicago: Home Vision, 1985. Recorded at the War Memorial Opera House, San Francisco, March 1, 1985.

    The dance work "Great Galloping Gottschalk" includes *Manchega, O! Ma charmante, Tournament Galop, Le bananier,* and *The Dying Poet,* arranged by Jack Elliott and Victoria Bond.

F2.   *Gottschalk: A Musical Portrait.* VHS-format videocassette. Garland Robinette, narrator; New Orleans Symphony; Philippe Entremant, conductor. East Hampton, New York: FilmAmerica FA002, 1986/1994.

F3.   *Routes of Rhythm.* U-matic format videocassette. 57 minutes. Produced and directed by Eugene Rosow and Howard Dratch. Written by Linda Post. Hosted by Harry Belafonte. Los Angeles: KCET-TV, 1989.

    Gottschalk's visits to Cuba and the influence of Cuba on his compositions are discussed in one segment of this film.

F4.   *Balanchine Celebration.* U-matic-format videocassette. Choreography by George Balanchine; Photography by Jay Millard. New York: The George Balanchine Trust, 1993.

    The ballet video contains a performance of *Tarantella,* as reconstructed and orchestrated by Hershy Kay. Videotaped in performance at New York State Theater, New York on May 27, 1993, during New York City Ballet's *Balanchine Celebration.*

F5.   *Dance Faculty in Concert.* VHS-format videocassette. Yasuko
        Tokunaga, artistic director. Boston: Boston Conservatory, 1993.
               The dance work "A Night in the Tropics" uses the music of
        Gottschalk's *Symphonie romantique ("La nuit des tropiques")*.

F6.   *New York City Ballet.* U-Matic format videocassette. Michael
        Truppin, photographer; George Balanchine, choreographer. New
        York: New York Public Library, 1995.
               Contains a ballet sequence to Gottschalk's *Tarantella*,
        reconstructed and orchestrated by Hershey Kay.

F7.   *The Black Boots.* VHS-format videocassette. Produced, written,
        directed and edited by Bridget Murnane; Marcus Schulkind,
        choreographer. BAM Productions, 1996.
               Part of this twelve-minute dance video utilizes Gottschalk's *O,
        Ma charmante, épargez-moi*, performed by Fredrik Wanger.

F8.   *Fall Ballet.* VHS-format videocassette. Indiana University Ballet
        Theater, Lynne Taylor-Corbett, choreographer. Bloomington:
        Indiana University, 1997.
               The dance work "Great Galloping Gottschalk" includes
        Manchega, O! *Ma charmante*, *Tournament Galop*, *Le bananier*, and
        The Dying Poet, arranged by Jack Elliott and Victoria Bond.

General Bibliography

B1.   Concert review. *Revue et gazette musicale* (Paris) April 6, 1845.
        A review of Gottschalk's Paris debut.

B2.   Hawes, William L. Concert review. *New Orleans Courier* May 17,
        1845.
                A review of Gottschalk's April 2, 1845 Paris debut. (See also:
        B142)

B3.   Escudier, Léon. *La France musicale* April 27, 1850.
                One of several brief news accounts of Gottschalk, his
        performances, and his compositions written by the Paris publisher.
        (See also: B4, B13, B16)

B4.   Escudier, Léon. *La France musicale* August 18, 1850.
                One of several brief news accounts of Gottschalk, his
        performances, and his compositions written by the Paris publisher.
        (See also: B3, B13, B16)

B5.   "Gottschalk's Second Geneva Concert." *New Orleans Times-
        Picayune* August 20, 1850. Reprinted in "Flashback: New Orleans a
        Century Ago." *New Orleans Times-Picayune* August 20, 1950.

B6.   Eichberg, Julius. Concert Review. *Nouvelliste vaudois* (Geneva)
        October 26, 1850.
                This concert review is reprinted in *Notes of a Pianist* (See:
        B113, p. 46).

B7.   Escudier, Marie. "Gottschalk en Suisse." *La France musicale*
         (October 27, 1850).
             This report on Gottschalk's concert activities in Switzerland is
         reprinted in *Notes of a Pianist* (See: B113, pp. 46-47)

B8.   Commettant, Oscar. *Feuilleton du siècle* (Paris) November 1, 1850.
             An article telling about Gottschalk's abduction by a young
         woman, showing the near hysteria he created as a performer.

B9.   Witterson. "Gottschalk en Lausanne." *La France musicale*
         November 10, 1850.

B10.   Schiriwaneck, C. Concert Review. *Feuilleton de la Gazette de
         Lausanne* November 28, 1850.
             A concert review reprinted in *Notes of a Pianist* (See: B113,
         47-48).

B11.   Fiorentino, P.A. Concert Review. *Le Constitutionnel* (Paris) c1850-
         51.
             The review is mentioned in Fors (See: B112, p. 18) and
         Loggins (See: B267, pp. 99-100).

B12.   Willis, N. Parker. *Hurry-graphs: Sketches of Scenery, Celebrities
         and Society Taken from Life.* New York, 1851.

B13.   Escudier, Léon. *La France musicale* January 12, 1851.
             One of several brief news accounts of Gottschalk, his
         performances, and his compositions written by the Paris publisher.
         (See also: B3, B4, B16)

B14.   Fiorentino, P.A. Concert Review. *Feuilleton du corsaire* (Paris)
         March 16, 1851.
             Concert review, reprinted in a number of other sources,
         including *Notes of a Pianist* (See: B113, pp. 52-53) and Fors (See:
         B112, pp. 12-13).

B15.   Delord, Taxile. Concert Review. *Le Charivari* (Paris). March 22,
         1851.
             Concert review, reprinted in a number of other sources,
         including *Notes of a Pianist* (See: B113, p. 53) and Loggins (See:
         B267, p. 100).

B16.   Escudier, Léon. *La France musicale* March 23, 1851.
        One of several brief news accounts of Gottschalk, his
        performances, and his compositions written by the Paris publisher.
        (See also: B3, B4, B13)

B17.   Gautier, Théophile. Concert Review. *Feuilleton de la presse* (Paris)
        March 31, 1851.
        A concert review reprinted in Clara Gottschalk Peterson's
        edition of *Notes of a Pianist* (See: B113, pp. 53-54); Jeanne
        Behrend's edition of the same (See: B113, p. xxii), and Loggins'
        Where the Word Ends (See: B267, p. 100).

B18.   Berlioz, Hector. "Gottschalk." *Feuilleton du Journal des débats*
        (Paris) April 3, 1851.
        Very positive review of Gottschalk's playing.

B19.   Adam, Adolphe. *Feuilleton de l'Assemblée nationale* April 29,
        1851.
        A review of Gottschalk's benefit concert for Pleyel's workers.
        Reprinted in *Notes of a Pianist* (See: B113).

B20.   Barthélemon, G. Concert Review. *L'Agent dramatique* (Toulouse)
        June 8, 1851.
        This concert review is reprinted in Clara Gottschalk Peterson's
        edition of *Notes of a Pianist* (B113, p. 55).

B21.   Dupouy, J. Saint-Rieul. Concert Review. *Mémorial des Pyrénées*
        (Pau) June 14, 1851.
        This concert review is reprinted in Clara Gottschalk Peterson's
        edition of *Notes of a Pianist* (B113, p. 56).

B22.   Barthélemon, G. Concert Review. *L'Ami des arts* (Bordeaux) June
        15, 1851.
        This concert review is reprinted in Clara Gottschalk Peterson's
        edition of *Notes of a Pianist* (B113, p. 55).

B23.   Boudin, A. Concert Review. *Courrier de la Gironde* (Bordeaux)
        June 20, 1851.
        A positive review of a Gottschalk performance. Reprinted in
        Clara Gottschalk Peterson's edition of *Notes of a Pianist* (B113, p.
        55).

B24.   Boudin, A. Concert Review. *Courrier de la Gironde* (Bordeaux) June 21, 1851.
        A favorable review of a Gottschalk performance. Reprinted in Clara Gottschalk Peterson's edition of *Notes of a Pianist* (B113, p. 55).

B25.   Dupouy, J. Saint-Rieul. Performance Review. *Courrier de la Girone* July 7, 1851.

B26.   Barthélemon, G. Concert Review. *L'Ami des arts* (Bordeaux) July 20, 1851.
        This concert review is reprinted in Clara Gottschalk Peterson's edition of *Notes of a Pianist* (B113, p. 56).

B27.   O'Quin, Patrick. Biography of Louis Moreau Gottschalk. *Mémorial des Pyrénées* (Pau) August 6, 1851.
        This biographical sketch is reproduced in *Notes of a Pianist* (See: B113).

B28.   Costa, H. da. "Gottschalk." *L'International* (Bayonne) September 15, 1851.
        This preview of Gottschalk's appearance in Madrid is a reprint from an undatable issue of *Tribune del Pueblo* (Madrid).

B29.   Escudier, Marie. "Gottschalk à Vallabolid." *La France musicale* (February 1, 1852).
        This report on Gottschalk's concert activities is reprinted in Clara Gottschalk Peterson's edition of *Notes of a Pianist* (B113, p. 62).

B30.   Arpin, Paul. *Biographie de L.M. Gottschalk, pianiste américain.* New York: Imprimerie du Courrier des États-Unis, 1853. English translation by Henry C. Watson. New York, 1853.
        The Arpin biography provides important lists of published and unpublished compositions, which were of particular interest to later indexers such as Offergeld (See: B378) and Doyle (See: B484). The book is also important for its treatment of contemporary criticism of Gottschalk, providing an excellent view portrait of how the pianist/composer was viewed by his contemporaries. Note that the Watson translation is significantly shorter and less detailed than the original.

B31.   D., H. [Didimus, Henry]. *Biography of Louis Moreau Gottschalk, the American Pianist and Composer.* Philadelphia: Deacon & Peterson, 1853.
        Note: The Didimus booklet was reprinted from *Grahams Magazine*, January 1853.

B32.   Concert Program. *New York Herald* February 11, 1853:22.
        A reproduction of Gottschalk's debut program.

B33.   "Mr. Gottschalk—Great Success of the American Pianist." *New York Herald* February 12, 1853.
        Favorable review of Gottschalk's New York debut.

B34.   "Gottschalk Arrives on the *Belle Key* from Louisville." *New Orleans Times-Picayune* March 29, 1853. Reprinted in "Flashback: New Orleans a Century Ago." *New Orleans Times-Picayune* March 29, 1953.

B35.   Portrait of Louis Moreau Gottschalk. *Gleason's Pictorial Drawing-Room Companion* 4:109 (April 2, 1853).

B36.   Mason, Lowell. *Musical Letters from Abroad.* New York, 1854.

B37.   Willis, N. Parker. *Famous Persons and Places.* New York, 1854.

B38.   Estorch, D.M. *Apuntes para la historia sobre la administración del Marqués de la Pezuela en la isla de Cuba, desde 3 de Diciembre de 1853 hasta 21 de Septiembre de 1854.* Madrid, 1856.
        The political scene in Cuba during the first part of Gottschalk's tour of the island are detailed.

B39.   "Comments on Gottschalk." *Godey's Lady's Book and Magazine* 52:377 (January-June 1856).
        A positive review of Gottschalk.

B40.   "Gottschalk, the Great Drawing-Card of the New York Season." *New Orleans Times-Picayune* April 1, 1856. Reprinted in "Flashback: New Orleans a Century Ago." *New Orleans Times-Picayune* April 1, 1956.

B41.   Clare, Ada. "Whips and Scorns of Time." *Atlas* December 7, 1856.
        (See also: B42, B43, B44)

B42.   Clare, Ada. "Whips and Scorns of Time." *Atlas* December 14, 1856.
        (See also: B41, B43, B44)

B43.   Clare, Ada. "Whips and Scorns of Time." *Atlas* December 21, 1856.
        (See also: B41, B42, B44)

B44.   Clare, Ada. "The Pangs of Despised Love." *Atlas* December 28,
        1856.

B45.   Adam, Adolphe. *Souvenirs d'un musicien*. Paris, 1857.
        Contains references to Gottschalk.

B46.   Barival, Mennechet de. "Gottschalk." *L'Art musical* April 5, 1857.
        The author provides a rave review of Gottschalk's piano
        playing in this Parisian newspaper.

B47.   Gottschalk, Louis Moreau. "La Musique à la Havane." *La France
        musicale* (January 24, 1858; December 11, 1859; October 28, 1860).

B48.   Dana, Richard Henry. *To Cuba and Back*. Boston, 1859.

B49.   Clare, Ada. "Thoughts and Things." *Saturday Press* (c1859-60).
        An article, cited in Loggins (See: B267, p. 179) and Doyle
        (See: B484, p. 34) about the bohemian circle in which Gottschalk
        moved in New York City. Doyle further notes that Ada Clare (the
        pseudonym of Jane McElhenny) was said to have been the mother of
        a child by Gottschalk.

B50.   Gottschalk, Louis Moreau. "La Musica, el Piano, los Pianistas,
        Espadero y 'La Plainte du poete.'" *Diario de la Marina* April 27,
        1860; April 28, 1860; May 3, 1860. Reprinted in *Liceo de la Habana*
        (May 1860).
        In this major article Gottschalk discusses music and the piano,
        as well as his personal likes and dislikes. The article is reprinted in
        Fors (See: B112, pp. 323-52).

B51.   Gottschalk, Louis Moreau. *Pocket Diary*, vol. 1. 1862.
        Gottschalk's French-language diary has been widely
        reproduced. (See also: B60 and B70).

B52.   Gamma. Article about Gottschalk's compositions. *L'Art musical*
        (February 6, 1862).

The pseudonymous critic acknowledges Gottschalk's expertise in Caribbean styles, but urges him to pursue larger, European-based forms.

B53.   Gottschalk, Louis Moreau. "Souvenirs de voyage d'un pianiste." *L'Art musical* (July 31, 1862).
Gottschalk's short articles about his travels, written for this Paris musical journal, later found their way, sometimes in slightly altered form, into *Notes of a Pianist* (See: B113).

B54.   Curtis, George W. "Gottschalk." *Harper's New Monthly Magazine* 25:418-19 (September 1862).

B55.   Lanas, Juan. "Gottschalk en el desierto." *El Continental* September 18, 1862.

B56.   Lanas, Juan. "Gottschalk en el desierto." *El Continental* September 22, 1862.

B57.   "Louis Moreau Gottschalk, Prince of the Piano-Forte." *Vanity Fair* October 11, 1862.

B58.   Moises (no first name give). Concert review. *La Tribuna* (Buenos Aires) 15:2 November 7, 1862.
This concert review is cited by Stevenson (See: B363, p. 1).

B59.   *Gottschalk's Illustrated Concert Book.* New York: 1863.
The present work contains Gottschalk's biography, a list of his compositions and excerpts from reviews.

B60.   Gottschalk, Louis Moreau. *Pocket Diary*, vol. 2. 1863.
Gottschalk's French-language diary has been widely reproduced. (See also: B51 and B70).

B61.   *The Life of Louis Moreau Gottschalk.* New York, 1863.
The brochure contains biographical material, copies of press notices and a list of Gottschalk's compositions.

B62.   Gottschalk, Louis Moreau. "Dramatic Feuilleton." June 1863.
An article from an unidentified newspaper. Contained in the New York Public Library's Gottschalk Collection.

B63.   Gottschalk, Louis Moreau. "Souvenirs de voyage d'un pianiste."
            L'Art musical (August 13, 1863).
                 Gottschalk's short articles about his travels, written for this
            Paris musical journal, later found their way, sometimes in slightly
            altered form, into *Notes of a Pianist* (See: B113).

B64.   Gottschalk, Louis Moreau. "Souvenirs de voyage d'un pianiste."
            L'Art musical (August 20, 1863).
                 Gottschalk's short articles about his travels, written for this
            Paris musical journal, later found their way, sometimes in slightly
            altered form, into *Notes of a Pianist* (See: B113).

B65.   Gottschalk, Louis Moreau. "Souvenirs de voyage d'un pianiste."
            L'Art musical (August 27, 1863).
                 Gottschalk's short articles about his travels, written for this
            Paris musical journal, later found their way, sometimes in slightly
            altered form, into *Notes of a Pianist* (See: B113).

B66.   Gottschalk, Louis Moreau. Letter. *El Siglo* (Havana) August 29,
            1863.
                 A letter from Gottschalk reprinted in Spanish translation in
            Fors (See: B112, pp. 124-34). The musician describes his
            experiences as an opera conductor in Matanzas and discusses his
            feelings about the operatic genre.

B67.   Gottschalk, Louis Moreau. "Souvenirs de voyage d'un pianiste."
            L'Art musical (September 3, 1863).
                 Gottschalk's short articles about his travels, written for this
            Paris musical journal, later found their way, sometimes in slightly
            altered form, into *Notes of a Pianist* (See: B113).

B68.   Gottschalk, Louis Moreau. "Souvenirs de voyage d'un pianiste."
            L'Art musical (September 24, 1863).
                 Gottschalk's short articles about his travels, written for this
            Paris musical journal, later found their way, sometimes in slightly
            altered form, into *Notes of a Pianist* (See: B113).

B69.   Gottschalk, Louis Moreau. "Souvenirs de voyage d'un pianiste."
            L'Art musical (October 15, 1863).
                 Gottschalk's short articles about his travels, written for this
            Paris musical journal, later found their way, sometimes in slightly
            altered form, into *Notes of a Pianist* (See: B113).

B70. Gottschalk, Louis Moreau. *Pocket Diary*, vol. 3. 1864.
      Gottschalk's French-language diary has been widely
      reproduced. (See also: B51 and B60).

B71. Nazareno. "Sobre Gottschalk, Luis Moreau." In Cosas de los
      Estados Unidos. New York: Imprenta del Porvenir, 1864.
      Simon Comacho, using the pseudonym Nazareno, presents
      recollections of Gottschalk's travels throughout the United States and
      the Caribbean.

B72. Chouquet, Gustave. "Clavecinists et pianistes." *L'Art musical*
      (Paris) March 3, 1864:108-09.
      The author includes Gottschalk in a list of pianist/composers
      who "have completely changed the piano from the piano of
      Beethoven."

B73. Gottschalk, Louis Moreau. "Souvenirs de voyage d'un pianiste."
      L'Art musical (May 19, 1864).
      Gottschalk's short articles about his travels, written for this
      Paris musical journal, later found their way, sometimes in slightly
      altered form, into *Notes of a Pianist* (See: B113).

B74. Gottschalk, Louis Moreau. "Souvenirs de voyage d'un pianiste."
      L'Art musical (July 14, 1864).
      Gottschalk's short articles about his travels, written for this
      Paris musical journal, later found their way, sometimes in slightly
      altered form, into *Notes of a Pianist* (See: B113).

B75. Gottschalk, Louis Moreau. "Notes of a Pianist." *Atlantic Monthly*
      15:177-81 (no. 88, February 1865).
      This material is reproduced in French in *Notes of a Pianist*
      (See: B113).

B76. Gottschalk, Louis Moreau. "Notes of a Pianist." *Atlantic Monthly*
      15:350-52 (no. 89, March 1865).
      This material is reproduced in French in *Notes of a Pianist*
      (See: B113).

B77. Gottschalk, Louis Moreau. "Notes of a Pianist." *Atlantic Monthly*
      15:573-75 (no. 91, May 1865).
      This material is reproduced in French in *Notes of a Pianist*
      (See: B113).

B78.   "Obsequio a Gottschalk." *El Comercio* (Lima, Peru) October 23, 1865:2.
        An article about Gottschalk's achievements and medals cited by Stevenson (See: B364, p. 10).

B79.   "Louis Moreau Gottschalk." *Watson's Weekly Art Journal* pp56+ (November 11, 1865).
        A report defending Gottschalk in light of the San Francisco "scandal" that drove him from the United States.

B80.   Clare, Ada. *Only a Woman's Heart.* New York: M. Doolady, 1866.
        The character Victor Doria is supposedly based on Gottschalk.

B81.   Fors, Luis Ricardo. *La Tribuna* (Montevideo) p2 (June 20, 1867).
        An announcement of Gottschalk's decoration from the Queen of Spain.

B82.   Moreno, Jacinto. Concert review. *El Nacional* (Montevideo) 1:1 (no. 40, September 17, 1867).
        Moreno's review, cited in Fors (See: B112, p. 12), mentions that Gottschalk played the piano works of Beethoven in private concerts and for his own enjoyment more frequently than he performed them in concert halls.

B83.   Fors, Luis Ricardo. *La Tribuna* (Montevideo) p24 (September 26, 1867).
        Reprinted in the author's *Gottschalk* (See: B112).

B84.   Nunez, Julio and Gustave Nessler. Concert reviews. *El Nacional* (Buenos Aires) November 6, 1867.
        These reviews of the same Gottschalk performance are cited by Gesualdo (See: B285, pp. 248-49).

B85.   Escudier, Léon. *Mes souvenirs: les virtuoses.* Paris: Dentu, 1868.
        Gottschalk is profiled, pp. 173-195. Doyle (See: B484, p. 48) and Starr's account of Gottschalk's life (See: B524) suggest that some details may be incorrect. As a well-known writer on music and friend of Gottschalk during the composer's years in France, and because these are first-hand accounts, Escudier's memoires are an important source. Portions were included in Fors (See: B112).

B86.   Thomson, Juan Jacapo. Article about Gottschalk. *Las Bellas artes, periodic semanal* (Chile) 1:23 (April 19, 1869).
        Cited in Stevenson (See: B364)

B87.   Cybrão, Ernest. "Gottschalk." *A Semana illustrada* (Rio de Janeiro) n443:3543 (June 6, 1869).
        Concert review.

B88.   Menezes, Ferreira de, "O Poeta do Piano." *O Ypiranga* (São Paulo) n21 (August 29, 1869).
        This article praising Gottschalk is cited by Lange (See: B245, p. 68).

B89.   Meirelles, Soares de. Article on Gottschalk. *O Ypiranga* (São Paulo) n24 (September 5, 1869).
        This article is cited by Lange (See: B245, p. 73).

B90.   Thomson, Juan Jacapo. Article about Gottschalk. *Las Bellas artes, periodic semanal* (Chile) 1:235 (October 18, 1869).
        Cited by Stevenson (See: B364)

B91.   Camacho, Simon Bolivar. "Gottschalk en Rio de Janeiro." *Jornal do commercio* (no. 326, November 24, 1869).

B92.   Verejão, Achilles. "Noticiario." *Diario do Rio de Janeiro* v351 (December 21, 1869).
        An eulogy quoted in Lange (See: B245, pp. 117-120)

B93.   Cardoso de Menezes, Antonio. "Noticiaro Gottschalk." *Diario do Rio de Janeiro* (no. 352, December 22, 1869).
        The eulogy given at Gottschalk's funeral. Reprinted in Lange (See: B245, pp. 120-23).

B94.   Menezes, Ferreia de. "Literature: Gottschalk. A morte de Gottschalk." *Correio Paulistano* (São Paulo) n4051 (December 24, 1869).
        This eulogy is cited by Lange (See: B245, p. 76).

B95.   Hensel, Octavia. *Life and Letters of Louis Moreau Gottschalk.* Boston: Ditson, 1870.
        Hensel, whose real name was Mary Alice Seymour, studied with Gottschalk and was later one of his close friends.

Unfortunately, her biography does not deal in a substantive way with Gottschalk's teaching technique or with his interpretation of his own compositions. This book was reprinted using the author's real name, Mary Alice Seymour (See: B479).

B96.   Estrada, Santiago. "Luis Moreau Gottschalk." *Revista Argentina* 6:57-64 (January 1870).

B97.   Cybrão, Ernest. Special Supplement in *A Semana illustrada* (Rio de Janeiro) n473 (January 2, 1870).
A biography and review of Gottschalk's final concert appearance.

B98.   Camacho, Simon Bolivar. "Gottschalk." *La Discussion* (Buenos Aires) January 25, 1870.

B99.   Escudier, Léon. "Mort de Gottschalk." *L'Art musical* (January 27, 1870).

B100.   Espadero, Nicolás Ruiz. "À propos de Gottschalk." *L'Art musical* (March 31, 1870).

B101.   Aymar, Marguerite F. "Gottschalk's Grave." *Musical Bulletin* (February 1871).

B102.   Drake, Francis S. *Dictionary of American Biography, Including Men of the Time, and a Supplement.* Boston: Osgood, 1872.
Although I have not included some of the shorter biographical sketches of Gottschalk that appear in encyclopedias and biographical dictionaries, I have included this entry (pp. 371-72) as an illustration of the extent to which Gottschalk remained, just a few years after his death, a notable figure—notable enough to be included in a general reference work such as this.

B103.   Espadero, Nicolás Ruiz. "Prefatory Remarks by an Artist Friend of the Great Composer." Preface to Posthumous Works of Louis Moreau Gottschalk. Boston: Oliver Ditson, 1872-74. Also published in Spanish as *Obras postumas de L.M. Gottschalk.* Havana, 1873.
(See also: B105 and B106)

B104.   Landaluze, Victor P. de. "*Célebre Tarantella* de Gottschalk y obras

postumas de este artista." *Diario de la Marina* (Havana) (1874).
Reprinted in Fors (See: B112, pp. 284-90).

B105.   Espadero, Nicolás Ruiz. "Les Oeuvres posthumes de L.M.
Gottschalk." *L'Art musical* (February 5, 1874).
(See also: B103 and B106)

B106.   Escudier, Léon. Preface to the Publication of Gottschalk's
Posthumous Works. *L'Art musical* (February 5, 1874).
According to Fors (See: B112, 291-92), Escudier's preface
represents a mutilation of Espadero's Spanish-language Preface to
Posthumous Works of Louis Moreau Gottschalk (See: B103).

B107.   Apthorp, William Foster. "Recent Music." *Atlantic Monthly* 35:380-
81 (March 1875).

B108.   Marmontel, Antoine François. *Art classique et moderne du piano.*
Paris: Heugel, 1876.
The inclusion of several of Gottschalk's solo piano works in
this graded list of pieces for study suggests the esteem in which the
composer continued to be held in France.

B109.   "Gottschalk." *Orchestra* (July 1877).

B110.   Marmontel, Antoine François. *Les Pianistes célèbre.* Paris: Heugel,
1878. 2nd ed., 1888.
Gottschalk is included among the celebrated pianists. It
should be noted that Marmontel had been a friend of Gottschalk,
knew him well, and had numerous opportunities to hear him perform.

B111.   Jullien, Adolphe. *A Dictionary of Music and Musicians*, ed. George
Grove. s.v. "Gottschalk." London: Macmillan, 1880.
Although superceeded by later editions of the reference work,
the article is interesting as a document of how Gottschalk was
viewed a decade after his death.

B112.   Fors, Luis Ricardo. *Gottschalk.* Havana: La Propaganda Literaria;
New York: "La Razalatina," 1880. English translation by J. Peter
Heinrich. Rochester, New York, 1973.
Doyle (See: B484) views the Fors book as an important
source of documentation on Gottschalk's career, although he writes

that "Fors' enthusiasm for LMG led him sometimes to excesses, perhaps pardonable" (See: B484, p. 54).

B113.   Gottschalk, Louis Moreau. *Notes of a Pianist*, ed. Clara Gottschalk Peterson. Philadelphia, 1881. Also published with English translation by Robert E. Peterson. London: J.B. Lippincott, 1881. Republished in an edition with commentary and a new introduction by Jeanne Behrend. New York: Knopf, 1964. The Behrend edition was reissued New York: Da Capo, 1979.

This posthumous book consists primarily of a collection of articles Gottschalk wrote for New York and Paris newspapers during his concert tours. For reviews of the original edition, see: B114, B115, B116. For reviews of the 1964 edition by Jeanne Behrend, see: B297-B304, B306, B308-B313, B318, B321.

B114.   Holt, Charles. "Gottschalk's Diary." *Dial* pp141-43 (November 1881).
A review of Gottschalk's *Notes of a Pianist* (See: B113).

B115.   "Gottschalk's Journals." *Atlantic Monthly* 48:859 (December 1881).
A review of Gottschalk's *Notes of a Pianist* (See: B113).

B116.   Finck, Henry T. (W.J. Henderson) "Gottschalk's Tour in the United States." *Nation* 34:16 (January 5, 1882).
A review of Gottschalk's *Notes of a Pianist* (See: B113). Doyle (See: B484) lists the author as Henderson, while Starr (See: B524) names Finck.

B117.   Allain, Helen d'Aquin. *Souvenirs d'Amérique et de France, par une Créole*. Paris, 1883.

B118.   Fillmore, John Comfort. *Pianoforte Music: Its History, with Biographical Sketches and Critical Estimates of Its Greatest Masters*. Chicago: Townsend MacCoun, 1883.

Fillmore praises Gottschalk as a perfomer but criticizes his compositions as being shallow and sentimental. There are some incorrect dates in the biographical sketch.

B119.   Jones, F.O. *A Handbook of American Music and Musicians*. Canaseraga, New York: F.O. Jones, 1886. Reprint, New York: Da Capo, 1971.

B120.   Ferris, George T. *Great Pianists and Great Violinists*, 2nd ed.
         London: Reeves, c1890.
             Ferris (pp. 202-32) profiles Gottschalk, asserting that the
         composer/pianist never fulfilled the promise of his early career. As
         was the case with many of the writings on Gottschalk of the era,
         some biographical details are incorrect.

B121.   Liebling, Emil. "A Pianistic Retrospect, Part II." *Music* 1:585 (April
             1892).
             The author discusses Gottschalk's influence on his
         contemporaries.

B122.   Mathews, William Smythe Babcock. "Gottschalk: A Successful
         American Composer." *Music* 2:117-32 (June 1892).

B123.   Leland, Charles G. *Memoirs*. New York, 1893.

B124.   Castellanos, Henry C. *New Orleans as It Was: Episodes of
         Louisiana Life*. New Orleans, 1895.

B125.   Ferris, George T. *Great Violinists and Pianists*. New York, 1895.

B126.   Mathews, William Smythe Babcock. "Editorial Bric-A-Brac."
         Music 8:188-91 (June 1895).
             Includes a generally negative reaction to Gottschalk's
         compositions. Mathews praises the works of William Mason.
         Ironically, Mason himself later praised Gottschalk's Creole works
         (See: B143). Mathews' attitude toward Gottschalk seemed to
         change over the course of the next three years (See: B133). (See
         also: B151)

B127.   Gilder, John Francis. "An Appreciation of Gottschalk by One Who
         Knew Him." *Musical Record* (November 1896). Reprinted in as
         "Recollections of Gottschalk." *Etude* 15:271 (October 1897).
         Reprinted as "An Appreciation of Gottschalk by One Who Knew
         Him." *Etude* 32:424 (June 1914).

B128.   Gottschalk, L. Gaston. "Carreño and L.M. Gottschalk." *Music*
         11:468 (February 1897).

B129.   de Vivo, Diego. "Gottschalk, the Adored." *New York Sun* March 29,
         1897.

An important figure in Gottschalk's Civil War tours of the United States and Canada, de Vivo acted as advance man for tour manager Max Strakosch. (See also: B130)

B130.   de Vivo, Diego. "De Vivo's Jolly Season." *New York Sun* April 4, 1897.
An important figure in Gottschalk's Civil War tours of the United States and Canada, de Vivo acted as advance man for tour manager Max Strakosch. (See also: B129)

B131.   Cooke, George Willis. *John Sullivan Dwight*. Boston: Small & Maynard, 1898. Reprint: New York: Da Capo, 1969.
This book is of interest due to the intensely negative criticism of Gottschalk by Dwight.

B132.   Kobbé, Gustav. *Appleton's Cyclopedia of American Biography*, ed. James Grant Wilson and John Fiske. s.v. "Gottschalk." New York: Appleton, 1898.
A short biographical sketch that reflects a John S. Dwight-inspired negative bias against Gottschalk's compositions.

B133.   Mathews, William Smythe Babcock. "An Evening with American Composers." *Music* 13:351-59 (January 1898).
Mathews gives significant coverage to Gottschalk in a longer article about a number of American composers. The author seems to have undergone something of a transformation since his 1895 article (See: B126) attacking Gottschalk; Mathews speaks well of Gottschalk's compositional achievements in the present article. (See also: B151)

B134.   Gates, W. Francis. "A Pioneer American Pianist: Gottschalk." *Etude* 16:231 (August 1898).

B135.   Hawes, William L. "Gottschalk in New Orleans, 1853." *New Orleans Times-Democrat* May 8, 1899.

B136.   Oliver Ditson Company. *Catalog of Instrumental Music*, no. 11. Boston: Oliver Ditson Company, c1900.
Cited by Doyle (See: B484, p. 130). Over 100 of Gottschalk's compositions are included. (See also: B180)

B137.   "Gottschalk Momentoes." *Musical Courier* 40:23 (March 7, 1900).

An article concerning the collection of memorabilia exhibited by the Louisiana Historical Society.

B138.   Hawes, William L. "Reminiscences of Louis Moreau Gottschalk." *Musical Courier* 40:14-15 (March 21, 1900).

B139.   "Gottschalk Momentoes at New Orleans." *Music* 17:663-64 (April 1900).
   An article concerning the collection of memorabilia exhibited by the Louisiana Historical Society.

B140.   "Gottschalk." *Musical Standard* 14:95 (August 11, 1900).
   The article contains quotations from William L. Hawes. (See also: B138)

B141.   Swayne, Egbert. "Gottschalk: The First American Pianist." *Music* 18:519-29 (October 1900).
   A biographical sketch that has Gottschalk traveling back to Europe for a second visit later in his career (he did not make such a voyage).

B142.   Hawes, William L. "Louis Moreau Gottschalk." *Musical Courier* 43:17 (September 11, 1901).
   A reprint of the author's account of Gottschalk's Paris debut in 1845. It was originally printed in the *New Orleans Courier* (See: B2).

B143.   Mason, William. *Memories of a Musical Life.* New York: Century, 1902. Reprint: New York: AMS Press, 1973.
   Mason praises Gottschalk's Creole compositions and his pianistic talents (pp. 205-09).

B144.   Peterson, Clara Gottschalk. *Creole Songs from New Orleans.* New Orleans, 1902.
   This collection, by Gottschalk's sister, includes a number of songs used by the composer in his Creole works.

B145.   "Moreau Gottschalk." *Masters in Music, a Monthly Magazine* p117 (no. 2, 1903).

B146.   Clay, Virginia. *A Belle of the Fifties.* New York, 1904.

B147.   Elson, Louis Charles. *The History of American Music*. New York: Macmillan, 1904. Reprint: New York: Gordon Press, 1972.
          Gottschalk's work as a composer and as a pianist is given coverage on pages 281-83 and 290. Although many music academicians, such as John S. Dwight, reacted negatively to Gottschalk's output, Elson treats his work sympathetically.

B148.   Stoddard, Charles Warren. "Ada Clare, Queen of Bohemia." *National Magazine* (September 1905).

B149.   Jullien, Adolphe. *Grove's Dictionary of Music and Musicians*, 2nd ed. s.v. "Gottschalk." London: Macmillan, 1906.

B150.   Finck, Henry T. "What Is American Music?" *Etude* 24:356-57 (no. 6, June 1906).
          Finck's article is concerned primarily with composers who used Native American and African-American resources in concert music.

B151.   Mathews, William Smythe Babcock. "The Great American Composer, the Where, the Why, and the When." *Etude* 19:422-23 (July 1906).
          Mathews, in his seemingly ever-evolving appraisal of Gottschalk, reaches a middle ground and describes the musician as "a lower-grade composer who, never-the-less, shows genius." (See also: B126 and B133)

B152.   *Musical Courier* (May 1, 1907).
          An anonyomous article, cited by Doyle (See: B484, 121), that lists the Gottschalk memorabilia in New Orleans.

B153.   Tracy, T. James. "The World's Greatest Pianists." *Etude* (September 1907).

B154.   Apthorp, William Foster. *Musicians and Music Lovers*. New York: Scribner's, 1908.
          Apthorp (pp. 212, 277-86) quotes Boston pianist and critic Otto Dresel on Gottschalk's tone quality as a performer and comments on Gottschalk nemesis John S. Dwight's qualifications as a critic.

B155.   Upton, George P. Musical Memories: *My Recollections of*

Celebrities of the Half Century 1850-1900. Chicago: McClurg, 1908.

> Includes a number of references to Gottschalk.

B156.   Harwood, Bertha. "Reminiscences of Louis Moreau Gottschalk." *Musical Courier* 56:39-40 (May 13, 1908).

B157.   Law, Frederic S. "Some Forgotten Worthies." *Musician* 13:262-63 (June 1908).

> Gottschalk, just forty years after his death, is included among the forgotten important musicians of the past. The author is of the opinion that the popularity of Gottschalk's compositions was due in large part to his popularity as a performer; others were not capable of playing his pieces effectively. (See also: B163)

B158.   *Musical Courier.* (June 7, 1908).

> An anonymous article, cited by Doyle (See: B484, p. 121), describing the Catalogue of the Louisiana State Museum, which includes a list of Gottschalk memorabilia housed in the city.

B159.   "Louis Moreau Gottschalk." *Musical Leader* 15:6 (June 11, 1908).

B160.   Fisher, William Arms. "Louis Moreau Gottschalk, the First American Pianist and Composer: A Life Sketch." *Musician* 13:437+ (October 1908).

B161.   "Gottschalk's Farewell Concert, New Orleans, 1841." *Musician* 13:441 (October 1908).

B162.   Hawes, William L. "Gottschalk's Views Regarding Beethoven's Sonatas." *Musician* 13:440 (October 1908).

B163.   Liebling, Emil. "Gottschalk and His Period." *Musician* 13:487 (October 1908).

> The author's primary stance is that Gottschalk was so concerned with his current popularity that his music quickly fell out of favor after his death. (See also: B157 for a related opinion about Gottschalk from the same year)

B164.   Mathews, William Smythe Babcock. "Louis Moreau Gottschalk, the Most Popular of American Composers." *Musician* 13:439-40 (October 1908).

While Mathews expresses the attitude that Gottschalk was, all-in-all, an inferior composer, he does state that Gottschalk was somewhat ahead of his time when he returned to America after his years in France.

B165.   Sherwood, William H. "An Appreciation of Gottschalk As a Composer." *Musician* 13:441 (October 1908).

B166.   Storer, H.J. "Gottschalk's Thoughts on Music." *Musician* 13:441 (October 1908).

B167.   Peterson, Clara Gottschalk. "On Gottschalk." *Musical Courier* (December 16, 1908).

B168.   Bacardi y Moreau, Emilio. *Cronicas de Santiago de Cuba*, 3 vols. Barcelona: Carbonell y Esteva, 1908-13.
          Gottschalk's activities in Santiago de Cuba are mentioned in volume 2 (p. 415) and volume 3 (p. 83).

B169.   Escragnolle-Doria, L.G. "Gottschalk" in "Cousas do Passado," Separata del Tmo LXXXII, Parte II. *Revista do Instituto Histórico e Geográfico Brazileiro*, 61-75. Rio de Janeiro, 1909.
          Includes some information about Gottschalk's stay in Brazil.

B170.   Winter, William. *Old Friends: Being Literary Recollections of Other Days.* New York, 1909.

B171.   Davis, George Ade. *The Theatre Magazine* pp. 67-8 (August 1909).
          An interview with tenor William Castle in which several stories about Gottschalk are told. Preserved in the Castle clipping file, Music Division, New York Public Library.

B172.   Escoto, José. *Gertrudis Gomez de Avellaneda: Cartas ineditas y documentos relativos a su vida en Cuba de 1859 a 1864.* Matanzas: La Pluma de Oro, 1911.
          Escoto mentions a letter written (October 29, 1861) by Gottschalk to Ambrosio Santo in which he offers to assist in a fund-raising project for the Matanzas theater.

B173.   Converse, Charles Crozat. "Reminiscences of Some Famous Musicians." *Etude* 30:695-696 (October 1912).
          A first-hand account of Gottschalk's ability to create

orchestral textures at the keyboard. *The Last Hope* (See: W139), in particular, is cited as a highpoint in Gottschalk's compositional command of the piano's resources. On the subject of Gottschalk as a person, Converse writes that "his ease of manner and his personal magneticism were remarkable."

B174.   Currier, T.P. "American Pioneers of Modern Piano Playing and Their Successors." *Musician* 17:810-11 (December 1912).
　　　　 Currier credits Gottschalk with being the first American pianist "to put piano playing on a distinctly higher footing."

B175.   Kellogg, Clara Louise. *Memoirs of an American Prima Donna.* New York: Putnam's, 1913.
　　　　 Contains several references to Gottschalk.

B176.   "Gottschalk's Period." *Etude* v32 (June 1914).

B177.   "The Real Gottschalk." *Etude* 32:423-25 (June 1914).

B178.   Elson, Louis Charles. "Old Times in American Music." *Musician* 19:805+ (December 1914).
　　　　 Elson briefly discusses the musical "feud" between John S. Dwight and Gottschalk.

B179.   *Art of Music*, ed. Daniel Gregory Mason. New York: The National Society of Music, 1915.
　　　　 Gottschalk is mentioned in several sections of this fourteen-volume work. *Le bananier* (See: W78) is included as one of the musical examples.

B180.   Oliver Ditson Company. *Complete Catalog of Piano Music.* Boston: Oliver Ditson Company, 1915.
　　　　 Cited by Doyle (See: B484, p. 130). Even as Gottschalk had faded from public memory, 55 of his compositions were still listed by the publisher. (See also: B136)

B181.   Winter, William. *Vagrant Memories: Being Further Recollections of Other Days.* New York, 1915.

B182.   Bartlett, Homer N. "First of American Pianists to Gain Recognition Abroad." *Musical America* 30:35 (January 1915).

B183.   Fors, Luis Ricardo. "Las grandes pianistas contemporaneous: Louis

Moreau Gottschalk." *Correo musical sud-americano Ano* 3 (April 4, 1917).

Fors defends Gottschalk against his detractors and provides a brief biographical sketch. That Fors wrote the piece suggests the extent to which Gottschalk's music had fallen somewhat out of favor a half-century after his death.

B184.   Bromwell, Henry P.H. *The Dying Poet*. Denver, 1918.

B185.   Saerchinger, César. "Musical Landmarks in New York." *Musical Quarterly* 6:70 (January 1920); 6:244-46 (April 1920).
         The Gottschalk grave sight is included.

B186.   Fay, Amy. *Music Study in Germany from the Home Correspondence of Amy Fay*, ed. Fay Pierce. New York: Macmillan, 1922.
         Originally published in 1880.
         Fay, who had heard Gottschalk perform, found his piano playing to compare well with other virtuosi of the era.

B187.   Huenker, James Gibbons. *Steeplejack*. New York: Scribner's, 1922.
         Gottschalk's piano technique receives positive mention. (See also: B189)

B188.   Saunders, Whitelaw. "What Gottschalk Said to Carreño." *Etude* 42:525 (August 1924).

B189.   Huenker, James Gibbons. *Mezzotints in Modern Music*, 6th ed. New York: Scribner's, 1925.
         The author gives Gottschalk's piano technique positive notice. (See also: B187)

B190.   Aubry, Jean. "A Forgotten Pioneer." *Christian Science Monitor* December 26, 1925.
         Even the title of this article suggests the extent to which Gottschalk had faded in popularity a little more than a half-century after his death.

B191.   Cernicchiaro, Vincenzo. *Storia della musica nel Brazile, 1549-1925*. Milan: Riccioni, 1926.
         According to Cernicchiaro, Gottschalk's performances in Brazil helped to foster a taste for piano music in the country.

B192.   Cooke, James Francis. *Louis Moreau Gottschalk*. Philadelphia: Presser, 1928.
         This is a brief, eighteen-page booklet, included as part of the *Etude* Musical Booklet Library.

B193.   Espadero, Nicolás Ruiz, *et al*. "El centenario Luis Moreau Gottschalk." *Revista bimestre Cubano* (Havana) pp254-63 (November-December 1930).

B194.   Cole, Fannie L. Gwinner. *Dictionary of American Biography*, ed. Allen Johnson and Dumas Malone. s.v. "Gottschalk." New York: Scribner's, 1931.
         This biographical dictionary entry is interesting for the author's assertion that Gottschalk had no Jewish ancestry.

B195.   Kirkpatrick, John. *Observations on Four Volumes and Supplement of the Works of Louis Moreau Gottschalk in the New York Public Library*. New York, c1931.
         A typescript owned by the New York Public Library on early holdings. Also indexed in OCLC, accession no. 42677284. Also reproduced on microfilm, OCLC accession no. 45587226.

B196.   Howard, John Tasker. "Good Old Days. The Last Hope." *Musical Digest* 16:27+ (March 1931).

B197.   Magendanz, Johannes. *Gottschalk in Utica*. Utica, New York, 1932.
         A typescript detailing Gottschalk's activities in Utica. Also indexed in OCLC, accession no. 42677294. (See also: B202)

B198.   Shaw, George Bernard. *Music in London 1890-1894*. London: Constable, 1932. New, complete edition published as *Shaw's Music, The Complete Music Criticism in Three Volumes*, ed. Dan H. Laurence. New York: Dodd, Mead, 1981.
         Playwright and music critic George Bernard Shaw criticized Teresa Carreño for performing Gottschalk's piano works.

B199.   Howard, John Tasker. "Louis Moreau Gottschalk, as Portrayed by Himself." *Musical Quarterly* 18:120-33 (January 1932).
         Based primarily upon *Notes of a Pianist* (See: B113). The subject of Gottschalk's portrayal of himself and the "spin" he put on his career and activities is discussed to some extent in Starr (See: B524).

B200.   Bolling, Ernest L. "Our First Musical Ambassador, Louis Moreau
         Gottschalk." *Etude* 50:97+ (February 1932).
             Bolling deals such topics as the tropical influence in
         Gottschalk's compositions and in his playing, the composer/pianist's
         engaging personality and musical virtuosity. Bolling also notes
         Gottschalk's abilities as an improviser and claims to find direct
         references to Gottschalk's *Le banjo* in Claude Debussy's *Minstrels*.

B201.   Galloway, Tod B. "A Forgotten American Musician." *General
         Magazine and Historical Chronicle* 35:56-64 (October 1932).
             Galloway's article suggests the extent to which Gottschalk had
         faded from memory.

B202.   Magendanz, Johannes. "Gottschalk in Utica." *Town Topics of the
         Mohawk Valley* (October-December 1932; January-May 1933).
             Concerning Gottschalk's performances in Utica, New York.
         (See also: B197)

B203.   Darrell, Robert D. "An Early Pan-American Exhumed." *Musical
         Mercury* 1:18-21 (January-February 1934).
             Darrell takes his contemporaries to task for "hack shuffling
         among the same material" instead of doing original research.

B204.   Rogers, M. Robert. "Jazz Influence on French Music." *Musical
         Quarterly* 21:67 (January 1935).
             Rogers credits Gottschalk with anticipating the blues and the
         Charleston rhythms.

B205.   Locke, Alain Leroy. *The Negro and His Music*. Washington, D.C.:
         The Associates in Negro Folk Education, 1936. Reprint: New York:
         Kennikat Press, 1968.
             Locke mentions that noted composer George Antheil reported
         believed that Gottschalk was a mulatto. There are also references to
         a Gottschalk composition, *Cubano*, a title found nowhere else in the
         Gottschalk literature; probably the closest documented Gottschalk
         title is "danse cubaine," used as the subtitle of several compositions.

B206.   Ayars, Christine Merrick. *Contributions to the Art of Music in
         America by the Music Industries in Boston, 1640 to 1936*. New
         York: Wilson, 1937.
             Gottschalk's endorsement of Chickering pianos is mentioned
         (p. 122).

B207.   Foster, Lois M. *Annals of the San Francisco Stage.* Berkeley:
         Bancroft Library (manuscript), 1937.

B208.   Agüero, Gaspar. "El Compositor Nicolás Ruiz Espadero." *Revista
         Cubana* pp160-78 (April-June 1938).
         (See: B209)

B209.   Agüero y Barreras, Gaspar. *El Compositor Nicolás Ruiz Espadero.*
         Havana: Dirección de Cultura, 1939.
              The author speculates (pp. 11-15) that in Gottschalk's
         posthumously published compositions, Espadero composed the
         harmony, with Gottschalk supplying only the melody. Although
         Espadero edited the Gottschalk works, this appears to be a singular,
         unlikely claim about the Cuban composer/pianist's contributions to
         the final published product. (See also: B208)

B210.   *Celebrities in El Dorado, 1850-1906, History of Music in San
         Francisco*, vol. 4, ed. Cornel Lengyel. San Francisco: Works
         Progress Administration, 1940. Reprint, New York: AMS Prss,
         1972.

B211.   Stengel, Theophil. *Lexikon der Juden in der Musik.* Berlin:
         Hahnefeld, 1940.
              Gottschalk is included in this official Nazi list of Jewish
         musicians.

B212.   Gates, W. Francis. "The First American Pianist." *Etude* (July 1940).
              A biographical sketch of Gottschalk that includes some
         dubious material.

B213.   Chase, Gilbert. *The Music of Spain.* New York: W.W. Norton,
         1941. Reprint: New York: Dover, 1959.
              Chase deals with Gottschalk in chapter 17, "Hispanic Music in
         the Americas."

B214.   Lang, Paul Henry. *Music in Western Civilization.* New York:
         Norton, 1941.
              The Lang book is one of the rare early-to-mid-twentieth-
         century works in which Gottschalk is said to measure up to his
         European contemporaries.

B215.   Almeida, Renato. *História da música brasiliera*, 2nd ed. Rio de

Janeiro: F. Briguiet, 1942.

The author mentions Gottschalk as the composer of *Variations de concert sur l'hymne portugais* (p. 393) and Gottschalk's festivals in Brazil (p. 414).

B216.   Erskine, John. *The Philharmonic Society of New York*. New York: Macmillan, 1943.

This book may be of some minor interest to Gottschalk biographers and genealogists as brief mention is made of his surviving nieces and nephews (pp. 58-59).

B217.   Pereira-Salas, Eugenio. *Notes on the History of Music Exchange Between the Americas Before 1940*, trans. Josefina de Roman. Washington, D.C.: Music Division, Pan-American Union, 1943.

Contains a number of references to Gottschalk.

B218.   Rooks, Mary Rachel, Sister, S.C.N. *The Life and Piano Music of Louis Moreau Gottschalk*. Thesis: University of Cincinnati, 1943.

B219.   Overmyer, Grace. *Famous American Composers*. New York: Thomas Y. Crowell, 1944.

Biographies of Gottschalk, Francis Hopkinson, Lowell Mason, Stephen Collins Foster, Theodore Thomas, John Phillip Sousa, Edward Alexander MacDowell, Harry Thacker Burleigh, Louise Home, Charles Wakefield Cadman, George Gershwin, and Aaron Copland are included.

B220.   Pereira-Salas, Eugenio. "La Embajada musical de Gottschalk en Chile." *Andean Quarterly* pp5-11 (Winter 1944).

B221.   Escragnolle-Doria, L.G. "Cousas não ditas (Os Gottschalk)." *Revista da semana* (Rio de Janeiro) April 8, 1944.

B222.   Chase, Gilbert. *A Guide to Latin American Music*. Washington, D.C.: Library of Congress, Music Division, 1945.

Chase mentions the importance of Gottschalk in bridging inter-American musical cultures.

B223.   Lindstrom, Carl E. "The American Quality in the Music of Louis Moreau Gottschalk." *Musical Quarterly* 31:356-66 (July 1945).

Concerned primarily with Gottschalk's music as a precursor of jazz and Tin Pan Alley.

B224.   Carpentier, Alejo. *La Musica en Cuba*. Mexico: Fondo de Cultura
         Economica, 1946.
             In a section on Nicolás Ruiz Espadero, Gottschalk's use of
         Latin American percussion instruments and the relationship of
         Espadero and Gottschalk are discussed. (See also: B228)

B225.   Ewen, David. *Music Comes to America*. New York: Allen, Towne
         & Heath, 1947.
             Includes discussion (pp. 39-40) on Gottschalk's success in
         attracting audiences.

B226.   Minor, Andrew C. *Piano Concerts in New York City, 1849-1865*.
         Thesis: University of Michigan, 1947.
             Minor's thesis contains numerous references to Gottschalk's
         performances in New York City and is a most valuable work for
         documenting the same.

B227.   Shpall, Leo. "Louis Moreau Gottschalk." *Louisiana Historical
         Quarterly* 30:120-27 (January 1947).
             A biographical article, largely concerned with the musician's
         genealogy.

B228.   Carpentier, Alejo. "Music in Cuba," trans. Ethel S. Cohen. *Musical
         Quarterly* 33:365-80 (July 1947).
             A translation of excerpts from B224.

B229.   Duran, Juan Carlos. "Gottschalk en Buenos Aires." *La Prensa*
         (Buenos Aires) (1948).

B230.   Lowens, Irving. "The First Matinée Idol: Louis Moreau
         Gottschalk." *Musicology* 2:23-34 (1948).
             (See also: B297)

B231.   Kendall, John Smith. "The Friend of Chopin, and Some Other New
         Orleans Musical Celebrities." *Louisiana Historical Quarterly*
         31:130-49 (January 1948).

B232.   Barrenda, E. M. "Un Pianista que hace ochenta anos hizo la delicia
         de las porteñas." *Atlantida* (Buenos Aires) (February 1948).
             The author deals with Gottschalk's private appearances in
         Buenos Aires and his friends in the Argentine city. Note that during
         his years of travel, particularly in South American, Gottschalk

presented numerous private concerts; these accounted for a most important part of his performance activities.

B233.   "News of the Month." *Bulletin of The New York Public Library* 52:371 (July 1948).
         A report including the announcement of the acquisition of a number of Gottschalk autograph manuscripts.

B234.   Kendall, John Smith. "The Friend of Chopin, and Some Other New Orleans Musical Celebrities." *Louisiana Historical Quarterly* 31:856-76 (October 1948).

B235.   Downes, Olin. Concert Preview. *New York Times* December 19, 1948.
         A preview of a concert of American piano music, on which works of a wide variety of American composers were performed.

B236.   "Piano Americana." *New York Herald-Tribune* December 19, 1948.
         A preview of a concert of American piano music, on which works of a wide variety of American composers were performed.

B237.   Downes, Olin. "Six Pianists Heard in Special Concert." *New York Times* December 23, 1948:23.
         A review of the December 22, 1948 Concert of American Piano Music at New York City's Times Hall.

B238.   Thomson, Virgil. "Music: American Piano Music." *New York Herald-Tribune* December 23, 1948.
         A review of the December 22, 1948 Concert of American Piano Music at New York City's Times Hall.

B239.   Sabin, Robert. "American Piano Concert for Library Musical Collection." *Musical America* 69:5 (January 1, 1949).
         A review of the December 22, 1948 Concert of American Piano Muisc at New York City's Times Hall.

B240.   Blesh, Rudi and Harriet Janis. *They All Played Ragtime*. New York: Knopf, 1950.
         Although the authors include some inaccuracies, they do make a valid connection between Gottschalk's compositional work and late nineteenth-century ragtime.

B241.   Tolon, Edwin T. and Jorge A. Gonzales. "Dos interesantes cartas de
         Gottschalk." *Mensuario* (January 1950).
              A discussion of two Gottschalk letters published in Fors (See:
         B112) and *Notes of a Pianist* (See: B113).

B242.   "Un gran pianista norteamericano dió concíertos a los campesinos.
         Conquistó fama en Europa y America, y en 1866, estuvo en Chile."
         El Campesino (Santiago de Chile) 82:47 (July 1950).

B243.   Barbacci, Rodolfo. "Actividades de L. M. Gottschalk en el Peru
         (1865-1866)." *Revista de estudios musicales* 2:343-50 (December
         1950-April 1951).
              The author used newspaper resources to document
         Gottschalk's activities in Peru.

B244.   Lange, Francisco Curt. "Vida y muerte de Louis Moreau Gottschalk
         en Rio de Janeiro, 1869." *Revista de estudios musicales* (Mendoza,
         Argentina) v2 (August 1950; December 1950; April 1951).
              The present is a serialized version of B245.

B245.   Lange, Francisco Curt. *Vida y muerte de Louis Moreau Gottschalk
         en Rio de Janeiro, 1869.* Mendoza, Argentina: Universidad
         Nacional de Cuyo, 1951.
              A reprint of B244 in book form. Doyle (See: B484, p. 89)
         refers to Lange's book as "the definitive work on Gottschalk's life
         and death in Rio de Janeiro." (See also: B254, B255, B256, B268,
         B288)

B246.   Dufour, Charles "Pie." "Gottschalk at Fifteen Won Fame." *New
         Orleans Times-Picayune* March 18, 1951:4.
              This article deals with Gottschalk's early success in Paris.

B247.   Rezende, Carlos Penteado de. "O Poeta do Piano." *Revista do
         Departamento de Investigações* (São Paulo) 3:21-42 (December
         1951).
              This article deals with Gottschalk's concerts in São Paulo and
         his death and funeral in Rio de Janeiro.

B248.   "Gottschalk." *Jornal de Musica* (Rio de Janeiro) (February 1952).

B249.   Schonberg, Harold C. "Facing the Music." *Musical Courier* 145:10;
         4 (February 15; March 1, 1952).

An article largely about Gottschalk's performing career and drawn from *Notes of a Pianist* (See: B113).

B250.   Ayestarán, Lauro. *La Música en el Uruguay.* Montevideo: Servicio Oficial de Defusion Radio Eléctrica, 1953.
　　　　　In volume 1, page 96 and following, musicians associated with Gottschalk during his time in Uruguay are discussed.

B251.   Loesser, Arthur. *Men, Women, and Pianos: A Social History.* New York: Simon & Schuster, 1954.
　　　　　Commentary on Gottschalk's career and impact are scattered throughout the second half of the book.

B252.   Chase, Gilbert. *America's Music from the Pilgrims to the Present.* New York: McGraw-Hill, 1955. Several later editions are also available.
　　　　　Chase deals extensively with Gottschalk in chapter 15, "The Exotic Periphery."

B253.   Schonberg, Harold C. "A Crude and Blustering Nation." *Musical Courier* 151:29-30 (February 1, 1955).
　　　　　Schonberg credits Gottschalk with "giving us the best picture of provincial musical life in America at the time of the Civil War," largely through documentation provided in *Notes of a Pianist* (See: B113).

B254.   Review of *Vida y muerte de Louis Moreau Gottschalk en Rio de Janeiro, 1869* by Francisco Curt Lange. *La Rassegna musicale* 25:153-54 (April-June 1955).
　　　　　A review of B245.

B255.   Pereira-Salas, Eugenio. Review of *Vida y muerte de Louis Moreau Gottschalk en Rio de Janeiro, 1869* by Francisco Curt Lange. *Revista Musical Chilena* 10:59 (July 1955).
　　　　　A review of B245.

B256.   Redlich, Hans F. Review of *Vida y muerte de Louis Moreau Gottschalk en Rio de Janeiro, 1869* by Francisco Curt Lange. *Music Review* 16:249-250 (August 1955).
　　　　　A review of B245.

B257.   Gottschalk, Louis Moreau. *Piano Music by Louis Moreau*

Gottschalk, ed. Jeanne Behrend. Bryn Mawr, Pennsylvania: Theodore Presser, 1956.

For reviews of Behrend's edition of Gottschalk's scores, see: B262 and B264.

B258.   Schonberg, Harold C. "Americana: Gottschalk Piano Works Recall Vanished Age." *New York Times* 106:17, section 2 September 23, 1956.

Includes a review of *The Banjo and Other Creole Favorites*, recorded by Eugene List (See: R68a, *etc.*).

B259.   Eyer, Ronald. "Musical Pioneer." *Musical America* 76:28 (December 15, 1956).

A review of *The Banjo and Other Creole Favorites*, recorded by Eugene List (See: R68a, *etc.*).

B260.   List, Eugene and Sidney Finkelstein. Liner notes for *The Banjo and Other Creole Favorites*. Eugene List, piano. 33-1/3 rpm phonodisc. Vanguard VRS-485, 1957.

(See: R68a, *etc.*)

B261.   Behrend, Jeanne. "Louis Moreau Gottschalk: First American Concert Pianist." *Etude* 75:14+ (January 1957).

Behrend deals with Gottschalk's personality, his reasons for playing mostly only his own compositions, and the problems caused in the quality of his compositions by his ever-increasing commercialism. (See also: B266)

B262.   Eyer, Ronald. Review of *Piano Music by Louis Moreau Gottschalk*, ed. Jeanne Behrend. *Musical America* 77:229 (February 1957).

A review of B257.

B263.   Lowens, Irving. Review of *Piano Music by Louis Moreau Gottschalk*, recorded by Eugene List. *Musical Quarterly* 43:270-73 (April 1957).

A favorable review of the List recording (See: R68a, *etc.*), although the assertion by Sidney Finkelstein in the liner notes (See: B260) that Gottschalk only wished to perform for the common people is called into question. Regarding the compositions themselves, Lowens praises *La Bamboula*, *Le bananier*, and *La savane*, as being deserving of serious consideration. The author characterizes the late Gottschalk repertoire as being comprised primarily of commercial potboilers.

B264.   Lowens, Irving. Review of *Piano Music by Louis Moreau Gottschalk*, ed. Jeanne Behrend. *Notes* 14:441-42 (June 1957).
A review of B257. Lowens praises Behrend's editing and choice of works for inclusion in this Gottschalk collection.

B265.   Kipnis, Igor. Review of *Piano Music by Louis Moreau Gottschalk*, recorded by Jeanne Behrend and *The Banjo and Other Creole Favorites*, recorded by Eugene List. *American Record Guide* 23:172 (August 1957).
While Behrend's musicianship (See: R68b, *etc.*) is praised, Kipnis laments the large amount of overlap between the repertoire on this recording and that on the earlier Gottschalk recording (Vanguard VRS-485) by Eugene List (See: R68a, *etc.*). He suggests that the virtuosic approach, rather than the folkish approach taken by Behrend, will tend to "wear better in the long run."

B266.   Behrend, Jeanne. "America's First Concert Pianist." *Jewish Digest* 2:67-9 (September 1957).
The present is a condensed version of B261.

B267.   Loggins, Vernon. *Where the Word Ends: The Life of Louis Moreau Gottschalk*. Baton Rouge: Louisiana State University Press, 1958.
This much-anticipated biography ultimately failed to impress reviewers and Gottschalk scholars, due in part to the inclusion of fictionalized conversations between Gottschalk and his contemporaries. (See: B270, B271, and B276, for example) (See also: B269, B272, B273, B275, B281)

B268.   Bose, Fritz. Review of *Vida y muerte de Louis Moreau Gottschalk en Rio de Janeiro, 1869* by Francisco Curt Lange. *Die Musikforschung* 11:241-43 (no. 2, 1958).
A review of B245.

B269.   Miller, C.K. Review of *Where the Word Ends* by Vernon Loggins. *Library Journal* p1792 (June 1958).
A review of B267.

B270.   Schonberg, Harold C. Review of *Where the Word Ends* by Vernon Loggins. *Musical Courier* 158:30 (August 1958).

A generally negative review of *Where the Word Ends* (See: B267). According to Schonberg, a biography of Gottschalk was sorely needed, but "Loggins lets us down." Schonberg writes that Gottschalk does not come to life in the Loggins account and that the book is overly sentimental.

B271.   Chase, Gilbert. Review of *Where the Word Ends* by Vernon Loggins. *Notes* 15:575-76 (no. 4, September 1958).

    Although Chase praises Loggins for preparing a well-researched, "picturesque" biography of Gottschalk, he finds the lack of any serious analysis of Gottschalk's compositions to be a serious deficiency. (See: B267)

B272.   Kammerer, Rafael. Review of *Where the Word Ends* by Vernon Loggins. *American Record Guide* 25:106+ (no. 2, October 1958).

    Kammerer attributes the renewed interest in Gottschalk that led to the Loggins book to "a reawakened curiosity about our cultural beginnings." The author praises the Loggins book for presenting a colorful picture of the United States of Gottschalk's day and suggests that Gottschalk's music has not been well represented on sound recordings and acknowledges a need for a complete edition of the composer's works. (See: B267)

B273.   Peterson, Melva. Review of *Where the Word Ends* by Vernon Loggins. *Pan Pipes* 51:35-6 (January 1959).

    A review of B267.

B274.   Pasarell, Emilio J. "El centenario de los conciertos de Adelina Patti y Luis Moreau Gottschalk en Puerto Rico." *Revista del Instituto de cultura Puertoriqueña* 2:52-55 (January-March 1959).

    An article dealing with the Gottschalk-Adelina Patti concerts in Puerto Rico. It is helpful in dating a number of works composed during the tour. Note that Doyle (See: B484, p. 132) incorrectly dates this article as being from 1859. A shortened version appeared in 1970 (See: B379).

B275.   Eyer, Ronald. "Louis Moreau Gottschalk: America's First Musical Celebrity." *Musical America* 69:10-12 (February 1959).

    A review of B267.

B276.   Kinscella, Hazel Gertrude. Review of *Where the Word Ends* by Vernon Loggins. *Journal of Research in Music Education* 7:152-53

(Spring 1959).

While the Loggins book features "excellence of research" and "literary charm," its effect "is greatly lessened by the inclusion of so much fictional material." Interestingly, the review itself contains some dubious factual material. (See: B267)

B277.   Lowens, Irving. "The Curious State of American Music on Records." *Notes* 16:371-76 (June 1959).

Longtime Gottschalk champion Lowens includes the composer among those underrepresented on sound recordings.

B278.   Behrend, Jeanne. "The Peripatetic Gottschalk: America's First Concert Pianist." *Américas* 11:21-26 (October 1959).

(See also: B261 and B266).

B279.   Doyle, John Godfrey. *The Piano Music of Louis Moreau Gottschalk, 1829-1869*. Dissertation: New York University, 1960.

Doyle's dissertation was, according to its author, the first systematic study of Gottschalk's music, including extensive work on the identification of folk melodies used by the composer. The study of Gottschalk's compositional style is also important. Also indexed in *Dissertation Abstracts International* 21-A/10 (April 1961), p. 3113.

B280.   "Piano Music." [Review of *Piano Music by Louis Moreau Gottschalk*, ed. Jeanne Behrend.] *Musical Opinion* (London) (June 1960).

B281.   Ferraro, Louis. Review of *Where the Word Ends* by Vernon Loggins. *Louisiana History* 1:272 (no. 3, Summer 1960).

A review of B267.

B282.   "Piano Music." [Review of *Piano Music by Louis Moreau Gottschalk*, ed. Jeanne Behrend.] *Musical Times* (August 1960).

B283.   "Piano Music." [Review of *Piano Music by Louis Moreau Gottschalk*, ed. Jeanne Behrend.] *South African Music Teacher* v41 (December 1960).

B284.   Broder, Nathan. "The Evolution of the American Composer." In *One Hundred Years of Music in America*, ed. Paul Henry Lang. New York: Schirmer, 1961.

B285.   Gesualdo, Vincente. *Historia de la musica en la Argentina*. Buenos
         Aires: Beta, 1961.
             The author deals with Gottschalk's activies in Argentina
         extensively in volume 2.

B286.   Schonberg, Harold C. "Civil War Pianist." *New York Times* April
         23, 1961:section 2, 13.

B287.   Keefer, Lubow. *Baltimore's Music: The Haven of the American
         Composer*. Baltimore: J.H. Furst, 1962.
             Contains a number of references to Gottschalk.

B288.   Andrade, Muricy. "Gottschalk no Rio de Janeiro." [Review of *Vida
         y muerte de Louis Moreau Gottschalk en Rio de Janeiro, 1869* by
         Francisco Curt Lange] *Jornal de musica* v1 (February 1962).
             A review of B245.

B289.   Breslin, Howard. *Concert Grand*. New York: Dodd and Mead,
         1963.
             A novel in which Gottschalk is named. (See also: B295)

B290.   Schonberg, Harold C. *The Great Pianists*. New York: Simon &
         Schuster, 1963.
             Schonberg includes a number of references to Gottschalk; his
         take on the pianist/composer is quite positive.

B291.   Williams, Jonathan and Ronald B. Kitaj. *The Macon County, North
         Carolina Meshuga Sound Society, Jonathan Williams, Musical
         Director, Presents: Lullabies Twisters Gibbers Drags (á la manière
         de M. Louis Moreau Gottschalk, Late of the City of New Orleans)*.
         Highlands, North Carolina: The Nantahala Foundation, 1963.
         Republished, Indiana University, 1967.
             Of the most peripheral interest in Gottschalk study, despite the
         inclusion of the composer's name in the title.

B292.   Williamson, Jerry Max. *The Transitional Period between
         Romanticism and Realism in the American Arts*. Dissertation:
         Florida State University, 1963.
             Also indexed in *Dissertation Abstracts International* 24-1
         (July 1963), p. 245.

B293.   Korn, Bertram Wallace. "A Note on the Jewish Ancestry of Louis

Moreau Gottschalk." *American Jewish Archives* 15 (no. 2, 1963).

B294.   "Around the Town." *Williamsport Sun-Gazette* February 25, 1963.
A report on the excitement caused by Gottschalk's visit to
Williamsport, Pennsylvania in 1863.

B295.   Walker, Alyce. "New Orleans Composer Got Short Shrift."
Birmingham News (Alabama) November 10, 1963.
A review of Howard Breslin's *Concert Grand* (See: B289).

B296.   Gottschalk, Louis Moreau. *Notes of a Pianist*, ed. Clara Gottschalk
Peterson. Philadelphia, 1881. Also published with English
translation by Robert E. Peterson. London: J.B. Lippincott, 1881.
Republished in an edition with commentary and a new introduction
by Jeanne Behrend. New York: Knopf, 1964. The Behrend edition
was reissued New York: Da Capo, 1979.
This posthumous book consists primarily of a collection of
articles Gottschalk wrote for New York and Paris newspapers during
his concert tours. For reviews of the 1964 edition by Jeanne
Behrend, see: B298-B304, B306, B308-B313, B318, B321. (See
also: B113)

B297.   Lowens, Irving. "The First Matinée Idol: Louis Moreau
Gottschalk." In *Music and Musicians in Early America*, 223-33.
New York: Norton, 1964.
A reprint of B230.

B298.   Miller, C.K. Review of *Notes of a Pianist*, ed. Jeanne Behrend.
Library Journal 89:2597 (June 15, 1964).
A review of Jeanne Behrend's revised edition of Gottschalk's
Notes of a Pianist (See: B296).

B299.   Review of *Notes of a Pianist*, ed. Jeanne Behrend. *Civil War Times*
(August 1964).
An obscure citation listed by Doyle (See: B484, p. 66). (See
also: B296)

B300.   Strongin, Theodore. Review of *Notes of a Pianist*, ed. Jeanne
Behrend. *New York Times* August 3, 1964:23.
A review of Jeanne Behrend's revised edition of Gottschalk's
Notes of a Pianist (See: B296).

B301.　"Book Notes." *Clavier* 3:10 (September 1964).
　　　　Includes a brief review of Jeanne Behrend's revised edition of
Gottschalk's *Notes of a Pianist* (See: B296).

B302.　Finch, A. Review of *Notes of a Pianist*, ed. Jeanne Behrend. *Book
of the Month Club News* p11 (September 1964).
　　　　A review of Jeanne Behrend's revised edition of Gottschalk's
Notes of a Pianist (See: B296).

B303.　Lowens, Irving. Review of *Notes of a Pianist*, ed. Jeanne Behrend.
Americas p39 (September 1964).
　　　　A review of Jeanne Behrend's revised edition of Gottschalk's
Notes of a Pianist (See: B296).

B304.　Sektberg, W. Review of *Notes of a Pianist*, ed. Jeanne Behrend.
Music Journal 22:48 (October 1964).
　　　　A review of Jeanne Behrend's revised edition of Gottschalk's
Notes of a Pianist (See: B296).

B305.　Webster, Daniel. "Eugene List Masters Difficulties Posed by
Gottschalk Music." *Philadelphia Inquirer* November 2, 1964.

B306.　Dawes, Frank. Review of *Notes of a Pianist*, ed. Jeanne Behrend.
Musical Times 105:903-904 (December 1964).
　　　　A review of Jeanne Behrend's revised edition of Gottschalk's
Notes of a Pianist (See: B296).

B307.　Mellers, Wilfred. *Music in a New Found Land*. New York: Knopf,
1965.
　　　　Mellers, a musicologist perhaps best known for giving early,
serious attention to music of The Beatles, deals fairly extensively
with Gottschalk in his book on music in America.

B308.　Peterson, Melva. Review of *Notes of a Pianist*, ed. Jeann Behrend.
Pan Pipes 57:35-36 (January 1965).
　　　　A review of Jeanne Behrend's revised edition of Gottschalk's
Notes of a Pianist (See: B296).

B309.　Review of *Notes of a Pianist*, ed. Jeanne Behrend. *International
Musician* 63:43 (January 1965).
　　　　A review of Jeanne Behrend's revised edition of Gottschalk's
Notes of a Pianist (See: B296).

B310.   Chapin, Louis. Review of *Notes of a Pianist*, ed. Jeanne Behrend.
         Christian Science Monitor January 16, 1965:9.
               A review of Jeanne Behrend's revised edition of Gottschalk's
         Notes of a Pianist (See: B296).

B311.   Sargent, Winthrop. "Have Piano, Will Travel." *New Yorker* 41:189-
         94 (April 17, 1965).
               A review of Jeanne Behrend's revised edition of Gottschalk's
         Notes of a Pianist (See: B296).

B312.   Kammerer, Rafael. Review of *Notes of a Pianist*, ed. Jeanne
         Behrend. *American Record Guide* 31:886-87 (May 1965).
               A review of Jeanne Behrend's revised edition of Gottschalk's
         Notes of a Pianist (See: B296).

B313.   Garrett, Allen M. Review of *Notes of a Pianist*, ed. Jeanne Behrend.
         Music Educators Journal 52:147-48 (September-October 1965).
               A brief review of Jeanne Behrend's revised edition of
         Gottschalk's *Notes of a Pianist* (See: B296).

B314.   Johnson, H. Earle. Review of *Notes of a Pianist*, ed. Jeanne
         Behrend. *Journal of the American Musicological Society* 18:259-62
         (Summer 1965).
               A review of Jeanne Behrend's revised edition of Gottschalk's
         Notes of a Pianist (See: B296).

B315.   *The American Composer Speaks*, ed. Gilbert Chase. Baton Rouge:
         Louisiana State University Press, 1966.
               The book contains excerpts from *Notes of a Pianist* (See:
         B113) on pp. 5-6 and 59-65. (See also: B324, B331)

B316.   Béhague, Gerard Henri. *Popular Musical Currents in the Art Music
         of the Early Nationalistic Period in Brazil, circa 1870-1920.*
         Dissertation: Tulane University, 1966.

B317.   Bernard, Kenneth A. *Lincoln and the Music of the Civil War.*
         Caldwell, Idaho: Caxton Printers, 1966.
               The author quotes newspaper accounts of Gottschalk's March
         24, 1864 performance for President and Mrs. Lincoln.

B318.   Chase, Gilbert. Review of *Notes of a Pianist*, ed. Jeanne Behrend.
         Anuario: Yearbook for Inter-American Musical Research 2:172

(1966).
A review of Jeanne Behrend's revised edition of Gottschalk's *Notes of a Pianist* (See: B296).

B319.   Horton, Charles Allison. *Serious Art and Concert Music for Piano in America in the 100 Years from Alexander Reinagle to Edward MacDowell.* Dissertation: University of North Carolina at Chapel Hill, 1966.
Also indexed in *Dissertation Abstracts International* 27-A/10 (April 1967), p. 3481.

B320.   Snook, Gerald O'Brien. *The Gottschalk Legacy.* Thesis: University of Nebraska, Lincoln, 1966.

B321.   Zelenka, K. "Louis Moreau Gottschalk ein zu Unrecht Vergessener." *Neue Zeitschrift für Musik* 127:98-99 (March 1966). Reprinted in *Das Orchester* 14:149-51 (April 1966).
A review of Jeanne Behrend's revised edition of Gottschalk's *Notes of a Pianist* (See: B296).

B322.   Young, Percy M. *Keyboard Musicians of the World.* New York: Abelard-Schuman, 1967.
Young includes several references to Gottschalk.

B323.   Barker, John W. "Gottschalk in Brooklyn: A Morbid Epilogue to a Brilliant Career." Paper read at a Midwest chapter meeting of the American Musicological Society, Newberry Library, Chicago, November 11-12, 1967.

B324.   Ringo, James. Review of *The American Composer Speaks*, ed. Gilbert Chase. *American Record Guide* 34:318 (December 1967).
A review of B315.

B325.   Clemons, Bonnie Lazenby. *Louis Moreau Gottschalk.* Thesis: Central Missouri State College, 1968.

B326.   Dwight, John S. *Dwight's Journal of Music and Literature.* Boston, 1852-81. Reprint, New York: Arno Press, 1968.
References to Gottschalk can be found in articles from the following dates: January 22, 1853; February 5, 1853; February 19, 1853 (includes reviews of Gottschalk's American debut); April 9, 1853; August 13, 1853; September 10, 1853; October 22, 1853 (a

review of Gottschalk's Boston debut); November 12, 1853;
November 19, 1853; May 20, 1854; May 27, 1854; April 26, 1856;
September 13, 1856; October 18, 1856; October 25, 1856; November
1, 1856; November 8, 1856; November 15, 1856; December 20,
1856; December 27, 1856; January 17, 1857; February 7, 1857;
February 8, 1862; February 15, 1862; February 22, 1862; March 1,
1862; March 8, 1862; March 22, 1862; June 7, 1862; June 12, 1862;
July 12, 1862; August 9, 1862; September 6, 1862; September 13,
1862; September 20, 1862; October 11, 1862; October 18, 1862 (an
article in which Dwight defends his earlier criticism of Gottschalk,
apparently in reaction to the popularity of the musician on his concert
tour); November 8, 1862; November 15, 1862; December 20, 1862;
January 10, 1863; March 14, 1863; April 4, 1863; April 18, 1863;
May 16, 1863; May 30, 1863; June 13, 1863; September 5, 1863;
September 19, 1863; October 3, 1863; October 17, 1863; October 31,
1863; November 14, 1863; November 28, 1863; December 13, 1863;
March 19, 1864; April 16, 1864; June 25, 1864; October 29, 1864;
December 24, 1864; January 5, 1865; January 21, 1865; February 4,
1865; March 4, 1865; April 15, 1865; April 29, 1865; May 13, 1865;
August 5, 1865; September 2, 1865; June 23, 1866; August 29, 1868;
and January 29, 1870 (a death notice for Gottschalk).

B327.   Strongin, Theodore. "A Pair of Originals." *New York Times* January
          28, 1968:II, D24.
               A review of *The Piano Music of Louis Moreau Gottschalk*
          (See: R78d, *etc.*), recorded by Amiram Rigai.

B328.   Schonberg, Harold C. "Let's Get to Gottschalk." *New York Times*
          February 25, 1968:19.
               An article dealing with the New York Public Library's
          acquisition of Gottschalk manuscripts.

B329.   Kammerer, Rafael. Review of *The Piano Music of Louis Moreau
          Gottschalk*, recorded by Amiram Rigai. *American Record Guide*
          p660 (April 1968).
               A review of R78d, *etc.*

B330.   Offergeld, Robert. Review of *The Piano Music of Louis Moreau
          Gottschalk*, recorded by Amiram Rigai. *Hi-Fi Stereo Review* pp88+
          (April 1968).
               A review of R78d, *etc.*

B331.   Hansen, Peter S.   Review of *The American Composer Speaks*, ed.
        Gilbert Chase. *Notes* 24:717 (June 1968).
        A review of B315.

B332.   "Composers: A Real Pioneer." *Time* (June 14, 1968).
        Although this article deals with the more sensational aspects
        of Gottschalk's life and career, it is significant that it signifies his
        story's exposure to a much wider public.

B333.   Ericson, Raymond. "105 Years Later, It's Gottschalk Time Again."
        New York Times July 7, 1968.
        A report on Jeanne Behrend's upcoming recital in New
        London, Connecticut on the anniversary of Gottschalk's appearance
        there on July 13, 1863.

B334.   Offergeld, Robert. "Louis Moreau Gottschalk." *High Fidelity/*
        Stereo Review 21:53-67 (September 1968).
        A biography reproduced as part of B378.

B335.   Offergeld, Robert. "Music of the Presidents." *Stereo Review* 21:80
        (November 1968).
        Offergeld mentions Gottschalk's performance for Abraham
        Lincoln and his encounters as a youth with Andrew Jackson.

B336.   "Primer concurso internacional Louis Moreau Gottschalk para
        pianistas y compositores." *Boletin interamericano de musica*
        n68:22-26 (November 1968).
        An announcement of the First Louis Moreau Gottschalk
        International Competition for Pianists and Composers. Although
        announced for the Conservatory of Music, San Juan, Puerto Rico,
        December 8-15, 1969, the event eventually took place at Dillard
        University, New Orleans, June 3-7, 1970.

B337.   Gottschalk, Louis Moreau. *The Piano Works of Louis Moreau*
        Gottschalk, ed. Vera Brodsky Lawrence and Richard Jackson. New
        York: Arno Press and *The New York Times*, 1969-70.
        For reviews of this collection, see: B375, B386, B390, B404,
        B409.

B338.   Hitchcock, H. Wiley. *Music in the United States: A Historical*
        Introduction. Englewood Cliffs, New Jersey: Prentice-Hall, 1969.
        Later reprints available.

Hitchcock provides detailed analysis of the work of
Gottschalk, Charles Ives, Aaron Copland, Edgar Varese, and Stephen
Foster. (See also: B368 and B391)

B339.   Lebow, Marcia Wilson. *A Systematic Examination of the "Journal
of Music and Art" Edited by John Sullivan Dwight: 1852-1881,
Boston, Massachusetts.* Dissertation: University of California, Los
Angeles, 1969.
    Also indexed in *Dissertation Abstracts International* 30-
A/8:3493 (February 1970). The author accuses Gottschalk of over-
reacting to Dwight's justifiable criticism of his compositons. Lebow
also discredits the story of Gottschalk fooling Dwight by making an
unannounced substitution of an obscure Beethoven piece for one of
his own compositions.

B340.   Offergeld, Robert. "The Gottschalk Legend: Grand Fantasy for a
Great Many Pianos." In *The Piano Works of Louis Moreau
Gottschalk*, ed. Vera Brodsky Lawrence and Richard Jackson. New
York: Arno Press and *The New York Times*, 1969:xiii-xxxiv.

B341.   Russell, Theodore C. *Theodore Thomas: His Role in the
Development of Musical Culture in the United States, 1835-1905.*
Dissertation: University of Minnesota, 1969.
    The author includes references to concerts jointly performed
by Thomas and Gottschalk. Also indexed in *Dissertation Abstracts
International* 31-A/5 (November 1970), p. 2425.

B342.   "Gottschalk Competition." *Inter-American Music Bulletin* n69-70:8
(January-March 1969).
    An announcement of the First Louis Moreau Gottschalk
International Competition for Pianists and Composers. Although
announced for the Conservatory of Music, San Juan, Puerto Rico,
December 8-15, 1969, the event eventually took place at Dillard
University, New Orleans, June 3-7, 1970.

B343.   Barker, John W. "Gottschalk's Grave." *Stereo Review* 22:6
(February 1969).

B344.   Eyer, Ronald. "Louis Moreau Gottschalk, America's First Musical
Celebrity." *Musical America* 69:10-12 (February 1969).

B345.   Goode, William M. "Letter to the Editor: Who's Got Gottschalk?"

Stereo Review 22:6+ (February 1969).

B346.　Offergeld, Robert. "Letter to the Editor: Who's Got Gottschalk?"
Stereo Review 22:6+ (February 1969).

B347.　Jackson, Richard. "Gottschalk and New Orleans." Paper presented
at the Louisiana State Museum at the opening of the Centennial
Exhibition: The World of Louis Moreau Gottschalk, February 21,
1969. Typescript housed at the Library of the Performing Arts, New
York Public Library.

B348.　Lorue, Marie-Thérèse. "Exhibit, Program, Reception Slated at
Presbytère Today." *New Orleans Times-Picayune* February 23,
1969.

B349.　"Commemorating the 100th Anniversary of the Death of Louis
Moreau Gottschalk. In *The New Orleans Philharmonic Society,
Program Notes* (February 25, 1969).

B350.　Dufour, Charles L. "Gottschalk Memorial Concert Honors N.O.
Piano Prodigy." *New Orleans States-Item* February 25, 1969.
　　　A preview of the Gottschalk centennial concert in New
Orleans and report on a memoral plaque honoring the composer;
contains a brief biography.

B351.　"Gottschalk Memorial." *New Orleans Times-Picayune* February 25,
1969.

B352.　"Plaque, Wreath Honor Composer-Pianist." *New Orleans Times-
Picayune* February 27, 1969.

B353.　Ericson, Raymond. "In a Gottschalk Year, a Contest." *New York
Times* March 2, 1969:2.
　　　An announcement of the First Louis Moreau Gottschalk
International Competition for Pianists and Composers. Although
announced for the Conservatory of Music, San Juan, Puerto Rico,
December 8-15, 1969, the event eventually took place at Dillard
University, New Orleans, June 3-7, 1970.

B354.　Grossman, James A. "Music Competition Will Be Held Here." *San
Juan Star* March 27, 1969.
　　　An announcement of the First Louis Moreau Gottschalk

International Competition for Pianists and Composers. Although announced for the Conservatory of Music, San Juan, Puerto Rico, December 8-15, 1969, the event eventually took place at Dillard University, New Orleans, June 3-7, 1970.

B355.   Rodriguez, Wilda. "Concurso mundial para pianistas se realizara en Puerto Rico." *EL Mundo* (San Juan) March 27, 1969.
    An article pertaining to the First Louis Moreau Gottschalk International Competition for Pianists and Composers.

B356.   Valdes, Ada Nivia Guerra. "Isla sera sede de concurso y homenaje a compositor EU." *El Imparcial* (San Juan) March 27, 1969.
    An article pertaining to the First Louis Moreau Gottschalk International Competition for Pianists and Composers.

B357.   Hume, Paul. "An American Composer, Good God!" *Washington Post* April 27, 1969:K,4.

B358.   Green, Alan H. "Gottschalk's Grave." *Stereo Review* 22:12 (May 1969).
    A letter to the editor about the poor condition of Gottschalk's grave in a Brooklyn, New York cemetery.

B359.   Bach, Eleanor and Robert Offergeld. "An Experiment in Astro-Musicology." *Stereo Review* 23:72-73 (July 1969).
    An article about Gottschalk's astrological signs.

B360.   "Special Merit Picks." *Billboard* (October 4, 1969).
    Includes a listing for *Gottschalk: 40 Works for Piano*, recorded by Alan Mandel (See: R67a, *etc.*).

B361.   Weinstock, Herbert. "Bread and Lollipops." *Saturday Review* 52:81 (October 25, 1969).
    Review of *Gottschalk: 40 Works for Piano*, recorded by Alan Mandel (See: R67a, *etc.*).

B362.   Webster, Daniel. "Centennial Discs Sample Gottschalk Piano Compositions." *Philadelphia Inquirer* October 26, 1969.
    Review of *Gottschalk: 40 Works for Piano*, recorded by Alan Mandel (See: R67a, *etc.*).

B363.   Stevenson, Robert. "Gottschalk in Buenos Aires." *Inter-American*

Music Bulletin 74:1-7 (November 1969).

B364.   Stevenson, Robert. "Gottschalk in Western South America." *Inter-American Music Bulletin* 74:7-16 (November 1969).

B365.   Klein, Howard. "Should We Dig up the Rare Romantics?" *New York Times* November 23, 1969:M14.
         Review of *Gottschalk: 40 Works for Piano*, recorded by Alan Mandel (See: R67a, *etc.*).

B366.   Croche, Florestan. "Mandel 'Revives' Gottschalk." *Baltimore Sunday Sun* November 30, 1969.
         Review of *Gottschalk: 40 Works for Piano*, recorded by Alan Mandel (See: R67a, *etc.*).

B367.   Doyle, John G. "Gottschalk: Nationalistic Composer, Native Virtuoso." *Music Educators Journal* 56:25+ (December 1969).
         The article contains examples of some of the folk melodies used by Gottschalk, primarily in his piano compositions.

B368.   Finney, Ross Lee. Review of *Music in the United States: A Historical Introduction* by H. Wiley Hitchcock. *Notes* 2:271-72 (December 1969).
         A review of B338.

B369.   Trimble, Lester. "Alan Mandel's Big Box Set of Gottchalk." *Stereo Review* 23:110 (December 1969).
         Review of *Gottschalk: 40 Works for Piano*, recorded by Alan Mandel (See: R67a, *etc.*).

B370.   Kriegsman, Alan M. "New Gottschalk Set." *Washington Post* December 14, 1969.
         Review of *Gottschalk: 40 Works for Piano*, recorded by Alan Mandel (See: R67a, *etc.*).

B371.   Schaden, Herman. "Backward Look." *Washington Sunday Star* December 15, 1969.
         Review of *Gottschalk: 40 Works for Piano*, recorded by Alan Mandel (See: R67a, *etc.*).

B372.   "City to Get Gottschalk Material." *Philadelphia Inquirer* December 18, 1969.

An article concerning Jeanne Behrend's gift of Gottschalk-related materials to the Free Library of Philadelphia.

B373.   Marrocco, W. Thomas. "Gottschalkiana II: Miscellanea." Paper read at the American Musicological Society Annual Meeting, St. Louis, December 29, 1969.

B374.   Baker, David N. "Indiana University's Black Music Committee." In *Black Music in Our Culture*, comp. Dominique-René de Lerma. Kent State University Press, 1970.

As described by Doyle (See: B484, p. 21), "undocumented speculation about [Gottschalk's] ancestry." Note that a number of scholars have mistakenly identified Gottschalk as being of mixed race, due to basic differences between the use of the term "Creole" during the composer's time and its use throughout much of the twentieth century; some writers, particularly those working before World War II, have questioned Gottschalk's Jewish heritage.

B375.   Chase, Gilbert. "Review Article: The Music of Gottschalk." *Anuario: Yearbook for Inter-American Musical Research* 6:105-110 (1970).

A review of *The Piano Works of Louis Moreau Gottschalk*, ed. Vera Brodsky Lawrence, with introductory material by Richard Jackson (See: B337), and *Gottschalk: 40 Works for Piano*, recorded by Alan Mandel (See: R67a, *etc.*).

B376.   "Eugene List in Gottschalk Centenary Concert." *Music Clubs Magazine* 49:11 (no. 3, Special Issue 1970).

B377.   Jackson, Richard. "A Note on Gottschalk Manuscripts in New York." *Anuario: Yearbook for Inter-American Musical Research* 6:111-12 (1970).

Jackson describes the recent acquisitions of the New York Public Library.

B378.   Offergeld, Robert. *The Centennial Catalogue of the Published and Unpublished Compositions of Louis Moreau Gottschalk.* New York: *Stereo Review*, 1970.

A most important catalog of Gottschalk's works when it first appeared. Although more recent scholarship has clarified some of the questions posed by Offergeld in relation to lost compositions and has suggested a revision of the dates of a number of works,

Offergeld's work remains important. (See also: B387, B413)

B379.   Pasarell, Emilio J. *Orígenes y desarrollo de la afición teatral en Puerto Rico.* San Juan: Editorial de Departamento de Instrucción Pública, Estado Libre Asociado de Puerto Rico, 1970.
        Includes references on pages 99-105 to Adelina Patti and Gottschalk's joint concerts in Puerto Rico. Pasarell's earlier article (See: B274) includes more detail.

B380.   Rigai, Amiram. Liner notes for *The Piano Music of Louis Moreau Gottschalk.* Amiram Rigai, piano. 33-1/3 rpm phonodisc. Decca DL 710143, 1970.

B381.   Schonberg, Harold C. *The Lives of the Great Composers.* New York, 1970.

B382.   Thompson, Donald. "Gottschalk in the Virgin Islands." *Anuario: Yearbook for Inter-American Musical Research* 6:95-104 (1970).
        Thompson deals with Gottschalk and Ademina Patti's sojourn to St. Thomas, Virgin Islands for three concerts in June 1857.

B383.   Sterling, Manuel Márquez. "Gottschalk: Musical Humboldt." *Américas* 22:10-18 (January 1970).

B384.   Frankenstein, Alfred. "Gottschalk: Works for Piano." *High Fidelity Magazine* (no. 2, 1970).

B385.   "A Gamut of Americana." *Pan Pipes* 62:33 (no. 2, 1970).
        Includes details (some incorrect) pertaining to events of the Gottschalk centennial.

B386.   Schonberg, Harold C. "A Prophet Without Honor in His Own Land." *New York Times* February 22, 1970. Reprinted in *American Musical Digest* 1:6-8 (no. 6, 1970).
        A review of *The Piano Works of Louis Moreau Gottschalk*, ed. Vera Brodsky Lawrence and Richard Jackson (See: B337).

B387.   Offergeld, Robert. "On the Trail of Louis Moreau Gottschalk." *Stereo Review* 24:81-84 (March 1970).
        An abridged version of the introduction to the author's *The Centennial Catalogue* (See: B378) in which Offergeld discusses his efforts to construct a catalog of Gottschalk's works.

B388.   "Forty Works for Piano." *Time* p63 (March 30, 1970).
　　　　　　Review of *Gottschalk: 40 Works for Piano*, recorded by Alan
　　　　Mandel (See: R67a, *etc.*).

B389.   Lowens, Irving. "A Revival." *Washington Sunday Star* March 8,
　　　　1970. Reprinted in *American Musical Digest* 1:6 (no. 6, 1970).
　　　　　　A review of *The Piano Works of Louis Moreau Gottschalk*, ed.
　　　　Vera Brodsky Lawrence and Richard Jackson.

B390.   Haskins, John. "Louis Moreau Gottschalk: The Piano Works in
　　　　Print." *Kansas City Star* March 22, 1970. Reprinted in *American
　　　　Musical Digest* 1:6 (no. 6, 1970).
　　　　　　A review of *The Piano Works of Louis Moreau Gottschalk*, ed.
　　　　Vera Brodsky Lawrence and Richard Jackson (See: B337).

B391.   Covey, Cyclone. Review of *Music in the United States: A Historical
　　　　Introduction* by H. Wiley Hitchcock. *American Historical Review*
　　　　75:1177-78 (no. 4, 1970).
　　　　　　A review of B338.

B392.   Schonberg, Harold C. "The Black Swan That Sang for the Nobility."
　　　　New York Times April 12, 1970.
　　　　　　Includes references to Gottschalk's relationship with Joseph
　　　　White and Lucien Lambert.

B393.   "World Piano Competition to Be Held at Dillard." *New Orleans
　　　　Times-Picayune* April 12, 1970. Reprinted in *American Musical
　　　　Digest* 1:9 (no. 6, 1970).
　　　　　　An announcement that the venue for the First Louis Moreau
　　　　Gottschalk International Competition for Pianists and Composers has
　　　　been changed from Puerto Rico to Dillard University, New Orleans.

B394.   Lange, Francisco Curt. "Louis Moreau Gottschalk." *Inter-American
　　　　Bulletin (Boletin interamericano de musica)* 77:3-14 (May 1970).
　　　　　　Lange deals with Gottschalk's work in Montevideo in 1867.

B395.   Gagnard, Frank. "New Orleans Birthplace of Gottschalk Contest."
　　　　New Orleans Times-Picayune May 24, 1970.

B396.   Frankenstein, Alfred. Review of *Gottschalk: 40 Works for Piano*,
　　　　recorded by Alan Mandel. *American Musical Digest* 1:8-10 (no. 6,
　　　　1970).

A review of R67a, *etc.*

B397. "Three Pianists to Play Today." *New Orleans Times-Picayune* June 3, 1970.
An announcement pertaining to the First Louis Moreau Gottschalk International Competition for Pianists and Composers.

B398. "Nine Composers Are Finalists." *New Orleans Times-Picayune* June 4, 1970.
A brief announcement pertaining to the First Louis Moreau Gottschalk International Competition for Pianists and Composers.

B399. "Pianist Here As Judge in Dillard Event." *New Orleans Times-Picayune* June 5, 1970.
An announcement of the arrival of pianist Guiomar Novaës to judge the First Louis Moreau Gottschalk International Competition for Pianists and Composers. Novaës had made some of the earlier recordings of Gottschalk's works (See: R258a, for example)

B400. Hansen, Peter S. Letter to the Editor. *New Orleans Times-Picayune* June 16, 1970.
The writer complains about the public and press neglect of the First Louis Moreau Gottschalk International Competition for Pianists and Composers. Obviously, from other *New Orleans Times-Picayune* articles pertaining to the competition, there was local press coverage; established music journals, however, did virtually ignore it.

B401. "Medallas de oro y plata a pianists de Cuba y Chile." *El Diario-La Prensa* (New York) June 19, 1970.
An announcement of the results of the First Louis Moreau Gottschalk International Competition for Pianists and Composers.

B402. Ericson, Raymond. "In New Orleans." *New York Times* June 28, 1970:23.
An announcement of the results of the First Louis Moreau Gottschalk International Competition for Pianists and Composers.

B403. Rubin, Libby. "Louis Moreau Gottschalk and the 1860-61 Opera Season in Cuba." *Inter-American Bulletin* (*Boletin interamericano de musica*) 78:1-7 (July-October 1970).
Documentation of Gottschalk's frustrating experiences as an

opera conductor in Cuba. Note that Starr's *Bamboula!* (See: B524) also provides much material on this, one of Gottschalk's least successful endeavors.

B404.   Doyle, John G. Review of *The Piano Works of Louis Moreau Gottschalk*, ed. Vera Brodsky Lawrence and Richard Jackson. *Music Educators Journal* 57:69-70 (October 1970).
A review of B337.

B405.   Mandel, Alan. "The Piano Music of Louis Moreau Gottschalk." Lecture/recital for the American Liszt Society Festival, October 15-17, 1970. 7-1/2 ips reel-to-reel audio tape. Recorded in Gheens Lecture Hall, Southern Baptist Theological Seminary.

B406.   Lewis, John Cary. *A Study and Edition of Recently Discovered Works of Louis Moreau Gottschalk.* Dissertation: The University of Rochester, 1971.
Also indexed in *American Doctoral Dissertations* (1972), p. 359. Lewis deals with "Andante" from *Symphony No. 1 ("A Night in the Tropics")*, *Grand marcha solemne*, *Variations de concert sur l'hymne portugais du roi Luis I*, *Tarantella for Piano and Orchestra*, *Symphony No. 2 ("A Montevideo")*, *Marcha triunfal y final de opera*, and *Escenas campestraes*.

B407.   Weiser, Bernhard D. *Keyboard Music.* Dubuque, Iowa: William C. Brown, 1971.
Even with the renewed interest in and appreciation of Gottschalk's compositional contributions, Weiser heavily criticizes the composer (pp. 125-26). As John Doyle writes (See: B484, p. 157), Weiser "outdoes John S. Dwight..."

B408.   Marrocco, W. Thomas. "Gottschalkiana: New Light on the Gottschalks and the Bruslés." *Louisiana History* 12:59-66 (Winter 1971).

B409.   Hitchcock, H. Wiley. Review of *The Piano Works of Louis Moreau Gottschalk*, ed. Vera Brodsky Lawrence and Richard Jackson. *Notes* 27:544-45 (March 1971).
A review of W337.

B410.   Ambrose, Jane. "Louis Moreau Gottschalk's Visit to Vermont in 1862." *Vermont History* pp. 125-27 (Spring 1971).

B411.   Prophit, Willie Sword. "The Crescent City's Charismatic Celebrity:
         Louis Moreau Gottschalk's New Orleans Concerts, Spring, 1853."
         Louisiana History 12:243-54 (Summer 1971).

B412.   Rubin, Libby Antarsh. "Louis Moreau Gottschalk and the 1860-61
         Opera Season in Cuba." *Inter-American Music Bulletin* 78:1-7 (July-
         October 1971).

B413.   Mandel, Alan. Review of *The Centennial Catalogue of the
         Published and Unpublished Compostions of Louis Moreau
         Gottschalk* by Robert Offergeld. *Notes* 28:42-43 (September 1971).
             A review of B378.

B414.   Leipold, L. Edmond. *Famous American Musicians.* Minneapolis:
         T.S. Denison, 1972.
             In a truly eclectic set of biographical sketches for children,
         Leipold profiles Gottschalk, James Bland, John Phillip Sousa, Irving
         Berlin, Louis Armstrong, Marian Anderson, Lena Horne, Van
         Cliburn, Leonard Bernstein, and the rock group Paul Revere and the
         Raiders.

B415.   Frankenstein, Alfred. Review of *Louis Moreau Gottschalk: A
         Centennial Concert* by various pianists. *High Fidelity* 22:108
         (January 1972).
             A review of R112c, *etc.*

B416.   Robinson, Florence Crim. "A View of Louis Moreau Gottschalk."
         Musical Analysis 1:12-18 (no. 1, winter 1972).
             A biographical sketch of Gottschalk that incorrectly identifies
         him as a mulatto due to confusion about the meaning of the term
         "Creole."

B417.   McCabe, John. Review of *The World of Louis Moreau Gottschalk*,
         recorded by Eugene List and others. *Records and Recordings* 15:56
         (April 1972).
             A review of RR34b, *etc.*

B418.   Prophit, Willie Sword. "Composer from the Crescent City." *Music
         Journal* pp24+ (July 1972).

B419.   Anderson, William. "Editorially Speaking: Home Sweet Home."
         Stereo Review 29:4 (October 1972).

Anderson discusses the growing public interest in such American composers as Gottschalk, John Phillip Sousa, and Scott Joplin.

B420.   Jackson, Richard. "Gottschalk of Louisiana." In *Piano Music of Louis Moreau Gottschalk*. New York: Dover Publications, 1973.

B421.   Loesser, Arthur. "Louis Moreau Gottschalk." In Krueger, Karl. *The Musical Heritage of the United States—The Unknown Portion*. New York: Society for the Preservation of the American Musical Heritage, 1973.

B422.   Mandel, Alan. "Louis Moreau Gottschalk." In *The New Music Lover's Handbook*, ed. Elie Siegmeister. Irvington-on-Hudson, New York: Harvey House, 1973:509-12.

B423.   Marrocco, W. Thomas. "America's First Nationalist Composer: Louis Moreau Gottschalk (1829-1869)." In *Scitti in onore di Ligi Ronga*, 293-313. Milan and Naples: Riccardo Ricciardi, 1973.
A biographical sketch.

B424.   "Gottschalk Compositions in New Book by Amiram Rigai." *Piano Guild News* 22:32 (January-February 1973).
A notice of Rigai's edition of Gottschalk piano works.

B425.   Abraham, Kenneth. "Mr. Dwight's Blind Spot: Louis Moreau Gottschalk." *Musart* pp47-50 (Winter 1973).
Abraham speculates about the causes of critic John S. Dwight's antagonism toward Gottschalk.

B426.   Cott, Jonathan. "Our Musical Past Rediscovered." *New York Times* March 11, 1973:II, D27, 35.
Review of *Monster Concert: Ten Pianos, Sixteen Pianists*, recorded by Eugene List and others (See: R277a and R298a)

B427.   Offergeld, Robert. "A Monster Concert." *Stereo Review* 30:109-09 (April 1973).
Review of *Monster Concert: Ten Pianos, Sixteen Pianists*, recorded by Eugene List and others (See: R277a and R298a)

B428.   Thompson, Sue. "Music: The Pianist Who Composed His Own Requiem." *New Orleans Magazine* 7:30-31 (April 1973).

B429.   Rockwell, John. Record review. *High Fidelity* 32:103 (May 1973).
         Review of *Monster Concert: Ten Pianos, Sixteen Pianists*,
         recorded by Eugene List and others (See: R277a and R298a)

B430.   Rockwell, John. "Bicentennial Music." *New York Times* May 16,
         1973.
         Review of *The Piano in America*, vol. 1, recorded by Neely
         Bruce (See: R91a and R142g).

B431.   Southern, Eileen. "Needs for Research in Black-American Music."
         College Music Symposium 13:43-52 (Fall 1973).
         Southern points to Gottschalk as one white composer who was
         inspired by African-American music.

B432.   Salzman, Eric. "Parlor Plinks: The Piano in America." *Stereo
         Review* 31:148 (October 1973).
         Review of *The Piano in America*, vol. 1, recorded by Neely
         Bruce (See: R91a and R142g).

B433.   Sargent, Winthrop. "Musical Events: Concert Records." *New
         Yorker* pp151-56 (October 8, 1973).
         Review of *Monster Concert: Ten Pianos, Sixteen Pianists*,
         recorded by Eugene List and others (See: R277a and R298a)

B434.   Frankenstein, Alfred. Record review. *High Fidelity* 23:130
         (November 1973).
         Review of *The Piano in America*, vol. 1, recorded by Neely
         Bruce (See: R91a and R142g).

B435.   Gerig, Reginald R. *Famous Pianists and Their Techniques.*
         Washington and New York, 1974.

B436.   Hines, James Robert. *Musical Activity in Norfolk, Virginia, 1680-
         1972.* Dissertation: University of North Carolina at Chapel Hill,
         1974.
         The author documents Gottschalk performances in Norfolk on
         April 4, 5, and 6, 1864. Also indexed in *Dissertation Abstracts
         International* 35-A/6 (December 1974), p. 3793.

B437.   Korf, William E. *The Orchestral Music of Louis Moreau Gottschalk.*
         Dissertation: The University of Iowa, 1974. Also published as
         Wissenschaftliche Abhandlungen, Vol. 28. Henryville,

Pennsylvania: Institute of Mediaeval Music, 1983.
Also indexed in *Dissertation Abstracts International* 35-A/7 (January 1975), p. 4589.

B438.   Logsdon, Leann Frances. *Louis Moreau Gottschalk: His Style and Significance.* Undergraduate honors thesis: Tulane University, 1974.

B439.   Rubin, Libby Antarsh. *Gottschalk in Cuba.* Dissertation: Columbia University, 1974.
The Rubin dissertation provides an account of Gottschalk's travels and performances in Cuba, as well as analysis of some of his works composed on the island and/or based on Cuban themes. Doyle (See: B484, p. 140) takes the author to task for relying on the European editions of many of these works, editions that differ to some degee from the earlier, sketchier, more improvisatory Edelmann editions from Cuba. Also indexed in *Dissertation Abstracts International* 35-A/10 (April 1975), p. 6755.

B440.   Denton, David. Record review. *Records and Recordings* 17:66-67 (June 1974).
Review of *Louis Moreau Gottschalk: A Centennial Concert,* recorded by various pianists (See: R112c, *etc.*).

B441.   Anderson, William. "Editorially Speaking: Musical Nutrition." *Stereo Review* 33:6 (November 1974).
Anderson discusses the problems that Gottschalk encountered in trying to break new musical ground while influential music critics, John S. Dwight in particular, urged American composers to follow Germanic musical traditions. Doyle (See: B484) takes Anderson to task for singling out Leonard Pennario (See: R68i, *etc.*) as a supporter of Gottschalk, while ignoring the likes of John Kirkpatrick, Jeanne Behrend, Eugene List, and others.

B442.   Offergeld, Robert. "The Patience of Louis Moreau Gottschalk." *Stereo Review* 33:130 (November 1974).
A review of *Music of Louis Moreau Gottschalk,* recorded by Leonard Pennario (See: R68i, *etc.*).

B443.   Bauer, Margaret Spearly. Salon Piano Music in America as Compared to the Piano Works of Louis Moreau Gottschalk during the Years 1853 to 1869. Thesis: Indiana University of Pennsylvania,

1975.

B444.   Cole, Ronald Fred. *Music in Portland, Maine, from Colonial Times Through the Nineteenth Century.* Dissertation: Indiana University, 1975.
         Gottschalk's concerts in Portland are included. Also indexed in *Dissertation Abstracts International* 36-A/8 (February 1976), p. 4836.

B445.   Whorf, Mike. *The Wizard of the Ivories Louis Gott Schalk* [*sic*]. 1-7/8 ips audio cassette. Birmingham, Michigan: Mike Whorf, Inc., c1975.
         This thirty-seven minute recording presents Gottschalk's biography and was recorded for the radio program *Kaleidoscope.*

B446.   Darrell, R.D. Record review. *High Fidelity* 20:78 (March 1975).
         Review of *Music of Louis Moreau Gottschalk*, recorded by Leonard Pennario (See: R68i, *etc.*)

B447.   Dart, Harold. "What Is American Music?" *Clavier* 14:12-13 (April 1975).
         The author presents some of Gottschalk's accomplishments.

B448.   Taylor, William J. "Music by Gottschalk." *Clavier* 14:16 (April 1975).
         A poem praising Gottschalk. Reprinted on the title page of Doyle (See: B484).

B449.   Bush, Robert D. and Blake Touchstone. "A Survey of Manuscript Holdings in The Historic New Orleans Collection." *Louisiana History* 16:89-96 (Winter 1975).

B450.   Offergeld, Robert. "More Worthy Gottschalk from Angel." *Stereo Review* 35:120 (December 1975).
         A review of *Music of Louis Moreau Gottschalk*, vol. 2, recorded by Leonard Pennario (See: R68i, *etc.*).

B451.   *American Music Before 1865 in Print and on Records.* I.S.A.M. Monographs, no. 6. Brooklyn, New York: Institute for Studies in American Music, Brooklyn College, City University of New York, 1976.
         Several modern editions and discographical citations for

Gottschalk works are provided.

B452.   Darrell, R.D. Record review. *High Fidelity* 26:88 (March 1976).
Review of *Music of Louis Moreau Gottschalk*, vol. 2, recorded
by Leonard Pennario (See: R68i, *etc.*).

B453.   Morrison, Jean Romer, *et al.* "Selective List of American Music for
the Bicentennial Celebration—Piano." *Music Educators Journal*
62:87+ (April 1976).
Several modern editions of Gottschalk works and collections
are included.

B454.   Offergeld, Robert. "Louis Moreau Superstar." *Stereo Review* 36:119
(April 1976).
Review of *Great Galloping Gottschalk*, recorded by Ivan
Davis (See: R78g, *etc.*).

B455.   Darrell, R.D. "Gottschalk: Piano Works." *High Fidelity* 26:83-84
(May 1976).
Review of *Great Galloping Gottschalk*, recorded by Ivan
Davis (See: R78g, *etc.*).

B456.   Jones, Robert. "An Angel for Louis." *New York Daily News* May
16, 1976:14 (Leisure Section).
An announcement of an Eugene List benefit concert to help
restore Gottschalk's grave.

B457.   Jacobson, Bernard. "A Basic Library of American Music." *Stereo
Review* 37:70-75 (July 1976).
Jacobson includes *Le banjo*, *Grande tarentelle*, and *La Nuit
des tropiques*.

B458.   Offergeld, Robert. "Gottschalk by Eugene List (and Others)."
Stereo Review 37:124 (October 1976).
Review of *Louis Moreau Gottschalk: Music for Piano, Four
Hands and Two Pianos*, recorded by Eugene List and others (See:
R277a and R298a).

B459.   Clarke, Garry E. *Essays on American Music*. Contributions in
American History series. Westport, Connecticut: Greenwood Press,
1977.
This book contains a chapter on Gottschalk.

B460.   Hill, Mark Lewis. *Louis Moreau Gottschalk and the American Public.* Thesis: University of Texas at Austin, 1977.

B461.   "Record of the Year Awards for 1976." [Review of *Great Galloping Gottschalk,* recorded by Ivan Davis] *Stereo Review* 38:63-65 (February 1977).
         The Davis recording (See: R78g, *etc.*) received an "Honorable Mention."

B462.   Darrell, R.D. Record review. *High Fidelity* 27:100-101 (March 1977).
         Review of *Louis Moreau Gottschalk: Music for Piano, Four Hands and Two Pianos,* recorded by Eugene List and others (See: R275a, *etc.*).

B463.   "Critics' Choice." *High Fidelity* 27:93 (April 1977).
         Review of *Louis Moreau Gottschalk: Music for Piano, Four Hands and Two Pianos,* recorded by Eugene List and others (See: R275a, etc.).

B464.   Logsdon, Leann F. "Gottschalk and Meyerbeer." Paper read at the Southern Chapter meeting of the American Musicological Society, March 10, 1978.

B465.   Saltzman, Joe. "Gottschalk: Early American Superstar." *Los Angeles Times* November 23, 1978:Section IV, 35.
         Primarily biographical, coinciding with the issue of several recordings of Gottschalk's piano music.

B466.   Kingman, Daniel. *American Music, a Panorama.* New York: Schirmer Books, 1979.
         A general survey of American music, but notable for its substantial coverage of Gottschalk and his importance.

B467.   Kolankiewicz, Gerald J. *Louis Moreau Gottschalk: Professional Musician in Mid-Nineteenth Century America.* Thesis: George Mason University, 1979.

B468.   Rigai, Amiram. Liner notes to *Louis Moreau Gottschalk, 1829-1869: American Piano Music.* Amiram Rigai, piano. 33-1/3 rpm phonodisc. Folkways Records FSS 37485, 1979. Reissued on compact disc, Smithsonian Folkways 40803, 1992.

(See also: R68f, *etc.*)

B469.   Davis, Peter. "A Landmark Series of American Music Recordings."
New York Times January 14, 1979:II, D19+.
Review of *Night in the Tropics and The Ornithological
Combat of Kings*, recorded by Anthony and Joseph Paratore (See:
R297a).

B470.   Schonberg, Harold C. "The Delights of Salon Music." *New York
Times* February 25, 1979:II, 21+.

B471.   Schonberg, Harold C. "Gottschalk's Monster Concert." *New York
Times* April 22, 1979:II, 23+.

B472.   Chase, Gilbert. *The New Grove Dictionary of Music and Musicians*,
ed. Stanley Sadie. *s.v.* "United States of America, Art Music (2),
Romantic Nationalism and The Classical Ideal." London:
Macmillan, 1980.

B473.   Gojowy, Detlef. "Ernesto Nazareth—ein brasilianischer Zeitgenosse
von Alexander Skrjabin und Scott Joplin." *Hamburger Jahrbuch fur
Musikwissenschaft* 4:163-80 (1980).
Dealing with Brazilian composer Ernesto Nazareth and his
similarities with Skrjabin and Joplin, the article also traces the
influence of Gottschalk on Brazilian concert music.

B474.   Lowens, Irving. *The New Grove Dictionary of Music and Musicians*,
ed. Stanley Sadie. *s.v.* "Gottschalk, Louis Moreau." London:
Macmillan, 1980.
The works list is somewhat limited as it includes only the
published compositions of Gottschalk. A throrough encyclopedia
entry, although it has been superceded by Lowens and Starr (See:
B543).

B475.   McKnight, Mark Curtis. *Music Criticism in "The New York Times"
and "The New York Tribune," 1851-1876.* Dissertation: The
Louisiana State University and Agricultural and Mechanical College,
1980.
Also indexed in *Dissertation Abstracts International* 41-A/8
(February 1981), p. 3315. The author deals with the period in which
Gottschalk was most active in New York.

B476.   Zuck, Barbara. *A History of Musical Americanism*. Ann Arbor, 1980.

B477.   Kurth, Ulrich. *Aus der Neuen Welt. Untersuchungen zur Rezeption afro-amerikanischer Musik in europaischer Kunstmusik des 19. und fruhen 20. Jahrhunderts*. Dissertation: U. Kiel, 1981.
         Discussion of Gottschalk's role in disseminating African-American music in Europe is included, although the focus of this dissertation is on the use African-American musical styles by European composers.

B478.   Lupton, Peggy Williams. *The Concert Tours of Louis Moreau Gottschalk in the Context of Secular Musical Life in Mid-Nineteenth Century America*. Thesis: East Carolina University, 1981.

B479.   Seymour, Mary Alice. *Life and Letters of Louis Moreau Gottschalk*. Ann Arbor, Michigan: University Microfilms International, 1981.
         This is a reprint of *Life and Letters of Louis Moreau Gottschalk* by Octavia Hensel (pseudonym of Mary Alice Seymour) (See: B95). I have included a separate entry for the reprint, as it was issued under the author's original name.

B480.   Sadowski, Susan. *Louis Moreau Gottschalk: His European Years, 1842-1852*. Thesis: Peabody Conservatory of Johns Hopkins University, c1981.

B481.   Schonberg, Harold C. Facing the Music. New York: Simon & Schuster, 1981.
         Facing the Music includes articles previously published in the *New York Times*, including several of the author's earlier writings on Gottschalk.

B482.   VanTilburg, Dave. *Louis Moreau Gottschalk, United States Ethnic and Patriotic Music*. Thesis: Bowling Green State University, 1981.

B483.   Mowder, William J. "Gottschalk and Dwight: America's First Composer vs. America's First Critic." *Journal of American Culture* 4:160-166 (no.4, winter 1981).

B484.   Doyle, John G. *Louis Moreau Gottschalk, 1929-1869: A Bibliographical Study and Catalog of Works*. Detroit, Michigan: Published for the College Music Society by Information

Coordinators, 1982.

The premiere bibliographical source for information on Gottschalk, publications, iconography, and recordings up to 1982. Doyle includes even the most trivial mention of Gottschalk in the various sources and evaluates the quality and quantity of each citation; however, some manuscripts have come to light, numerous articles and books have been written, and numerous recordings and reissues of older recordings have appeared since the publication of Doyle's book. (See also: B490, B493, B495)

B485.   Lange, Francisco Curt. "Louis Moreau Gottschalk (1829-1869)." In *Die Musikkulturer Lateinamerikas im 19. Jahrhundert*, ed. Robert Günther. Regensburg, 1982.

B486.   Henahan, Donal. "Composers Who Loved the Big Bang." *New York Times* May 30, 1982:Section 2, D21.

An article about "monster" concerts in which Gottschalk is mentioned.

B487.   Landre, Nikki. American Piano Duets." *American Music Teacher* 31:6+ (June-July 1982).

B488.   Andrews, Peter. "'The King of Pianists': Was Louis Moreau Gottschalk America's First Musical Genius or Simply the Purveyor of Melodic Claptrap?" *American Heritage* v34 (December 1982).

B489.   Stevenson, Robert. "Gottschalk Programs Wagner." *Inter-American Music Review* 5:89-94 (no. 2, 1983).

Gottschalk was responsible for bringing Wagnerian opera to South America through his performances of piano paraphrases between 1865 and 1869.

B490.   Hitchcock, H. Wiley. Review of *Louis Moreau Gottschalk, 1929-1869: A Bibliographical Study and Catalog of Works* by John G. Doyle. *Fontes artis musicae* 30:169-70 (no. 3, July-September 1983).

Review of B484.

B491.   Hihn, Richard Randall. *Boston, Dwight, and Pianists of Nineteenth Century America: The European Connection*. Dissertation: University of Colorado at Boulder, 1984.

Also indexed in *Dissertation Abstracts International* 45-A/7

(January 1985), p. 1910. Gottschalk was among the visiting pianists who greatly influenced the style of concert performance prevalent in Boston in the mid-nineteenth century.

B492. Gottschalk, Louis Moreau and Serge Berthier. *Les voyages extraordinaires de L. Moreau Gottschalk, pianiste et aventurier.* Lausanne: P.-M. Favre, 1985.

  The story of Gottschalk's career as told by his writings as collected and organized by Serge Berthier.

B493. Kirkpatrick, John. Review of *Louis Moreau Gottschalk, 1929-1869: A Bibliographical Study and Catalog of Works* by John G. Doyle. *American Music* 3:359-60 (fall 1985).

  A review of B484.

B494. Offergeld, Robert. "More on the Gottschalk-Ives Connection." *Newsletter of the Institute for Studies in American Music* 6:1-2 (September 1986).

B495. Kearns, William. Review of *Louis Moreau Gottschalk, 1929-1869: A Bibliographical Study and Catalog of Works* by John G. Doyle. *The Sonneck Society Newsletter* 12:19-20 (spring 1986).

  A review of B484.

B496. De Vries, Alan F. *The Spanish and Caribbean Influence in Selected Piano Works of Louis Moreau Gottschalk.* Thesis: California State University, Fullerton, 1987.

B497. Berry, Jason. "African Cultural Memory in New Orleans Music." *Black Music Research Journal* n1 (1988).

B498. Dicus, Kent Timothy. *A Stylistic Analysis of Selected Piano Works of Louis Moreau Gottschalk.* Thesis: The University of Arizona, 1988.

  Also indexed in *Masters Abstracts International* 27 (no. 1, 1988), p. 8. The author discusses Gottschalk as a link between the Romantic virtuosity of Chopin and the conscious Americanism of Charles Ives. Dicus deals with Gottschalk's experimentations with expansions of basic ABA form.

B499. Pendle, Karin. *Teresa Carreno: Pianist, Teacher, and Composer.* Dissertation: University of Cincinnati, 1988.

Also indexed in *Dissertation Abstracts International* 50-A/2, (August 1989), p. 289. Nicknamed the "Walkure of the Piano," pianist Teresa Carreno made her New York debut at the age of eight, shortly thereafter catching the attention of Gottschalk.

B500.   Jackson, Richard. *Notes of a Pianist: The Great Gottschalk Collection in The New York Public Library.* New York: New York Public Library Music Division, 1989.
An exhibition catalog. (See also: B505)

B501.   Stevenson, Robert M. *American Music: A Diversity Experience.* Los Angeles: Copymat, 1989.
Among the essays is a study of Latin American contexts in American concert music, including discussion of Gottschalk.

B502.   Brockett, Clyde W. "An Influential American in Paris." *Sonneck Society Bulletin* pp8-9 (no. 1, 1989).

B503.   Fiehrer, Thomas. "Saint Domingue—Haiti: Louisiana's Caribbean Connection." *Louisiana History* pp431-34 (no. 4, 1989).

B504.   Echevarria Saumell, Francisco. "Gottschalk el desconocido." *Clave* n15:24-30 (October-December 1989).
The author's article "The Unknown Gottschalk" chronicles the musician's 1854 travels and performances in the Caribbean.

B505.   Jackson, Richard. "More Notes of a Pianist: A Gottschalk Collection Surveyed and a Scandal Revisited." *Notes* 46:352-375 (no. 2, December 1989).
A survey of the materials acquired by the New York Public Library for the Performing Arts in 1984. Among items of interest are a draft letter from Gottschalk presenting his version of the romantic scandal that forced him to flee the United States in 1865, notebooks, playbills, and two drafts of Clara Gottschalk Peterson's edition of the composer's diary.

B506.   Hostetter, Elizabeth Ann. *Jeanne Behrend: Pioneer Performer of American Music, Pianist, Teacher, Musicologist, and Composer.* Dissertation: Arizona State University, 1990.
The subject of this dissertation, Jeanne Behrend, was one of the most important Gottschalk performers of and writers about Gottschalk, especially in the late 1950s. Also indexed in

Dissertation Abstracts International 51-A/9 (March 1991).

B507.   Wallace, Elizabeth Ann. *The Effect of War on the Lives and Work of Piano Composers and the Evolution of Compositional Technique in War-Related Piano Pieces from 1849 through the Second World War*. Dissertation: Texas Tech University, 1990.
           Also indexed in *Dissertation Abstracts International* 51-A/9 (March 1990), p. 2920.

B508.   Ruiz Tarazona, Andres. "Musicos extranjeros en España: Luis Moreau Gottschalk." *Temporadas de la musica* 8:67-71 (no. 1, 1990).
           A survey of Gottschalk's 1851-52 tours of Spain.

B509.   Thompson, Donald. "El joven Tavarez: Nuevos documentos y nuevas perspectivas." *Revista del Centro de Estudios Avanzados de Puerto Rico y el Caribe* n11:64-74 (July-December 1990).
           Includes a brief mention of Gottschalk and refutiation of suggestions that Gottschalk and Adelina Patti played a role in his family's decision to send Puerto Rican pianist Manuel Gregorio Tavarez Ropero to Paris to study.

B510.   Gojowy, Detlef. "Nationalismus und Kosmopolitismus: Paradoxe Kehrseiten der europaischen Belle Epoque." In *Wissenschaftliche Buchgesellschaft*. Darmstadt, Germany, 1991:20-36.
           Gojowy deals with the paradox of nationalism and internationalism in nineteenth-century European culture. Gottschalk and several European musicians are considered.

B511.   Marsh, Ellen. "Music of the Gas Light Era." *Humanities* 12:26-29 (January-February 1991).
           Based primarily on the diary of George Templeton Strong, this is an account of concert life in New York. In addition to Gottschalk, Marsh describes the roles of figures such as P.T. Barnum, Jenny Lind, and Louis Jullien.

B512.   Brockett, Clyde W. "Footnotes of a Pianist: A Waltz for a Living Princess." *Sonneck Society Bulletin* (Spring 1991).

B513.   Brockett, Clyde W. "Gottschalk in Madrid: A Tale of Ten Pianos." *Musical Quarterly* pp279-315 (no. 3, 1991).

B514.   *The Complete Published Songs of Louis Moreau Gottschalk, with a Selection of Other Songs of Mid-Nineteenth-Century America,* ed. Richard Jackson. Newton Centre, Massachusetts: Margun Music, 1992.

Jackson includes notes about each of the Gottschalk songs, including some information not previously available.

B515.   Maxwell, Grant L. *Music for Three or More Pianists: An Historical Survey.* University of Alberta, 1992.

Also indexed in *Dissertation Abstracts International* 53-A/12 (June 1993).

B516.   Mann, Brian. "A Gottschalk Letter at Vassar College." *Sonneck Society Bulletin* 18:5-7 (no. 1, spring 1992).

Gottschalk's writing style shines forth in this letter, dated August 2, 1863. The composer discusses his brother Edward's declining health. Of special interest are the newspaper articles to which he refers; some of the articles written by Gottschalk were previously unknown to researchers.

B517.   Brockett, Clyde W. "Gottschalk in Biscay, Castile and Andalusia: A Man for All Classes." *Revista de musicologia* 15:815-849 (no. 2-3, 1992).

The author deals with Gottschalk's performances in Spain and the ways in which he related personally and as a performer with the army, Spanish royalty, street people, and artists from a variety of disciplines.

B518.   Rabinowitz, Peter J. "'With Our Own Dominant Passions': Gottschalk, Gender, and the Power of Listening." *Nineteenth-Century Music* 16:242-252 (no. 3, spring 1993).

The author explores nineteenth-century concepts of gender roles in the context of Gottschalk's sentimental piano works.

B519.   Brockett, Clyde W. "Autobiographer Versus Biographer: How Factual Is Gottschalk?" *Sonneck Society Bulletin* 19:9-12 (no. 3, fall 1993).

The article deals with incorrect dates in some of Gottschalk's accounts of his activities.

B520.   Gojowy, Detlef. "Darius Milhaud et Ernesto Nazareth, ou La découverte de la musique brésilienne." In *Honegger et Milhaud:*

Musique et esthetique, 1994:215-224.
The author deals with Gottschalk's influence on Brazilian composer/pianist Ernesto Nazareth, who in turn influenced Darius Milhaud's Brazilian compositions.

B521.   Magaldi, Cristina. *Concert Life in Rio de Janeiro, 1837-1900.* Dissertation: University of California, Los Angeles, 1994.
Also indexed in *Dissertation Abstracts International* 55-A/11 (May 1995), 3347. The author deals extensively with the Paris-oriented music being performed in the Brazilian capital during the time of Gottschalk. The Emperor Pedro II was most responsible for European virtuosi and Gottschalk performing in Rio de Janeiro. Also mentioned and of note in the context of Gottschalk's compositional work was the practice of incorporating African percussion music into performances of European operas. The author also notes that shortly after Gottschalk's death, German "classic" works began dominating programs.

B522.   Allman, Kevin. Review of *Bamboula! The Life and Times of Louis Moreau Gottschalk* by S. Frederick Starr. *Book World* 24:2 (November 20, 1994).
A review of B524.

B523.   Offergeld, Robert. "Louis Moreau Gottschalk." Liner notes to *Gottschalk: 40 Works for Piano.* Four 33-1/3 rpm phonodiscs. Desto DC 6470-73, 1969. Reissued on three compact discs, VoxBox CD3X 3033, 1995.

B524.   Starr, S. Frederick. *Bamboula! The Life and Times of Louis Moreau Gottschalk.* New York: Oxford University Press, 1995. Paperback edition: Urbana: University of Illinois Press, 2000.
Starr's book combines excellent scholarship with a writing style that truly brings Gottschalk's career to life. Of particular note are several compositions the author uncovered that were not listed by previous researchers. Although some reviewers, notably Donald W. Krummel (See: B527) found Starr's chapter on the relationship between music critic John S. Dwight and Gottschalk to be of questionable usefulness, I find that it gives the reader considerable insight into Gottschalk's psyche and into the religious and regional conflicts that characterized mid-nineteenth-century America. The bibliography contains a number of errors, including incorrect dates and redundant entries caused by typographical errors. (See also:

B522, B527, B528, B531, B532, B537)

B525.   Rabinowitz, Peter J. Review of *Gottschalk: Piano Music, Vol. 2*, recorded by Philip Martin, piano. *Fanfare* (January 1, 1995).
       A thoroughly positive review of the recording and Martin's choice of repertoire (See: R76f, *etc.*).

B526.   Tacuchian, Ricardo. "Louis Moreau Gottschalk: Atraves de uma bibliografia seletiva e comentada." *Boletim de Sociedade Brasileira de Musicologia* pp39-51 (no. 1, 1995).
       An annotated and selectived bibliography related to Gottschalk. The author's primary focus is on tracing changes in the academic reaction to the musician.

B527.   Krummel, Donald W. Review of *Bamboula! The Life and Times of Louis Moreau Gottschalk* by S. Frederick Starr. *Notes* 52:476-77 (no. 2, 1995).
       A very positive review of the Starr book (See: B524), although the chapter delving into the possible motivations behind John S. Dwight's criticisms of Gottschalk is described as "irrelevant." Krummel makes the interesting point that the reality of Gottschalk's life and the mystique surrounding the pianist/composer (enhanced and maintained by Gottschalk's press notices and correspondance, "with their ample puffery and personal self-promotion") blur together "disturbingly well."

B528.   Mellers, Wilfrid Howard. Review of *Bamboula! The Life and Times of Louis Moreau Gottschalk* by S. Frederick Starr. *TLS: The Times Literary Supplement* n4810:20 (June 9, 1995).
       A review of B524.

B529.   Rabinowitz, Peter J. Review of *Gottschalk: Piano Music* by Alan Mandel. *Fanfare* (September 1, 1995).
       A decidedly mixed review of the compact disc reissue of Mandel's recording of forty Gottschalk works (See: R67a, *etc.*). Rabinowitz prefers the Philip Martin recordings (See: R76f, *etc.*).

B530.   Hamel, Réginald. *Louis-Moreau Gottschalk et son temps (1829-1869)*. Montréal: Guérin, 1996.
       An extensive, 645-page, French-language work on Gottschalk. Important features include a detailed intinerary of Gottschalk's performances and discussion of the circles in which Gottschalk

moved and their relationship to his career.

B531. Rollins, Peter. Review of *Bamoula! The Life and Times of Louis Moreau Gottschalk* by S. Frederick Starr. *Journal of Popular Culture* 30:224-25 (no. 2, 1996).

According to Rollins, *Bamboula!* (See: B524) "deserves high praise" for restoring "the eminent position held by Gottschalk during his lifetime," and for doing so in a way that is "culturally comprehensive."

B532. Tischler, Barbara L. Review of *Bamboula! The Life and Times of Louis Moreau Gottschalk* by S. Frederick Starr. *The American Historical Review* 101:913 (no. 3, 1996)

A review of B524.

B533. North, James H. Review of *Piano Portraits from Nineteenth-Century America*, recorded by Noël Lester, piano. *Fanfare* (March 22, 1996).

A mixed review, praising Lester's technical brilliance in the Gottschalk works, but indicating that the works do not sound as "fun" as they should. (See: R142u, *etc.*)

B534. Starr, Frederick. "Louis Moreau Gottschalk: Almost Forgotten." *Clavier* 35:14 (October 1996).

B535. Thompson, David Bruce. *Piano Music in the South during the Civil War Period, 1855-1870.* Dissertation: University of South Carolina, 1997.

Also indexed in *Dissertation Abstracts International* 58-A/3 (September 1997).

B536. Taranto, Cheryl. "Thomas Maguire in Virginia City." *The Sonneck Society for American Music Bulletin* 23:33+ (no. 2, summer 1997).

Gottschalk's performances at Maguire's Opera House in Virginia City, Nevada are mentioned.

B537. Yellin, Victor Fell. Review of *Bamboula! The Life and Times of Louis Moreau Gottschalk* by S. Frederick Starr. *American Music* 15:233-238 (no. 2, summer 1997).

A review of B524.

B538. Rabinowitz, Peter J. Review of *Gottschalk: Piano Music, Vol. 3,* recorded by Philip Martin. *Fanfare* (July 24, 1997).

A positive review of Martin's performance (See: R681, *etc.*); however, the reviewer detects some distortion in some of the recording's louder passages.

B539.   Starr, S. Frederick. "Louis Moreau Gottschalk: An Almost Forgotten Celebrity." *The Instrumentalist* 53:56 (September 1998).

B540.   Falconer-Salkeld, Bridget. "From Albion to Albany: On the Tracks of Gottschalk in the Hudson Valley." *The Sonneck Society for American Music Bulletin* 25:76+ (no. 3, fall 1999).

B541.   Moore, Laura. *Bombastic Bamboulas and Bostonian Brahmins: L.M. Gottschalk, J.S. Dwight, and Their Viewpoints on American Music.* Thesis: Florida State University, 2000.

B542.   Crawford, Richard. *The New Grove Dictionary of Music and Musicians,* 2nd ed. s.v. "United States of America, Art Music (2), Nineteenth Century." London: Macmillan, 2001.

B543.   Lowens, Irving and S. Frederick Starr. *The New Grove Dictionary of Music and Musicians,* 2nd ed. s.v. "Gottschalk, Louis Moreau." London: Macmillan, 2001.

A strong biography and assessment of Gottschalk's importance as a pianist and as a composer. The works list is limited primarily to published scores, thereby not including a substantial number of Gottschalk's documented lost works.

B544.   Haley, Mary. *Louis Moreau Gottschalk. Ragtimers.org* [World Wide Web Resource]. http://www.ragtimers.org/%7eragtimers/artists/gttschlk. Accessed January 6, 2001.

This web page provides two jpg-format photographs of Gottschalk and a biographical sketch. The author provides links to other internet resources for information on ragtime-related composers, performers, and organizations.

B545.   Webster, Michael. "Louis Moreau Gottschalk: The New Orleans/French Connection." Lecture/recital presented at the International Clarinet Association's ClarinetFest 2001, New Orleans, August 15-19, 2001.

The presentation included performance of a number of

Gottschalk works arranged for flute, clarinet, and piano by Webster.

B546.   Lange, Francisco Curt. "Louis Moreau Gottschalk (1829-1869):
         Correspondencia recientement descubierta sobre su personalidad y
         obra realizada en el Uruguay y el Brasil." In *Die Musikkulturen
         Lateinamerikas*, 371-449. Unknown location, unknown date.
              Lange details Gottschalk's activities in Montevideo, Buenos
         Aires, and Rio de Janeiro in the 1867-1869 period. Texts of
         Gottschalk's correspondence from the period are also provided.

Alphabetical List of Compositions

Addio, mio solo amor, *See*: My Only Love, Good Bye!
Adieu funèbre pour violoncello et piano, W49.
Adiós à Cuba, W141.
Adiós a la Habana, W301.
Agnus Dei, W8.
L'Alianza, W243.
Alone, W10.
Amalia Warden, W3.
Amour chevaleresque, Op. 97, *See*: Love and Chivalry, Op. 97.
Andante de la symphonie romantique, W177.
Andante, pour violon et piano, W50.
Andes, The (George William Warren), W316.
Apothéose, grande marche solennelle, Op. 29, W157.
Autrefrois, ballade, W118.
Ave Maria, W24.
Ay! Lunarcitos!, contradanza, W208.
Ay pimpillo, no me mates!, contradanza, W213.
Bailemos, Creole Dance, W224.
Ballade (in A-flat Major), W119.
Ballade, Op. 83 (85), W265.
Ballade, Op. 87, W266.
Ballade, Op. 90, W267.
Ballades en F, W89.
Ballo in Maschera, La, fantaisie triomphale, W219, W303.
Ballo in Maschera Quartet, W54.
Bamboula, danse des nègres, Op. 2, W68.
Bananier, Le, chanson nègre, Op. 5, W78, W273.
Banjo, Op. 82, W110.

Banjo, Le, grotesque fantaisie, esquisse américaine, Op. 15, W142, W290.
Bataille, Op. 63 (64), W245.
Bataille de Carabova, La, W35.
Battle Cry of Freedom, grand caprice de concert, Op. 55, W229.
Bengali au réveil, bluette en form d'étude, W115.
Berceuse (Cradle Song), Op. 47, W212.
Berceuse (O mon trésor, dors d'un calme sommeil), W28.
Berceuse, La Même, W51.
Brise, La, valse de concert, W234.
Bunker's Hill, fantaisie triomphale, W121.
Cakewalk: Ballet (Hershy Kay), W319.
Camagüay Fantasy, W137.
Caña, La, chanson andalouse, W106.
Canadian Boat Song, W22.
Canto de los pájaros, El, *See*: Chant des oiseaux.
Canto del gitano, *See*: Chanson du gitano.
Caprice cubain, W130.
Caprice élégiaque, Op. 56, W252.
Caprice en A-flat, W120.
Caprice on Peruvian Airs, W235.
Caprice-polka, Op. 79, W158.
Caprice sur la danse créole, W166.
Caprichos sobre danses de Puerto Principe, W138.
Carnaval de Venise, Le, W12.
Carnaval de Venise, Le, grand caprice et variations, Op. 89, W90.
Célèbre tarentelle, *See*: Grande tarentelle, Op. 67.
Chanson du gitano, W107.
Chant de guerre, Op. 78, W169.
Chant des Caraïbes, W164.
Chant des oiseaux, W47.
Chant du martyr, grand caprice religieux, W145.
Chant du soldat, grand caprice de concert, Op. 23, W144.
Charles IX (Carlos IX), W2.
Charme du foyer, *See*: Home, Sweet Home, caprice, Op. 51.
Chasse de jeune Henri, La, Op. 10, W85, W274.
Chute des feuilles, La, nocturne, Op. 42, W209.
Clermont Mass, The, W7.
Cocoyé, El, grand caprice cubain de bravura, Op. 80, W135.
Colliers d'or, deux mazurkas, Op. 6, W67.
Colombe, La, petite polka, Op. 49, W226.
Columbia, caprice américain, Op. 34, W178.
Concerto in F minor for Piano and Orchestra, W29.

Cri de délivrance, Le, *See*: Battle Cry of Freedom, grand caprice de concert, Op. 55.

Dans les nuages, *See*: Fairy Land, schottische de concert.

Danse des sylphes, caprice de concert, Op. 86, W96.

Danse ossianique (Danse des ombres), Op. 12, W91.

Danza, Op. 33, W167.

Danza en A-flat, No. 1, W188.

Danza en A-flat, No. 2, W189.

Danza en E, W179.

Danza en F, W180.

Dernier amour, Op. 62 (63), W246.

Deuxième Banjo, *See*: Banjo, Op. 82.

Deuxième Reflects de passé, *See*: Reflects de passé, rêverie, Op. 28.

Dove, The, *See*: Colombe, La, petite polka, Op. 49.

Drums and Cannon, military polka, W217.

Dying Poet, Meditation, W227.

Dying Swan, The, Op. 100, W254.

Escenas campestres, W4.

Esquisse, W160.

Esquisses créoles, W268.

L'Étincelle, *See*: Scintilla, La.

Étude, W61.

Étude de force en B Major, W211.

Étude en A-flat, W127.

Étude in C-sharp minor, W271.

Étude in D-flat Major, W86.

Étude in G Major, W73.

Étude pour un main, W181.

Études de concert, W196.

L'exile, W27.

Fair Butterfly, *See*: Papillon, Le.

Fairy Land, schottische de concert, W183.

Fandango, W117.

Fantaisie sur des airs matiniquais, W174.

Fantaisie sur Fille du Regiment, W148.

Fantaisie sur *I Puritani*, W206.

Fantaisie sur *La Norma*, W207.

Fantaisie sur *Lucia*, W147.

Fantasia sobre la *Lucrezia Borgia*, W238.

Fantôme de bonheur, Op. 36, W200.

Fatma (Le Caïd), W87.

Favorita, La, grand fantaisie triomphale, Op. 68, W194, W299.

Festival, El, W202.
Fleur de lys, gallop brillante, W269, W315.
Flor que ella me envia, La, W26, W248.
Forest Glade Polka, Op. 25, W122, W284.
Forget Me Not, mazurka caprice, W255.
Gallina, La, danse cubaine, Op. 53, W204, W302.
Gaselle, La: Andante elegant, W155.
Gitanella, La, caprice caractéristique, Op. 35, W168.
Glaneuse, La, W82.
Gloires italiennes, W289.
God Save the Queen (America), morceau de concert, Op. 41, W92.
Gran Galopada según Quidant, W293.
Gran marcha solemne, W251.
Grand March for the Sultan, W46.
Grand National Symphony for Ten Pianos, Bunker's Hill, W285.
Grand scherzo, Op. 57, W257.
Grande étude de concert, W74.
Grande Fantaisie de *Lucia*, W314.
Grande fantaisie triomphale sur l'hymne national brésilien, Op. 69, W258.
Grande Marche de *Athalia*, W45.
Grande Marche de *Faust*, W40, W308.
Grande Marche de *Tannhauser*, W39.
Grande Méditation poétique sobre *Faust* de Gounod, W56, W57.
Grande Phantasia sobre motives de *Norma*, W313.
Grande phantasie sobre *Martha*, W242.
Grande tarantelle, Op. 67, W37, W247, W311, W312.
Grande Valse de concert, W75.
Grande Valse poétique concertante, W11.
Hercule, grande étude de concert, Op. 88, W259.
Home, Sweet Home, caprice, Op. 51, W221.
Huitième Ballade, *See*: Ballade, Op. 90.
Hurrah Galop, pas redoublé de concert, W186.
I Don't See It, Mamma!, W20.
Idol of Beauty, W14.
I'll Pray for Thee, W125.
Im Hochland, W306.
Impromptu, Op. 54, W256.
Innocence, grand valse de concert, W270.
Isaura di Salerno, W1.
Italian Glories, W129.
Jerusalem, grande fantaisie triomphale, Op. 13, W93.
Jerusalem, grande fantaisie triomphale, Op. 84, W276.

Jeune Fille aux yeux noirs, W184.
Jeunesse, mazurka brillante, Op. 70, W195.
Jota aragonesa, La, caprice espagnol, Op. 14, W105, W282.
Last Hope, The, Religious Meditation, Op. 16, W139, W288.
Last Rose of Summer, *See*: Ultima rosa.
Love and Chivalry, Op. 97, W175.
Lucrezia Borgia, Transcription du Final, W123.
Madeleine, étude, W264.
Maiden's Blush, The, Grande valse de concert, Op. 106, W230.
Mancenillier, La, W88.
Manchega, étude de concert, Op. 38, W103.
Marcha real española, W102.
Marcha Triunfal y Final de Opera, W36.
Marche, W38.
Marche de nuit, Op. 17, W146, W291.
Marche de *Tannhäuser*, W304.
Marche funèbre, Op. 61, W132, W286.
Marche funèbre, Op. 64, W133.
Marche in E-flat Major, W241.
Marche scandinave, W70.
Marche solennelle, W44.
Marguerite, Op. 76, W244.
Maria la O, W136.
Marlborough, s'en va t'en guerre, W173.
Mazeppa, Étude dramatique, W84.
Mazurk in F-sharp minor, W272.
Mazurka in A Major, W98.
Mazurka in A minor, W77.
Mazurka rustique, Op. 81, W97.
Mélancolie, La, etude caractéristique, W80.
Mélodie pour voix d'homme, W9.
Melody, W59.
Minuit à Séville, caprice, Op. 30, W112.
Miserere du *Trovatore*, paraphrase de concert, Op. 52, W162, W295.
Moissonneuse, La, mazurka caractéristique, Op. 8, W81.
Moripont, W116.
Morte!! (She Is Dead), Op. 60 (55), W249.
Mountaineer's Song, The, W17.
Murmures éoliens, Op. 46, W176.
My Only Love, Good Bye!, W18.
Ne m'oubliez pas, *See*: Forget Me Not, mazurka caprice.
Nocturne, W131.

O Loving Heart, Trust On!, W19.
O, Ma charmante, épargnez-moi!, Op. 44, W203.
Ojos criollos, danse cubaine, Op. 37, W191, W298.
Orfa, grande polka, Op. 71, W231, W307.
Ossian, deux ballades, Op. 4, W69.
Overture de *Guillaume Tell*, grande morceau de concert, W277.
Overture d'*Oberon*, Op. 83.
Pange linguae, W5.
Papillon, Le, W15.
Pasquinade, caprice, Op. 59, W228.
Pastorella e cavalliere, W23.
Pastorella e cavalliere, Op. 32, W185.
Patitas de mi sobrina, Las, W170.
Paulina, sérénade pour voix d'homme, W13.
Pensée poétique (L'extase), Op. 61/62, W153.
Pensée poétique, nocturne, Op. 18, W111.
Pensez à moi, *See*: Rapelle-toi.
Pensive, polka-rédowa, Op. 68, W225.
Piano Septet, W58.
Piano Trio: Two Tarentelles, W52.
Piano Quintet, *Ballo in Maschera*, W55.
Poète mourant, Le, *See*: Dying Poet, The, Meditation.
Polka caracteristica sobre Le mancenillier, W108.
Polka de concert, W63.
Polka de salon, Op. 1, W64.
Polka di bravura, W222.
Polka in A-flat Major, W187.
Polka in B-flat Major, W199.
Polka militaire, W215.
Polka poétique, W128.
Polonia, grande caprice de concert, Op. 35 (43), W190.
Ponceñas, Las, Contradanzas: Quadrilles, W32.
Prelude, W154.
Première Reflects du passé, W71.
Prière, W126.
Printemps d'amour, mazurka, caprice de concert, Op. 40, W149, W292.
Puertorrequeña, La, W30.
Quadrille créole, W317.
Radieuse, grande valse de concert, Op. 72, W232, W305.
Rapelle-toi, W25.
Raytons d'azur, polka de salon, Op. 77, W150.
Recuerdo de la Vuelta de Abajo, W143.

Recuerdos de la Habana, *See*: Souvenir de la Havane, Op. 39.
Recuerdos de Puerto-Princípe, W287.
Reflects de passé, rêverie, Op. 28, W161.
Regarde moi, idylle, W261.
Réponds-moi, danse cubaine, Op. 50, W193, W300.
Réveil de l'aigle, Le, W109.
Rex altissime, W6.
Ricordati, Op. 26, W156.
Rigoletto Quartet, transcription de bravura, W218.
Romance in E-flat Major, W201.
Rome, étude, W182.
Savane, La, ballade créole, Op. 3, W76.
Scherzo Romantique, Op. 73, W99.
Scintilla, La, Op. 20/21, W83, W275.
Second Banjo, *See*: Banjo, Op. 82.
Septième Ballade, *See*: Ballade, Op. 87.
Ses yeux, polka de concert, Op. 66, W237, W309, W310.
Silvido, El, contradanza, W172.
Sitio de Zaragoza, El, W101, W279.
Sixième Ballade, *See*: Ballade, Op. 83 (85).
Slumber on, Baby Dear, W16.
Solemne Marcha Triunfal a Chile, W43.
Solitude, Op. 65, W151.
Sonate, W60.
Songe d'une nuit d'été, caprice élégant, Op. 9, W94.
Sospiro, valse poétique, Op. 24, W152.
Sourire d'une jeune fille, Le, *See*: Maiden's Blush, Grande valse de concert,
      Op. 106.
Souvenir de Cuba, mazurka, Op. 75, W198.
Souvenir de la Havane, grande caprice de concert, Op. 39, W192
Souvenir de la Louisiane, W140.
Souvenir de Lima, mazurka, Op. 74, W210.
Souvenir de *Lucrezia Borgia*, W240.
Souvenir de Porto Rico, Marche des Gibaros, Op. 31, W165.
Souvenir des Ardennnes, W66.
Souvenirs d'Andalousie, caprice de concert, Op. 22, W100, W278.
Souvenirs de Bellini, W283.
Spirito gentil, W263.
Stay, My Charmer, W21.
Suis-moi!, Op. 45, W216.
Sylphe, Le, W79.
Symphonie romantique ("La nuit des tropiques"), W34, W297.

Symphony No. 2 ("À Montevideo"), W41.

Tarantelle, W48.

Tennessee, W163.

Trovatore, Il, Grand Duo di bravura, W159, W294.

Tournament Galop, W95.

Tremelo, grande étude de concert, Op. 58, W250.

Tres Romanzas, W197.

Ultima rosa, W239.

Unadilla Waltz, W233.

L'Union, paraphrase de concert, Op. 48, W220.

Vallisoletana, La, W280.

Valse brillant, W65.

Valse de concert in G, W113.

Valse de *Faust*, W223.

Valse de salon, W62.

Valse di bravura (piano duet), W281.

Valse di bravura (solo piano), W33.

Valse en A flat, W114.

Valse en D minor, W205.

Valse en E flat, W124.

Valse poétique, W31.

Vamos a la azotea, *See*: Suis-moi!, Op. 45.

Variaciones de aires nacionales del Perú, *See*: Caprice on Peruvian Airs.

Variations de concert sur l'hymne portugais, Op. 91, W42, W260.

Variations on "Auld Lang Syne," W236.

Variations on "Dixie's Land," W214.

Variations on "Old Folks at Home," W134.

Variations sur le dernière pensée de Weber, W262.

Variations sur un theme français, W72.

Vision, étude, W253.

Water Sprite, The, polka de salon, Op. 27, W104.

Workbook, W318.

Yearning, *See*: Ricordati, Op. 26.

Yeux créoles, Les, *See*: Ojos criollos, Op. 37.

Ynés, danza in E-flat Major, W171.

Young Shepherdess and the Knight, The, *See*: Pastorella e cavalliere.

Index

The mnemonics used in this Index include "W" for "Work," "WB" for "Work Bibliography" (numbered sequentially in the various works chapters), "R" for "Recording," "F" for "Filmography," and "B" for "Bibliography" (General Bibliography entries).

About the Author

JAMES E. PERONE is Associate Professor of Music at Mount Union College. He is the author of *Paul Simon: A Bio-Bibliography* (Greenwood Press, 2000) and *Songs of the Vietnam Conflict* (Greenwood Press, 2001).

**Recent Titles in
Bio-Bibliographies in Music**

Cyril Scott: A Bio-Bibliography
Laurie J. Sampsel

Irwin Bazelon: A Bio-Bibliography
David Harold Cox

Sergei Rachmaninoff: A Bio-Bibliography
Robert E. Cunningham

Witold Lutosławski: A Bio-Bibliography
Stanisław Bedkowski and Stanisław Hrabia

Pietro Mascagni: A Bio-Bibliography
Roger Flury

Toru Takemitsu: A Bio-Bibliography
James Siddons

Emma Lou Diemer: A Bio-Bibliography
Ellen Grolman Schlegel

Ernst von Dohnányi: A Bio-Bibliography
James A. Grymes

Steve Reich: A Bio-Bibliography
D.J. Hoek

Vivian Fine: A Bio-Bibliography
Judith Cody

Benjamin Britten: A Bio-Bibliography
Stewart R. Craggs

George Crumb: A Bio-Bibliography
David Cohen

2057